THE WILEY BICENTENNIAL—KNOWLEDGE FOR GENERATIONS

*E*ach generation has its unique needs and aspirations. When Charles Wiley first opened his small printing shop in lower Manhattan in 1807, it was a generation of boundless potential searching for an identity. And we were there, helping to define a new American literary tradition. Over half a century later, in the midst of the Second Industrial Revolution, it was a generation focused on building the future. Once again, we were there, supplying the critical scientific, technical, and engineering knowledge that helped frame the world. Throughout the 20th Century, and into the new millennium, nations began to reach out beyond their own borders and a new international community was born. Wiley was there, expanding its operations around the world to enable a global exchange of ideas, opinions, and know-how.

For 200 years, Wiley has been an integral part of each generation's journey, enabling the flow of information and understanding necessary to meet their needs and fulfill their aspirations. Today, bold new technologies are changing the way we live and learn. Wiley will be there, providing you the must-have knowledge you need to imagine new worlds, new possibilities, and new opportunities.

Generations come and go, but you can always count on Wiley to provide you the knowledge you need, when and where you need it!

WILLIAM J. PESCE
PRESIDENT AND CHIEF EXECUTIVE OFFICER

PETER BOOTH WILEY
CHAIRMAN OF THE BOARD

www.wiley.com/college/microsoft *or* call the MOAC Toll-Free Number: 1+(888) 764-7001

Microsoft Certified Application Specialist (MCAS)

Approved Courseware

▪ What does this logo mean?

It means this courseware has been approved by the Microsoft® Certified Application Specialist program to be among the finest available for learning Microsoft® Office Word 2007, Microsoft® Office Excel 2007, Microsoft® Office PowerPoint 2007, Microsoft® Office Access 2007, or Microsoft® Office Outlook 2007. It also means that upon completion of this courseware, you may be prepared to take an exam for Microsoft Certified Application Specialist qualification.

▪ What is a Microsoft Certified Application Specialist?

A Microsoft Certified Application Specialist is an individual who has passed exams for certifying his or her skills in one or more of the Microsoft Office desktop applications such as Microsoft Word, Microsoft Excel, Microsoft PowerPoint, Microsoft Outlook, or Microsoft Access. The Microsoft Certified Application Specialist program is the only program approved by Microsoft for testing proficiency in Microsoft Office desktop applications. This testing program can be a valuable asset in any job search or career development.

▪ More Information

To learn more about becoming a Microsoft Certified Application Specialist and exam availability, visit www.microsoft.com/learning/msbc.

Microsoft, the Microsoft Office Logo, PowerPoint, and Outlook are trademarks or registered trademarks of Microsoft Corporation in the United States and/or other countries, and the Microsoft Certified Application Specialist logo is used under license from the owner.

Microsoft® Official Academic Course

Microsoft® Office Excel® 2007

Credits

EXECUTIVE EDITOR	John Kane
SENIOR EDITOR	Gary Schwartz
DIRECTOR OF MARKETING AND SALES	Mitchell Beaton
EDITORIAL ASSISTANT	Jennifer Lartz
PRODUCTION MANAGER	Kelly Tavares
DEVELOPMENT AND PRODUCTION	Custom Editorial Productions, Inc
PRODUCTION ASSISTANT	Courtney Leshko
CREATIVE DIRECTOR	Harry Nolan
COVER DESIGNER	Harry Nolan
INTERIOR DESIGN	Brian Salisbury
TECHNOLOGY AND MEDIA	Phyllis Bregman
COVER PHOTO	Corbis

Wiley 200th Anniversary logo designed by: Richard J. Pacifico

This book was set in Garamond by Aptara, Inc. and printed and bound by Bind Rite Graphics.
The covers were printed by Phoenix Color.

Foreword from the Publisher

Wiley's publishing vision for the Microsoft Official Academic Course series is to provide students and instructors with the skills and knowledge they need to use Microsoft technology effectively in all aspects of their personal and professional lives. Quality instruction is required to help both educators and students get the most from Microsoft's software tools and to become more productive. Thus our mission is to make our instructional programs trusted educational companions for life.

To accomplish this mission, Wiley and Microsoft have partnered to develop the highest quality educational programs for Information Workers, IT Professionals, and Developers. Materials created by this partnership carry the brand name "Microsoft Official Academic Course," assuring instructors and students alike that the content of these textbooks is fully endorsed by Microsoft, and that they provide the highest quality information and instruction on Microsoft products. The Microsoft Official Academic Course textbooks are "Official" in still one more way—they are the officially sanctioned courseware for Microsoft IT Academy members.

The Microsoft Official Academic Course series focuses on *workforce development*. These programs are aimed at those students seeking to enter the workforce, change jobs, or embark on new careers as information workers, IT professionals, and developers. Microsoft Official Academic Course programs address their needs by emphasizing authentic workplace scenarios with an abundance of projects, exercises, cases, and assessments.

The Microsoft Official Academic Courses are mapped to Microsoft's extensive research and job-task analysis, the same research and analysis used to create the Microsoft Certified Application Specialist (MCAS) and Microsoft Certified Application Professional (MCAP) exams. The textbooks focus on real skills for real jobs. As students work through the projects and exercises in the textbooks they enhance their level of knowledge and their ability to apply the latest Microsoft technology to everyday tasks. These students also gain resume-building credentials that can assist them in finding a job, keeping their current job, or in furthering their education.

The concept of life-long learning is today an utmost necessity. Job roles, and even whole job categories, are changing so quickly that none of us can stay competitive and productive without continuously updating our skills and capabilities. The Microsoft Official Academic Course offerings, and their focus on Microsoft certification exam preparation, provide a means for people to acquire and effectively update their skills and knowledge. Wiley supports students in this endeavor through the development and distribution of these courses as Microsoft's official academic publisher.

Today educational publishing requires attention to providing quality print and robust electronic content. By integrating Microsoft Official Academic Course products, *WileyPLUS*, and Microsoft certifications, we are better able to deliver efficient learning solutions for students and teachers alike.

Bonnie Lieberman
General Manager and Senior Vice President

Preface

Welcome to the Microsoft Official Academic Course (MOAC) program for the 2007 Microsoft Office system. MOAC represents the collaboration between Microsoft Learning and John Wiley & Sons, Inc. publishing company. Microsoft and Wiley teamed up to produce a series of textbooks that deliver compelling and innovative teaching solutions to instructors and superior learning experiences for students. Infused and informed by in-depth knowledge from the creators of Microsoft Office and Windows Vista™, and crafted by a publisher known worldwide for the pedagogical quality of its products, these textbooks maximize skills transfer in minimum time. With MOAC, students are hands on right away—there are no superfluous text passages to get in the way of learning and using the software. Students are challenged to reach their potential by using their new technical skills as highly productive members of the workforce.

Because this knowledgebase comes directly from Microsoft, architect of the 2007 Office system and creator of the Microsoft Certified Application Specialist (MCAS) exams, you are sure to receive the topical coverage that is most relevant to students' personal and professional success. Microsoft's direct participation not only assures you that MOAC textbook content is accurate and current; it also means that students will receive the best instruction possible to enable their success on certification exams and in the workplace.

■ The Microsoft Official Academic Course Program

The *Microsoft Official Academic Course* series is a complete program for instructors and institutions to prepare and deliver great courses on Microsoft software technologies. With MOAC, we recognize that, because of the rapid pace of change in the technology and curriculum developed by Microsoft, there is an ongoing set of needs beyond classroom instruction tools for an instructor to be ready to teach the course. The MOAC program endeavors to provide solutions for all these needs in a systematic manner in order to ensure a successful and rewarding course experience for both instructor and student—technical and curriculum training for instructor readiness with new software releases; the software itself for student use at home for building hands-on skills, assessment, and validation of skill development; and a great set of tools for delivering instruction in the classroom and lab. All are important to the smooth delivery of an interesting course on Microsoft software, and all are provided with the MOAC program. We think about the model below as a gauge for ensuring that we completely support you in your goal of teaching a great course. As you evaluate your instructional materials options, you may wish to use the model for comparison purposes with available products.

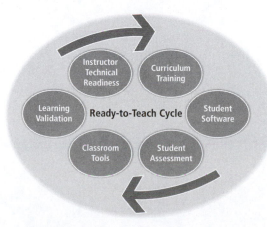

▪ Organization

MOAC for 2007 Microsoft Office system is designed to cover all the learning objectives in the MCAS exams, referred to as "objective domains." The Microsoft Certified Application Specialist (MCAS) exam objectives are highlighted throughout the textbooks. Unique features of our task-based approach include a Lesson Skills Matrix that correlates skills taught in each lesson to the MCAS objectives; Certification, Workplace, and Internet Ready exercises; and three levels of increasingly rigorous lesson-ending activities: Competency, Proficiency, and Mastery Assessment.

Following is a list of key features in each lesson designed to prepare your students for success on these exams and in the workplace:

- Each lesson begins with a **Lesson Skill Matrix.** More than a standard list of learning objectives, the Skill Matrix correlates each software skill covered in the lesson to the specific MCAS "objective domain."

- Every lesson features a real-world **Business Case** scenario that places the software skills and knowledge to be acquired in a real-world setting.

- Every lesson opens with a **Software Orientation.** This feature provides an overview of the software features students will be working with in the lesson. The orientation includes a large, labeled screen image.

- Engaging point-of-use **Reading Aids** provide students with hints, introduce alternative methods for producing results, alert them to pitfalls, provide learning cross-references, and tell them the names of files found on the Student CD.

- **Certification Ready?** features throughout the text signal students where a specific certification objective is covered. It provides students with a chance to check their understanding of that particular MCAS objective and, if necessary, review the section of the lesson where it is covered. MOAC offers complete preparation for MCAS certification.

- Concise and frequent **Step-by-Step** instructions teach students new features and provide an opportunity for hands-on practice.

- **Circling Back.** These integrated projects provide students with an opportunity to review and practice skills learned in previous lessons.

- **Competency, Proficiency, and Mastery Assessment** provide three progressively more challenging lesson-ending activities.

- **Internet Ready.** Projects combine the knowledge students acquire in a lesson with a Web-based research task.

- **Workplace Ready.** These features preview how 2007 Microsoft Office system applications are used in real-world situations.

■ Pedagogical Features

Many pedagogical features have been developed specifically for *Microsoft Official Academic Course* programs. Presenting the extensive procedural information and technical concepts woven throughout the textbook raises challenges for the student and instructor alike. The Illustrated Book Tour that follows provides a guide to the rich features contributing to *Microsoft Official Academic Course* program's pedagogical plan.

Each book within the *Microsoft Official Academic Course* series features:

- **Lesson Skill Matrix:** The skill matrix lists the instructional goals for the lesson so that you know what skills you will be asked to master. The Matrix previews the lesson structure, helping you grasp key concepts and prepares you for learning software skills. These skills are also linked directly to the Microsoft Certified Application Specialist (MCAS) certification skill, when appropriate.

- **Key Terms:** Important technical vocabulary is listed at the beginning of the lesson. When these terms are used later in the lesson, they appear in bold italic type and are defined. The Glossary contains all of the key terms and their definitions.

- **Software Orientation:** This feature provides an overview of the software you will be using in the lesson. The orientation will detail the general properties of the software or specific features, such as a ribbon or dialog box.

- **The Bottom Line:** Each main topic within the lesson has a summary of why this topic is relevant.

- **Hands-on practice:** Numbered steps give detailed, step-by-step instructions to help you learn software skills. The steps also show results and screen images to match what you should see on your computer screen.

- **Student CD:** The companion CD contains the data files needed for each lesson. These files are indicated by the CD icon in the margin of the textbook.

- **Informational text for each topic:** Easy-to-read, technique-focused information can be found following each exercise.

- **Illustrations:** Screen images provide visual feedback as you work through the exercises. The images reinforce key concepts, provide visual clues about the steps, and allow you to check your progress.

- **Reader aids:** Helpful hints, such as *Take Note,* and alternate ways to accomplish tasks (*Another Way*) are located throughout the lessons. Reader aids provide additional relevant or background information that adds value to the lesson. Reader aids, such as *Troubleshooting,* also point out things to watch out for or things to avoid.

- **Button images:** When the text instructs you to click a particular toolbar button, an image of the button is shown in the margin.

- **Certification Ready?:** This feature signals the point in the text where a specific certification objective is covered. It provides you with a chance to check your understanding of that particular MCAS objective and, if necessary, review the section of the lesson where it is covered.

- **New Feature:** The New Feature icon appears in the margin next to any software feature that is new to Office 2007.

- **Workplace Ready:** These special features provide a glimpse of how the software application can be put into practice in a real-world situation.
- **Circling Back:** This feature provides you with an opportunity to review and practice skills learned in previous lessons.
- **Knowledge Assessment:** True/false, multiple choice, matching, or fill-in-the-blank questions test or reinforce your understanding of key lesson topics.
- **Competency Assessment:** These projects are similar to the exercises you completed within the lesson. Specific steps for completion are provided so that you can practice what you have learned.
- **Proficiency Assessment:** These projects give you additional opportunity to practice skills that you learned in the lesson. Not all the steps for completion are provided. Completing these exercises helps you verify whether you understand the lesson and reinforces your learning.
- **Mastery Assessment:** These projects require you to work independently—as you would in the workplace. Steps needed to complete the problems are not supplied. You must apply the knowledge you have acquired in the lesson to complete the problems successfully.
- **Internet Ready:** These projects combine what you have learned with research on the Internet.
- **Glossary:** Technical vocabulary is defined in the Glossary. Terms in the Glossary also appear in boldface italic type and are defined within the lessons.
- **Index:** All Glossary terms and application features appear in the Index.

■ Lesson Features

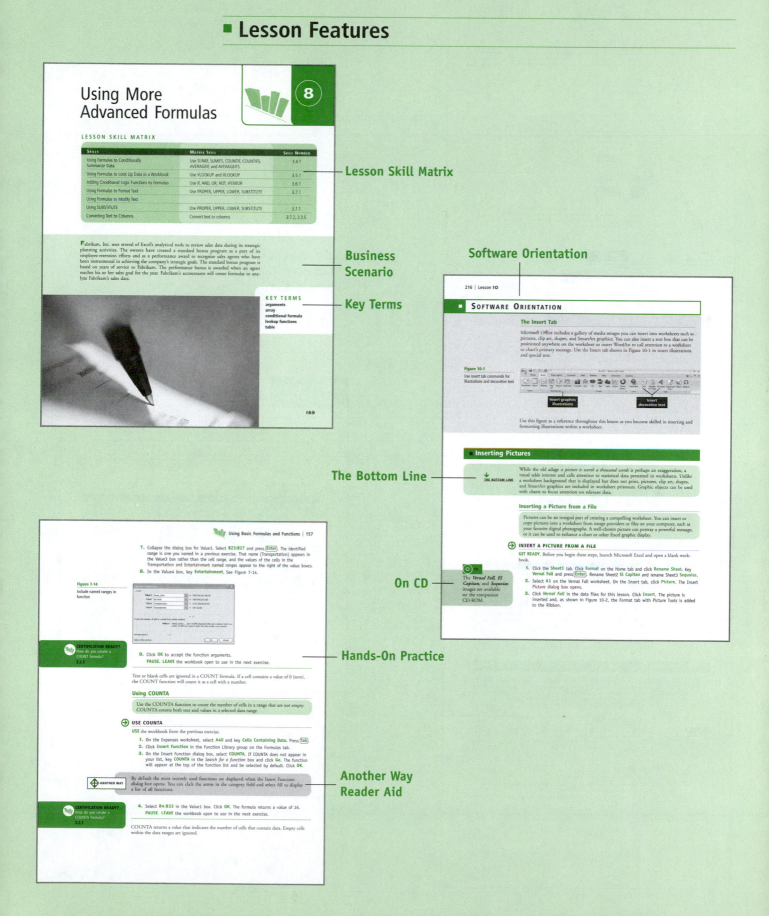

Lesson Skill Matrix

Business Scenario

Key Terms

Software Orientation

The Bottom Line

On CD

Hands-On Practice

Another Way Reader Aid

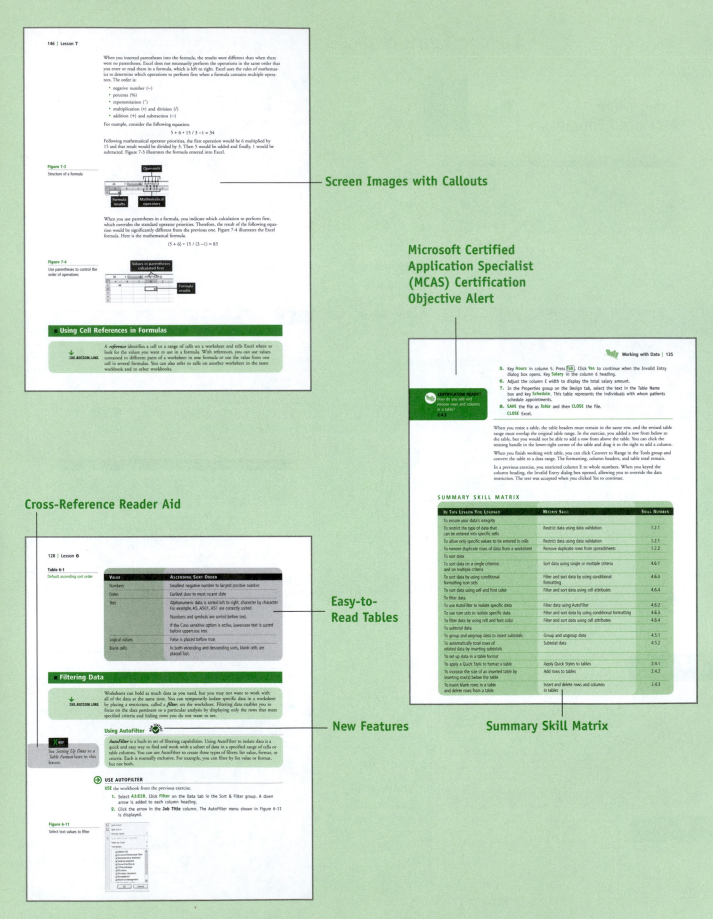

Screen Images with Callouts

Microsoft Certified Application Specialist (MCAS) Certification Objective Alert

Cross-Reference Reader Aid

Easy-to-Read Tables

New Features

Summary Skill Matrix

210 | Lesson 9

■ **Knowledge Assessment**

Matching

a. axis   f. data marker
b. chart   g. data series
c. chart area   h. embedded chart
d. chart sheet   i. legend
e. data labels   j. title

_____ 1. A box that identifies the patterns or colors that are assigned to a data series or categories in a chart.

_____ 2. A graphical representation of numeric data in a worksheet.

_____ 3. A bar, area, dot, slice, or other symbol in a chart that represents a single data point or value that originates from a worksheet cell.

_____ 4. A chart that is placed on a worksheet rather than on a separate sheet.

_____ 5. A sheet in a workbook that contains only a chart.

_____ 6. The entire chart and all its elements.

_____ 7. Related data points that are plotted in a chart.

_____ 8. A line bordering the chart plot area used as a frame of reference for measurement.

_____ 9. Descriptive text that is automatically aligned to an axis or centered at the top of a chart.

_____ 10. A label that provides additional information about a data marker, which represents a single data point or value that originates from a worksheet cell.

Multiple Choice

Circle the choice that best completes the following statements.

1. Which chart type shows values as parts of a whole?
   a. column
   b. bar
   c. area
   d. pie

2. A(n) _____ chart appears on a worksheet with other data.
   a. chart sheet
   b. embedded
   c. Pivot chart
   d. mixed

3. What part of a chart do you click when you want to select the entire chart?
   a. chart area
   b. plot area
   c. chart title
   d. legend

Knowledge Assessment Questions

Proficiency Assessment Projects

234 | Lesson 10

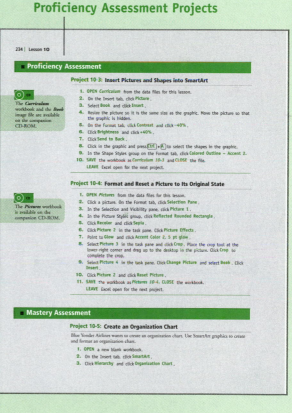

■ **Proficiency Assessment**

Project 10-3: Insert Pictures and Shapes into SmartArt

The **Curriculum** workbook and the **Book** image file are available on the companion CD-ROM.

1. OPEN _Curriculum_ from the data files for this lesson.
2. On the Insert tab, click **Picture**.
3. Select **Book** and click **Insert**.
4. Resize the picture so it is the same size as the graphic. Move the picture so that the graphic is hidden.
5. On the Format tab, click **Contrast** and click **−40%**.
6. Click **Brightness** and click **+40%**.
7. Click **Send to Back**.
8. Click in the graphic and press **Ctrl + A** to select the shapes in the graphic.
9. In the Shape Styles group on the Format tab, click **Colored Outline − Accent 2**.
10. SAVE the workbook as _Curriculum 10-3_ and **CLOSE** the file.
    LEAVE Excel open for the next project.

Project 10-4: Format and Reset a Picture to Its Original State

The **Pictures** workbook is available on the companion CD-ROM.

1. OPEN _Pictures_ from the data files for this lesson.
2. Click a picture. On the Format tab, click **Selection Pane**.
3. In the Selection and Visibility pane, click **Picture 1**.
4. In the Picture Styles group, click **Reflected Rounded Rectangle**.
5. Click **Recolor** and click **Sepia**.
6. Click **Picture 2** in the task pane. Click **Picture Effects**.
7. Point to **Glow** and click **Accent Color 2, 5 pt glow**.
8. Select **Picture 3** in the task pane and click **Crop**. Place the crop tool at the lower right corner and drag up to the desktop in the picture. Click **Crop** to complete the crop.
9. Select **Picture 4** in the task pane. Click **Change Picture** and select **Book**. Click **Insert**.
10. Click **Picture 2** and click **Reset Picture**.
11. SAVE the workbook as _Pictures 10-4_. **CLOSE** the workbook.
    LEAVE Excel open for the next project.

■ **Mastery Assessment**

Project 10-5: Create an Organization Chart

Blue Yonder Airlines wants to create an organization chart. Use SmartArt graphics to create and format an organization chart.

1. OPEN a new blank workbook.
2. On the Insert tab, click **SmartArt**.
3. Click **Hierarchy** and click **Organization Chart**.

Competency Assessment Projects

212 | Lesson 9

■ **Competency Assessment**

Project 9-1: Create a Pie Chart

Blue Yonder Airlines has created a workbook to analyze sales for its first four years of operation. The manager wants to create charts that reflect an analysis of the data.
GET READY. Launch Excel.

The **BY Financials** workbook is available on the companion CD-ROM.

1. OPEN _BY Financials_ from the data files for this lesson.
2. On the Income worksheet, select A3:A7. Press **Ctrl** and select E3:E7.
3. Click the **Insert** tab. Click **Pie** and click **Pie in 3-D**.
4. Click **Layout 1** in the Chart Layouts group on the Design tab.
5. Click **Move Chart Location**.
6. Select **New Sheet** and click **OK**.
7. Right-click the **Chart1** tab and click **Rename**.
8. Key **2008 Income Chart** and press **Enter**.
9. SAVE the workbook as _BY Financials 9-1_.
10. CLOSE the workbook.
    LEAVE Excel open for the next project.

Project 9-2: Create a Bar Chart

The **Financial History** workbook is available on the companion CD-ROM.

Create a bar chart to analyze trends in Fourth Coffee's income before taxes.

1. OPEN _Financial History_ from the data files for this lesson.
2. Make the Income worksheet active. Select A4:F9 and click the **Insert** tab.
3. Click **Bar** in the Charts group and click **100% Stacked Horizontal Cylinder**.
4. Click in the **Chart Area** and click the **Layout** tab.
5. Click **Legend** and click **Legend at Bottom**.
6. Click the **Chart Area** to display the move handles. Move the chart so that the top-left corner is aligned with B12.
7. Click the bottom-right sizing handle and increase the size of the chart so that it fills B12:G29.
8. SAVE the workbook as _Financial History 9-2_.
    LEAVE the workbook open to use in the next project.

■ **Proficiency Assessment**

Project 9-3: Modify a Bar Chart

In the previous project, you created a bar chart to analyze trends in Fourth Coffee's income before taxes. Modify the chart by adding additional chart elements.
USE the workbook from the previous project.

1. Select the chart area and click **Chart Title** in the Labels group on the Layout tab.
2. Click **More Title Options** and click **Gradient fill**.
3. In the Preset colors box, click **Moss** and click **Close**. The Chart Title text box is selected.

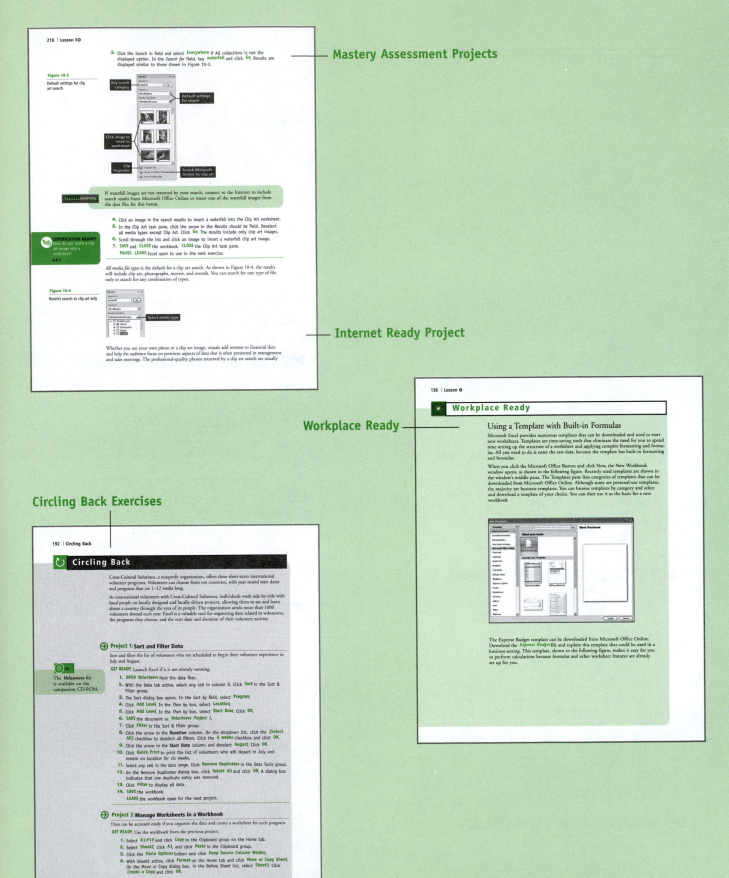

Mastery Assessment Projects

Internet Ready Project

Workplace Ready

Circling Back Exercises

Conventions and Features Used in This Book

This book uses particular fonts, symbols, and heading conventions to highlight important information or to call your attention to special steps. For more information about the features in each lesson, refer to the Illustrated Book Tour section.

CONVENTION	MEANING
NEW FEATURE ✓	This icon indicates a new or greatly improved Office 2007 feature in this version of the software.
↓ **THE BOTTOM LINE**	This feature provides a brief summary of the material to be covered in the section that follows.
CLOSE	Words in all capital letters and in a different font color than the rest of the text indicate instructions for opening, saving, or closing files or programs. They also point out items you should check or actions you should take.
CERTIFICATION READY?	This feature signals the point in the text where a specific certification objective is covered. It provides you with a chance to check your understanding of that particular MCAS objective and, if necessary, review the section of the lesson where it is covered.
◎ **CD**	This indicates a file that is available on the student CD.
TAKE NOTE *	Reader aids appear in shaded boxes found in your text. *Take Note* provides helpful hints related to particular tasks or topics.
✦ **ANOTHER WAY**	*Another Way* provides an alternative procedure for accomplishing a particular task.
TROUBLESHOOTING	*Troubleshooting* covers common problems and pitfalls.
X REF	These notes provide pointers to information discussed elsewhere in the textbook or describe interesting features of Office 2007 that are not directly addressed in the current topic or exercise.
SAVE 🖬	When a toolbar button is referenced in an exercise, the button's picture is shown in the margin.
[Alt] + [Tab]	A plus sign (+) between two key names means that you must press both keys at the same time. Keys that you are instructed to press in an exercise will appear in the font shown here.
A *cell* is the area where data is entered.	Key terms appear in bold italic.
Key **My Name is.**	Any text you are asked to key appears in color.
Click **OK**.	Any button on the screen you are supposed to click on or select will also appear in color.
OPEN *FitnessClasses*.	The names of data files will appear in bold, italic, and color for easy identification.

Instructor Support Program

The *Microsoft Official Academic Course* programs are accompanied by a rich array of resources that incorporate the extensive textbook visuals to form a pedagogically cohesive package. These resources provide all the materials instructors need to deploy and deliver their courses. Resources available online for download include:

- **6-Month Office 2007 Trial Edition (available in North America only).** Students receive 6-months' access to Microsoft Office Professional 2007 when you adopt a MOAC 2007 Microsoft Office system textbook. The textbook includes the trial CD and a product key that allows students to activate the CD for a 6-month period.

- The **Instructor's Guide** contains Solutions to all the textbook exercises, Syllabi for various term lengths, Data Files for all the documents students need to work the exercises. The Instructor's Guide also includes chapter summaries and lecture notes. The Instructor's Guide is available from the Book Companion site (http://www.wiley.com/college/microsoft) and from *WileyPLUS*.

- The **Test Bank** contains hundreds of multiple-choice, true-false, and short answer questions and is available to download from the Instructor's Book Companion site (http://www.wiley.com/college/microsoft) and from *WileyPLUS*. A complete answer key is provided.

- **PowerPoint Presentations and Images.** A complete set of PowerPoint presentations is available on the Instructor's Book Companion site (http://www.wiley.com/college/microsoft) and in *WileyPLUS* to enhance classroom presentations. Approximately 50 PowerPoint slides are provided for each lesson. Tailored to the text's topical coverage and Skills Matrix, these presentations are designed to convey key Office 2007 concepts addressed in the text.

  All figures from the text are on the Instructor's Book Companion site (http://www.wiley.com/college/microsoft) and in *WileyPLUS*. You can incorporate them into your PowerPoint presentations, or create your own overhead transparencies and handouts.

  By using these visuals in class discussions, you can help focus students' attention on key elements of Office 2007 and help them understand how to use it effectively in the workplace.

- **Microsoft Business Certification Pre-Test and Exams**. With each MOAC textbook, students receive information allowing them to access a Pre-Test, Score Report, and Learning Plan, either directly from Certiport, one of Microsoft's exam delivery partners, or through links from *WileyPLUS* Premium. They also receive a code and information for taking the certification exams.

- The **MSDN Academic Alliance** is designed to provide the easiest and most inexpensive way for university departments to make the latest Microsoft software available to faculty and students in labs, classrooms, and on student PCs. A free 1-year membership is available to qualified MOAC adopters.

- **The Wiley Faculty Network** lets you tap into a large community of your peers effortlessly. Wiley Faculty Network mentors are faculty like you, from educational institutions around the country, who are passionate about enhancing instructional efficiency and effectiveness through best practices. Faculty Network activities include technology training and tutorials, virtual seminars, peer-to-peer exchanges of experience and ideas, personal consulting, and sharing of resources. To register for a seminar, go to www.wherefacultyconnect.com or phone 1-866-4FACULTY.

WileyPLUS

Broad developments in education over the past decade have influenced the instructional approach taken in the Microsoft Official Academic Course programs. The way that students learn, especially about new technologies, has changed dramatically in the Internet era. Electronic learning materials and Internet-based instruction is now as much a part of classroom instruction as printed textbooks. *WileyPLUS* provides the technology to create an environment where students reach their full potential and experience academic success that will last them a lifetime!

WileyPLUS is a powerful and highly-integrated suite of teaching and learning resources designed to bridge the gap between what happens in the classroom and what happens at home and on the job. *WileyPLUS* provides Instructors with the resources to teach their students new technologies and guide them to reach their goals of getting ahead in the job market by having the skills to become certified and advance in the workforce. For students, *WileyPLUS* provides the tools for study and practice that are available to them 24/7, wherever and whenever they want to study. *WileyPLUS* includes a complete online version of the student textbook; PowerPoint presentations; homework and practice assignments and quizzes; links to Microsoft's Pre-Test, Learning Plan, and a code for taking the certification exam (in *WileyPLUS* Premium); image galleries; test-bank questions; gradebook; and all the instructor resources in one easy-to-use website.

Organized around the everyday activities you and your students perform in the class, *WileyPLUS* helps you:

- **Prepare & Present** outstanding class presentations using relevant PowerPoint slides and other *WileyPLUS* materials—and you can easily upload and add your own.
- **Create Assignments** by choosing from questions organized by lesson, level of difficulty, and source—and add your own questions. Students' homework and quizzes are automatically graded, and the results are recorded in your gradebook.
- **Offer context-sensitive help to students, 24/7.** When you assign homework or quizzes, you decide if and when students get access to hints, solutions, or answers where appropriate—or they can be linked to relevant sections of their complete, online text for additional help whenever—and wherever they need it most.
- **Track Student Progress:** Analyze students' results and assess their level of understanding on an individual and class level using the *WileyPLUS* gradebook, or export data to your own personal gradebook.
- **Administer Your Course:** *WileyPLUS* can easily be integrated with another course management system, gradebook, or other resources you are using in your class, providing you with the flexibility to build your course, your way.
- **Seamlessly integrate all of the rich *WileyPLUS* content and resources with WebCT and Blackboard**—with a single sign-on.

Please view our online demo at **www.wiley.com/college/wileyplus**. Here you will find additional information about the features and benefits of *WileyPLUS*, how to request a "test drive" of *WileyPLUS* for this title, and how to adopt it for class use.

MICROSOFT BUSINESS CERTIFICATION PRE-TEST AND EXAMS AVAILABLE THROUGH *WILEYPLUS* PREMIUM

Enhance your students' knowledge and skills and increase their performance on Microsoft Business Certification exams with adoption of the Microsoft Official Academic Course program for Office 2007.

With the majority of the workforce classified as *information workers*, certification on the 2007 Microsoft Office system is a critical tool in terms of validating the desktop computing knowledge and skills required to be more productive in the workplace. Certification is the primary tool companies use to validate the proficiency of desktop computing skills among employees. It gives organizations the ability to help assess employees' actual computer skills and select job candidates based on verifiable skills applying the latest productivity tools and technology.

Microsoft Pre-tests, delivered by Certiport, provide a simple, low-cost way for individuals to identify their desktop computing skill level. Pre-Tests are taken online, making the first step towards certification easy and convenient. Through the Pre-Tests, individuals can receive a custom learning path with recommended training.

To help students to study for and pass the Microsoft Certified Application Specialist, or MCAS exam, each MOAC textbook includes information allowing students to access a Pre-Test, Score Report, and Learning Plan, either directly from Certiport or through links from the *WileyPLUS* Premium course. Students also receive a code and information for taking the certification exams. Students who do not have access to *WileyPLUS* Premium can find information on how to purchase access to the Pre-Test and a code for taking the certification exams by clicking on their textbook at:

http://www.wiley.com/college/microsoft.

The Pre-Test can only be taken once. It provides a simple, low-cost way for students to evaluate and identify their skill level. Through the Pre-Test, students receive a recommended study plan that they can print out to help them prepare for the live certification exams. The Pre-Test is comprised of a variety of selected response questions, including matching, sequencing exercises, "hot spots" where students must identify an item or function, and traditional multiple-choice questions. After students have mastered all the certification objectives, they can use their code to take the actual Microsoft Certified Application Specialist (MCAS) exams for Office 2007.

WileyPLUS Premium includes a complete online version of the student textbook, PowerPoint® presentations, homework and practice assignments and quizzes, links to Microsoft's Pre-Test, Learning Plan and a certification voucher, image galleries, test bank questions, gradebook, and all the instructor resources in one, easy-to-use website. Together, with *WileyPLUS* and the MCAS Pre-Test and exams delivered by Certiport, we are creating the best of both worlds in academic learning and performance based validation in preparation for a great career and a globally recognized Microsoft certification—the higher education learning management system that accesses the industry-leading certification pre-test.

Contact your Wiley rep today about this special offer.

MSDN ACADEMIC ALLIANCE—FREE 1-YEAR MEMBERSHIP AVAILABLE TO QUALIFIED ADOPTERS!

MSDN Academic Alliance (MSDN AA) is designed to provide the easiest and most inexpensive way for universities to make the latest Microsoft software available in labs, classrooms, and on student PCs. MSDN AA is an annual membership program for departments teaching Science, Technology, Engineering, and Mathematics (STEM) courses. The membership provides a complete solution to keep academic labs, faculty, and students on the leading edge of technology.

As a bonus to this free offer, faculty will be introduced to Microsoft's Faculty Connection and Academic Resource Center. It takes time and preparation to keep students engaged while giving them a fundamental understanding of theory, and the Microsoft Faculty Connection is designed to help STEM professors with this preparation by providing articles, curriculum, and tools that professors can use to engage and inspire today's technology students.

Software provided in the MSDN AA program carries a high retail value but is being provided here through the Wiley and Microsoft publishing partnership and is made available to your department free of charge with the adoption of any Wiley qualified textbook.*

* Contact your Wiley rep for details.

For more information about the MSDN Academic Alliance program, go to:

http://msdn.microsoft.com/academic/

Adoption Options

To provide you and your students with the right choices for learning, studying, and passing the MCAS certification exams, we have put together various options for your adoption requirements.

All selections include the student CD. Please contact your Wiley rep for more information:

- Textbook with 6-month Microsoft Office Trial
- Textbook, 6-month Microsoft Office Trial, *WileyPLUS*
- Textbook, 6-month Microsoft Office Trial, *WileyPLUS* Premium (includes access to Certiport)
- *WileyPLUS* (includes full e-book)
- *WileyPLUS* Premium (includes full e-book and access to Certiport)

Important Web Addresses and Phone Numbers

To locate the Wiley Higher Education Rep in your area, go to the following Web address and click on the "*Who's My Rep?*" link at the top of the page.

http://www.wiley.com/college

Or Call the MOAC Toll Free Number: 1 + (888) 764-7001

To learn more about becoming a Microsoft Certified Application Specialist and exam availability, visit www.microsoft.com/learning/msbc.

http://www.wiley.com/college/microsoft *or* call the MOAC Toll-Free Number: 1+(888) 764-7001

Book Companion Website (www.wiley.com/college/microsoft)

The book companion site for the MOAC series includes the Instructor Resources and Web links to important information for students and instructors.

WileyPLUS

WileyPLUS is a powerful and highly-integrated suite of teaching and learning resources designed to bridge the gap between what happens in the classroom and what happens at home and on the job. For students, *WileyPLUS* provides the tools for study and practice that are available 24/7, wherever and whenever they want to study. *WileyPLUS* includes a complete online version of the student textbook; PowerPoint presentations; homework and practice assignments and quizzes; links to Microsoft's Pre-Test, Learning Plan, and a code for taking the certification exam (in *WileyPLUS* Premium); image galleries; test bank questions; gradebook; and all the instructor resources in one easy-to-use website.

WileyPLUS provides immediate feedback on student assignments and a wealth of support materials. This powerful study tool will help your students develop their conceptual understanding of the class material and increase their ability to answer questions.

- A **Study and Practice** area links directly to text content, allowing students to review the text while they study and answer. Access to Microsoft's Pre-Test, Learning Plan, and a code for taking the MCAS certification exam is available in Study and Practice. Additional Practice Questions tied to the MCAS certification that can be re-taken as many times as necessary, are also available.

- An **Assignment** area keeps all the work you want your students to complete in one location, making it easy for them to stay on task. Students have access to a variety of interactive self-assessment tools, as well as other resources for building their confidence and understanding. In addition, all of the assignments and quizzes contain a link to the relevant section of the multimedia book, providing students with context-sensitive help that allows them to conquer obstacles as they arise.

- A **Personal Gradebook** for each student allows students to view their results from past assignments at any time.

Please view our online demo at www.wiley.com/college/wileyplus. Here you will find additional information about the features and benefits of *WileyPLUS*, how to request a "test drive" of *WileyPLUS* for this title, and how to adopt it for class use.

6-MONTH MICROSOFT OFFICE 2007 TRIAL EDITION

MOAC textbooks provide an unparalleled value to students in today's performance-based courses. All MOAC 2007 Microsoft Office system textbooks sold in North America are packaged with a 6-month trial CD of Microsoft Office Professional 2007. The textbook includes the CD and a product key that allows students to activate Microsoft Office Professional 2007 for the 6-month trial period. After purchasing the textbook containing the Microsoft Office Professional 2007 Trial CD, students must install the CD onto their computer and, when prompted, enter the Office Trial product key that allows them to activate the software.

Installing the Microsoft Office Professional 2007 Trial CD provides students with the state-of-the-art 2007 Microsoft Office system software, allowing them to use the practice files on the Student CD and in *WileyPLUS* to learn and study by doing, which is the best and most effective way to acquire and remember new computing skills.

TAKE NOTE *

For the best performance, the default selection during Setup is to uninstall previous versions of Office. There is also an option to remove previous versions of Office. With all trial software, Microsoft recommends that you have your original CDs available to reinstall if necessary. If you want to return to your previous version of Office, you need to uninstall the trial software. This should be done through the Add or Remove Programs icon in Microsoft Windows Control Panel (or Uninstall a program in the Control Panel of Windows Vista).

Installation of Microsoft Office Professional 2007 6-Month Trial software will remove your existing version of Microsoft Outlook. However, your contacts, calendar, and other personal information will not be deleted. At the end of the trial, if you choose to upgrade or to reinstall your previous version of Outlook, your personal settings and information will be retained.

Installing the 2007 Microsoft Office System 6-Month Trial

1. Insert the trial software CD-ROM into the CD drive on your computer. The CD will be detected, and the Setup.exe file should automatically begin to run on your computer.
2. When prompted for the Office Product Key, enter the Product Key provided with the software, and then click **Next.**
3. Enter your name and organization user name, and then click **Next.**
4. Read the End-User License Agreement, select the *I Accept the Terms in the License Agreement* check box, and then click **Next.**
5. Select the install option, verify the installation location or click **Browse** to change the installation location, and then click **Next.**
6. Verify the program installation preferences, and then click **Next.**
7. Click **Finish** to complete the setup.

Upgrading Microsoft Office Professional 2007 6-Month Trial Software to the Full Product

You can convert the software into full use without removing or reinstalling software on your computer. When you complete your trial, you can purchase a product license from any Microsoft reseller and enter a valid Product Key when prompted during Setup.

Uninstalling the Trial Software and Returning to Your Previous Office Version

If you want to return to your previous version of Office, you need to uninstall the trial software. This should be done through the Add or Remove Programs icon in Control Panel (or Uninstall a program in the Control Panel of Windows Vista).

Uninstall Trial Software

1. Quit any programs that are running.
2. In Control Panel, click **Add or Remove Programs** (or **Uninstall a program** in Windows Vista).
3. Click **Microsoft Office Professional 2007,** and then click **Remove** (or **Uninstall** in Windows Vista).

TAKE NOTE If you selected the option to remove a previous version of Office during installation of the trial software, you need to reinstall your previous version of Office. If you did not remove your previous version of Office, you can start each of your Office programs either through the Start menu or by opening files for each program. In some cases, you may have to recreate some of your shortcuts and default settings.

Student CD

The CD-ROM included with this book contains the practice files that you will use as you perform the exercises in the book. By using the practice files, you will not waste time creating the samples used in the lessons, and you can concentrate on learning how to use Microsoft Office 2007. With the files and the step-by-step instructions in the lessons, you will learn by doing, which is an easy and effective way to acquire and remember new skills.

IMPORTANT This course assumes that the 2007 Microsoft Office system has already been installed on the PC you are using. Note that Microsoft Product Support does not support this trial version.

Copying the Practice Files

Your instructor might already have copied the practice files before you arrive in class. However, your instructor might ask you to copy the practice files on your own at the start of class. Also, if you want to work through any of the exercises in this book on your own at home or at your place of business after class, you may want to copy the practice files. Note that you can also open the files directly from the CD-ROM, but you should be cautious about carrying the CD-ROM around with you as it could become damaged.

ANOTHER WAY

If you only want to copy the files for one lesson, you can open the Excel Data folder and right-click the desired Lesson folder within the Excel Data folder.

1. Insert the CD-ROM in the CD-ROM drive of your computer.
2. Start Windows Explorer.
3. In the left pane of Explorer, locate the icon for your CD-ROM and click on this icon. The folders and files contained on the CD will appear listed on the right.
4. Locate and select the **Excel Data** folder. This is the folder which contains all of the practice files, separated by Lesson folders.
5. Right-click on the **Excel Data** folder and choose **Copy** from the menu.
6. In the left pane of Windows Explorer, locate the location to which you would like to copy the practice files. This can be a drive on your local PC or an external drive.
7. Right-click on the drive/location to which you want to copy the practice files and choose **Paste.** This will copy the entire Excel Data folder to your chosen location.
8. Close Windows Explorer.

Deleting the Practice Files

Use the following steps when you want to delete the practice files from your hard disk or other drive. Your instructor might ask you to perform these steps at the end of class. Also, you should perform these steps if you have worked through the exercises at home or at your place of business and want to work through the exercises again. Deleting the practice files and then reinstalling them ensures that all files and folders are in their original condition if you decide to work through the exercises again.

1. Start Windows Explorer.
2. Browse through the drives and folders to locate the practice files.
3. Select the **Excel Data** folder.
4. Right-click on the **Excel Data** folder and choose **Delete** from the menu.
5. Close Windows Explorer.

Locating and Opening Practice Files

After you (or your instructor) have copied the practice files, all the files you need for this course will be stored in a folder named Excel Data located on the disk you choose.

1. Click the **Office Button** in the top left corner of your application.
2. Choose **Open** from the menu.
3. In the Open dialog box, browse through the Folders panel to locate the drive and folder where you copied the files.
4. Double-click on the **Excel Data** folder.
5. Double-click on the **Lesson** folder for the lesson in which you are working.
6. Select the file that you want and click **Open** or double-click on the file that you want.

Wiley Desktop Editions

Wiley MOAC Desktop Editions are innovative, electronic versions of printed textbooks. Students buy the desktop version for 50% off the price of the printed text, and get the added value of permanence and portability. Wiley Desktop Editions provide students with numerous additional benefits that are not available with other e-text solutions:

Wiley Desktop Editions are NOT subscriptions; students download the Wiley Desktop Edition to their computer desktops. Students own the content they buy to keep for as long as they want. Once a Wiley Desktop Edition is downloaded to the computer desktop, students have instant access to all of the content without being online. Students can also print out the sections they prefer to read in hard copy. Students also have access to fully integrated resources within their Wiley Desktop Edition. From highlighting their e-text to taking and sharing notes, students can easily personalize their Wiley Desktop Edition as they are reading or following along in class.

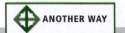

ANOTHER WAY

If you only want to delete only the files for one lesson, you can open the Excel Data folder and right-click the desired Lesson folder within the Excel Data folder.

ANOTHER WAY

You can use the Search function in the Open dialog box to quickly find the specific file for which you are looking.

Please visit Microsoft Office Online for help using Office 2007, Clip Art, Templates, and other valuable information:
http://office.microsoft.com/

Preparing to Take the Microsoft Certified Application Specialist (MCAS) Exam

The Microsoft Certified Application Specialist program is part of the new and enhanced Microsoft Business Certifications. It is easily attainable through a series of verifications that provide a simple and convenient framework for skills assessment and validation.

For organizations, the new certification program provides better skills verification tools that help with assessing not only in-demand skills on the 2007 Microsoft Office system, but also the ability to quickly complete on-the-job tasks. Individuals will find it easier to identify and work towards the certification credential that meets their personal and professional goals.

To learn more about becoming a Microsoft Certified Application Specialist and exam availability, visit www.microsoft.com/learning/msbc.

Microsoft Certified Application Specialist (MCAS) Program

The core Microsoft Office Specialist credential has been upgraded to validate skills with the 2007 Microsoft Office system as well as the new Windows Vista operating system. The Application Specialist certifications target information workers and cover the most popular business applications such as Word 2007, PowerPoint 2007, Excel 2007, Access 2007, and Outlook 2007.

By becoming certified, you demonstrate to employers that you have achieved a predictable level of skill in the use of a particular Office application. Employers often require certification either as a condition of employment or as a condition of advancement within the company or other organization. The certification examinations are sponsored by Microsoft but administered through exam delivery partners like Certiport.

Preparing to Take an Exam

Unless you are a very experienced user, you will need to use a test preparation course to prepare to complete the test correctly and within the time allowed. The *Microsoft Official Academic Course* series is designed to prepare you with a strong knowledge of all exam topics, and with some additional review and practice on your own. You should feel confident in your ability to pass the appropriate exam.

After you decide which exam to take, review the list of objectives for the exam. This list can be found in the MCAS Objectives Appendix at the back of this book. You can also easily identify tasks that are included in the objective list by locating the Lesson Skill Matrix at the start of each lesson and the Certification Ready sidebars in the margin of the lessons in this book.

To take the MCAS test, visit *www.microsoft.com/learning/msbc* to locate your nearest testing center. Then call the testing center directly to schedule your test. The amount of advance notice you should provide will vary for different testing centers, and it typically depends on the number of computers available at the testing center, the number of other testers who have already been scheduled for the day on which you want to take the test, and the number of times per week that the testing center offers MCAS testing. In general, you should call to schedule your test at least two weeks prior to the date on which you want to take the test.

When you arrive at the testing center, you might be asked for proof of identity. A driver's license or passport is an acceptable form of identification. If you do not have either of these items of documentation, call your testing center and ask what alternative forms of identification will be accepted. If you are retaking a test, bring your MCAS identification number, which will have been given to you when you previously took the test. If you have not prepaid or if your organization has not already arranged to make payment for you, you will need to pay the test-taking fee when you arrive.

Test Format

All MCAS certification tests are live, performance-based tests. There are no true/false or short-answer questions. Instructions are general: you are told the basic tasks to perform on the computer, but you aren't given any help in figuring out how to perform them. You are not permitted to use reference material.

As you complete the tasks stated in a particular test question, the testing software monitors your actions. An example question might be:

Open the file named *Wiley Guests* and select the word *Welcome* in the first paragraph. Change the font to 12 point, and apply bold formatting. Select the words *at your convenience* in the second paragraph, move them to the end of the first paragraph using drag and drop, and then center the first paragraph.

When the test administrator seats you at a computer, you will see an online form that you use to enter information about yourself (name, address, and other information required to process your exam results). While you complete the form, the software will generate the test from a master test bank and then prompt you to continue. The first test question will appear in a window. Read the question carefully, and then perform all the tasks stated in the test question. When you have finished completing all tasks for a question, click the Next Question button.

You have 45 to 50 minutes to complete all questions, depending on the test that you are taking. The testing software assesses your results as soon as you complete the test, and the test administrator can print the results of the test so that you will have a record of any tasks that you performed incorrectly. If you pass, you will receive a certificate in the mail within two to four weeks. If you do not pass, you can study and practice the skills that you missed and then schedule to retake the test at a later date.

Tips for Successfully Completing the Test

The following tips and suggestions are the result of feedback received from many individuals who have taken one or more MCAS tests:

- Make sure that you are thoroughly prepared. If you have extensively used the application for which you are being tested, you might feel confident that you are prepared for the test. However, the test might include questions that involve tasks that you rarely or never perform when you use the application at your place of business, at school, or at home. You must be knowledgeable in all the MCAS objectives for the test that you will take.

- Read each exam question carefully. An exam question might include several tasks that you are to perform. A partially correct response to a test question is counted as an incorrect response. In the example question on the previous page, you might apply bold formatting and move the words *at your convenience* to the correct location, but forget to center the first paragraph. This would count as an incorrect response and would result in a lower test score.

- You are not allowed to use the application's Help system. The Help function is always disabled for all exams.

- The test does display the amount of time that you have left. The test program also displays the number of items that you have completed along with the total number of test items (for example, "35 of 40 items have been completed"). Use this information to gauge your pace.

- If you skip a question, you can return to it later.

If You Do Not Pass the Test

If you do not pass, you can use the assessment printout as a guide to practice the items that you missed. There is no limit to the number of times that you can retake a test; however, you must pay the fee each time that you take the test. When you retake the test, expect to see some of the same test items on the subsequent test; the test software randomly generates the test items from a master test bank before you begin the test. Also expect to see several questions that did not appear on the previous test.

Acknowledgments

MOAC Instructor Advisory Board

We would like to thank our Instructor Advisory Board, an elite group of educators who has assisted us every step of the way in building these products. Advisory Board members have acted as our sounding board on key pedagogical and design decisions leading to the development of these compelling and innovative textbooks for future Information Workers. Their dedication to technology education is truly appreciated.

Catherine Binder, Strayer University & Katharine Gibbs School–Philadelphia

Catherine currently works at both Katharine Gibbs School in Norristown, PA, and Strayer University in King of Prussia, PA. Catherine has been at Katharine Gibbs School for 4 years. Catherine is currently the Department Chair/Lead instructor for PC Networking at Gibbs and the founder/advisor of the TEK Masters Society. Since joining Strayer University a year and a half ago she has risen in the ranks from adjunct to DIT/Assistant Campus Dean.

Catherine has brought her 10+ year's industry experience as Network Administrator, Network Supervisor, Professor, Bench Tech, Manager and CTO from such places as Foster Wheeler Corp, KidsPeace Inc., Victoria Vogue, TESST College, AMC Theatres, Blue Mountain Publishing and many more to her teaching venue.

Catherine began as an adjunct in the PC Networking department and quickly became a full-time instructor. At both schools she is in charge of scheduling, curricula and departmental duties. She happily advises about 80+ students and is committed to Gibbs/Strayer life, her students, and continuing technology education every day.

Penny Gudgeon, CDI College

Penny is the Program Manager for IT curriculum at Corinthian Colleges, Inc. Until January 2006, Penny was responsible for all Canadian programming and web curriculum for five years. During that time, Corinthian Colleges, Inc. acquired CDI College of Business and Technology in 2004. Before 2000 she spent four years as IT instructor at one of the campuses. Penny joined CDI College in 1997 after her working for 10 years first in programming and later in software productivity education. Penny previously has worked in the fields of advertising, sales, engineering technology and programming. When not working from her home office or indulging her passion for life long learning, and the possibilities of what might be, Penny likes to read mysteries, garden and relax at home in Hamilton, Ontario, with her Shih-Tzu, Gracie, and husband, Al.

Jana Hambruch, School District of Lee County

Ms. Hambruch currently serves as Director for the Information Technology Magnet Programs at The School District of Lee County in Ft Myers, Florida. She is responsible for the implementation and direction of three schools that fall under this grant program. This program has been recognized as one of the top 15 most innovative technology programs in the nation. She is also co-author of the grant proposal for the IT Magnet Grant prior to taking on the role of Director.

Ms. Hambruch has over ten years experience directing the technical certification training programs at many Colleges and Universities, including Barry University, the University of

South Florida, Broward Community College, and at Florida Gulf Coast University, where she served as the Director for the Center for Technology Education. She excels at developing alternative training models that focus on the tie between the education provider and the community in which it serves.

Ms. Hambruch is a past board member and treasurer of the Human Resources Management Association of SW Florida, graduate of Leadership Lee County Class of 2002, Steering Committee Member for Leadership Lee County Class of 2004 and a former board member of the Career Coalition of Southwest Florida. She has frequently lectured for organizations such as Microsoft, American Society of Training and Development, Florida Gulf Coast University, Florida State University, University of Nevada at Las Vegas, University of Wisconsin at Milwaukee, Canada's McGill University, and Florida's State Workforce Summit.

Dee Hobson, Richland College

Dee Hobson is currently a faculty member of the Business Office Systems and Support Division at Richland College. Richland is one of seven colleges in the Dallas County Community College District and has the distinction of being the first community college to receive the Malcolm Baldrige National Quality Award in 2005. Richland also received the Texas Award for Performance Excellence in 2005.

The Business Office Systems and Support Division at Richland is also a Certiport Authorized Microsoft Office testing center. All students enrolling in one of Microsoft's application software courses (Word, Excel, PowerPoint, and Access) are required to take the respective Microsoft certification exam at the end of the semester.

Dee has taught computer and business courses in K-12 public schools and at a proprietary career college in Dallas. She has also been involved with several corporate training companies and with adult education programs in the Dallas area. She began her computer career as an employee of IBM Corporation in St. Louis, Missouri. During her ten-year IBM employment, she moved to Memphis, Tennessee, to accept a managerial position and to Dallas, Texas, to work in a national sales and marketing technical support center.

Keith Hoell, Katharine Gibbs School–New York

Keith has worked in both non-profit and proprietary education for over 10 years, initially at St. John's University in New York, and then as full-time faculty, Chairperson and currently Dean of Information Systems at the Katharine Gibbs School in New York City. He also worked for General Electric in the late 80's and early 90's as the Sysop of a popular bulletin board dedicated to ASCII-Art on GE's pioneering GEnie on-line service before the advent of the World Wide Web. He has taught courses and workshops dealing with many mainstream IT issues and varied technology, especially those related to computer hardware and operating system software, networking, software applications, IT project management and ethics, and relational database technology. An avid runner and a member of The New York Road Runners, he won the Footlocker Five Borough Challenge representing Queens at the 2005 ING New York City Marathon while competing against the 4 other borough reps. He currently resides in Queens, New York.

Michael Taylor, Seattle Central Community College

Michael worked in education and training for the last 20 years in both the public and private sector. He currently teaches and coordinates the applications support program at Seattle Central Community College and also administers the Microsoft IT Academy. His experience outside the educational world is in Travel and Tourism with wholesale tour operations and cruise lines.

Interests outside of work include greyhound rescue. (He adopted 3 ex-racers who bring him great joy.) He also enjoys the arts and is fortunate to live in downtown Seattle where there is much to see and do.

MOAC Office 2007 Reviewers

We also thank the many reviewers who pored over the manuscript providing invaluable feedback in the service of quality instructional materials.

Access

Susan Fry, Boise State University
Leslie Jernberg, Eastern Idaho Technical College
Dr. Deborah Jones, South Georgia Technical College
Suzanne Marks, Bellevue Community College
Kim Styles, Tri-County Technical College & Anderson School District 5

Excel

Christie Hovey, Lincoln Land Community College
Barbara Lave, Portland Community College
Donna Madsen, Kirkwood Community College
James M. Veneziano, Davenport University—Caro
Dorothy Weiner, Manchester Community College

PowerPoint

Barbara Gillespie, Cuyamaca College
Tatyana Pashnyak, Bainbridge College
Michelle Poertner, Northwestern Michigan College
Janet Sebesy, Cuyahoga Community College

Outlook

Julie Boyles, Portland Community College
Joe LaMontagne, Davenport University—Grand Rapids
Randy Nordell, American River College
Echo Rantanen, Spokane Community College

Project

Janis DeHaven, Central Community College
Dr. Susan Jennings, Stephen F. Austin State University
Diane D. Mickey, Northern Virginia Community College
Linda Nutter, Peninsula College
Marika Reinke, Bellevue Community College

Word

Diana Anderson, Big Sandy Community & Technical College
Donna Hendricks, South Arkansas Community College
Dr. Donna McGill-Cameron, Yuba Community College—Woodland Campus
Patricia McMahon, South Suburban College
Nancy Noe, Linn-Benton Community College
Teresa Roberts, Wilson Technical Community College

Focus Group and Survey Participants

Finally we thank the hundreds of instructors who participated in our focus groups and surveys to ensure that the Microsoft Official Academic Courses best met the needs of our customers.

Jean Aguilar, Mt. Hood Community College
Konrad Akens, Zane State College
Michael Albers, University of Memphis
Diana Anderson, Big Sandy Community & Technical College
Phyllis Anderson, Delaware County Community College

Judith Andrews, Feather River College
Damon Antos, American River College
Bridget Archer, Oakton Community College
Linda Arnold, Harrisburg Area Community College–
    Lebanon Campus

www.wiley.com/college/microsoft *or* **call the MOAC Toll-Free Number: 1+(888) 764-7001**

Neha Arya, Fullerton College

Mohammad Bajwa, Katharine Gibbs School–New York

Virginia Baker, University of Alaska Fairbanks

Carla Bannick, Pima Community College

Rita Barkley, Northeast Alabama Community College

Elsa Barr, Central Community College – Hastings

Ronald W. Barry, Ventura County Community College District

Elizabeth Bastedo, Central Carolina Technical College

Karen Baston, Waubonsee Community College

Karen Bean, Blinn College

Scott Beckstrand, Community College of Southern Nevada

Paulette Bell, Santa Rosa Junior College

Liz Bennett, Southeast Technical Institute

Nancy Bermea, Olympic College

Lucy Betz, Milwaukee Area Technical College

Meral Binbasioglu, Hofstra University

Catherine Binder, Strayer University & Katharine Gibbs School–Philadelphia

Terrel Blair, El Centro College

Ruth Blalock, Alamance Community College

Beverly Bohner, Reading Area Community College

Henry Bojack, Farmingdale State University

Matthew Bowie, Luna Community College

Julie Boyles, Portland Community College

Karen Brandt, College of the Albemarle

Stephen Brown, College of San Mateo

Jared Bruckner, Southern Adventist University

Pam Brune, Chattanooga State Technical Community College

Sue Buchholz, Georgia Perimeter College

Roberta Buczyna, Edison College

Angela Butler, Mississippi Gulf Coast Community College

Rebecca Byrd, Augusta Technical College

Kristen Callahan, Mercer County Community College

Judy Cameron, Spokane Community College

Dianne Campbell, Athens Technical College

Gena Casas, Florida Community College at Jacksonville

Jesus Castrejon, Latin Technologies

Gail Chambers, Southwest Tennessee Community College

Jacques Chansavang, Indiana University–Purdue University Fort Wayne

Nancy Chapko, Milwaukee Area Technical College

Rebecca Chavez, Yavapai College

Sanjiv Chopra, Thomas Nelson Community College

Greg Clements, Midland Lutheran College

Dayna Coker, Southwestern Oklahoma State University–Sayre Campus

Tamra Collins, Otero Junior College

Janet Conrey, Gavilan Community College

Carol Cornforth, West Virginia Northern Community College

Gary Cotton, American River College

Edie Cox, Chattahoochee Technical College

Rollie Cox, Madison Area Technical College

David Crawford, Northwestern Michigan College

J.K. Crowley, Victor Valley College

Rosalyn Culver, Washtenaw Community College

Sharon Custer, Huntington University

Sandra Daniels, New River Community College

Anila Das, Cedar Valley College

Brad Davis, Santa Rosa Junior College

Susan Davis, Green River Community College

Mark Dawdy, Lincoln Land Community College

Jennifer Day, Sinclair Community College

Carol Deane, Eastern Idaho Technical College

Julie DeBuhr, Lewis-Clark State College

Janis DeHaven, Central Community College

Drew Dekreon, University of Alaska–Anchorage

Joy DePover, Central Lakes College

Salli DiBartolo, Brevard Community College

Melissa Diegnau, Riverland Community College

Al Dillard, Lansdale School of Business

Marjorie Duffy, Cosumnes River College

Sarah Dunn, Southwest Tennessee Community College

Shahla Durany, Tarrant County College–South Campus

Kay Durden, University of Tennessee at Martin

Dineen Ebert, St. Louis Community College–Meramec

Donna Ehrhart, State University of New York–Brockport

Larry Elias, Montgomery County Community College

Glenda Elser, New Mexico State University at Alamogordo

Angela Evangelinos, Monroe County Community College

Angie Evans, Ivy Tech Community College of Indiana

Linda Farrington, Indian Hills Community College

Dana Fladhammer, Phoenix College

Richard Flores, Citrus College

Connie Fox, Community and Technical College at Institute of Technology West Virginia University

Wanda Freeman, Okefenokee Technical College

Brenda Freeman, Augusta Technical College

Susan Fry, Boise State University

Roger Fulk, Wright State University–Lake Campus

Sue Furnas, Collin County Community College District

Sandy Gabel, Vernon College

Laura Galvan, Fayetteville Technical Community College

Candace Garrod, Red Rocks Community College

Sherrie Geitgey, Northwest State Community College

Chris Gerig, Chattahoochee Technical College

Barb Gillespie, Cuyamaca College

Jessica Gilmore, Highline Community College

Pamela Gilmore, Reedley College

Debbie Glinert, Queensborough Community College

Steven Goldman, Polk Community College

Bettie Goodman, C.S. Mott Community College

Mike Grabill, Katharine Gibbs School–Philadelphia

Francis Green, Penn State University

Walter Griffin, Blinn College

Fillmore Guinn, Odessa College

Helen Haasch, Milwaukee Area Technical College

John Habal, Ventura College

Joy Haerens, Chaffey College
Norman Hahn, Thomas Nelson Community College
Kathy Hall, Alamance Community College
Teri Harbacheck, Boise State University
Linda Harper, Richland Community College
Maureen Harper, Indian Hills Community College
Steve Harris, Katharine Gibbs School–New York
Robyn Hart, Fresno City College
Darien Hartman, Boise State University
Gina Hatcher, Tacoma Community College
Winona T. Hatcher, Aiken Technical College
BJ Hathaway, Northeast Wisconsin Tech College
Cynthia Hauki, West Hills College – Coalinga
Mary L. Haynes, Wayne County Community College
Marcie Hawkins, Zane State College
Steve Hebrock, Ohio State University Agricultural
    Technical Institute
Sue Heistand, Iowa Central Community College
Heith Hennel, Valencia Community College
Donna Hendricks, South Arkansas Community College
Judy Hendrix, Dyersburg State Community College
Gloria Hensel, Matanuska-Susitna College University
    of Alaska Anchorage
Gwendolyn Hester, Richland College
Tammarra Holmes, Laramie County Community College
Dee Hobson, Richland College
Keith Hoell, Katharine Gibbs School–New York
Pashia Hogan, Northeast State Technical
    Community College
Susan Hoggard, Tulsa Community College
Kathleen Holliman, Wallace Community College Selma
Chastity Honchul, Brown Mackie College/Wright
    State University
Christie Hovey, Lincoln Land Community College
Peggy Hughes, Allegany College of Maryland
Sandra Hume, Chippewa Valley Technical College
John Hutson, Aims Community College
Celia Ing, Sacramento City College
Joan Ivey, Lanier Technical College
Barbara Jaffari, College of the Redwoods
Penny Jakes, University of Montana College of Technology
Eduardo Jaramillo, Peninsula College
Barbara Jauken, Southeast Community College
Susan Jennings, Stephen F. Austin State University
Leslie Jernberg, Eastern Idaho Technical College
Linda Johns, Georgia Perimeter College
Brent Johnson, Okefenokee Technical College
Mary Johnson, Mt. San Antonio College
Shirley Johnson, Trinidad State Junior College–
    Valley Campus
Sandra M. Jolley, Tarrant County College
Teresa Jolly, South Georgia Technical College
Dr. Deborah Jones, South Georgia Technical College
Margie Jones, Central Virginia Community College
Randall Jones, Marshall Community and Technical College

Diane Karlsbraaten, Lake Region State College
Teresa Keller, Ivy Tech Community College of Indiana
Charles Kemnitz, Pennsylvania College of Technology
Sandra Kinghorn, Ventura College
Bill Klein, Katharine Gibbs School–Philadelphia
Bea Knaapen, Fresno City College
Kit Kofoed, Western Wyoming Community College
Maria Kolatis, County College of Morris
Barry Kolb, Ocean County College
Karen Kuralt, University of Arkansas at Little Rock
Belva-Carole Lamb, Rogue Community College
Betty Lambert, Des Moines Area Community College
Anita Lande, Cabrillo College
Junnae Landry, Pratt Community College
Karen Lankisch, UC Clermont
David Lanzilla, Central Florida Community College
Nora Laredo, Cerritos Community College
Jennifer Larrabee, Chippewa Valley Technical College
Debra Larson, Idaho State University
Barb Lave, Portland Community College
Audrey Lawrence, Tidewater Community College
Deborah Layton, Eastern Oklahoma State College
Larry LeBlanc, Owen Graduate School–
    Vanderbilt University
Philip Lee, Nashville State Community College
Michael Lehrfeld, Brevard Community College
Vasant Limaye, Southwest Collegiate Institute for the
    Deaf – Howard College
Anne C. Lewis, Edgecombe Community College
Stephen Linkin, Houston Community College
Peggy Linston, Athens Technical College
Hugh Lofton, Moultrie Technical College
Donna Lohn, Lakeland Community College
Jackie Lou, Lake Tahoe Community College
Donna Love, Gaston College
Curt Lynch, Ozarks Technical Community College
Sheilah Lynn, Florida Community College–Jacksonville
Pat R. Lyon, Tomball College
Bill Madden, Bergen Community College
Heather Madden, Delaware Technical &
    Community College
Donna Madsen, Kirkwood Community College
Jane Maringer-Cantu, Gavilan College
Suzanne Marks, Bellevue Community College
Carol Martin, Louisiana State University–Alexandria
Cheryl Martucci, Diablo Valley College
Roberta Marvel, Eastern Wyoming College
Tom Mason, Brookdale Community College
Mindy Mass, Santa Barbara City College
Dixie Massaro, Irvine Valley College
Rebekah May, Ashland Community & Technical College
Emma Mays-Reynolds, Dyersburg State
    Community College
Timothy Mayes, Metropolitan State College of Denver
Reggie McCarthy, Central Lakes College

Matt McCaskill, Brevard Community College
Kevin McFarlane, Front Range Community College
Donna McGill, Yuba Community College
Terri McKeever, Ozarks Technical Community College
Patricia McMahon, South Suburban College
Sally McMillin, Katharine Gibbs School–Philadelphia
Charles McNerney, Bergen Community College
Lisa Mears, Palm Beach Community College
Imran Mehmood, ITT Technical Institute–King of
    Prussia Campus
Virginia Melvin, Southwest Tennessee Community College
Jeanne Mercer, Texas State Technical College
Denise Merrell, Jefferson Community & Technical College
Catherine Merrikin, Pearl River Community College
Diane D. Mickey, Northern Virginia Community College
Darrelyn Miller, Grays Harbor College
Sue Mitchell, Calhoun Community College
Jacquie Moldenhauer, Front Range Community College
Linda Motonaga, Los Angeles City College
Sam Mryyan, Allen County Community College
Cindy Murphy, Southeastern Community College
Ryan Murphy, Sinclair Community College
Sharon E. Nastav, Johnson County Community College
Christine Naylor, Kent State University Ashtabula
Haji Nazarian, Seattle Central Community College
Nancy Noe, Linn-Benton Community College
Jennie Noriega, San Joaquin Delta College
Linda Nutter, Peninsula College
Thomas Omerza, Middle Bucks Institute of Technology
Edith Orozco, St. Philip's College
Dona Orr, Boise State University
Joanne Osgood, Chaffey College
Janice Owens, Kishwaukee College
Tatyana Pashnyak, Bainbridge College
John Partacz, College of DuPage
Tim Paul, Montana State University–Great Falls
Joseph Perez, South Texas College
Mike Peterson, Chemeketa Community College
Dr. Karen R. Petitto, West Virginia Wesleyan College
Terry Pierce, Onandaga Community College
Ashlee Pieris, Raritan Valley Community College
Jamie Pinchot, Thiel College
Michelle Poertner, Northwestern Michigan College
Betty Posta, University of Toledo
Deborah Powell, West Central Technical College
Mark Pranger, Rogers State University
Carolyn Rainey, Southeast Missouri State University
Linda Raskovich, Hibbing Community College
Leslie Ratliff, Griffin Technical College
Mar-Sue Ratzke, Rio Hondo Community College
Roxy Reissen, Southeastern Community College
Silvio Reyes, Technical Career Institutes
Patricia Rishavy, Anoka Technical College
Jean Robbins, Southeast Technical Institute

Carol Roberts, Eastern Maine Community College
    and University of Maine
Teresa Roberts, Wilson Technical Community College
Vicki Robertson, Southwest Tennessee Community College
Betty Rogge, Ohio State Agricultural Technical Institute
Lynne Rusley, Missouri Southern State University
Claude Russo, Brevard Community College
Ginger Sabine, Northwestern Technical College
Steven Sachs, Los Angeles Valley College
Joanne Salas, Olympic College
Lloyd Sandmann, Pima Community College–Desert
    Vista Campus
Beverly Santillo, Georgia Perimeter College
Theresa Savarese, San Diego City College
Sharolyn Sayers, Milwaukee Area Technical College
Judith Scheeren, Westmoreland County
    Community College
Adolph Scheiwe, Joliet Junior College
Marilyn Schmid, Asheville-Buncombe Technical
    Community College
Janet Sebesy, Cuyahoga Community College
Phyllis T. Shafer, Brookdale Community College
Ralph Shafer, Truckee Meadows Community College
Anne Marie Shanley, County College of Morris
Shelia Shelton, Surry Community College
Merilyn Shepherd, Danville Area Community College
Susan Sinele, Aims Community College
Beth Sindt, Hawkeye Community College
Andrew Smith, Marian College
Brenda Smith, Southwest Tennessee Community College
Lynne Smith, State University of New York–Delhi
Rob Smith, Katharine Gibbs School–Philadelphia
Tonya Smith, Arkansas State University–Mountain Home
Del Spencer – Trinity Valley Community College
Jeri Spinner, Idaho State University
Eric Stadnik, Santa Rosa Junior College
Karen Stanton, Los Medanos College
Meg Stoner, Santa Rosa Junior College
Beverly Stowers, Ivy Tech Community College of Indiana
Marcia Stranix, Yuba College
Kim Styles, Tri-County Technical College
Sylvia Summers, Tacoma Community College
Beverly Swann, Delaware Technical & Community College
Ann Taff, Tulsa Community College
Mike Theiss, University of Wisconsin–Marathon Campus
Romy Thiele, Cañada College
Sharron Thompson, Portland Community College
Ingrid Thompson-Sellers, Georgia Perimeter College
Barbara Tietsort, University of Cincinnati–Raymond
    Walters College
Janine Tiffany, Reading Area Community College
Denise Tillery, University of Nevada Las Vegas
Susan Trebelhorn, Normandale Community College
Noel Trout, Santiago Canyon College

Cheryl Turgeon, Asnuntuck Community College
Steve Turner, Ventura College
Sylvia Unwin, Bellevue Community College
Lilly Vigil, Colorado Mountain College
Sabrina Vincent, College of the Mainland
Mary Vitrano, Palm Beach Community College
Brad Vogt, Northeast Community College
Cozell Wagner, Southeastern Community College
Carolyn Walker, Tri-County Technical College
Sherry Walker, Tulsa Community College
Qi Wang, Tacoma Community College
Betty Wanielista, Valencia Community College
Marge Warber, Lanier Technical College–Forsyth Campus
Marjorie Webster, Bergen Community College
Linda Wenn, Central Community College
Mark Westlund, Olympic College
Carolyn Whited, Roane State Community College
Winona Whited, Richland College
Jerry Wilkerson, Scott Community College
Joel Willenbring, Fullerton College

Barbara Williams, WITC Superior
Charlotte Williams, Jones County Junior College
Bonnie Willy, Ivy Tech Community College of Indiana
Diane Wilson, J. Sargeant Reynolds Community College
James Wolfe, Metropolitan Community College
Marjory Wooten, Lanier Technical College
Mark Yanko, Hocking College
Alexis Yusov, Pace University
Naeem Zaman, San Joaquin Delta College
Kathleen Zimmerman, Des Moines Area
   Community College

We would also like to thank Lutz Ziob, Sanjay Advani,
Jim DiIanni, Merrick Van Dongen, Jim LeValley, Bruce
Curling, Joe Wilson, and Naman Kahn at Microsoft for
their encouragement and support in making the Microsoft
Official Academic Course programs the finest instructional
materials for mastering the newest Microsoft technologies
for both students and instructors.

Brief Contents

www.wiley.com/college/microsoft *or* call the MOAC Toll-Free Number: 1+(888) 764-7001

Contents

FOR INSTRUCTORS

WileyPLUS is built around the activities you perform in your class each day. With *WileyPLUS* you can:

Prepare & Present
Create outstanding class presentations using a wealth of resources such as PowerPoint™ slides, image galleries, interactive simulations, and more. You can even add materials you have created yourself.

Create Assignments
Automate the assigning and grading of homework or quizzes by using the provided question banks, or by writing your own.

Track Student Progress
Keep track of your students' progress and analyze individual and overall class results.

Now Available with WebCT and Blackboard!

"It has been a great help, and I believe it has helped me to achieve a better grade."

Michael Morris,
Columbia Basin College

FOR STUDENTS

You have the potential to make a difference!

WileyPLUS is a powerful online system packed with features to help you make the most of your potential and get the best grade you can!

With *WileyPLUS* you get:

A complete online version of your text and other study resources.

Problem-solving help, instant grading, and feedback on your homework and quizzes.

The ability to track your progress and grades throughout the term.

Access to Microsoft's Assessment, Learning Plan, and MCAS examination voucher.

For more information on what *WileyPLUS* can do to help you and your students reach their potential, please visit www.wiley.com/college/*wileyplus*.

76% of students surveyed said it made them better prepared for tests.*

www.wiley.com/college/microsoft *or* call the MOAC Toll-Free Number: 1+(888) 764-7001

Excel Essentials

LESSON SKILL MATRIX

SKILLS	MATRIX SKILL	SKILL NUMBER
Starting Excel		
Working in the Excel Window		
Changing Excel's View	Change views within a single window	1.4.1
Splitting a Window	Split windows	1.4.2
Opening a New Window	Open and arrange new windows	1.4.3
Working with an Existing Workbook		

Contoso, Ltd., provides specialty healthcare for the entire family—prenatal through geriatric care. The practice, owned by Dr. Stephanie Bourne, has an expanding patient list. It currently employs a staff of 36, which includes three additional family practice physicians. Each physician has unique patient-contact hours; the office is open from 7 a.m. to 7 p.m. on Mondays and from 8 a.m. to 4 p.m. other weekdays. The office manager must track revenue and expenses for the practice and maintain a large volume of employee data. Microsoft Excel is an ideal tool for organizing and analyzing such data. In this lesson, you will learn how to enter text and numbers into an Excel worksheet to keep up-to-date employee records.

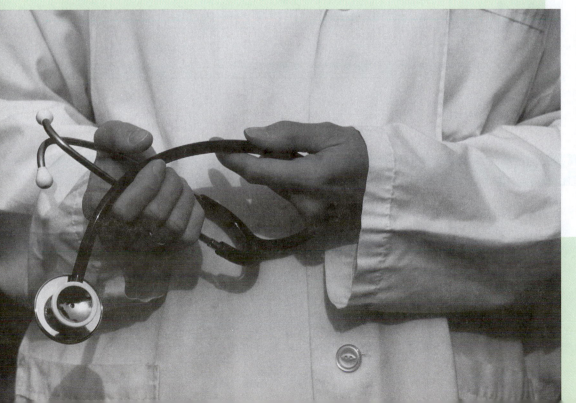

KEY TERMS

active cell
cell
column
command tab
Dialog Box Launcher
Microsoft Office Button
Quick Access Toolbar
Ribbon
row
ScreenTip
workbook
worksheet

■ SOFTWARE ORIENTATION

Microsoft Excel's Opening Screen

Microsoft Office Excel 2007 provides new and improved powerful tools that enable users to organize, analyze, manage, and share information easily. When you open Excel, you will immediately see that it has an entirely new look. A broad band, called the *Ribbon*, runs across the top of the window. The Ribbon is organized into task-oriented *command tabs*. Each tab is divided into task groups that are based on the type of work to be performed. The tabs and groups replace the menus and multiple toolbars that were present in Excel 2003.

When you first launch Excel, you will see a screen similar to the one shown in Figure 1-1. The Developer and Add-Ins tabs may not appear on your screen if default settings have been changed or other preferences have been set. Use Figure 1-1 as a reference throughout this lesson and the rest of this book.

Figure 1-1

Excel's opening screen

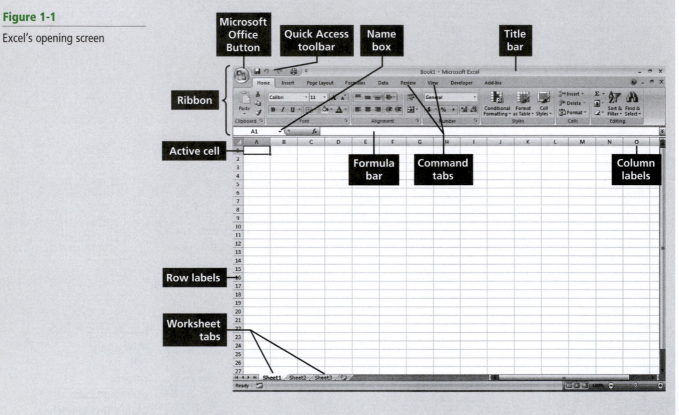

■ Starting Excel

THE BOTTOM LINE

To open Microsoft Office Excel 2007, click the Start menu, click All Programs, click Microsoft Office, and then click Microsoft Office Excel 2007. Excel opens with a blank workbook displayed (see Figure 1-1). The filename (Book1) and the program name (Microsoft Excel) appear in the title bar at the top of the screen. When you open a new *workbook*, it contains three worksheets—similar to pages in a document or a book. A worksheet (sometimes called a spreadsheet) is simply a workspace where you can enter information. The sheet tabs are located just above the Status bar and are identified as Sheet1, Sheet2, and Sheet3. Worksheets can be renamed to identify their content and additional worksheets can be added as needed.

→ START EXCEL

GET READY. The computer must be running and Excel must be installed.

1. Click the **Start** menu, and then click **All Programs**.
2. On the list of programs, click **Microsoft Office**.
3. Click **Microsoft Office Excel 2007**. A blank workbook will open.

   PAUSE. LEAVE the worksheet open to use in the next exercise.

The default filename (Book1) will remain in the title bar until you save the workbook with a name of your choice. A ***worksheet*** is a grid comprised of rows, columns, and cells. Worksheet ***columns*** go from top to bottom and are identified by letters; ***rows*** go from left to right and are identified by numbers. Information is entered into a cell. Each box on the grid is a ***cell*** and is identified by the intersection of a column and a row. Thus, the first cell in an open worksheet is A1. The ***active cell*** is outlined by a bold black line. When you key information, it will be entered in the outlined cell.

■ Working in the Excel Window

↓ THE BOTTOM LINE

When you launched Excel in the previous exercise, a blank workbook was displayed. You are ready to explore the Excel window components. Sheet1 is the active worksheet and A1 is the active cell.

Using the Onscreen Tools

The ***Quick Access Toolbar*** appears on the left side of the title bar, above the Ribbon. If you want the toolbar closer to your work area, you can move it below the Ribbon. This toolbar should contain the commands you use most frequently.

By default, the Quick Access Toolbar displays Save, Undo, and Redo. If you want a particular command to be more readily available, you can add it to the toolbar. You can also remove default items that you use infrequently.

→ USE ONSCREEN TOOLS

GET READY. Use the workbook you opened in the previous exercise.

1. Place the cursor at the bottom of each command on the Quick Access Toolbar and read the description that appears as a ScreenTip. **A *ScreenTip*** is a small window that displays descriptive text when you rest the pointer on a command or control.

TAKE NOTE*

Use ScreenTips to remind you of a command's function. Enhanced ScreenTips display in a larger window that contains more descriptive text than a ScreenTip. Most Enhanced ScreenTips contain a link to a Help topic.

2. Click the down arrow at the right side of the Quick Access Toolbar. From the dropdown list, select **Open**. The Open icon is added to the Quick Access Toolbar. Click the down arrow again and select **Quick Print** from the dropdown list (Figure 1-2).

Figure 1-2

Customize the Quick Access
Toolbar

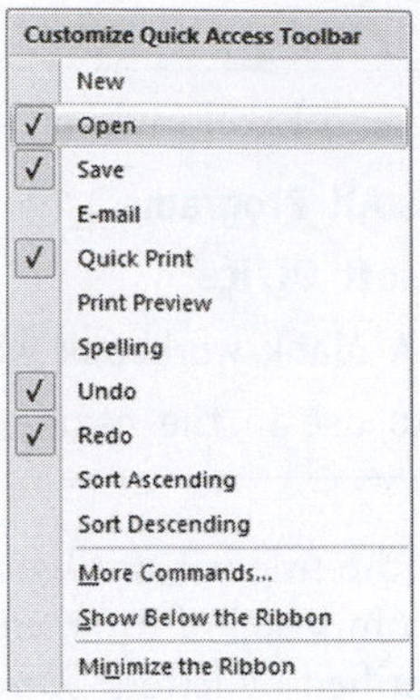

 ANOTHER WAY   To add a command to the Quick Access Toolbar, you can right-click any icon on the
Ribbon and then click Add to Quick Access Toolbar.

3. Right-click the toolbar and click **Show Quick Access Toolbar Below the Ribbon**.

4. Right-click the **Home** tab and click **Minimize the Ribbon**. Only the tabs are shown
and your workspace is increased.

5. Click the down arrow on the right side of the **Quick Access Toolbar**. Click
Minimize the Ribbon to turn off the option and make the Ribbon commands
visible.

6. Right-click the **Quick Access Toolbar** and click **Show Quick Access Toolbar Above
the Ribbon**.

7. Right-click the **Open** command and select **Remove from Quick Access Toolbar**.

TAKE NOTE *   If you want to add commands to the Quick Access Toolbar that do not appear in the
dropdown list, click More Commands on the dropdown list. The Excel Options dialog
box opens. You can also right-click the Quick Access Toolbar or any Ribbon tab and
select Customize Quick Access Toolbar to open the Excel Options window.

PAUSE. LEAVE the workbook open to use in the next exercise.

As you work in Excel, customize the Quick Access Toolbar so that it contains the commands
you use most often. Do not, however, remove the Undo and Redo commands. These commands are not available on the command tabs.

Using the Microsoft Office Button

The *Microsoft Office Button* at the top left of the screen opens a pane with the commands that were available in the File menu of Excel 2003. This button provides access to
the document commands, such as Save, Print, and Close. The Microsoft Office Button
also displays the new advanced commands Prepare, Send, and Publish.

USE THE MICROSOFT OFFICE BUTTON

USE the workbook from the previous exercise.

1. Click the **Microsoft Office Button**.

2. Click **Close**. Your workbook disappears, but Excel remains open.

3. Click the **Microsoft Office Button**, and then click **New**.

4. Click **Blank Workbook**, if necessary, and then click **Create**. A new blank workbook is opened.

   PAUSE. LEAVE the workbook open to use in the next exercise.

You can press Ctrl + N to open a blank workbook. As illustrated in this exercise, when you open a blank workbook, it contains three worksheets. You can enter data in each of the worksheets. The worksheets will be saved as one document. Worksheets related to one main topic are often placed in one workbook rather than saving each worksheet as a separate document.

Changing Excel's View

On the Ribbon, commands are grouped according to tasks normally performed in Excel. Commands are displayed on the work surface. Each time you click a tab, you will see a different group of commands. The Home tab contains the formatting commands—these are the commands Excel users need most frequently. The View tab has commands related to the appearance of the displayed document.

While you are working, you can see your worksheet as it will appear when printed. To preview your printed worksheet, click the Ribbon's View tab, then click Page Layout in the Workbook Views group (first section).

An arrow, called a *Dialog Box Launcher*, is located in the lower-right corner of many group headers. The arrow tells you that more options for that group of commands are available. Clicking the arrow will open a dialog box or a task pane.

➔ CHANGE EXCEL'S VIEW

USE the workbook from the previous exercise.

1. The Home tab should be active. If it is not, click **Home**.

2. Select the **A1** cell to make it active. Key **456** and press Tab.

3. Click the arrow in the lower-right corner of the Font group of commands. The Format Cells dialog box, shown in Figure 1-3, opens.

Figure 1-3

Format Cells dialog box

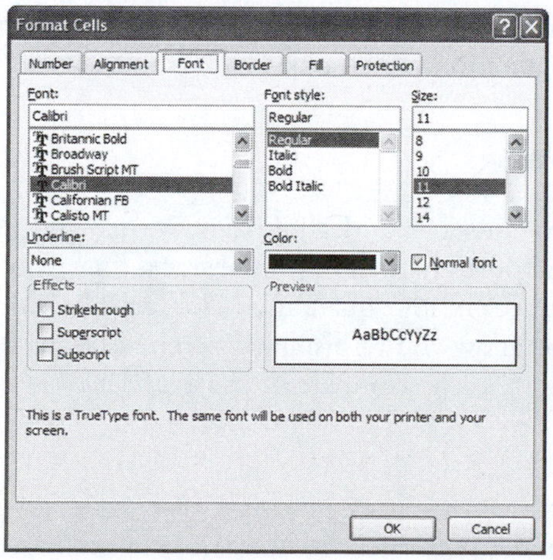

4. Notice that the Font tab of the box is active. Change the font to **Arial** and click **OK**.

5. Cell B1 should be the active cell. Key **456** and press **Tab**. Notice the difference in size and appearance between this number and the one you keyed in cell A1.

6. Click the **View** tab.

7. Click **Page Layout View**. Your workbook should look like Figure 1-4. From this view, you can see the margins, and you can add a header or footer in this view.

Figure 1-4

Worksheet in Page Layout View

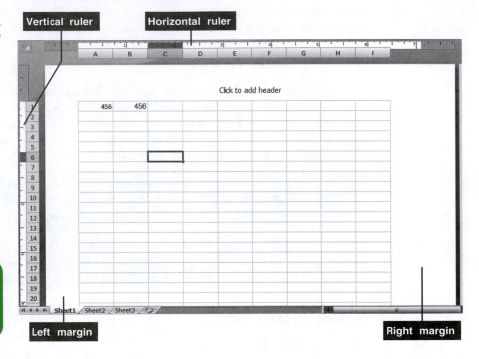

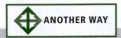

CERTIFICATION READY?
How do you change views within a single window?
1.4.1

ANOTHER WAY

You can also access the Format Cells dialog box by right-clicking in a cell or on a column or row label.

PAUSE. LEAVE the workbook open to use in the next exercise.

Page Layout view is useful when preparing your data for printing. This view enables you to fine-tune pages before printing. You can change the data's layout and format in this view as well as the Normal view. You can also use the rulers to measure the width and height of the data and determine whether you need to change the margins or print orientation. These commands will be presented in later lessons.

Splitting a Window

When a worksheet contains a great deal of data, Normal and Page Layout views allow you to see only a small portion of the worksheet at a time. The Split command allows you to view the worksheet in four quadrants. The scroll bars on the right and at the bottom of the window allow you to display different sections of the worksheet at the same time. You can more easily compare or contrast data.

⊙ SPLIT A WINDOW

USE the workbook from the previous exercise.

1. Press **Ctrl** + **Home** to make cell **A1** active.

2. With the **View** tab active, click the **Split** command in the Window group.

3. Choose the lower-right quadrant and scroll down to **row 30**.

4. Key **235** in cell **H30** and press **Enter**. The data you entered in cells A1 and B1 should be visible as well as what you just entered in cell H30. See Figure 1-5.

Figure 1-5

Split window

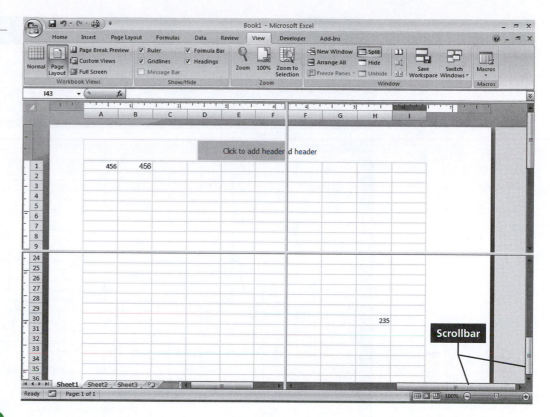

5. Click **Split** to remove the split. The data in cell H30 is no longer visible. If you click the **Split** command, you will again see all the data in this worksheet.

   PAUSE. LEAVE the workbook open to use in the next exercise.

TAKE NOTE The Split command is especially useful when you need to compare various portions of a long worksheet.

When you use a worksheet that contains a small amount of data, it is easy to scroll through the worksheet and focus on specific cells. Worksheets that you create and work with in the future, however, could be much larger. The ability to view more than one section of a worksheet at the same time is especially useful when you need to compare various sections of data.

Opening a New Window

Splitting a window allows you to look at two sections of a worksheet side by side. You can also view two sections of a worksheet by using the New Window command.

OPEN A NEW WINDOW

USE the workbook from the previous exercise.

1. Make **A1** the active cell.

2. With the **View** tab active, click **New Window** in the Window group. A new window titled Book1:2 opens.

3. Scroll down the window until cell **H30** is visible. As illustrated in Figure 1-6, you can see the data in H30. Although cell A1 is not visible, it is still the active cell. It is important to note that you have opened a new view of the active worksheet—not a new worksheet.

Figure 1-6

New window

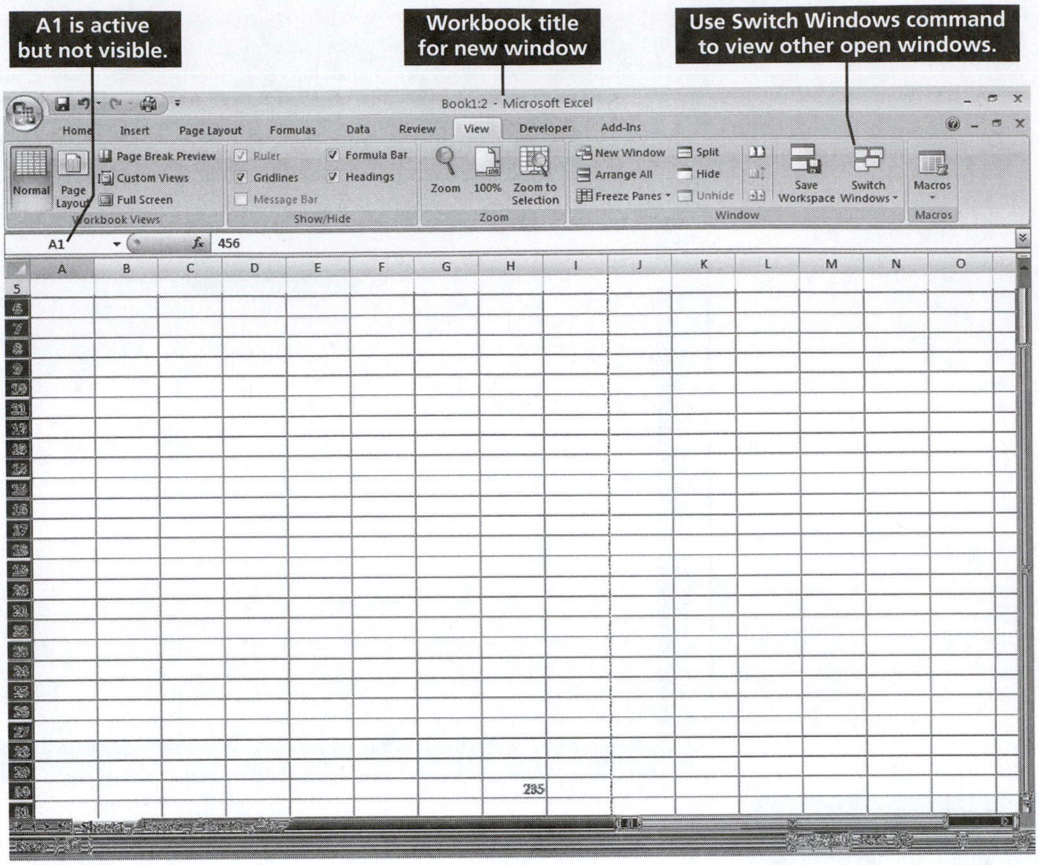

A1 is active but not visible.

Workbook title for new window

Use Switch Windows command to view other open windows.

4. Click **Switch Windows**. Book1:2 is checked, which indicates that it is the active window.

5. Click **Book1:1.** You see the original view of the worksheet with cell A1 active.

6. Click **Switch Windows** and make Book1:2 active.

7. Click the **Close** button (**X** in the corner of the window) to close Book1:2. The window closes and the title Book1 tells you that this is the only open view of this workbook.

TAKE NOTE *

If you use the Microsoft Office Button, you will close the workbook. The Close window option will close only the new window opened at the beginning of this exercise.

CERTIFICATION READY?
How do you open and arrange new windows?
1.4.3

8. Click the **Microsoft Office Button** and then click **Close**.

9. When asked if you want to save the changes to Book1, click **No**.

PAUSE. LEAVE Excel open to use in the next exercise.

TROUBLESHOOTING

Until you are well acquainted with the Ribbon tabs and the command groups within each tab, you may want to use Excel's Help to find the location of a particular command. To open Help, click the question mark on the right side of the Ribbon next to the last command tab.

When you open a new window, you can move between the windows as you did in this exercise. You can also use the Arrange All command on the View tab to display the windows side by side to compare or contrast various parts of a worksheet. This function is especially useful when you work with workbooks that contain more than one worksheet.

✳ Workplace Ready

Contoso, Ltd provides health insurance and other benefits to its employees who work 30 or more hours each week. The office manager has created a workbook for employee information so that he can more easily track which employees are eligible for benefits. In the following exercises, you will update existing data and add additional employees to an Excel worksheet.

■ Working with an Existing Workbook

THE BOTTOM LINE

Many workbooks require frequent updating because existing data has changed or new data must be added. Workers frequently open an existing workbook, update information, and then save the workbook again to be further revised at a later time. Often, files are created by one person, then used and/or updated by others.

Filenames should reflect the type of data contained in the file. A descriptive filename enables workers to locate and retrieve files quickly. Filenames can be up to 255 characters long, including the filename extension. However, most workers use short, descriptive filenames that clearly identify the content of the workbook.

Opening an Existing Workbook

When an Excel 2007 file is saved, the extension *xlsx* is automatically added to the name assigned to the file. When you want to open a file, the filename extension identifies the program in which the file can be opened. To open a file, you must identify the drive and folder that contains the file. In the following exercise, you will open a file created by Contoso's office manager.

ANOTHER WAY

To display the Open dialog box without using the Microsoft Office Button, press Ctrl+O.

➔ OPEN AN EXISTING WORKBOOK

CD

The *Contoso Employee Info* workbook is available on the companion CD-ROM.

BEFORE you begin this exercise, put the companion CD in the computer.

1. Click the **Microsoft Office Button**. Documents you recently created or edited will appear on the right side in the Recent Documents list.
2. Click **Open**. The Open dialog box will appear.
3. In the **Look in** box, click the location of the data files for this lesson.

TAKE NOTE ✳

By default, the Open dialog box lists only the files that were created in the program you are using—in this case, only Excel files. To see files created in other programs, you can select All Files in the Files of type box at the bottom of the Open dialog box.

4. Select *Contoso Employee Info* from the listed files, and then click **Open**. The open file is displayed in Figure 1-7 with the workbook name displayed in the title bar.

Figure 1-7

Existing worksheet

Figure 1-7

Existing worksheet

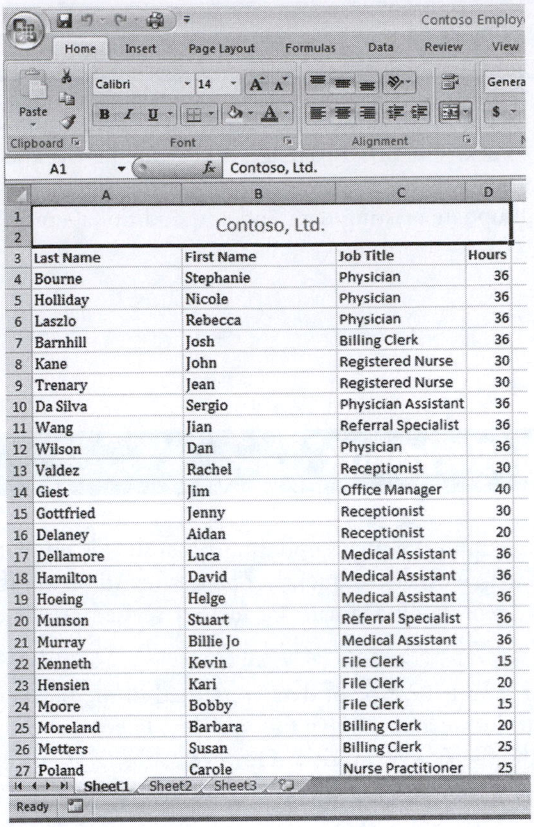

PAUSE. LEAVE the workbook open to use in the next exercise.

If you are familiar with Microsoft Word, you know that the beginning of the document is displayed when you open a file. When you open an Excel workbook, the active cell and view were determined when the file was saved. For example, when you opened the Contoso Employee Info workbook, A22 was the active cell displayed in Normal view because A22 was the active cell displayed in Normal view when the file was saved. This feature enables you to continue working in the same location when you return to the workbook.

Navigating a Worksheet

An Excel worksheet can contain more than a million rows and more than sixteen thousand columns. There are several ways to move through worksheets that contain numerous rows and columns. You can use the arrow keys, the scrollbars, or the mouse to navigate through a worksheet. In the following exercises, you will explore several ways to move through a worksheet.

→ **NAVIGATE A WORKSHEET**

USE the workbook you opened in the previous exercise.

1. Press [Ctrl] + [Home] to move to the beginning of the document (cell A1).
2. Press [Ctrl] + [End] to move to the end of the document (cell D27).
3. Make cell **A27** the active cell and press [Page Up]. The cursor moves to cell A1.
4. Click the **A3** cell to make it active, and press [Ctrl] + [Down Arrow] to go to the last row of data (cell A27).
5. Press [Ctrl] + [Right Arrow]. The cursor moves to D27, the last column in the range of data.
6. Press [Ctrl] + [Down Arrow]. The cursor moves to the last possible row in the worksheet. The unused cells below the data are considered a range.

TAKE NOTE*

Ctrl+Arrow allows you to move to the start and end of ranges of data. The title, which spans all the columns, is not considered part of the worksheet's data range.

7. Press **Ctrl** + **Home**.
8. Press **Scroll Lock** while you press the **Right Arrow** key. This moves the sheet one column to the right.

TAKE NOTE * When you use the scroll options, the view of the worksheet changes, but the active cell does not change.

9. Use the vertical *scrollbar* to move from the beginning to the end of the data.
10. If your mouse has a wheel button, roll the **wheel button** on the mouse forward and back to scroll quickly through the worksheet.

 ANOTHER WAY The name box is located below the Ribbon at the left end of the formula bar. You can key a cell location in this box and press Enter. The cursor moves to that cell.

TAKE NOTE * When Scroll Lock is on, *scroll lock* is displayed on the left side of the Status bar. If you want to use the arrow keys to move between cells, you must turn off Scroll Lock.

PAUSE. LEAVE the workbook open to use in the next exercise.

In the preceding exercise, you learned a variety of ways to view and navigate through data. As you continue to create and edit worksheets, you will select the navigation methods that work best for you.

Entering Data in a Worksheet

X REF

Other methods of entering worksheet data will be addressed in Lesson 2.

You can key data directly into a worksheet cell or cells. You can also copy and paste information from another worksheet or from other programs. To enter data in a cell within a worksheet, you must make the desired cell active and then key the data. To move to the next column after text has been entered, press Tab. When you have finished keying the entries in a row, press Enter to move to the beginning of the next row. You can also use the arrow keys to move to an adjacent cell. If the first few characters you key in a cell match an existing entry in that column, Excel enters the remaining characters automatically. Press Enter to accept the proposed entry or continue keying. In the following exercise, you will add a new employee's information to the worksheet.

⊕ **ENTER DATA IN A WORKSHEET**

USE the workbook from the previous exercise.

1. Move to cell **A28**.
2. Key **Simon** and press **Tab**.
3. Key **Britta** and press **Tab**.
4. Key **Administrative Assistant** and press **Tab**.
5. Key **36** and press **Enter**.
6. Double-click the **marker** between columns C and D to so that the entire text is visible in column C.

PAUSE. LEAVE the workbook open to use in the next exercise.

TAKE NOTE * When you key text that is longer than the cell, the text extends into the next cell. However, when you press Tab and move to the next cell, the overflow text is not displayed. The text is still there. You will learn more about adjusting the column width in Lesson 2.

You added data to an existing worksheet in this exercise. However, column width has been established based on the existing data. When you added an entry in column C that was longer than other entries in the column, it was necessary to adjust the column width to accommodate the entry.

Selecting, Editing, and Deleting a Cell's Contents

One advantage of electronic records versus manual ones is that changes can be made quickly and easily. To edit information in a worksheet, you can make changes directly in the cell or edit the contents of a cell in the formula bar. Before changes can be made, however, you must select the information that is to be changed. Selecting text means that you highlight the text that is to be changed. You can select a single cell, a row, a column, a range of cells, or an entire workbook.

➔ SELECT, EDIT, AND DELETE A CELL'S CONTENTS

USE the workbook from the previous exercise.

1. Select cell **A22** as shown in Figure 1-8.

Figure 1-8

Edit in the cell or in the formula bar

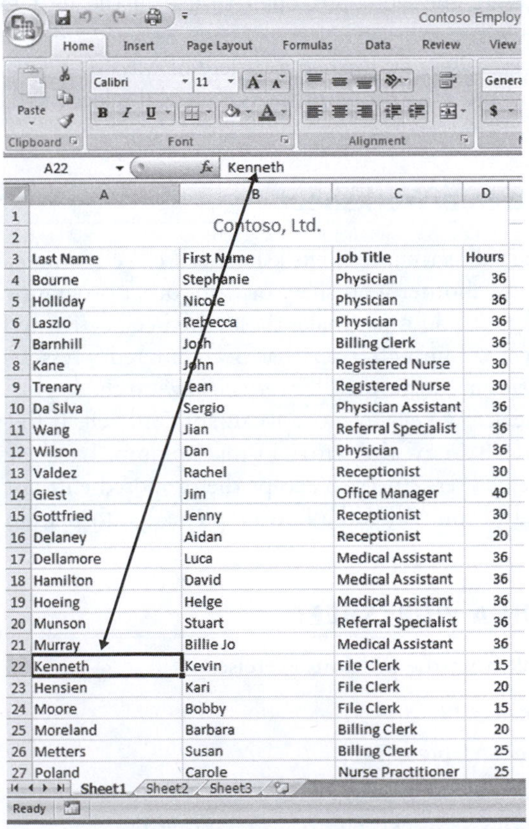

2. Select the existing text. Key **Kennedy** and press Enter.
3. Click cell **A15**. Hold down the **left mouse button** and drag to cell **D15**. You have selected the entire record for Jenny Gottfried.
4. Press Delete. The information is deleted and row 15 is now blank.
5. With cells A15 to D15 still selected, right-click to display the shortcut menu.
6. Press Delete. The Delete dialog box will be displayed.
7. Click **Entire row** as shown in Figure 1-9, and then click **OK**.

Figure 1-9

Delete a row from a worksheet

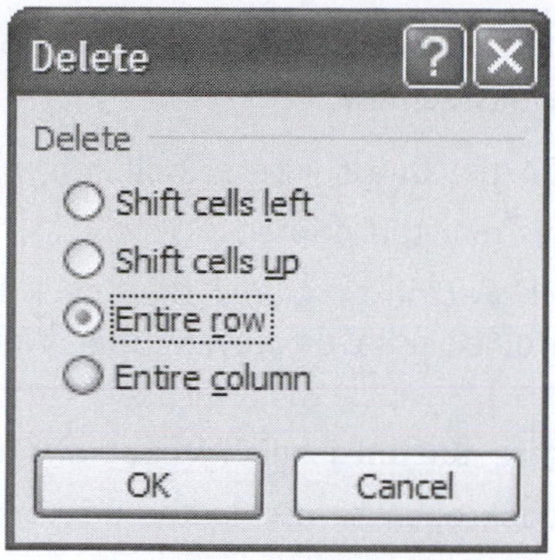

Delete

- ○ Shift cells left
- ○ Shift cells up
- ◉ Entire row
- ○ Entire column

OK   Cancel

8. Click the **Select All** button. As you can see in Figure 1-10, all cells on the worksheet are selected.

Figure 1-10

Select all cells

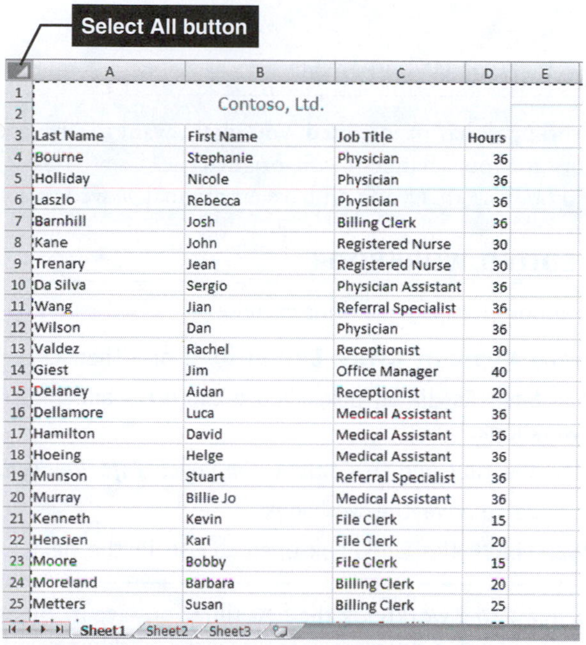

Select All button

	A	B	C	D	E
1		Contoso, Ltd.			
2					
3	Last Name	First Name	Job Title	Hours	
4	Bourne	Stephanie	Physician	36	
5	Holliday	Nicole	Physician	36	
6	Laszlo	Rebecca	Physician	36	
7	Barnhill	Josh	Billing Clerk	36	
8	Kane	John	Registered Nurse	30	
9	Trenary	Jean	Registered Nurse	30	
10	Da Silva	Sergio	Physician Assistant	36	
11	Wang	Jian	Referral Specialist	36	
12	Wilson	Dan	Physician	36	
13	Valdez	Rachel	Receptionist	30	
14	Giest	Jim	Office Manager	40	
15	Delaney	Aidan	Receptionist	20	
16	Dellamore	Luca	Medical Assistant	36	
17	Hamilton	David	Medical Assistant	36	
18	Hoeing	Helge	Medical Assistant	36	
19	Munson	Stuart	Referral Specialist	36	
20	Murray	Billie Jo	Medical Assistant	36	
21	Kenneth	Kevin	File Clerk	15	
22	Hensien	Kari	File Clerk	20	
23	Moore	Bobby	File Clerk	15	
24	Moreland	Barbara	Billing Clerk	20	
25	Metters	Susan	Billing Clerk	25	

Sheet1 Sheet2 Sheet3

9. Click any worksheet cell to deselect the worksheet.

10. To select all cells containing data, select **A1** and press $Ctrl$+A. Click any worksheet cell to deselect the cells.

PAUSE. LEAVE the workbook open to use in the next exercise.

You can begin editing by double-clicking the cell to be edited and then keying the change in the cell. Or you can click the cell and then click in the formula bar. When you are in Edit mode, the insertion point appears as a vertical bar and other commands are inactive.

In Edit mode, you can move the insertion point by using the direction keys. Use Home to move the insertion point to the beginning of the cell, and use End to move the insertion point to the end. You can add new characters at the location of the insertion point. To select multiple characters, press Shift while you press the arrow keys. You also can use the mouse to select characters while you are editing a cell. Just click and drag the mouse pointer over the characters that you want to select.

Quick Printing a Worksheet

The Quick Print option is used when you need to review a draft of a worksheet before you are ready to print the final document. If you click the Quick Print icon on the Quick Access Toolbar, the worksheet is sent directly to the printer.

TAKE NOTE*

If you edit a cell's contents and change your mind before you press Enter, press Esc and the original text will be restored. If you change the content of a cell and then do not want the change, click Undo on the Quick Access Toolbar. The deleted text will be restored.

QUICK PRINT A WORKSHEET

USE the workbook from the previous exercise.

1. Click **Quick Print** 🖨 on the Quick Access Toolbar.
2. Retrieve the printed copy from the printer.
3. Click the **Microsoft Office Button** 🔳, and then click the arrow next to Print. From this pane, you can quick print or preview the printout before sending it to the printer.
4. **CLOSE** the **Microsoft Office Button** menu without printing.

   PAUSE. LEAVE the workbook open to use in the next exercise.

ANOTHER WAY

Ctrl+P will open the Print dialog box. Click OK to print your worksheet.

The Quick Print command on the Quick Access Toolbar is useful because worksheets are frequently printed for review and editing or distribution to others. If the Quick Print command is not on the Quick Access Toolbar by default, follow the steps in an earlier exercise to add the command.

Saving an Edited Workbook

When a workbook has been edited, you might want to save a copy of the workbook rather than save your changes in the original file. Use the Save As command to save an edited workbook so that you will have an original as well as a revised workbook.

SAVE AN EDITED WORKBOOK

USE the workbook from the previous exercise.

1. Click the **Microsoft Office Button** 🔳 and then click **Save As**.
2. On the **Save As** dialog box, choose the drive and folder in which you want to save the workbook.
3. Change the filename to *Contoso Employee Info Revised*.
4. Click **Save** to save the workbook

   PAUSE. LEAVE the workbook open to use in the next exercise.

You assign a name to a workbook the first time you save it. By using the Save As command, you gave the workbook a different name than the workbook you opened from the CD files.

When you work in Excel, you should save frequently so that data is not lost. If you click the Save command on the Quick Access Toolbar, your file will be saved without changing its name or location.

Closing a Workbook

When you have finished editing, printing, and saving a workbook, you want to close the workbook. In the office, it is important that you close files when you are finished with them in order to maintain confidentiality and security.

CLOSE A WORKBOOK

USE the workbook you saved in the previous exercise.

1. Click the **Microsoft Office Button** 🔳 and then click **Close**.
2. If you have not saved the file after you edited it, you will be asked if you want to save the changes you made.
3. Because you saved the file, the workbook will be closed, but Excel remains open.

   CLOSE Excel.

As you have seen in the preceding exercises, there are several ways to modify the values or text you have entered into a cell:

- Erase the cell's contents.
- Replace the cell's contents with something else.
- Edit the cell's contents.

To erase the contents of a cell, simply double-click the cell and press Delete. To erase more than one cell, select all of the cells that you want to erase and then press Delete. Pressing Delete removes the cell's contents, but does not remove any formatting (such as bold, italic, or a different number format) that you may have applied to the cell.

 **ANOTHER WAY**

You can right-click a cell or a selected range of cells and choose Delete from the menu that appears.

ANOTHER WAY

Place the cursor in the cell you want to edit, press F2, and edit directly in the cell.

To replace the contents of a cell with something else, simply click the cell and key the new entry. This replaces the cell's previous contents. Any formatting that you previously applied to the cell remains in place and is applied to the new content.

If the cell contains only a few characters, replacing the contents by keying new data usually is easiest. But if the cell contains lengthy text or a complex formula and you need to make only a slight modification, it is probably easier to edit the cell rather than re-enter information.

SUMMARY SKILL MATRIX

IN THIS LESSON YOU LEARNED	MATRIX SKILL	SKILL NUMBER
To start Excel		
To work in the Excel window		
To change the views of a worksheet in a single window	Change views within a single window	1.4.1
To split windows	Split windows	1.4.2
To open and arrange new windows	Open and arrange new windows	1.4.3
To work with an existing workbook		
To open a workbook		
To navigate a worksheet		
To enter data		
To select and edit data		
To print a worksheet		

Knowledge Assessment

Fill in the Blank

Complete the following sentences by writing the correct word or words in the blanks provided.

1. An arrow at the bottom of a group header on the Ribbon tells you that a(n) _____ is available that will offer additional options.

2. A selected cell is called the _____.

3. Click the _____ to save, print, or close a file.

4. After a file has been saved, the filename appears in the _____.

5. When you split a window, the window is divided into _____ panes.

6. When you are changing the contents of a cell, you are in the _____ mode.

7. A cell is formed by the intersection of _____.

8. The _____ can be customized and should contain the commands you use most frequently.

9. A new Excel workbook opens with _____ worksheets.

10. The active cell is identified in the _____ that appears on the left side of the formula bar.

True / False

Circle T if the statement is true or F if the statement is false.

T F 1. Three worksheets is the maximum number that can be included in one workbook.

T F 2. **Ctrl + N** will open a new blank workbook.

T F 3. When data is too wide for a cell, the part of the data that will not fit is automatically deleted.

T F 4. After a file has been saved, the file name appears in the title bar.

T F 5. Excel opens with a new blank workbook displayed.

T F 6. The columns in a worksheet are indentified by numbers.

T F 7. The active cell is outlined by a bold black line.

T F 8. Use the **Save As** command to save a file with a new name.

T F 9. Using the **Delete** key will remove both text and formats from a cell.

T F 10. Edits can be made in the formula bar.

Competency Assessment

Project 1-1: Scenic Drives in the United States

Create a worksheet listing the top scenic drives in the United States (according to Orbitz.com). Identify the state and the scenic route.

GET READY. Launch Excel if it is not already running.

1. Click the **Microsoft Office Button**, click **New**, click Blank Workbook, and click Create.

2. Select **A1**, key **State**, and press (Tab).

3. In **B1**, key **Scenic Route**.

4. Beginning in cell **A2**, key the following data.

State	Scenic Route
AK	Seward Highway
CA	California 1
WY and MT	Beartooth Highway
UT	Zion National Park Scenic Byway
SD	Custer Scenic Byway
MN	North Shore Drive
LA	Old Spanish Trail
VT	Vermont 100
VA and NC	Blue Ridge Parkway
GA	Sea Islands

5. Double-click the boundary between columns B and C to adjust the width of column B to display all of the text.

6. Click the **Quick Print** icon on the Quick Access Toolbar.

7. **SAVE** the worksheet as *Road Trip* and then CLOSE the file.

LEAVE Excel open for the next project.

Project 1-2: Pro Football Hall of Fame

Eleven colleges have five or more of their football alumni who have been inducted into the Pro Football Hall of Fame.

College	Number of Inductees
Notre Dame	10
Southern California	10
Michigan	7
Alabama	6
Illinois	6
Ohio State	6
Minnesota	5
Oregon	5
Penn State	5
Southern Methodist	5
Syracuse	5

1. Press Ctrl + N to open a new blank workbook to enter the data.

2. Create columns for **College** and **Number of Inductees**. Enter the data.

3. Adjust column widths to fit the text contained in each column.

4. **SAVE** the worksheet as *Hall of Fame* and then **CLOSE** the file.

LEAVE Excel open for the next project.

■ Proficiency Assessment

Project 1-3: Fixing Approved Vendor List

An employee at Contoso, Ltd., has begun an Excel worksheet to identify approved vendors for office and medical supplies. The worksheet is not complete, but before additional entries are made, you need to edit the existing data. The worker who created the worksheet has not been consistent in the way addresses are entered and columns have not been adjusted to display all worksheet information. You need to review how the cells are set up and edit cell content. Use the techniques learned in this lesson to format the worksheet.

The **Contoso Vendor List** workbook is available on the companion CD-ROM.

1. **OPEN** *Contoso Vendor List* from the data files for this lesson.
2. Make necessary corrections to the worksheet. Two-letter state abbreviations should always be used in addresses. Find and correct inconsistencies within columns. Check each row to verify that information has been entered in the correct column.
3. **SAVE** the file as *Contoso Vendor List Revised* and **CLOSE** the file.
   LEAVE Excel open for the next exercise.

Project 1-4: Excel Grade Sheet

Create a worksheet that your professor might use for recording your achievement of the objectives for Lesson 1.

1. Click the **Microsoft Office Button**, click **New**, click Blank Workbook, and click Create.
2. Determine the column headings you will need for the worksheet. The worksheet will include student names and the numbers identifying each skill. Lesson 1 objectives are listed in the Skill Matrix at the beginning of the lesson and in the summary at the end of the lesson.
3. Enter the column headings for the worksheet. Select **A1** and key a heading for the first column. Press [Tab].
4. Key headings for the remaining columns and press [Enter].
5. In cell **A2**, enter your name in Last Name, First Name format. Press [Enter].
6. In **B2**, enter the name of one other student in your class.
7. **SAVE** the workbook as *Grade Sheet* and **CLOSE** the file.
   LEAVE Excel open for the next exercise.

■ Mastery Assessment

Project 1-5: Fortune's Best Companies

Create a worksheet that lists the ten best companies to work for as determined by employee satisfaction rankings.

1. Create a new blank workbook.
2. Review the data to be entered and determine the column headings you will use for this worksheet. You must have two columns.
3. Select **A1** and key a heading for the first column. Press [Tab].
4. Key a heading for column 2 and press [Enter].

5. Enter the following data, starting in cell **A2**.

Companies in Rank Order
Genentech
Wegmans
Valero Energy
Griffin Hospital
W. L. Gore
Container Store
Vision Service Plan
J. M. Smucker
REI
S. C. Johnson and Son

Source: Fortune.com

6. SAVE the workbook as *Best Companies* when all data has been entered.

7. CLOSE the workbook.

LEAVE Excel open for the next project.

Project 1-6: Updating an Existing Workbook

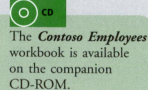

The *Contoso Employees* workbook is available on the companion CD-ROM.

1. OPEN *Contoso Employees* from the data files for this lesson.

2. Add your name as a new employee. You have been hired as a file clerk. You will work 15 hours each week.

3. With the Home tab active, select the entire worksheet.

4. Click the arrow in the Dialog Box Launcher in the Font command group. The Format Cells dialog box will open.

5. Change the font to **Times New Roman** and press Enter.

6. SAVE the workbook as *Contoso Employees 1-6* and **CLOSE** the file.

LEAVE Excel open for the next project.

INTERNET READY

In this lesson you learned how to select a cell, a row, and an entire worksheet. Use Excel's Help to gain further knowledge of selecting data.

1. Click the **question mark** on the right side of the Ribbon.
2. On the Excel Help dialog box, key **Select text** in the Search box at the top of the Help window.
3. Click **Search**. From the search result, open a topic that will provide information about selecting cells.
4. Print the topic. **CLOSE** Excel.

2

Creating and Editing a Workbook

LESSON SKILL MATRIX

Skills	Matrix Skill	Skill Number
Creating a Workbook		
Populating a Worksheet with Data		
Filling a Series with Auto Fill	Fill a series	1.1.1
Cutting, Copying, and Pasting Data	Cut, copy, and paste data and cell contents	1.3.1
Copying a Data Series with the Mouse	Copy a series	1.1.2
Editing a Workbook's Properties	Add key words and other information to workbook properties	5.3.3
Printing a Worksheet		
Setting the Print Area	Define the area of a worksheet to be printed	5.5.1
Saving a Workbook for the First Time		
Saving a Workbook for Use in a Previous Version of Excel	Save workbooks for use in a previous version of Excel	5.4.1
Choosing a Different File Format	Using the correct format, save a workbook as a template, a Web page, a macro-enabled document, or another appropriate format	5.4.2

KEY TERMS
auto fill
AutoComplete
command groups
copy
copy pointer
cut
document properties
fill handle
formula bar
label
move pointer
Office Clipboard
paste
range
template

Purchasing a home is usually the biggest financial investment most people make in a lifetime. Real estate agents advise and assist those who want to buy a new home or sell their present home. Agents must be licensed by the state. Many licensed agents also become Realtors®. This is a trademarked name that an agent can use only when he or she joins the local, state, and national associations of Realtors®. Fabrikam, Inc., located in Columbus, Ohio, is owned by Richard Carey and David Ortiz. Fabrikam has five full-time sales agents. Fabrikam uses an Excel workbook to track each agent's sales data with the date of the agent's last sale.

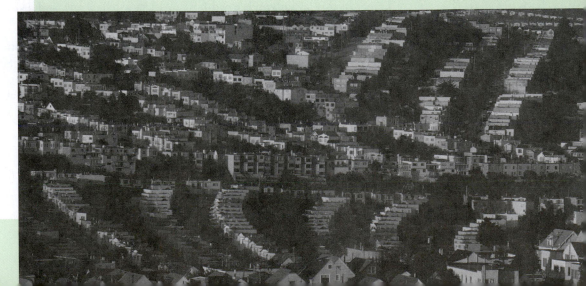

▪ SOFTWARE ORIENTATION

Excel's Home Tab

The Ribbon in Microsoft Office Excel 2007 is made up of a series of tabs, each related to specific kinds of tasks that workers do in Excel. The Home tab, the first one, contains the commands that people use the most. Having commands visible on the work surface enables you to work quickly and efficiently.

Commands are organized into related tasks called ***command groups***. For example, when the Home tab is displayed, you see the Clipboard group, which contains the command buttons to cut, copy, and paste data. These commands allow you to revise, move, and repeat data within a worksheet. Commands related to editing worksheet data are grouped together in the Editing group. Use commands in this group to fill adjacent cells, to sort and filter data, and to find specific data within a worksheet.

Figure 2-1

Home tab groups and commands

▪ Creating a Workbook

↓ **THE BOTTOM LINE**

There are three ways to create a new Microsoft Excel workbook. You can open a new, blank workbook using the Microsoft Office Button. You can open an existing Excel workbook, enter new or additional data, and save the file with a new name, thus creating a new workbook. You can also use a ***template*** to create a new workbook. A template is a model that has already been set up to track certain kinds of data, such as sales reports, invoices, etc.

Starting a Workbook from Scratch

When you want to create a new workbook, launch Excel and a blank workbook is ready for you to begin working. If you have already been working in Excel and want to begin a new workbook, click the Microsoft Office Button, click New, and then click Create to create a blank workbook.

Worksheets usually begin with a title. The primary title is often followed by a secondary title. A title sets the stage for the reader's interpretation of the data contained in a worksheet. You will create a sales report for Fabrikam in the following exercises.

ANOTHER WAY

When you are working in Excel, you can open a blank workbook with the shortcut combination Ctrl+N.

→ START A WORKBOOK FROM SCRATCH

1. Launch Excel. A blank workbook opens with A1 as the active cell.
2. Key **Fabrikam, Inc.** This is the primary title for the worksheet. Note that as you key, the text appears in the cell and in the formula bar.
3. Press Enter. The text is entered into cell A1, but looks like it flows over into B1.
4. In cell A2, key **Monthly Sales Report.** Press Enter.
5. Click the **Microsoft Office Button**, and then click **New** in the Options pane. The New Workbook dialog box will open. Sometimes you need to open a new workbook when you are already working in Excel.
6. In the right pane, click **Blank Workbook** if necessary.
7. Click the **Create** button. A second Excel workbook is opened.
8. Click the **Microsoft Office Button**, and then click **Close**. Book2 is closed. Book1 remains open.

    PAUSE. LEAVE the workbook open to use in the next exercise.

TAKE NOTE Text is stored in only one cell even when it appears to extend into adjacent cells. If an entry is longer than the cell width and the next cell contains data, the entry appears in truncated form.

■ Populating a Worksheet with Data

↓ THE BOTTOM LINE

You can enter three types of data into Excel: text, numbers, and formulas. In the following exercises, you will enter text (labels) and numbers (values). You will learn to enter formulas in Lesson 7. Text entries contain alphabetic characters and any other character that does not have a purely numeric value.

The real strength of Excel is its ability to calculate and to analyze numbers based on the numeric values you enter. For that reason, accurate data entry is crucial.

Entering Labels

Labels are used to identify the numeric data and are the most common type of text entered in a worksheet. Labels are also used to sort and group data. If the first few characters that you type in a column match an existing entry in that column, Excel automatically enters the remaining characters. This *AutoComplete* feature works only for entries that contain text or a combination of text and numbers.

ENTER LABELS

USE the workbook from the previous exercise.

To verify that AutoComplete is enabled, click the Microsoft Office Button, and then click Excel Options. Click Advanced. In the Editing options section, click the Enable AutoComplete for cell values check box if it is not already checked. Click OK.

1. Select **A4** to enter the first column label. Key **Agent** and press Tab.
2. Key **Last Closing** and press Tab.
3. In cell C4, key **January** and press Enter.

TAKE NOTE When you press Tab to enter data in several cells in a row and then press Enter at the end of the row, the selection moves to the beginning of the next row.

4. Select **A5** to enter the first row label and key **Richard Carey**.
5. Select **A6** and key **David Ortiz**.
6. Select **A7** and key **Kim Akers**.
7. Select **A8** and key **Nicole Caron**.
8. Select **A9** and key **R**. As shown in Figure 2-2, AutoComplete is activated when you key the *R* because it matches the beginning of a previous entry in this column. AutoComplete displays the entry for Richard Carey.

Figure 2-2

Excel's AutoComplete

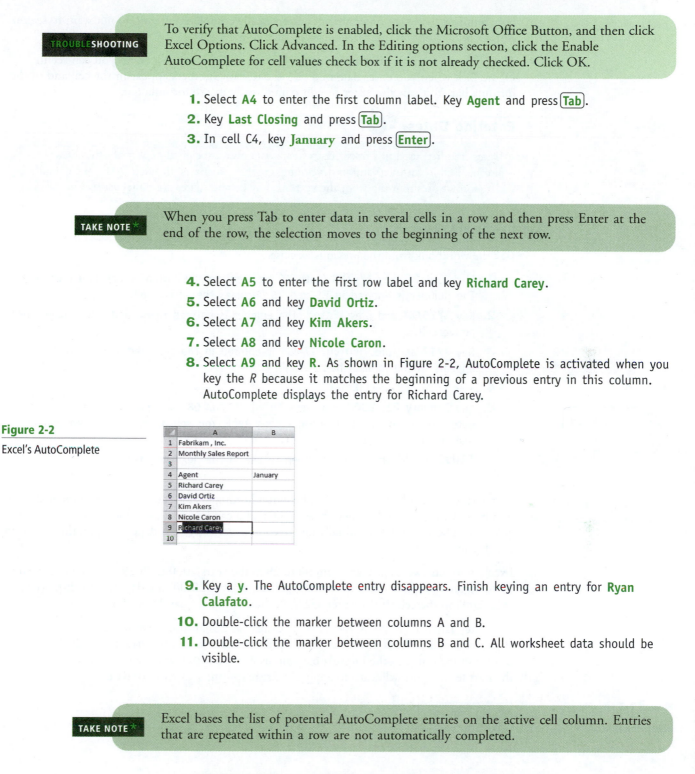

9. Key a **y**. The AutoComplete entry disappears. Finish keying an entry for **Ryan Calafato**.
10. Double-click the marker between columns A and B.
11. Double-click the marker between columns B and C. All worksheet data should be visible.

TAKE NOTE Excel bases the list of potential AutoComplete entries on the active cell column. Entries that are repeated within a row are not automatically completed.

PAUSE. LEAVE the workbook open to use in the next exercise.

As you experienced in the preceding exercise, when the beginning of a new column entry matches an existing entry and AutoComplete is activated, the remaining text is selected, and you can accept or reject it. To accept an AutoComplete entry, press Enter or Tab. When you accept AutoComplete, the completed entry will exactly match the pattern of uppercase and lowercase letters of the existing entry. To replace the automatically entered characters, continue keying. To delete the automatically entered characters, press Backspace. Entries that contain only numbers, dates, or times are not automatically completed. If you do not want to see the AutoComplete option, the feature can be turned off.

The *formula bar* is located between the Ribbon and the worksheet. As you can see in Figure 2-3, when you enter data in a cell, the text or numbers appear in the cell and in the formula bar. You can also enter or edit data directly in the formula bar.

Entering Dates NEW FEATURE ✓

> Dates are often used in worksheets to track data over a specified period of time. Dates can also be used in formulas and in developing graphs and charts. In Excel 2007, the default date format uses four digits for the year. Also by default, dates are right-justified in the cells.

➡ ENTER DATES

USE the workbook from the previous exercise.

1. Click cell **B5**, key **1/4/XX** (with XX representing the current year), and press Enter. The number is entered in B5 and B6 becomes the active cell.

2. Key **1/25/XX** and press Enter. The number is entered in B6 and B7 becomes the active cell.

3. Key **1/17** and press Enter. 17-Jan is entered in the cell, and 1/17/current year appears in the formula bar.

4. Key **1/28** and press Enter.

5. Key **January 21, 2008** and press Enter. 21-Jan-08 will appear in the cell. The date formats in column B are not consistent. You will apply a consistent date format in the next lesson.

   PAUSE. LEAVE the workbook open to use in the next exercise.

◆ ANOTHER WAY

Ctrl+; (semicolon) will enter the current date into a worksheet cell; Ctrl+: (colon) will enter the current time.

Like text, dates can be used as row and column headings. However, dates are considered serial numbers, which means that they are sequential and can be added, subtracted, and used in calculations. The way a date is initially displayed in a worksheet cell depends upon the format in which you enter it.

Excel interprets two-digit years from 00 to 29 as the years 2000 to 2029; two-digit years from 30 to 99 are interpreted as 1930 to 1999. If you enter 1/28/08, the date will be displayed as 1/28/2008 in the cell. If you enter 1/28/37, the cell will display 1/28/1937.

If you key January 28, 2008, the date will display as 28-Jan-08, as shown in Figure 2-3. If you key 1/28 without a year, Excel interprets the date to be the current year. 28-Jan will display in the cell, and the formula bar will display 1/28/ followed by the current year. In the next lesson, you will learn to apply a consistent format to series of dates.

Figure 2-3

Date formats

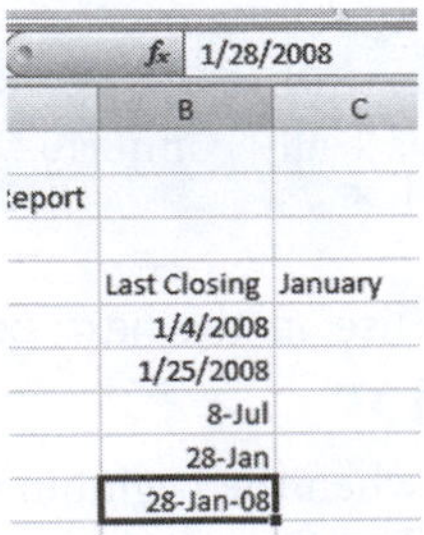

When you enter a date into a cell in a particular format, the cell is automatically formatted. Subsequent numbers entered in that cell will be converted to the date format of the original entry. In the preceding exercise, if you enter a date in a different format than what is specified and then key the format specified, your worksheet may not reflect the results described.

TAKE NOTE Regardless of the date format displayed in the cell, the formula bar displays the date in month/day/four-digit-year format because that is the format required for calculations and analyses.

Entering Values

Numeric values are the foundation for Excel's calculations, analyses, charts, and graphs. Numbers can be formatted as currency, percentages, decimals, and fractions. By default, numeric entries are right-justified in a cell.

Applying formatting to numbers changes their appearance but does not affect the cell value that Excel uses to perform calculations. The value is not affected by formatting or special characters that are entered with a number. The true value is always displayed in the formula bar.

→ ENTER VALUES

USE the workbook from the previous exercise.

1. Click cell **C5**, key **$275,000**, and press **Enter**. Be sure to include the $ and the comma in your entry. The number is entered in C5 and C6 becomes the active cell. The number is displayed in the cell with a dollar sign and comma; however, the formula bar displays the true value and disregards the special characters.

2. Key **125000** and press **Enter**.

3. Key **209,000** and press **Enter**. The number is entered in the cell with a comma separating the digits; the comma does not appear in the formula bar.

4. Key **258,000** and press **Enter**.

5. Key **145700** and press **Enter**. See Figure 2-4.

Figure 2-4

Value unaffected by formatting

	C5	▾	fx	275000	
	A	B	C	D	
1	Fabrikam, Inc.				
2	Monthly Sales Report				
3					
4	Agent	Last Closing	January		
5	Richard Carey	1/4/2008	$275,000		
6	David Ortiz	1/25/2008	125000		
7	Kim Akers	17-Jan	209,000		
8	Nicole Caron	28-Jan	258,000		
9	Ryan Calafato	21-Jan-08	145700		
10					

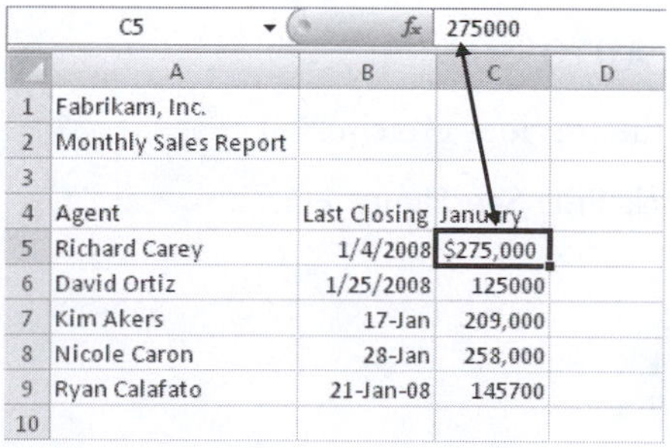

PAUSE. LEAVE the workbook open to use in the next exercise.

A numeric entry contains a combination of the digits 0 through 9. Special characters that indicate the type of value can also be included in the entry. The following chart illustrates special characters that can be entered with numbers.

CHARACTER	USED TO
+	Indicate a positive value
- or ( )	Indicate a negative value
$	Indicate a currency value
%	Indicate a percentage
/	Indicate a fraction
.	Indicate a decimal
,	Separate the digits of an entry

A number entered in Excel is considered positive unless it is combined with a special character to indicate otherwise. If you enter a plus sign with a number, Excel ignores it. Negative numbers can be entered with a minus sign or with parentheses. By default, Excel shows negative numbers with a minus sign. When you enter a dollar sign or another of the characters shown, Excel automatically assigns a number format to the entry.

Filling a Series with Auto Fill

Excel provides *auto fill* options that will automatically fill cells with data and/or formatting. To populate a new cell with data that exists in an adjacent cell, use the Fill command. You can choose the direction from which you want the data to be copied.

The *fill handle* is a small black square in the lower-right corner of the selected cell. When you point to the fill handle, the pointer changes to a black cross. You can drag the fill handle from a cell containing data to fill adjacent cells with existing data or have Excel automatically continue a series of numbers, numbers and text combinations, dates, or time periods, based on an established pattern.

⊙ **FILL A SERIES WITH AUTO FILL**

USE the workbook from the previous exercise.

1. Select **D4** and click **Fill**. See Figure 2-5.

Figure 2-5

Fill command

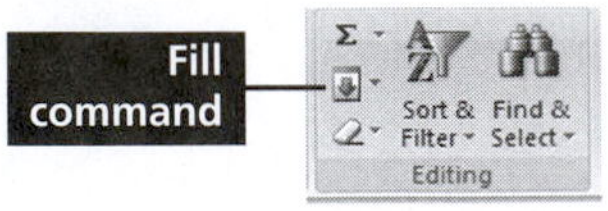

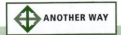

ANOTHER WAY

To quickly fill a cell with the contents of the cell above, press Ctrl+D; press Ctrl+R to fill the cell to the right.

2. From the Options box, click **Right**. The contents of C4 (January) is filled into cell D4.
3. Select **C10** and click the **Fill** button. Choose **Down**. The content of C9 is copied into C10.
4. Click the **fill** handle in C5, as shown in Figure 2-6, and drag to F5. The Auto Fill Options button appears in G6.

Figure 2-6

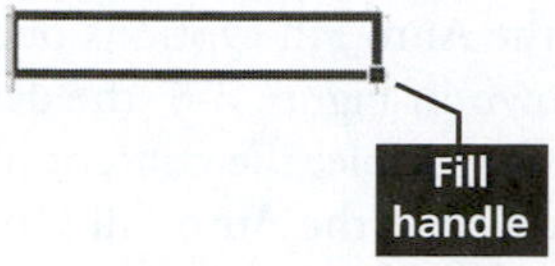

Fill handle

Fill handle

A **range** is a group of adjacent cells that you select to perform operations on all of the selected cells. When you refer to a range of cells, the first cell and last cell are written with a colon, for example, D5:F5.

5. Point to the **Auto Fill Options button**, click the arrow, and choose **Fill Formatting Only**.

6. Click the **fill handle** in C4 and drag to H4. Excel recognizes January as the beginning of a natural series and completes the series as far as you take the fill handle.

7. Select **C13**, key **2007**, and press [Enter].

8. Click the **fill handle** in C13 and drag to D13. The contents of C13 are copied.

9. In **D13**, key **2008** and press [Enter]. You have created a series of years.

10. Select **C13** and **D13**. Click the **fill handle** and drag to G13. The cells are filled with consecutive years. When you enter sufficient data for Excel to recognize a series, you can drag the fill handle to complete the series as far as you want.

When Excel recognizes a series, the default fill option is to complete the series. When you use the fill handle and a series is not present, the default is to copy the cell contents. The Fill Options button also allows you to fill formatting only or to fill without formatting.

11. Select cells **F4:H4**. With the range selected, press [Delete].

12. Select **C10:G13**. Press [Delete]. You have cleared your Sales Report worksheet of unneeded data. Your worksheet should look like Figure 2-7.

Figure 2-7

Sales Report worksheet

	A	B	C	D	E
1	Fabrikam , Inc.				
2	Monthly Sales Report				
3					
4	Agent	Last Closing	January	February	March
5	Richard Carey	1/4/2008	$275,000		
6	David Ortiz	1/25/2008	125000		
7	Kim Akers	8-Jul	209,000		
8	Nicole Caron	28-Jan	258,000		
9	Ryan Calafato	28-Jan-08	145700		
10					

PAUSE. LEAVE the workbook open to use in the next exercise.

CERTIFICATION READY?
How do you fill a series using Auto Fill?
1.1.1

To display the fill handle, hover the cursor over the lower-right corner of the cell until it turns into a +. Click and drag the handle from cells that contain data to the cells you want to fill with that data.

After you fill cells using the fill handle, the Auto Fill Options button appears so that you can choose how the selection is filled. As shown in Figure 2-8, the default is to copy the original content and formatting. In the illustrated example, the content of the original cell appears in each cell in the filled range. When you point to the Auto Fill Options button and click the arrow that appears, you can choose other fill options.

Figure 2-8

Auto Fill Options button

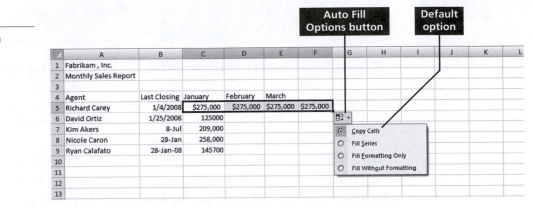

If you choose to fill formatting only, the contents are not copied, but any number that you key into a cell in the selected range will be formatted like the original cell, such as Currency. If you click Fill Series, the copied cells will read $275,001, $275,002, etc. The Auto Fill Options button remains until you perform another function.

The fill handle can be used to complete a natural series or any series that you create. For example, to record daily sales, you might want to have consecutive columns labeled with the days of the week. If you key Monday in the first cell, you can fill in the rest of the days by dragging the fill handle from the Monday cell to complete the series. When you key sufficient data for Excel to recognize a series, the fill handle will do the rest.

Cutting, Copying, and Pasting Data

↓
THE BOTTOM LINE

You can use Excel's Cut, Copy, and Paste commands to copy or move entire cells with their contents, formats, and formulas. You can also copy specific contents or attributes from the cells. For example, you can copy the format only without copying the cell value or copy the resulting value of a formula without copying the formula itself. You can also copy the value from the original cell but retain the formatting of the destination cell.

Copying a Data Series with the Mouse

By default, drag-and-drop editing is turned on so that you can use the mouse to **copy** (duplicate) or move cells. Just select the cells or range of cells you want to copy and hold down Ctrl while you point to the border of the selection. When the pointer becomes a **copy pointer**, you can drag the cell or range of cells to the new location. As you drag, a scrolling ScreenTip identifies where the selection will be copied if you released the mouse button.

COPY A DATA SERIES WITH THE MOUSE

USE the workbook from the previous exercise.

1. Select the range **A4:A9**.

2. Press Ctrl and point the cursor at the bottom border of the selected range. The copy pointer is displayed. Be sure to hold down the Ctrl key the entire time, or you will move the value instead of copying it.

3. With the copy pointer displayed, hold down the left mouse button and drag the selection down until **A12:A17** is displayed in the scrolling ScreenTip below the copy box.

4. Release the mouse button. The data in A4:A9 appears in A12:A17.

   PAUSE. LEAVE the workbook open to use in the next exercise.

After you have entered data into a worksheet, you frequently need to rearrange or reorganize some of it to make the worksheet easier to understand and analyze. As you practiced in this exercise, cut, copy, and paste functions can be performed in a variety of ways:

- using the mouse
- using Ribbon commands
- using shortcut commands
- using the Office Clipboard task pane

CERTIFICATION READY?
How do you copy a data series with the mouse?
1.1.2

Moving a Data Series with the Mouse

Data can be moved from one location to another within a workbook in much the same way as copying. To move a data series, select the cell or range of cells and point to the border of the selection. When the pointer becomes a ***move pointer***, you can drag the cell or range of cells to a new location. When data is moved, it replaces any existing data in the destination cells.

MOVE A DATA SERIES WITH THE MOUSE

USE the workbook from the previous exercise.

1. Select **B4:B9**.

2. Point the cursor at the **bottom border** of the selected range. The move pointer is displayed.

3. With the move pointer displayed, hold down the **left mouse button** and drag the selection down until B12:B17 is displayed in the scrolling ScreenTip below the box.

4. Release the mouse button. In your worksheet, the destination cells are empty; therefore, you are not concerned with replacing existing data. The data previously in B4:B9 is now in B12:B17.

5. Select the range of cells from **C4:E9**.

6. Point the cursor at the left border of the selection to display the move arrows.

7. Drag left and drop the range of cells in the same rows in column B.

   PAUSE. LEAVE the workbook open to use in the next exercise.

When you attempt to move a selection to a location that contains data, a caution dialog box, shown in Figure 2-9, opens. "Do you want to replace the contents of the destination cells?" is a reminder that moving data to a new location replaces the existing data.

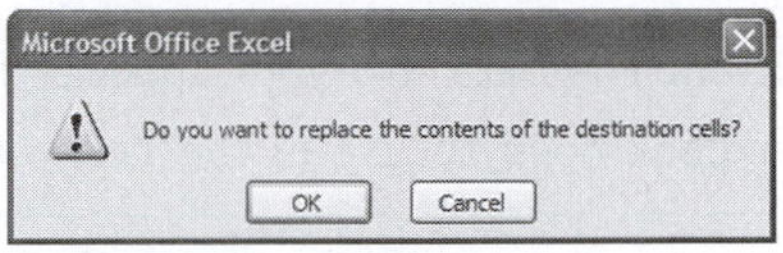

Figure 2-9

Dialog box to move cells

Microsoft Office Excel

! Do you want to replace the contents of the destination cells?

OK   Cancel

Copying and Pasting Data

The **Office Clipboard** collects and stores up to 24 copied or cut items. You can then **paste** (insert) selected items from the Clipboard to a new location in the worksheet. **Cut** data is removed from the worksheet but is still available for you to use in multiple locations. Items on the Office Clipboard are available to be used in the active workbook, in other workbooks, and in other Microsoft Office programs. To use more than the last item cut or copied, however, the Clipboard task pane must be open. If Collect Without Showing Office Clipboard is selected in Clipboard Options, cut or copied items will be stored on the Clipboard, but you must display the task pane to paste any item except the last one.

→ COPY AND PASTE DATA

USE the workbook from the previous exercise.

1. Click the **Clipboard Dialog Box Launcher** to open the Office Clipboard task pane. The Clipboard task pane opens on the left side of the worksheet. (Task panes opened on the right in Excel 2003.)

2. Select **C5** and key **305000**. Press ⌨Enter.

3. Select **C5** and click **Copy** in the Clipboard group. The border around C5 becomes a flashing marquee.

 **ANOTHER WAY**

To copy, you can use Ctrl+C or right-click and then click Copy on the shortcut menu. You can use Ctrl+V to paste the last cut or copied data.

4. Select **C8**; the flashing marquee identifies the item that will be copied. Click **Paste** in the Clipboard group.

5. Select **D5**. Right-click and then click **Paste** on the shortcut menu. The flashing border remains.

6. With D5 selected, press ⌨Delete to remove the data from D5. When you perform any function other than paste, the flashing border is removed from C5. You can no longer paste the item unless you use the Clipboard pane.

7. Select **C6**, key **185000**, and press ⌨Enter.

8. You can copy data from one worksheet or workbook and paste it to another worksheet or workbook. Select **A1:A9** and click **Copy**.

9. Click the **Sheet2** tab to open the worksheet.

10. Select **A1** and click **Paste**. Point to **Paste Options** and click the arrow. Click **Keep Source Column Widths**.

> **TAKE NOTE**✲ To paste a range of cells, select the first cell in the range to copy or select a range the same size as the one copied.

11. Click **Sheet1**. With C9 active, click the **$305,000** item in the task pane. The item is pasted. Click **Undo** to clear C9.

12. Close the Clipboard task pane.

PAUSE. LEAVE the workbook open to use in the next exercise.

You have just practiced using the commands in the Clipboard group. You can select a range of data, click copy, move the cursor to a new location, and click Paste. If you copy additional items and then click Paste, only the last item copied will be pasted. To access multiple items, open the Clipboard task pane.

> **TAKE NOTE**✲ When you cut or copy data and then paste the data using the Office Clipboard, the Paste command on the Ribbon, or press Ctrl+V, the default is to paste the original cell contents and formatting. Additional options are available when you click the arrow below the Paste command. You can copy a range of data in a column and click Transpose to paste the data into columns. Other options allow you to copy formulas, to copy values instead of formulas, and to copy cells containing borders and paste the data without the border. In Lesson 8, you will use some of the Paste Special options.

When you paste data, the Paste Options button appears below the pasted data. Click the button to choose how the destination cell or range will be formatted. Paste options are illustrated in Figure 2-10.

Figure 2-10

Paste options

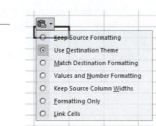

To display the Office Clipboard task pane, click the Clipboard Dialog Box Launcher. The most recently copied item is always added at the top and it is the item that will be copied when you click Paste or use a shortcut command. As illustrated in Figure 2-11, the Clipboard stores items copied from other programs as well as those from Excel. The program icon and the beginning of the copied text are displayed.

Figure 2-11

Office Clipboard task pane

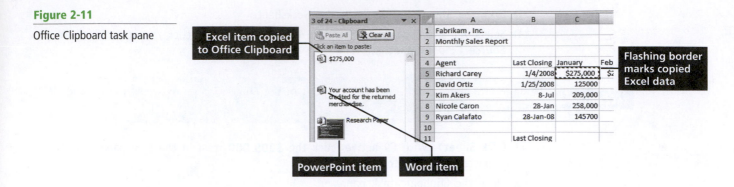

When you copy or cut data from a worksheet, a flashing border appears around the item and remains visible after you paste the data to one or more new locations. It will continue to flash until you perform another action or press Esc. As long as the marquee flashes, you can paste that item to multiple locations without the Clipboard being open.

When you move the cursor over a Clipboard item, an arrow appears on the right side that allows you to paste the item or delete it. You can delete individual items, or click Clear All to delete all Clipboard items. When the task pane is open, you can still use the command buttons or shortcuts to paste the last copied item.

Clipboard Options allow you to display the Clipboard automatically. If you do not have the Clipboard automatically displayed, it is a good idea to check Collect Without Showing Office Clipboard so that you can access items you cut or copied when you open the Clipboard.

To close the Clipboard task pane, click the Dialog Box Launcher or the Close button at the top of the pane. Clipboard items remain, however, until you exit all Microsoft Office programs. If you want the Clipboard task pane to be displayed when Excel opens, click the Options button at the bottom of the Clipboard task pane and check the Show Office Clipboard Automatically option.

ANOTHER WAY

Press Ctrl+C twice to display the Office Clipboard task pane. If this shortcut does not open the Clipboard, open the Clipboard with the Dialog Box Launcher, click Clipboard Options, and enable this shortcut.

CERTIFICATION READY?
How do you copy and paste a data series?
1.3.1

Cutting and Pasting Data

Most of the options for copying and pasting data also apply to cutting and pasting. The major difference is that data copied and pasted remains in the original location as well as in the destination cell or range. Cut and pasted data appears only in the destination cell or range.

⊕ CUT AND PASTE DATA

USE the workbook from the previous exercise.

1. Click **Sheet2** if necessary.
2. Select **A8** and click **Cut** in the Clipboard group.
3. Select **A9** and click **Paste**.

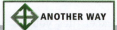

ANOTHER WAY

You can press Ctrl+Z to undo and Ctrl+Y to redo.

4. Click **Undo**. The data is restored to A8.

   PAUSE. LEAVE the workbook open to use in the next exercise.

If you complete an action and then change your mind, Excel's Undo 🔄 is extremely useful. If you mistakenly paste into a cell or range that already contains data, that data will not be available on the Clipboard. You must undo the paste to recover the data.

You can undo and repeat up to 100 actions in Excel. You can undo one or more actions by clicking Undo on the Quick Access Toolbar. To undo several actions at once, click the arrow next to Undo 🔄 and select the actions that you want to reverse. Click the list and Excel will reverse the selected actions.

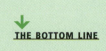 **CERTIFICATION READY?**
How do you cut and paste data and cell contents?
1.3.1

To redo an action that you undid, click Redo 🔄 on the Quick Access Toolbar. When all actions have been undone, the Redo command changes to Repeat.

In the preceding exercises you learned that Excel provides a number of options for populating a worksheet with data. There are also several ways you can accomplish each of the tasks. To cut, copy, and paste, you can use Ribbon commands, shortcut key combinations, or right-click and use a shortcut menu. As you become more proficient in working with Excel, you will decide which method is most efficient for you.

■ Editing a Workbook's Properties

THE BOTTOM LINE

Document properties are details that describe or identify a file. Document properties usually include details such as the title of the document, author name, subject, and keywords related to the document's topic or contents. Setting properties in a document enables you to easily organize and identify documents. You can use document properties to search for and locate documents.

Setting Basic Properties

You can use the Document Information Panel to view or change document properties for an open worksheet. To open the panel, click the Microsoft Office Button, point to Prepare, and then click Properties. The Document Information Panel displays directly above the workspace rather than in a dialog box as it did in earlier versions of Excel.

⊙ SET BASIC PROPERTIES

USE the workbook from the previous exercise.

1. Click the **Microsoft Office Button**.
2. Point to **Prepare**. The Prepare the document for distribution window opens. Click **Properties**. The Document Information Panel is displayed as shown in Figure 2-12. If text appears in the Author field, it is the person or institution whose name was entered in Windows user information.

Figure 2-12

Document Information Panel

Document Properties ▼			Location: Y:\Excel Project\Excel PDF Final Lessons\Lesson 02 Edits\Solutions\Le * Required field ×

Author: Title: Subject: Keywords: Category: Status:

Comments:

3. In the Author field, key your name as you want it to appear in Excel files you create. Press **Tab**.

4. In the Title field, key **Sales Report** and press **Tab**.

 PAUSE. LEAVE the workbook open to use in the next exercise.

TAKE NOTE *

If any Document Information fields are marked with a red asterisk, the field is required. Your organization most likely specified the requirement when it created customized property options.

Assigning Key Words

Assigning key words to document properties makes it easier to organize and find documents. You can assign your own text values in the Keywords field. For example, if you work for Fabrikam, Inc., you might assign the key word *seller* to worksheets that contain data about clients whose homes the company has listed for sale. You could then search for and locate all files containing information about owners of homes your company has listed. You can assign more than one key word to a document.

→ ASSIGN KEY WORDS

USE the workbook from the previous exercise.

1. In the Document Properties Panel, click the **Keywords** field and key **Agent, Closing**.

2. Click the arrow next to **Document Properties**. Click **Advanced Properties**. The Properties dialog box opens.

3. Click the **Summary** tab to see the properties you entered.

4. Click the **Statistics** tab to see the date you created the file (today).

5. Click **OK** to close the Properties dialog box.

6. Click the **Close** button (X) at the top of the Document Information Panel.

 PAUSE. LEAVE the workbook open to use in the next exercise.

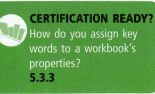

CERTIFICATION READY?
How do you assign key words to a workbook's properties?
5.3.3

After a file has been saved, the Statistics tab will record when the file was accessed and when it was modified. It also identifies the person who last saved the file. After a workbook has been saved, the Properties dialog box title bar will display the workbook name. Because you have not yet saved the workbook you have been using, the dialog box title bar said *Book1 Properties*. You can view a document's properties from the Open dialog box or from the Save As dialog box when the workbook is closed. You can also view properties from the Print dialog box.

■ Printing a Worksheet

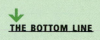
THE BOTTOM LINE

When you click Quick Print, the entire open worksheet is printed. That option does not allow you to customize the printed report. The Page Layout tab commands allow you to tailor how a worksheet looks when it is printed. The commands on this tab let you set a print area, determine the page orientation, adjust page breaks, and decide whether you want the grid lines to print.

Setting the Print Area

Defining a print area gives you more control over what shows up on the printed page. If a worksheet has a defined print area, Excel will print only the specified print area. The print options in the Print dialog box will not override a defined area. You can set print areas to print a completed portion of a worksheet or to restrict publication of some data.

SET THE PRINT AREA

USE the workbook from the previous exercise.

1. With **Sheet1** active, select **C1:C9**.
2. Click the **Microsoft Office Button** and select **Print**. The Print dialog box will open. The default printer will appear in the Name box.
3. In the Print what section, click **Selection**.
4. Click **OK**. Only the portion of the worksheet that you selected is printed. If you want to print a second copy of this portion of the worksheet, you have to repeat Steps 1–3.
5. Select **A1:B9**. On the Page Layout tab, click **Print Area** in the Page Setup command group as shown in Figure 2-13.

Figure 2-13

Use Page Layout commands to prepare for printing

If you click the Print Area without selecting the range of data you want to print, you will print only the active cell.

6. Click **Set Print Area** on the dropdown list. When you print from this worksheet, only the area **A1:B9** will be printed.

7. Click outside the print area to deselect it.

   PAUSE. LEAVE the workbook open to use in the next exercise.

With this print area setting, regardless of the method you use to print, only the January sales information will appear in the printed document. When a print area has been set, it will remain outlined on the worksheet as you continue to work. If you later want to print the entire worksheet, you must clear the print area or check Ignore print areas on the Print dialog box.

Using Print Preview

You have two options for seeing how your page will look when printed.

- Click the Microsoft Office Button, point to the Print arrow, and then click Print Preview.
- Click the Microsoft Office Button, click Print, and click Preview on the Print dialog box.

→ USE PRINT PREVIEW

USE the workbook from the previous exercise.

1. Click the **Microsoft Office Button** and point to the arrow next to **Print**.

2. Click **Print Preview** from the options panel. The worksheet is displayed as it will be printed. Only the cell contents will be printed; the gridlines will not be printed.

3. Click **Close Print Preview**.

4. Click the **Page Layout** tab if necessary. Check the Print box in the Gridlines section of the Sheet Options command group. Although gridlines are visible on the work surface, the lines will not print unless the Print box is checked.

5. Click the **Microsoft Office Button**, point to **Print**, and choose **Print Preview**. The gridlines are shown in the preview window.

6. **CLOSE** the Print Preview window.

   PAUSE. LEAVE the workbook open to use in the next exercise.

Choosing a Printer

Before you can print from Excel, printers must be set up for your computer. If more than one printer has been set up, you can choose the printer on which you want the document printed. Installed printers will be listed in the Name box on the Print dialog box.

→ CHOOSE A PRINTER

USE the workbook from the previous exercise.

1. Click the **Microsoft Office Button**.

2. Click **Print**. The Print dialog box is displayed as shown in Figure 2-14.

Figure 2-14

Print dialog box

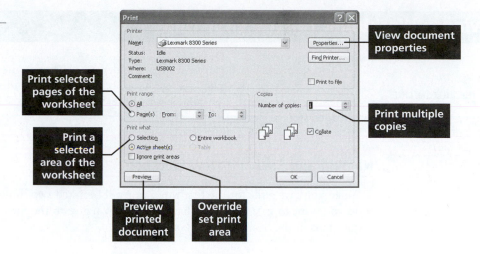

3. Click the arrow in the **Name** field. Available printers will be listed.

4. Click a printer choice.

5. Click **OK**. The print area set in the previous exercise is in effect. Your printed document displays A1:B9 only.

   PAUSE. LEAVE the workbook open to use in the next exercise.

Setting Other Printer Options

The Print dialog box options allow you to print multiple copies, print selected pages of a multi-page document, print an entire workbook, and ignore a set print area. You can also view document properties and preview the printed document.

⊕ SET OTHER PRINTER OPTIONS

USE the workbook from the previous exercise.

1. Click the **Microsoft Office Button**.

2. Click **Print**. The Print dialog box is displayed.

3. Click **Ignore print areas**. The print area will be ignored for this printing only. It will remain set and be visible in your worksheet.

4. Click **OK**. The active worksheet will be printed.

   PAUSE. LEAVE the workbook open to use in the next exercise.

■ Saving a Workbook for the First Time

↓ THE BOTTOM LINE

When you save a file, you can save it to a folder on your computer's hard drive, a network drive, a disk, CD, or any other storage location. You must first identify where the document is to be saved. The remainder of the Save process is the same, regardless of the location or storage device.

Naming and Saving a New Workbook

When you save a file for the first time, you will be asked two important questions: Where do you want to save the file? What name will you give to the file? You will answer these questions in the Save As dialog box.

→ NAME AND SAVE A NEW WORKBOOK

USE the workbook from the previous exercise.

1. Click the **Microsoft Office Button**, point to **Save As**, and click **Excel Workbook**. The files and folders that appear in the Save As dialog box depend upon the folder that was last used to save a workbook on your computer.

2. In the Save in box, select the drive and folder to which you save documents. Click **Create New Folder** to open the New Folder dialog box shown in Figure 2-15.

Figure 2-15

New Folder dialog box

3. In the New Folder dialog box, key **Excel Lesson 2** and click **OK**. The New Folder dialog box closes and the Save As name box shows that the file will be saved in the Excel Lesson 2 folder.

4. Click the **File name** box and key **Fabrikam First Qtr Sales**.

5. Click **Save**.

PAUSE. LEAVE the workbook open to use in the next exercise.

Electronic filing and manual filings operate on the same principles. Files are stored in folders. Folders are stored in file cabinets. In electronic filing, the file cabinets are drives and storage devices. The Save As dialog box is where you place the document in a folder and select the location to store it.

Saving a Workbook under a Different Name

You can rename an existing workbook to create a new workbook. For example, the sales report you created in the exercises is for the first quarter. When all first-quarter data has been entered, you can save the file with a new name and use it to enter second-quarter data. You can also use an existing workbook as a template to create new workbooks. Use the Save As dialog box to implement either of these options.

SAVE A WORKBOOK UNDER A DIFFERENT NAME

USE the workbook from the previous exercise.

1. Click the **Microsoft Office Button** and click **Save As**. The Excel Lesson 2 folder appears in the **Save As** dialog box because it was the folder that was last used to save a workbook.
2. Click the **File name** box and key **Fabrikam Second Qtr Sales**.
3. Click **Save**. You have created a new workbook by saving an existing workbook with a new name.
4. Click the **Microsoft Office Button** and click **Save As** to open the dialog box.
5. In the File name box, key **Fabrikam Sales Template**.
6. In the Save as type box, click **Excel Template**. Click the **Save** button.

   PAUSE. LEAVE the workbook open to use in the next exercise.

Creating a template to use for each new report eliminates the possibility that you might lose data because you neglected to save with a new name before you replaced one quarter's data with another.

Saving a Workbook for Use in a Previous Version of Excel

Files created in earlier versions can be opened and revised in Excel 2007. You can save a copy of an Excel 2007 workbook (xlsx) that is fully compatible with Excel 97 through Excel 2003 (xls) versions. The program symbol displayed with the filenames will be different, but it is a good idea to give the earlier edition file a different name.

SAVE A WORKBOOK FOR USE IN A PREVIOUS VERSION OF EXCEL

USE the workbook from the previous exercise.

1. Click the **Microsoft Office Button** and point to **Save As**.
2. In the Save a copy of the document pane, click **Excel 97-2003 Workbook**.
3. In the Save As dialog box, key **Fabrikam First Qtr Sales 97-03**. Click **Save**. Close the workbook.
4. Press **Ctrl** + **O** to display the Open dialog box. Select **Fabrikam First Qtr Sales 97-03**. Scroll right to view the file type and see that it is saved to be compatible with earlier Excel editions.
5. Click (but do not open) **Fabrikam First Qtr Sales**.
6. Click the arrow next to **Views**. Click **Properties** on the list. The properties you entered earlier are displayed. Click **Open**.

   PAUSE. LEAVE the workbook open to use in the next exercise.

CERTIFICATION READY?
How do you save a workbook for use in a previous version of Excel?
5.4.1

Choosing a Different File Format

You can save an Excel 2007 file in a format other than xlsx or xlx. The file formats that are available in the Save As dialog box depend upon what type of sheet is active. When you save a file in another file format, some of the formatting, data, and/or features may be lost.

➡ **CHOOSE A DIFFERENT FILE FORMAT**

USE the workbook from the previous exercise.

1. Click the **Microsoft Office Button** and point to **Save As**. Click **Other Formats**.
2. Choose **Single File Web Page** in the Save as type box.
3. Click **Change Title**. Key **January Sales**. Click **OK**.
4. Click **Selection:Sheet** and click **Publish**.
5. In the Publish as Web Page dialog box, select **Print Area**.
6. Click **Publish**. A browser window opens with January Sales displayed.
7. Close the browser window.
8. Click the **Microsoft Office Button** and click **Close**.
9. If prompted to save changes, click **Yes**. The workbook is closed but Excel remains open.

   CLOSE Excel.

CERTIFICATION READY?
How do you save a workbook in a different file format?
5.4.2

You can save an Excel file in a number of other formats such as an Excel Macro-Enabled Workbook or an XML Data file.

SUMMARY SKILL MATRIX

IN THIS LESSON YOU LEARNED	MATRIX SKILL	SKILL NUMBER
To create a new workbook		
To start a workbook from scratch		
To populate a worksheet with data		
To fill a series using Auto Fill	Fill a series	1.1.1
To cut, copy, and paste data	Cut, copy, and paste data and cell contents	1.3.1
To copy and move a data series	Copy a series	1.1.2
To edit a workbook's properties	Add key words and other information to workbook properties	5.3.3
To print a worksheet		
To set the print area	Define the area of a worksheet to be printed	5.5.1
To set printer options		
To name and save a new workbook		
To save a workbook for use in a previous version of Excel	Save workbooks for use in a previous version of Excel	5.4.1
To choose a different file format when saving a workbook	Using the correct format, save a workbook as a template, a Web page, a macro-enabled document, or other appropriate format	5.4.2

Knowledge Assessment

Matching

Match each vocabulary term with its definition.

a. auto fill
b. AutoComplete
c. copy
d. document properties
e. fill handle

f. formula bar
g. label
h. paste
i. range
j. template

_____ 1. A command used to insert a cut or copied selection to a cell or range of cells

_____ 2. Worksheets that are already set up to track certain kinds of data

_____ 3. A small black square in the lower-right corner of selected cells that you can use to copy one cell to adjacent cells or to create a series

_____ 4. A bar at the top of the Excel window where you can enter or edit cell entries or formulas

_____ 5. A group of adjacent cells that you select to perform operations on all of the selected cells

_____ 6. To place a duplicate of a selection on the Office Clipboard

_____ 7. An Excel feature that helps you quickly enter data into cells

_____ 8. An Excel feature that automatically fills cells with data from another cell or range or completes a data series

_____ 9. Entries that identify the numeric data in a worksheet

_____ 10. Details about a file that describe or identify it and include details such as the author

True / False

Circle T if the statement is true or F if the statement is false.

T F 1. You can accept an AutoComplete entry by pressing Tab or Enter.

T F 2. If you key **June 5** in a cell, the formula bar will display June 5 as well.

T F 3. Use Ctrl+: to enter the current date in a worksheet cell.

T F 4. When you paste data into a cell or range of cells that contain data, the data that is replaced is copied to the Office Clipboard.

T F 5. When you set a print area, the setting lasts for one printing only. If you want to print that range again, you will need to reset the print area.

T F 6. Use the fill handle to create a natural series such as the months of the year.

T F 7. You can use Quick Print to print selected pages of a long document.

T F 8. The Office Clipboard collects items cut or copied from Excel worksheets only.

T F 9. You cannot make changes to a worksheet in the Print Preview window.

T F 10. By default, gridlines will print in an Excel worksheet.

■ Competency Assessment

Project 2-1: Advertising Budget

Create a new workbook for Fabrikam, Inc., that can be used to compare actual expenses with budgeted amounts.

GET READY. Launch Excel if it is not already running.

1. Click the **Microsoft Office Button** and click **New**.
2. Click **Blank Workbook** and then click **Create**.
3. Select **A1** and key **Fabrikam, Inc.**
4. Select **A2** and key **Advertising Budget**.
5. Beginning in A4, key the following labels and values.

Media	Vendor	Monthly Budget
Print	Lucerne Publishing	2000
Radio	Northwind Traders	$1,500
Door-to-Door	Consolidated Messenger	1200
Print	Graphic Design Institute	500
Television	Southridge Video	3000

6. If necessary, double-click the **marker** between columns to adjust the column width to display all of the text.
7. **SAVE** the workbook in the Lesson 2 folder you created in an exercise. Save the workbook as *Advertising Budget 2-1*.
8. **CLOSE** the file.

LEAVE Excel open for the next project.

Project 2-2: Set Document Properties and Assign Key Words

Use the Document Properties panel to assign document properties to an existing workbook. **OPEN** *Employees* from the CD data files.

> 🔘 **CD**
>
> The *Employees* workbook is avilable on the companion CD-ROM.

1. Click the **Microsoft Office Button**.
2. Point to **Prepare** and then click **Properties**.
3. In the Author field, key your name. Press `Tab`.
4. In the Title field, key **Employees** and press `Tab`.
5. In the Subject field, key **Hours Worked** and press `Tab`.
6. In the Keywords field, key **Job Title, Hours**.
7. Click the **Close (X)** button at the top of the Document Information Panel.
8. **SAVE** the workbook as *Employees 2-2* and **CLOSE** the file.

LEAVE Excel open for the next project.

■ Proficiency Assessment

Project 2-3: Monthly Advertising Expense

> 🔘 **CD**
>
> The *Advertising Expense* workbook is available on the companion CD-ROM

Use an existing workbook to create a new workbook that will track monthly advertising costs.

OPEN *Advertising Expense* from the CD data files.

1. Select **D4** and key **January**.
2. Select **D4**. Use the **fill handle** to enter the months of the year.

3. Select **A10**. Click **Fill** in the Editing group on the Home tab.

4. Choose **Down** and press Enter.

5. Select **B10**, key **Trey Research**, and press Enter.

6. Select **C10**, key **2500**, and press Enter.

7. Open the Document Information Panel and key your name as the author, **Advertising Expense** as the title, and **Monthly Expenses** as the subject.

8. Close the Document Information Panel.

9. **SAVE** the workbook in your Lesson 2 folder as *Advertising Expense 2-3*.

10. **CLOSE** the workbook.

  LEAVE Excel open for the next project.

Project 2-4: Advertising Expenditures

Fourth Coffee specializes in unique coffee and tea blends. Create a workbook to track and classify expenditures for January.

1. Click the **Microsoft Office Button**. Open a new blank workbook.

2. In A1 key **Fourth Coffee**.

3. In A2 key **January Expenditures**.

4. Enter the following column headings in row 4.

Date	Check No.	Paid to	Category	Amount

5. Enter the following expenditures:

   • **January 3**, paid **$3000** to **Wide World Importers** for **coffee**, Check No. **4076**.
   • **January 20**, paid **$600** to **Northwind Traders** for **tea**, Check **4077**.
   • **January 22**, paid **$300** to **City Power and Light** for **utilities**.
   • **January 28**, paid **$200** to **A. Datum Corporation** for **advertising**.

6. Checks are written sequentially. Use the fill handle to enter the missing check numbers.

7. Adjust column headings as needed.

8. **SAVE** the workbook as *Expenses 2-4*. **CLOSE** the workbook.

  LEAVE Excel open for the next project.

■ Mastery Assessment

Project 2-5: Home Sales Data

Fabrikam receives sales research data from the local association of Realtors, which it uses as a benchmark for evaluating its sales performance.

OPEN *Sales Research* from the CD data files.

1. **OPEN** the **Office Clipboard**. If it contains items, click **Clear All** so that only data for this project will be on the Clipboard.

2. Use AutoFill to add the remaining months in column A.

3. The data for March and April are reversed. Use the Copy command to place the data for March (B6:G6) on the Clipboard. Copy the data as one item.

4. Use the mouse to move B7:G7 to B6:G6. Paste the April data from the Clipboard to B7:G7.

5. Beginning with A1, set the Print Area to include all data for January through June. Print the selected area.

6. Click the **Select All** button in the upper-left corner of the worksheet. Copy the entire worksheet to the Clipboard.

7. Paste the data to Sheet2. Adjust column widths if necessary.

8. **SAVE** the workbook as *Sales Research 2-5*. **CLOSE** the workbook.

   LEAVE Excel open for the next project.

Project 2-6: Fourth Coffee

An employee has begun an inventory worksheet for Fourth Coffee. You want to use the company name and logo from the inventory sheet to create a banner for a website.

OPEN *FC Inventory* from the CD data files.

The *FC Inventory* workbook is available on the companion CD-ROM.

1. **SAVE** the workbook as a Single File Web Page.

2. **PUBLISH** Selection A1:E1.

3. Click **Publish**. You have just created the banner for the company's new Web page.

4. **CLOSE** the browser and all other open files.

   LEAVE Excel open for the next project.

INTERNET READY

More than fifteen shortcut combinations were given in the first two lessons. Create a worksheet to list at least fifteen shortcut combinations. Decide how many columns you will need. Each column must have a label that identifies its contents.

Use the Excel Help on your computer and Microsoft Help online. Save your file as *Excel Shortcuts.*

When you have finished, **CLOSE** Excel.

Formatting Cells and Ranges

3

LESSON SKILL MATRIX

SKILLS	MATRIX SKILL	SKILL NUMBER
Inserting and Deleting Cells	Insert and delete cells, rows, and columns	2.2.1
Manually Formatting Cell Contents	Format text in cells	2.3.4
Filling Cells with Color	Create custom cell formats	2.3.2
Applying Number Formats	Apply number formats	2.3.1
Merging and Splitting Merged Cells	Merge and split cells	2.3.6
Placing Borders around Cells	Add and remove cell borders	2.3.7
Copying Cell Formatting with the Format Painter		
Formatting Cells with Styles	Apply and modify cell styles	2.3.3
Working with Hyperlinked Data	Insert, modify, and remove hyperlinks	2.3.8
Applying Conditional Formatting to Cells		
Using the Rule Manager to Apply Conditional Formats	Manage conditional formats using the rule manager	4.3.1
Allowing Multiple Conditional Formatting Rules to Be True	Allow more than one rule to be true	4.3.2
Applying Specific Conditional Formats	Apply conditional formats	4.3.3
Clearing a Cell's Formatting		

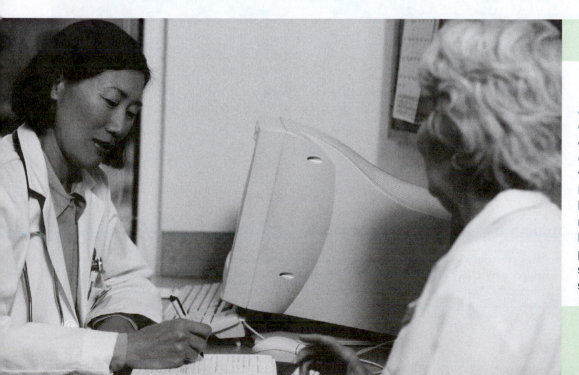

KEY TERMS
attribute
character
conditional formatting
default
font
Format Painter
hyperlink
merged cells
Mini toolbar
point
select
style

Contoso Ltd.'s income is generated by the four physicians and the physician assistant (PA). Ideally, physicians are scheduled to see no more than 35 patients per day, but every effort is made to accommodate patients who need immediate medical attention. Working in collaboration with the physicians, the PA sees patients who need an appointment when all the physicians' schedules are full. Many chronically ill patients whose conditions require frequent monitoring are scheduled with the PA. By law, a PA can treat no more than 25 patients a day. The firm is considering adding a nurse practitioner (NP) to balance the patient load. An NP is a registered nurse who provides some of the same care as physicians. In most states, an NP can prescribe medications.

■ SOFTWARE ORIENTATION

Formatting Excel Worksheets

The Home tab displayed in Figure 3-1 contains the formatting commands that you will use to enhance the appearance of the worksheets you create. You will use commands from every group as you learn to insert and delete cells, apply basic formatting to text, copy formatting, and apply styles and conditional formatting.

Figure 3-1

Apply formatting using the Home tab

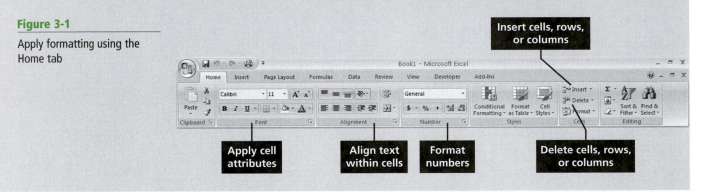

■ Inserting and Deleting Cells

↓
THE BOTTOM LINE

As shown in Figure 3-2, when you click the arrow next to Insert, you can insert cells, worksheet rows, worksheet columns, or a new worksheet into a workbook.

Similar options apply to deleting cells. You can delete a cell, a worksheet row, a worksheet column, or a worksheet from a workbook. In the exercises that follow, you will add and delete cells.

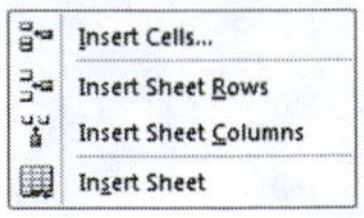

Figure 3-2

Insert options

Looking Ahead

In Lesson 4, you will insert and delete worksheet rows and columns. In Lesson 5 you will add a worksheet to an existing workbook and delete a worksheet from a workbook.

Adding a New Cell to a Worksheet

After creating a worksheet, you may decide that you need to add additional data or delete unnecessary data. To enter additional text or values within the existing data, you need to insert cells. You can insert a cell or cells and shift down other cells in the same column, or you can shift other cells in the same row to the right.

ADD A NEW CELL TO A WORKSHEET

GET READY. Before you begin these steps, be sure to turn on or log on to your computer.

1. Launch Excel. The Home tab should be active.
2. **OPEN** *Contoso Patient Visits* from the data files for this lesson.
3. Click **F5** and click **Insert** in the Cells group. F5 is now blank and the cells in the range F5:F8 have shifted down one row.
4. Key **604** and press Enter.
5. Select **J4**.
6. Click the **Insert** arrow, and click **Insert Cells**. The Insert dialog box opens.
7. Click **Shift cells right** and click **OK**. A blank cell is inserted and the data is shifted to the right.

 CD

The *Contoso Patient Visits* workbook is available on the companion CD-ROM.

ANOTHER WAY

You can select a cell or range, right-click, and click Insert to open the Insert dialog box. In the dialog box, click the direction in which you want to shift the cells.

8. Key **580** and press Enter.
9. Select **K7:L7** and click the **Insert** arrow.
10. Click **Insert Cells**.
11. Click **Shift cells right** and click **OK**. The data has shifted two cells to the right.

ANOTHER WAY

You can repeat the action of inserting a cell by clicking Redo on the Quick Access Toolbar.

12. Select **K7**, key **475**, and press Tab.
13. Key **611** and press Enter.
14. Select **N3:N9**. Click the **Insert** arrow and click **Insert Cells**.
15. Click **Shift cells right** and click **OK**. Cells are inserted so that November's data can be entered later.

   PAUSE. LEAVE the workbook open to use in the next exercise.

CERTIFICATION READY?
How do you insert a cell or a range of cells into a worksheet?
2.2.1

Additions and changes are common activities in Microsoft Office Excel 2007 workbooks. In the previous exercise, Contoso created an Excel workbook to track the number of patients treated during a month to determine whether to hire a nurse practitioner. After creating and saving the workbook, the administrative assistant discovered that corrections are needed and additional data must be added to the workbook.

If you click Insert in the Cells group, a blank cell is inserted and, by default, existing cells move down in the column. When you click the arrow next to Insert and click Insert Cells, the Insert dialog box shown in Figure 3-3 opens, and you can choose to shift cells to the right. The dialog box also allows you to insert a row or a column in a worksheet.

Figure 3-3

Insert dialog box

To insert blank cells in a worksheet, select the cell or the range of cells where you want to insert the new blank cells. Select the number of cells that you want to insert. As Figure 3-4 illustrates, if you want to insert two cells, you must select two cells.

	A	B	C	D	
1	ontoso, Ltd.				
2					
3	Last Name	First Name	Job Title	January	Febr
4	Bourne	Stephanie	Physician	640	
5	Holiday	Nicole	Physician	589	
6	Laszlo	Rebecca	Physician	603	
7	Wilson	Dan	Physician	565	
8	Da Silva	Sergio	PA	300	

With the cells selected, click the arrow next to Insert, and then click Insert Cells. When the Insert dialog box opens, click the direction you want to shift the cells.

Deleting a Cell from a Worksheet

You can use Delete in the Cells group to delete cells, ranges, rows, or columns. The principles are the same as those you used to insert cells except that the direction the cells shift is reversed.

⊕ DELETE A CELL FROM A WORKSHEET

USE the workbook from the previous exercise.

1. Select **C3:C9**. Click **Delete** in the Cells group. The Job Title data is removed from the worksheet and the remaining columns are shifted left.
2. Select **A9:N9** and click **Delete**. The duplicate row of data is removed.
3. Select **K13:K18** and click **Cut** in the Clipboard group.
4. Select **M3** and click **Paste**.

   PAUSE. LEAVE the workbook open to use in the next exercise.

CERTIFICATION READY?
How do you delete cells from a worksheet?
2.2.1

Click Delete in the Cells group to eliminate cells from a worksheet. Any data to the right of the deleted cell or cells will automatically shift left. If you want to shift cells up rather than left, click the arrow next to Delete and click Delete Cells to open the Delete dialog box.

You can right-click and click Delete on the shortcut menu to open the Delete dialog box and delete cells. Remember that when you use the Delete command, the cells are deleted. When you use the Cut command or press Delete on the keyboard, only the cell contents are deleted. The cells and any formatting remain.

■ Manually Formatting Cell Contents

↓
THE BOTTOM LINE

The commands in the Font, Alignment, and Number groups (Figure 3-5) contain the basic formatting commands. Using only those groups, you can significantly change the appearance of a worksheet. Use Font commands to change the font and font size; to bold, italicize, and underline data; and to add color, fill, and borders. Use Alignment commands to choose how data is aligned within cells. Use Number commands to apply a format to values and to increase or decrease the number of digits after a decimal.

Selecting Cells and Ranges

To apply formatting to text and values in an existing worksheet, you must first **select** the data. When you select data, you identify the cell or range of cells in which you want to enter data or apply formatting. You can select cells, ranges, rows, columns, or the complete worksheet. The cells in a range can be adjacent or nonadjacent. You can also place a cell in editing mode and select all or part of its contents.

⊕ SELECT CELLS AND RANGES

USE the workbook from the previous exercise.

1. Select **A3**. Hold down the left mouse button and drag to **B8** to select the range.
2. Click the row 3 heading to select the entire row.
3. Click the column **C** header, press and hold (Ctrl), and click **E**, **G**, and **I** to select nonadjacent columns.

Looking Ahead If a worksheet has been protected, you may not be able to select cells on the worksheet. You will learn how to protect a worksheet in Lesson 11.

4. Click the **Microsoft Office Button** and then click **Save As**.
5. When the Save As dialog box opens, create a Lesson 3 folder.
6. **SAVE** your workbook in the folder and name it **Patient Visits**.

PAUSE. LEAVE the workbook open to use in the next exercise.

Table 3-1 illustrates a variety of ways to select portions or all of a worksheet.

Table 3-1

Options for selecting cells and ranges

TO SELECT	DO THIS
A single cell	Click the cell or press the arrow keys to move to the cell.
A range of cells	Click the first cell in the range and drag to the last cell, or hold down Shift while you press the arrow keys to extend the selection.
A large range of cells	Click the first cell in the range and hold down Shift while you click the last cell.
All cells on a worksheet	Click the Select All button (intersection of the column and row headings), or press Ctrl+A.
Nonadjacent cells or cell ranges	Select the first cell or range and hold down Ctrl while you select the other cells or ranges.
An entire row or column	Click the row or column heading.
Adjacent rows or columns	Drag across the row or column headings.
Nonadjacent rows or columns	Click the column or row heading of the first row or column of the selection. Hold down Ctrl while you click the column or row headings of other rows or columns you want to add to the selection.
The contents of a cell	Double-click the cell and then drag across the contents that you want to select.

When you make a selection, the cell or range is highlighted on the screen. These highlights do not appear in a printout, however. If you want cells to be highlighted when you print a worksheet, you must use formatting features to apply shading.

Excel provides many ways to format labels and values in a worksheet. In the business world, worksheets are usually printed or shared with others electronically. Therefore, you want your worksheet or workbook to be as eye-catching and understandable as possible. You can improve the design of a worksheet in several ways.

- Change the alignment.
- Change the font style and enlarge the text for titles.
- Format titles and labels in bold and/or italics.
- Apply special formatting attributes.

Aligning Cell Contents

Text and numbers in a worksheet can be aligned to the left, to the right, or at the center. By default, when you enter alphabetic characters or alphabetic characters combined with numbers or symbols, the cell content is left-aligned. When you enter numbers, the content is right-aligned. You can use Alignment commands to change default alignment or to override previous alignment formatting.

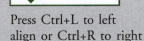

ANOTHER WAY

Press Ctrl+L to left align or Ctrl+R to right align text.

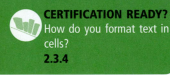

CERTIFICATION READY?
How do you format text in cells?
2.3.4

ALIGN CELL CONTENTS

USE the workbook from the previous exercise.

1. Select **A3:N3**.
2. In the Alignment group, click **Center**. The column labels are horizontally centered.
3. Click **C4**, press **Shift**, and click **N8**. The cell range containing the values is selected. Click **Align Text Right**. All cells containing values are now right-aligned.

   PAUSE. LEAVE the workbook open to use in the next exercise.

As illustrated in Figure 3-6, the alignment that has been applied to the active cell is shown by the highlighted commands in the Alignment group. Proper alignment and spacing greatly improve the readability of worksheet data.

Figure 3-6

Active cell alignment is highlighted

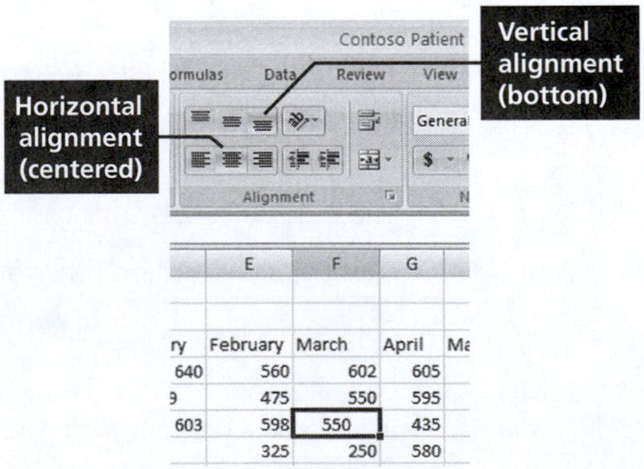

Choosing Fonts and Font Sizes

A *font* is a set of text characteristics designed to appear a certain way. The font determines the appearance of the cell contents. The *default,* or predefined, font for Excel 2007 is 11-point Calibri. This is an easy-to-read font that takes up less space than Arial, which was the default in earlier Excel versions.

⊕ CHOOSE FONTS AND FONT SIZES

USE the workbook from the previous exercise.

1. Select the column labels in **row 3**.
2. Click the **Font** arrow. Scroll up the list of font names and click **Arial**. Notice that the font size is unchanged (still 11 point), but Arial is larger than the default Calibri font.
3. With row 3 still selected, click **Decrease Font Size**. The number 10 appears in the Font Size box and the labels now fit within the column width.

   PAUSE. LEAVE the workbook open to use in the next exercise.

CERTIFICATION READY?
How do you format text in cells?
2.3.4

You can change the default font in Excel Options. If you chose a different default font and/or font size, that font is used only in new workbooks that you create after you change the default and restart Excel. Existing workbooks are not affected.

You can change the font for a selected cell, a range of cells, or for characters within text. To change the font, select the font that you want in the Font box `Calibri ▾`. You can change the size in the Font Size box `11 ▾` or click Increase Font Size **A˄** or Decrease Font Size **A˅** until the size you want is displayed in the Font Size box. To improve the overall design of a worksheet, the font size is usually enlarged for titles and labels.

Font size is measured in points. Each time you click Decrease Font Size or Increase Font Size, the size changes by a set amount that matches the size options on the Font Size list. Points refer to the measurement of height of characters in a cell. A point is equal to 1/72 inch.

Applying Special Character Attributes 🟢 NEW FEATURE

> In addition to changing the font and font size, you can apply special **attributes** to the font that add visual appeal. An attribute is a formatting characteristic, such as bold, italic, or underlined text. Applying special characteristics to specific text or values adds interest to a worksheet and calls attention to specific data.

⊕ APPLY SPECIAL CHARACTER ATTRIBUTES

USE the workbook from the previous exercise.

1. Select **A4**. Hold down the left mouse button and drag to **B8**. Click **Bold** **B** in the Font group.
2. Click **A3**. Press Shift and click **N3** to select the column labels. Click **Italic** **I** in the Font group, then click **Bold**.

   PAUSE. LEAVE the workbook open to use in the next exercise.

CERTIFICATION READY?
How do you format text in cells?
2.3.4

Although you are adding multiple special formatting to the worksheet in these exercises to improve your skills, it is wise to have a clear, logical design plan that presents the data in an easy-to-understand format. It is best not to overuse special character attributes. Keep in mind that the focus is on the data and the information that it conveys.

When you select text for formatting, you can use the **Mini toolbar**, shown in Figure 3-7, to apply selected formatting features. This unique formatting tool is new in Excel 2007. When you right-click, the Mini toolbar displays above the shortcut menu. Just click any of the available features to apply them to selected text. Unlike the Quick Access Toolbar, which can be customized, you cannot customize the Mini toolbar. You can turn off the Mini toolbar in Excel Options.

Figure 3-7

Mini toolbar

Changing Font Color

Color enhances the visual appeal of a worksheet. You can change the color of the text in cells. To add color, select the cell, range of cells, text, or *characters* that you want to format with a different color. A character can be a letter, number, punctuation mark, or symbol.

➜ CHANGE FONT COLOR

USE the workbook from the previous exercise.

1. Select the column labels. Click the **Font Color** arrow.
2. Click **Blue** in the standard colors.
3. Select **A4:B8**. Click the **Font Color** arrow. Click **Red** in the standard colors.

    PAUSE. LEAVE the workbook open to use in the next exercise.

TAKE NOTE *

If you choose a color and change your mind, click Undo on the Quick Access Toolbar or press Ctrl+Z.

CERTIFICATION READY?
How do you format text in cells?
2.3.4

Black is the default, or automatic, font color, but you can easily change the color. The most recently applied color appears on the Font Color button . To apply that color, make a selection and click Font Color. To apply a different text color, click the arrow next to Font Color. You can choose a theme color or a standard color. You can also click More Colors to open the Colors dialog box where you can choose from additional standard colors or create colors to your specifications.

Looking Ahead
You will learn about Document Themes in Lesson 4. The default Office theme is the basis for the colors that appear under Theme Colors and Standard Colors on the Font Color menu.

Filling Cells with Color

You can call attention to cells by adding a background color and pattern. You can use a solid color or apply special effects, such as gradients, textures, and pictures. Use the Fill Color command in the Font group to change the background color. The most recently used fill color appears on the Fill Color button.

➜ FILL CELLS WITH COLOR

USE the workbook from the previous exercise.

1. Select **A3:N3**.
2. Click the **Font** Dialog Box Launcher.
3. Click the **Fill** tab.
4. In the Background Color section, click the **light blue** color (second box) in column 5.
5. Add a second color in the Pattern Color box. Click the arrow and click the **third box** in column 5.
6. Click the **Pattern Style** arrow and click the pattern at the end of the first row. At the bottom of the dialog box, you can see a sample of how the pattern and color will look in the selected cells.
7. Click **OK** to apply the color and the fill pattern.
8. **SAVE** and **CLOSE** the *Patient Visits* workbook.

    PAUSE. LEAVE Excel open to use in the next exercise.

CERTIFICATION READY?
How do you create custom cell formats?
2.3.2

No color (clear) is the default background. To add color and shading, select cells to which you want to add special effects. The color palate you used to apply font color is also used for background color. To apply the color shown on the Fill Color button, make a selection and click the button. To apply a different fill color, click the arrow next to Fill Color and apply a theme color or a standard color. You can also click More Colors to open the Colors dialog box and custom blend colors.

You can apply a background color and add a pattern effect. Select the range of cells to which you want to apply a background color with fill effects. Click the Font group's Dialog Box Launcher. The Format Cells dialog box opens. Click the Fill tab. As shown in Figure 3-8, make a selection in the Pattern Style box to add a pattern to the background color.

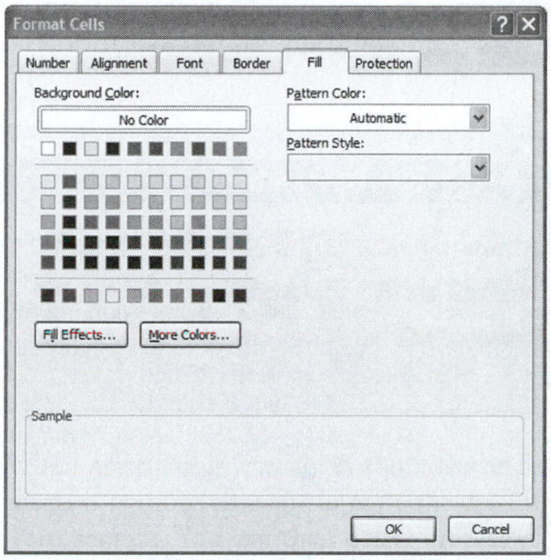

Figure 3-8

Add a pattern to cell background color

Applying Number Formats

Most of the data that you use in Excel is numeric. Applying accurate formatting to numeric data makes it easier to interpret and, therefore, more useful. Number formatting can be applied to cells before data is entered, or data can be selected and formatted after it has been entered. Formatting changes the appearance of numbers; it does not change their value. The actual value is always displayed in the formula bar.

APPLY NUMBER FORMATS

GET READY. Before you begin these steps, be sure that Microsoft Excel is running.

1. **OPEN** *Contoso Revenue*. Click the **Sheet1** tab if necessary to make it the active worksheet.
2. Select **B4:D10** and click **Accounting Number Format ($)** in the Number group. The data is reformatted to monetary values, the decimal points are aligned, and column width is increased to accommodate the selected number format.
3. With the text still selected, click **Decrease Decimal** in the Number group twice. The data is rounded to whole dollars.
4. Select **B10:D10**. Click **Comma Style (,)**. Click **Decrease Decimal** twice to show whole numbers. Row 10 data relates to the number of patients, not monetary values. Accounting style was inappropriately applied to this data.
5. Click the **Sheet2** tab.
6. Select **B7:B11**. Click the **Number** Dialog Box Launcher.
7. Click **Number** in the Category area. Key **0** in the Decimal places box and check the **Use 1000 Separator** box. Click **OK**.
8. Format B6 with **Accounting** and zero decimals.
9. Select **C7:C11**. Click the **Number** Dialog Box Launcher.

The *Contoso Revenue* workbook is available on the companion CD-ROM.

CERTIFICATION READY?
How do you apply number formats?
2.3.1

10. On the Number tab, click **Date** in the Category area. Click the **03/14/01** date style. Click **OK**.
11. **SAVE** the workbook as *Revenue*.

PAUSE. LEAVE the workbook open to use in the next exercise.

In this exercise you applied formatting to Contoso's first-quarter revenue data. When you enter a number in Excel, the default format is General, which displays the data exactly as you enter it. If you include a special character such as $ or % when you enter a number, the special character will appear in the cell. The format does not affect the actual cell value.

To change how numeric data appears, you can select one of the formatting options in the Number group on the Home tab, or you can launch the Format Cells dialog box and click the Number tab. The most commonly applied number formats are summarized in Table 3-2.

Table 3-2

Number-formatting categories

FORMAT CATEGORY	DESCRIPTION
General	This is the default number format that Excel applies when you key a number. Numbers are displayed just the way you key them. If a cell is not wide enough to show the entire number, a number with decimals will be rounded.
Number	This format is used for the general display of numbers. You can specify the number of decimal places that you want to use, whether you want to use a thousands separator, and how you want to display negative numbers.
Currency	This format is used for general monetary values and displays the default currency symbol with numbers. You can specify the number of decimal places that you want to use, whether you want to use a thousands separator, and how you want to display negative numbers.
Accounting	This format is also used for monetary values. Currency symbols and decimal points are aligned.
Date	Displays days, month, and years in various formats such as January 7, 2008, 7-Jan, and 1/7/2008.

If number symbols (###) appear in a cell, it means that the number entered is wider than the cell. If you plan to apply a number format to the data, it is not necessary to adjust column width because the column width is adjusted automatically when you apply a number format.

After you choose a number format, you will need to further specify how you want the numbers to appear. You can use the commands in the Number group to apply formats and to increase or decrease the number of decimal places displayed in worksheet data. When you decrease the decimal, data becomes less precise because numbers following the decimal are rounded. The lack of preciseness is insignificant, however, when you deal with large numbers.

Wrapping Text in a Cell

When a cell is formatted to wrap text, data in the cell wraps to fit the column width. If you change the column width, text wrapping adjusts automatically. When text is wrapped, row height is adjusted to accommodate the wrap.

➔ WRAP TEXT IN A CELL

USE the workbook from the previous exercise.

1. Select **Sheet1**. Select **A7** and click **Wrap Text** in the Alignment group. The row height is adjusted and the cell's full text is displayed on two lines.

TAKE NOTE＊ If you format a cell for text wrapping and all wrapped text is not visible, it may be because the row is set to a specific height. You will learn to modify row height in Lesson 4.

CERTIFICATION READY?
How do you wrap text in a cell?
2.3.4

2. Double-click **A4**. *Edit* is displayed on the Status bar, indicating that the cell is in edit mode.
3. Place the cursor just to the left of the word *Coverage* and press [Alt] + [Enter]. A manual line break is inserted. Press **Enter**.

PAUSE. LEAVE the workbook open to use in the next exercise.

TAKE NOTE＊
Remember that you can edit a cell in the formula bar as well as in the cell.

If you want the text in a cell to appear on multiple lines, you can format the cell so that the text wraps automatically, or you can enter a manual line break. To wrap text automatically, select the text you want to format and click Wrap Text in the Alignment group. To start a new line of text at a specific point in a cell, double-click the cell to place it in edit mode. Click the location where you want to break the line and press Alt+Enter.

Merging and Splitting Merged Cells

You can use the Merge and Center command in the Alignment group to merge cells. A **merged cell** is created by combining two or more adjacent horizontal or vertical cells. When you merge cells, the selected cells become one large cell that spans multiple columns or rows. You can split cells that have been merged into separate cells again, but you cannot split a single worksheet cell that has not been merged.

➔ MERGE AND SPLIT MERGED CELLS

USE the workbook from the previous exercise.

1. Select **A1:D1**. Click **Merge & Center** in the Alignment group. The content previously in A1 is now centered across columns A, B, C, and D.
2. Select **A2:D2**. Click **Merge & Center**.
3. Select **A4:A5** and click **Merge & Center**. A dialog box opens to remind you that the data in A5 will be deleted in the merge.
4. Click **OK**. A4 and A5 are merged and the data originally in A4 is centered in the merged cell.
5. Click the arrow next to **Merge & Center** and click **Unmerge Cells**. The cells are unmerged, but the data from A5 has been deleted.
6. Select **A5**, key **Medicare/Medicaid**, and press **Enter**.
7. Select **A4:A5** and click **Align Text Left** in the Alignment group.

PAUSE. LEAVE the workbook open to use in the next exercise.

 **ANOTHER WAY**

With a merged cell active, you can click Merge and Center to unmerge the cells.

When you merge cells, the data that you want to appear in the merged cells must be in the upper-left cell of the selected range. Only the data in the upper-left cell will remain in the merged cell. Data in the other cells to be merged will be deleted. Cells can be merged in a row or column, and the content of the upper-left cell will be centered in the merged cell. If the cells to be merged contain information that will be deleted in the merge, the Excel dialog box shown in Figure 3-9 opens to caution you that if you merge the cells, only the content of the upper-left cell will remain after the merge.

CERTIFICATION READY?
How do you merge cells and split merged cells?
2.3.6

Figure 3-9

Merge cells warning

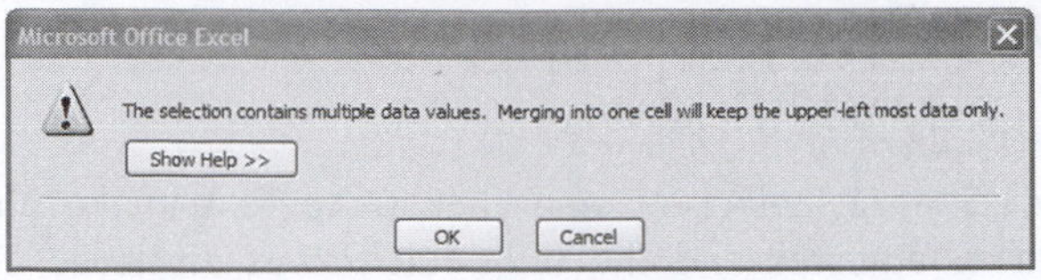

> Microsoft Office Excel
>
> ⚠ The selection contains multiple data values. Merging into one cell will keep the upper-left most data only.
>
> Show Help >>
>
> OK   Cancel

To merge cells without centering the contents of the upper-left cell, click the arrow next to Merge & Center, and click Merge Cells. Text you enter in such a merged cell will be left aligned.

With a merged cell active, click Merge & Center to split the merged cell. You can also use the arrow next to Merge & Center and choose Unmerge Cells.

TROUBLESHOOTING If the Merge & Center button is unavailable, the selected cells may be in editing mode. To cancel editing mode, press Enter or Escape (Esc).

A merged cell takes the name of the original upper-left cell. As shown in Figure 3-10, when you merged A1:D1 in the previous exercise, the merged cell is named A1.

Figure 3-10

Merged cells have one name

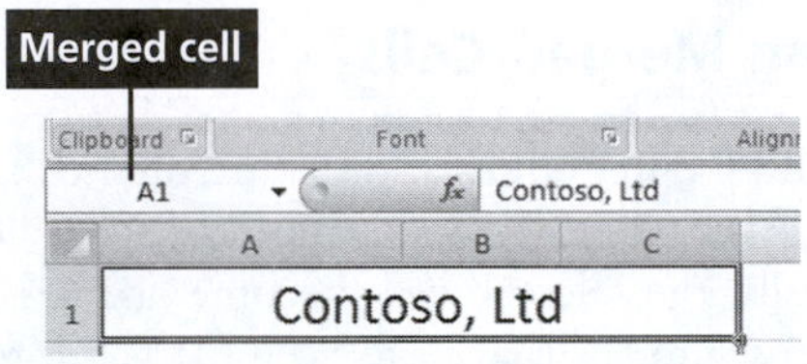

Merged cell

	A	B	C
1		Contoso, Ltd	

A1 ▼ fx Contoso, Ltd

Placing Borders around Cells

> You can use borders to enhance a worksheet's visual interest and to make it easier to read. You can apply Excel's predefined border styles, or you can customize borders by specifying a line style and a color of your choice. Borders are often used to set off headings, labels, or totals.

➔ PLACE BORDERS AROUND CELLS

USE the workbook from the previous exercise.

1. Select **A1** and click the arrow next to **Bottom Border**.
2. Click **More Borders**. The Format Cells dialog box opens with the Border tab displayed.
3. Under Line, click the Style displayed in the lower-right corner.
4. Click the **Color** arrow and then click **Red**.
5. Under Presets, click **Outline**. The red border is previewed in the Border box.
6. Click **OK**. The dialog box closes and the border is applied to A1.
7. With **A1** selected, click **Increase Font Size** until the value in the Font Size box is 20 points.

   PAUSE. LEAVE the workbook open to use in the next exercise.

CERTIFICATION READY?
How do you place borders around a cell?
2.3.7

To add a border, select the cell or range of cells to which you want to call attention. For example, you may want to place a border around the titles, around the cells displaying the total revenue for the first quarter, or around the labels that identify the months.

In the Font group, the Border button displays the most recently used border style, and the button's name changes to that style name. Click the Border button (not the arrow) to apply that style, or you can click the arrow and choose a different border style. Click More Borders to apply a custom or diagonal border. On the Border tab of the Format Cells dialog box, click a Line Style and a color. Select a border style from the Presets or create a style with line-placement options in the Border area. Notice that Figure 3-11 displays the two diagonal borders.

Figure 3-11

Borders options

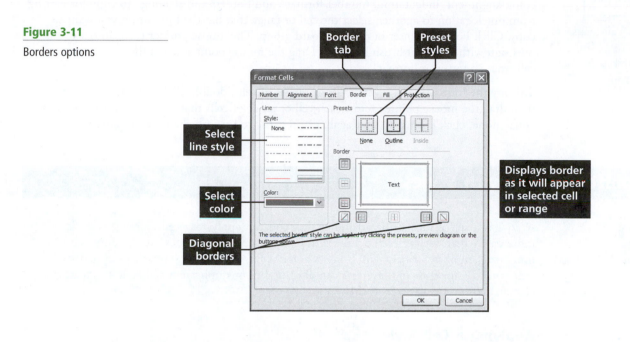

TAKE NOTE* If you apply two different types of borders to a shared cell boundary, the most recently applied border is displayed.

■ Copying Cell Formatting with the Format Painter

THE BOTTOM LINE

The **Format Painter** is an Excel feature that allows you to copy formatting from a cell or range of cells to another cell or range of cells. Located in the Clipboard group on the Home tab, it is one of Excel's most useful tools. It allows you to quickly copy attributes that you have already applied and "paint" those attributes to other data.

⊕ COPY CELL FORMATTING WITH THE FORMAT PAINTER

USE the workbook from the previous exercise.

1. With A1 active, click **Format Painter**. A flashing border appears around A1, the formatting to be copied.
2. Click **A2**.
3. Select **A2** and right-click to display the Mini toolbar. Click the **Font Size** arrow and click **14**. The font size of the subtitle is reduced.
4. Select **A1:A2** and click **Format Painter**.

5. Click the **Sheet2** tab and select **A1:A2**. The formatting from the Sheet1 titles have been applied to the Sheet2 titles.

6. Click the **Sheet1** tab.

   PAUSE. LEAVE the workbook open to use in the next exercise.

You can use the Format Painter to copy formats, including font, font size, font style, font color, alignment, indentation, number formats, and borders and shading. To copy formatting from one location to another, select the cell or range that has the formatting you want to copy. Click Format Painter in the Clipboard group. The mouse pointer turns into a white plus sign with the paint brush beside it. Drag the mouse pointer across the cell or range of cells that you want to format.

To copy the formatting to several cells or ranges of cells, double-click Format Painter, and then drag the mouse pointer across each cell or range of cells that you want to format. When you're done, click Format Painter again or press Esc to turn off the Format Painter.

■ Formatting Cells with Styles

THE BOTTOM LINE

A *style* is a set of formatting attributes that you can apply to a cell or range of cells more easily than setting each attribute individually. Style attributes include fonts and font sizes, number formats, and borders and shading. Excel has several predefined styles that you can apply or modify; you can also modify or duplicate a cell style to create a custom cell style.

Applying a Cell Style

To apply a cell style to an active cell or range, click Cell Styles in the Styles group on the Home tab. Click the cell style that you want to apply. You can apply more than one style to a cell or range.

→ APPLY A CELL STYLE

USE the workbook from the previous exercise.

1. Select **A1:A2** and click **Cell Styles** in the Styles group. The Cell Styles gallery opens.

2. Click **20% - Accent4** under Themed Cell Styles. The themed shading is applied to A1 and A2. The style changes the font size as well as adding the shading.

3. Select **A1** and click **Cell Styles**.

4. Click **Heading 1** under Titles and Headings.

5. Select **A2** and click **Cell Styles**.

6. Click **Heading 2** under Titles and Headings.

7. Select **A8:D8** and click **Cell Styles**.

8. Click **Total** under Titles and Headings.

   PAUSE. LEAVE the workbook open to use in the next exercise.

When you view defined styles in the Cell Styles gallery, you can see the formatting that will be used when you apply each style. This feature allows you to assess the formatting without actually applying it.

Experiment with combining styles to achieve the desired effect. For example, you can click a themed cell style, which will apply shading to the cell. Then, you can click Cell Styles again and click Heading 1, which applies font face, font size, and special formatting effects such as bold or italics.

If you are not pleased with a style you apply, you can Undo the style or apply another style
to the cell or range. To remove a cell style from selected cells without deleting the cell style,
select the cells that are formatted with that cell style. Click Cell Styles and click Normal. To
delete the cell style and remove it from all cells formatted with that style, right-click the cell
with the cell style, and then click Delete.

Modifying a Cell Style

You can modify or duplicate a cell style to create your own custom cell style. You can add
additional attributes to the style and delete attributes.

➔ MODIFY A CELL STYLE

USE the workbook from the previous exercise.

1. With A12 active, click **Cell Styles** in the Styles group. The Cell Styles gallery opens.
2. Right-click **20% - Accent6** under Themed Cell Styles. Click **Duplicate**. The Style dialog box opens.
3. Key **Accent Revised** in the Style name box.
4. Click **Format**. Click the **Font** tab.
5. Click **Italic** in the Font style box.
6. Click **12** in the Size box.
7. Click the **Border** tab and click your choice of a broken line in the Line Style box.
8. Click the two **diagonal borders** below the Border box. Click **OK**. Your formatting modifications will be shown in the Style dialog box.
9. Click **OK** to close the dialog box.
10. Click **Cell Styles** in the Styles group. Your **Accent Revised** cell style should be the first style in the Custom section. Click **Accent Revised** to apply the style to A12.
11. Use the Format Painter to apply your style to **B12:D12**.

   PAUSE. LEAVE the workbook open to use in the next exercise.

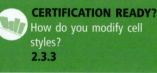
CERTIFICATION READY?
How do you modify cell
styles?
2.3.3

In this exercise, you duplicated a cell style and then modified the style to create your own
custom style. Your custom style was added to the styles gallery. If you had used the Modify
command, the existing style would have reflected the formatting changes you made.
Duplicating an existing style, and then modifying it is preferable. To modify an existing style,
click Cell Styles in the Styles group. When the styles gallery is displayed, right-click the cell
style that you want to change, and then click Modify. The Style dialog box shown in Figure 3-12
opens with the current style name displayed but not accessible. This tells you that any changes
you make to the style will be made to the existing style rather than a customized style.

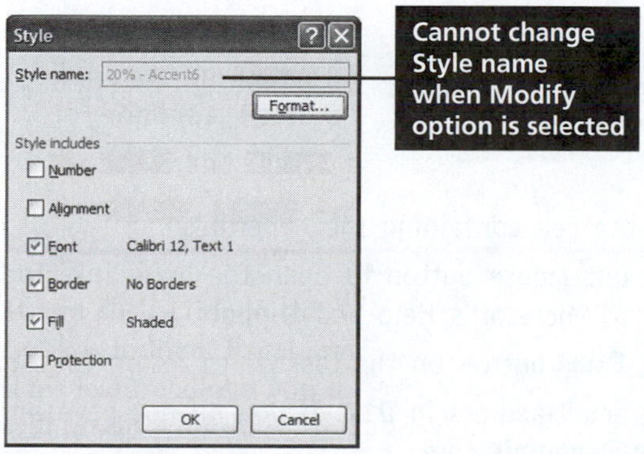

Figure 3-12

Style dialog box

Key an appropriate name for the new cell style you want to create. To change the cell style, click Format. The Format Cells dialog box opens. On the various tabs in the dialog box, select the formatting that you want for the new style. Click OK when you have completed your changes. The changes will be reflected on the Style dialog box. When you are satisfied with the style attributes, click OK. The new cell style is added to the styles gallery and identified as a custom style.

■ Working with Hyperlinked Data

↓
THE BOTTOM LINE

For quick access to related information in another file or on a Web page, you can insert a hyperlink in a worksheet cell. Hyperlinks enable you to supplement worksheet data with additional information and resources.

A *hyperlink* is an image or a sequence of characters that opens another file or Web page when you click it. The target file or Web page can be on the World Wide Web, on an intranet, or on your personal computer. In a workbook containing your personal banking records, for example, you might insert a hyperlink to jump to your bank's online bill-paying service.

Placing a Hyperlink in a Cell

It is easy to embed a hyperlink in a workbook cell. Just click the cell where you want to create a hyperlink and identify the source to which you want to connect. Each hyperlink appears in the cell as blue underlined text. When you point to a hyperlink, a ScreenTip describing the link or giving the location of the file appears.

⊕ PLACE A HYPERLINK IN A CELL

USE the workbook from the previous exercise. Verify that you can access the Internet.

1. Click **A15**.
2. Click the Ribbon's **Insert** tab.
3. Click **Insert Hyperlink** in the Links group. The Insert Hyperlink dialog box opens.
4. In the Text to display box, key **Microsoft**. This is the blue, underlined text that will appear in A15.
5. Click **ScreenTip**. The Set Hyperlink ScreenTip dialog box opens.
6. Key **Go to Microsoft's Help and Support Center**. Click **OK**. The text you keyed will replace the default ScreenTip.
7. In the Address box, key **www.support.microsoft.com** and click **OK**. The hyperlink appears in A15.

ANOTHER WAY

Ctrl+K will insert a hyperlink in a cell, or you can right-click and then click Hyperlink on the shortcut menu.

TAKE NOTE*

When you key www, Excel recognizes it as the beginning of a Web address and *http://* is supplied automatically.

8. Point to the cell containing the hyperlink.
9. Click the left mouse button to open the hyperlink. The Web browser opens and connects to Microsoft's Help and Support.
10. Click the **Excel** button on the taskbar to return to your workbook.
11. Key your email address in D17. If you do not have an email address, key **someone@example.com**.

   PAUSE. LEAVE the workbook open to use in the next exercise.

CERTIFICATION READY?
How do you create a hyperlink in a worksheet cell?
2.3.8

In this exercise, you created a hyperlink using the Hyperlink command on the Insert tab. You can also create a hyperlink to an email address or an Internet address by typing the address directly in the cell. For example, if you key someone@example.com or www.microsoft.com in a worksheet cell, an automatic hyperlink is created.

The default ScreenTip identifies the full address of the hyperlink and provides instructions for following the link. You can specify the information you want in the tip when you create the link or you can edit it later.

To edit a hyperlink, click and hold to select the cell containing the hyperlink. Right-click and then click Edit Hyperlink to open the Edit Hyperlink dialog box. You can edit the text that displays in the link, the ScreenTip text, or the address where the link will take you. You can cut or copy a hyperlink and paste it into another cell in the worksheet or paste it into another worksheet.

Removing a Hyperlink

You can delete a hyperlink and the text that represents it, turn off a single hyperlink, or turn off several hyperlinks at once.

➔ REMOVE A HYPERLINK

USE the workbook from the previous exercise.

1. Right-click the link in D17.
2. Click **Clear Contents** on the shortcut menu. The hyperlink and text are removed.
3. Right-click **B17** and click **Remove Hyperlink**. The hyperlink is removed and the text remains in the cell.
4. **SAVE** and **CLOSE** the *Revenue* workbook.

    PAUSE. LEAVE Excel open to use in the next exercise.

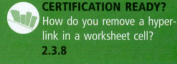

CERTIFICATION READY?
How do you remove a hyperlink in a worksheet cell?
2.3.8

As demonstrated in this exercise, you can remove a hyperlink and the associated text, or you can remove the link and retain the text. To remove multiple links, press Shift and select the hyperlinks to be removed or deleted. Right-click and click the appropriate action.

■ Applying Conditional Formatting to Cells

↓
THE BOTTOM LINE

There are times when you want to format cells in a particular way only if they meet a specific condition. Conditional formatting allows you to specify how cells that meet a given condition should be displayed. Thus, *conditional formatting* means that Excel applies formatting automatically, based on established criteria.

When you analyze data, you often ask questions, such as:

- Who are the highest performing sales representatives?
- In what months were revenues highest or lowest?
- What are the trends in profits over a specified time period?

Conditional formatting helps to answer such questions by highlighting interesting cells or ranges of cells. With conditional formatting, fonts become visual guides that help the reader understand data distribution and variation.

Using the Rule Manager to Apply Conditional Formats ✓ NEW FEATURE

On what conditions or criteria do you want to analyze the data contained in a worksheet? That is the basis for establishing conditional formats. Once data is selected, you can choose one of five preset specific conditional formats that provide a visual analysis of a worksheet or selected range of data.

For example, you can specify that when the value in a cell is greater than a given number, the value will be displayed with a particular font or background color. You can establish multiple conditional format rules for a data range.

⊕ USE THE RULE MANAGER TO APPLY CONDITIONAL FORMATS

GET READY. Open the *Patient Visit Data* file.

1. Select **A1:N1**. Merge and center the range and apply the **Heading 1** style.

2. Select **A2:N2**. Merge and center the range and apply the **Heading 2** style.

3. Select **C4:N7** and click **Conditional Formatting** in the Styles group.

4. Click **Highlight Cells Rules** and click **Greater Than**.

5. In the Greater Than dialog box, key **600** and click **OK**. The highlighted data represents the months in which the doctors were seeing more than the ideal number of patients.

6. With the range still selected, click **Conditional Formatting**.

7. Click **Highlight Cells Rules** and click **Less Than**.

8. In the Less Than dialog box, key **560**. In the *with* box, select **Green Fill with Dark Green Text** and click **OK**. The highlight now contrasts the months in which the patient load was less than expected.

9. Click **Conditional Formatting** and click **Top/Bottom Rules**.

10. Click **Top 10%**. In the dialog box, accept 10% and click **Yellow Fill with Dark Yellow Text**. Click **OK**.

11. Click **Conditional Formatting** and click **Manage Rules** at the bottom of the list.

12. In the *Show formatting rules for* box, click **This Worksheet**. The three conditional formatting rules you have applied are displayed. Position the Conditional Formatting Rules Manager dialog box below the worksheet data so you can view the data and the conditional formatting rules. Notice that the first and third rules apply to overlapping data. Therefore, if a cell value exceeds 600 and that value also falls within the top 10%, the 10% formatting will be applied.

13. Click the **Cell Value>600** rule and click the **up arrow** to move the rule to the top of the list. Click **Apply**. All values greater than 600 are formatted with the dark red font.

14. Click the **Close** button to close the dialog box.

    PAUSE. LEAVE the workbook open to use in the next exercise.

In this lesson's exercises, you have worked with data related to the number of patients treated each month at Contoso, Ltd. You can use Excel's Rule Manager to apply conditional formatting to provide visual analyses of the data in the *Patient Visit Data* workbook.

You can display the Conditional Rules Manager to see what rules are in effect for the worksheet and to apply those rules at an appropriate time. From the Conditional Formatting Rules Manager, you can add new rules, edit the existing rules, or delete one or all of the rules. The rules are applied in the order in which they are listed in the Conditional Formatting Rules Manager. You can apply all the rules or you can apply specific rules to analyze the data. As you can see in Figure 3-13, formatting is visible while the Conditional Formatting Rules Manager is open. Thus, you can experiment with the formats you want to apply and the order in which they are applied.

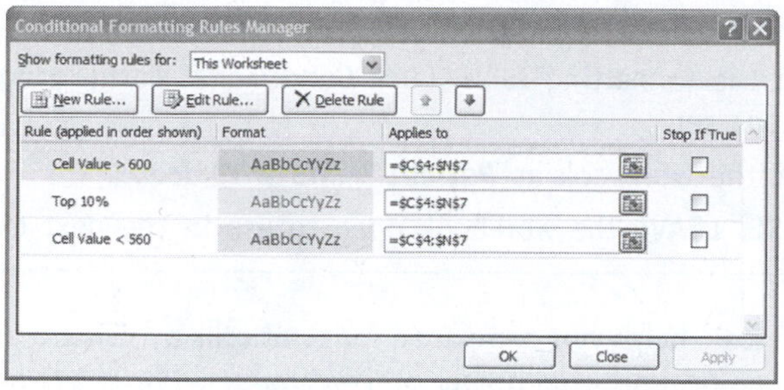

Figure 3-13

Conditional Formatting Rules Manager

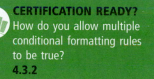

Conditional formatting is applied in the order it appears in the Rule Manager. The top rule is the latest condition created and it takes precedence. However, you can use the arrow keys to adjust rule precedence. If two rules conflict, the rule that is higher on the list is applied.

Allowing Multiple Conditional Formatting Rules to Be True

Multiple conditional formatting rules can be true. By default, new rules are always added to the top of the list and therefore have a higher precedence. Conditional formatting takes precedence over manual formatting that has been applied.

 ALLOW MULTIPLE CONDITIONAL FORMATTING RULES TO BE TRUE

USE the workbook from the previous exercise.

1. Select **C8:N8**. Click **Conditional Formatting** and click **Highlight Cells Rules**.
2. Click **Less Than**. Key **300** in the value box and click **Red Text**. Click **OK**.
3. Click **Conditional Formatting** and click **Manage Rules**. In the Show formatting rules for box, click **This Worksheet**. Although the last rule has the highest precedence, it applies only to the PA's schedule and therefore does not conflict with any of the rules that apply to the physicians' schedules.
4. Click the **Close** button to close the dialog box.

    PAUSE. LEAVE the workbook open to use in the next exercise.

CERTIFICATION READY?
How do you allow multiple conditional formatting rules to be true?
4.3.2

Applying Specific Conditional Formats

Excel has three preset conditional formats that use color and symbols to provide visual guides to help you understand data distribution and variation: color scales, icon sets, and data bars.

 APPLY SPECIFIC CONDITIONAL FORMATS

USE the workbook from the previous exercise.

1. Click **Conditional Formatting**.
2. Click **Clear Rules** and then click Clear Rules from **Entire Sheet**. All conditional formatting is cleared from the data.
3. Select **C4:N8**. Click **Conditional Formatting**.

4. Click **Data Bars** and click **Blue Data Bar**. The longer the dark blue portion of the bar is, the higher the value is in relation to other cells in the data range.

5. Clear the data bars. Select the data range and click **Conditional Formatting**.

6. Click **Color Scales** and click the **Yellow–Red Color Scale** (first option in the second row). The darker colors indicate the lower values.

7. Clear the formatting rules. Click **Conditional Formatting**. Click **Icon Sets**. Click the **3 Flags** set.

8. **SAVE** the workbook as *Patient Visits with Icons*.

PAUSE. LEAVE the workbook open to use in the next exercise.

A two-color scale helps you compare a range of cells by using a gradation of two colors. The shade of the color represents higher or lower values. The shade of the color in a three-color scale represents higher, middle, and lower values.

You can use an icon set to interpret and classify data into three to five categories. Each icon represents a range of values. For example, in the three-flag icon set, the green flag represents higher values, the yellow represents middle values, and the red represents lower values.

A data bar helps you see the value of a cell relative to other cells in the data range. The length of the data bar represents the value in the cell. A longer bar represents a higher value and a shorter bar represents a lower value. Data bars are useful in spotting higher and lower numbers, especially with large amounts such as a retailer's after-Thanksgiving sales report.

■ Clearing a Cell's Formatting

THE BOTTOM LINE

The Clear command in the Editing group on the Home tab lets you clear contents and formatting or allows you to selectively remove the contents or the formatting. When you want to redesign the appearance of an existing worksheet, click Clear and then click Clear Formats. The content will remain and you can choose to apply manual formatting, styles, or conditional formatting. Clearing all formatting ensures that you are starting with a clean formatting slate.

⊙ CLEAR A CELL'S FORMATTING

USE the workbook from previous exercise.

1. Click **Select All** to select the entire worksheet.

2. Click **Clear** in the Editing group.

3. Click **Clear Formats**. All formatting is cleared from the data. If you selected **Clear All**, the data would be removed as well as the formatting.

4. **CLOSE** the file without saving.

CLOSE Excel.

If you select Clear All, contents and formatting are removed. Selecting Clear Contents will remove the data within the selected range, but the formatting will remain.

SUMMARY SKILL MATRIX

IN THIS LESSON YOU LEARNED	MATRIX SKILL	SKILL NUMBER
To insert and delete cells in a worksheet	Insert and delete cells, rows, and columns	2.2.1
To manually format text in cells	Format text in cells	2.3.4
To fill cells with color	Create custom cell formats	2.3.2
To apply number formats	Apply number formats	2.3.1
To merge and split merged cells	Merge and split cells	2.3.6
To add and remove cell borders	Add and remove cell borders	2.3.7
To copy cell formatting with the Format Painter		
To format cells with styles	Apply and modify cell styles	2.3.3
To work with hyperlinked data	Insert, modify, and remove hyperlinks	2.3.8
To apply conditional formatting to cells		
To use the rule manager to apply conditional formats	Manage conditional formats using the rule manager	4.3.1
To apply multiple conditional formatting rules to selected data	Allow more than one rule to be true	4.3.2
To apply specific conditional formats to selected data	Apply conditional formats	4.3.3
To clear a cell's formatting		

■ Knowledge Assessment

True / False

Circle T if the statement is true or F if the statement is false.

T F **1.** When you insert a cell into a row, all data in that row is shifted down.

T F **2.** When you shift cells down and data in another cell is replaced, that data is copied to the Office Clipboard.

T F **3.** You can select a large range of cells by selecting the first cell in the range, pressing Shift, and selecting the last cell in the range.

T F **4.** You can merge cells horizontally, but not vertically.

T F **5.** If you want the dollar sign and decimals to align in a column, apply Accounting format.

T F **6.** When you wrap text in a cell, the row height is automatically adjusted to accommodate the multiple-line text.

T F **7.** Any cell in a worksheet can be split.

T F **8.** When you apply a style to text, any conflicting formatting in the cell or range is replaced by the style format.

T F **9.** When you remove a hyperlink, the link and the text are removed.

T F **10.** When you select the entire worksheet and click Clear and Clear All, the worksheet will be blank.

Fill in the Blank

Complete the following sentences by writing the correct word or words in the blanks provided.

1. When a single cell is created by combining two or more selected cells, the new cell is referred to as a(n) _____.

2. A(n) _____ is a set of formatting attributes that you can apply as a group to a selected cell or range of cells.

3. A shortcut or jump that opens a stored document or connects with the Internet is called a(n) _____.

4. When formatting is applied to data based on established criteria, it is said to be _____ formatting.

5. Bold, italic, or underlining are examples of formatting _____.

6. You can apply formatting to multiple cells with the _____.

7. By default, a new Excel 2007 feature called the _____ displays above the right-click shortcut menu.

8. Font sizes are measured in _____.

9. A letter, number, punctuation mark, or symbol is considered a(n) _____.

10. Small windows that display descriptive text when you rest the pointer on a command are called _____.

■ Competency Assessment

Project 3-1: Apply Basic Formatting

Apply formatting attributes to a workbook used to track annual utilities expenses.

GET READY. Launch Excel if it is not already running.

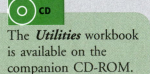

The *Utilities* workbook is available on the companion CD-ROM.

1. Click the **Microsoft Office Button** and click **Open**.
2. Open the *Utilities* file from the data files for this lesson.
3. Select **A8:G8**. Click the **Insert** arrow in the Cells group and click **Insert Cells**.
4. Click **OK** on the Insert dialog box to shift the cells down.
5. Select **A27:G27** and click **Cut** in the Clipboard group.
6. Select **A8** and click **Paste** in the Clipboard group.
7. Select **A2:G2**. Click **Bold** in the Font group.
8. Select the column labels and click **Center** in the Alignment group.
9. With the column labels still selected, click the **Font Color** arrow and click **Red**.
10. Click **Quick Print** on the Quick Access Toolbar.
11. Click the **Microsoft Office Button**. Click **Save As**.
12. **SAVE** the workbook as *Utilities 3-1* in your Lesson 3 folder.

    LEAVE the workbook open for the next project.

Project 3-2: Enhance Worksheet Appearance

Apply additional formatting attributes to an existing workbook.

USE the workbook from Project 3-1.

1. Select **A1**. Click the arrow in the Font box and click **Cambria**.
2. With A1 still selected, click **Increase Font Size** until the Font Size box shows 16 point.
3. Apply the **Green** font color to the title.
4. Select **A1:G1** and click **Merge & Center** in the Alignment group.
5. With only the merged A1 cell still selected, click **Middle Align** in the Alignment group.
6. Select **F2** and click **Wrap Text** in the Alignment group.
7. With F2 selected, click the **Format Painter** in the Clipboard group. Drag the Format Painter across all column labels.
8. Adjust column width if necessary so that column labels are completely visible.
9. Select the labels and click **Middle Align**.
10. Click **B3**, press Shift, and click **G15** to select the range that contains values. Apply the Number format to the range.
11. Print the worksheet.
12. **SAVE** the workbook as *Utilities 3-2* in the Lesson 3 folder.

    CLOSE the workbook; leave Excel open for the next project.

■ Proficiency Assessment

Project 3-3: Format Training Budget

Graphic Design Institute's Training Department provides in-house technical and soft-skills training for the firm's 1,200 employees. Apply the formatting skills you learned in Lesson 3 to give the Training Budget worksheet a professional finish.

OPEN *Training Budget* from the data files for this lesson.

CD

The *Training Budget* workbook is available on the companion CD-ROM.

1. Merge and center cells **A1:E1**.
2. Key **Graphic Design Institute** as the worksheet title.
3. Click **Cell Styles** in the Styles group and apply the **40% - Accent 1** style to the title.
4. Click *Cell Styles* and apply the **Heading 1** style.
5. Merge and center cells A2:E2. Key the subtitle **Training Department Budget**.
6. Apply the **20% - Accent 1** fill to the subtitle. Apply the Heading 2 style.
7. Merge and center the blank row above the column labels.
8. Select the column labels and apply the Note style.
9. Key **TOTAL** in A18 and apply the Total style to row 18.
10. Select **D6:E17**. Click the **Number** group Dialog Box Launcher. Click the **Number** category, set decimal places to 0, and check **Use 1000 separator**.
11. Select the nonadjacent cells **D5:E5**, **E18**. Apply the Currency format and reduce decimals to 0.
12. Print the worksheet.
13. **SAVE** the workbook as *Training Budget 3-3*.

    LEAVE the workbook open for the next project.

Project 3-4: Hyperlinks

Create and edit hyperlinks that connect a worksheet with selected web pages. Insert links to send e-mail messages to selected recipients.

Use the *Training Budget 3-3* workbook from Project 3-3.

1. Label column B **Contact**.
2. Click the **Insert** tab.
3. Select **B5** and click **Hyperlink**.
4. Key **A. Datum Corporation** as the text to display.
5. Key **www.adatum.com** in the address box. Click **OK**.
6. In B11, create a hyperlink that displays as Lucerne Publishing at www.lucernepublishing.com.
7. In B16 create a hyperlink for Margie's Travel. The address is www.margiestravel.com.
8. Select **B16** and click **Hyperlink** to open the Edit Hyperlink dialog box. Edit the ScreenTip to read **Corporate contract for all travel**.
9. Select **B13** and create an email link for the consultant: someone@example.com.
10. **PRINT** the worksheet. **SAVE** the workbook as *Training Budget 3-4*. **CLOSE** the workbook.

    LEAVE Excel open for the next project.

■ Mastery Assessment

Project 3-5: Format Sales Report

Litware, Inc. wants to apply Font and Alignment group formatting to enhance its sales report's appearance and readability.

OPEN *Litware Sales* from the data files for this lesson.

CD

The *Litware Sales* workbook is available on the companion CD-ROM.

1. Merge and center the title and apply the Heading 1 style.
2. Merge and center the subtitle and apply the Heading 2 style.
3. Select A1:G2 Click the **Border** arrow to open the Format Cells dialog box.
4. Under Line Styles, select the last line style in column 2.
5. Click the **Color** arrow and click **Red**.
6. Click **Outline** and **Inside** in Presets. Click **OK**.
7. Select **B4** and use the fill handle to extend the months across the remaining columns of data.
8. Select the labels in row 4. Center the labels and apply the Red font color. Add a Thick Box border.
9. Apply the Accounting format to the values in row 5. Reduce decimals to 0.
10. Select **B6:G12** and apply the Number format with comma separator and 0 decimals.
11. Apply the Total style to row 13.
12. **PRINT** the workbook. **SAVE** the workbook as *Litware Sales 3-5*.

    LEAVE the workbook open for the next project.

Project 3-6: Apply Conditional Formatting to Sales Report

Apply conditional formatting to the Litware, Inc. sales report to highlight the top performing sales representatives.

USE the workbook from Project 3-5.

1. Select **B13:G13**.
2. Click **Conditional Formatting** and click **Highlight Cells Rules**.
3. Click **Greater Than**. In the Greater Than dialog box, key **140,000** and click **OK**. Total sales exceed $140,000 for February and May.
4. Select **B5:G12**. Click **Conditional Formatting**, click **Top/Bottom Rules**, and then click **Top 10%**. When the dialog box opens, four cells are highlighted.
5. Drag the dialog box below the data range. Change the Top percentage number to 1. Format cells that rank in the Top 1% with a red border. Deborah Poe was the top sales performer with $25,874 for the month of May.
6. Click **Conditional Formatting** and click **Icon Sets**. Click **3 Flags**. Colored flags are applied to the sales data. Green flags mark the top 10%; red flags mark the bottom 10%; and yellow flags mark the middle range.
7. Print the worksheet.
8. Click **Conditional Formatting** and click **Manage Rules**.
9. On the dialog box, show the formatting for **This Worksheet**. The formatting rules are listed in the order you created them.
10. Delete the **Icon Set** rule.
11. **PRINT** the worksheet. **SAVE** the workbook as *Litware Sales 3-6*. **CLOSE** the workbook.

    LEAVE Excel open for the next project.

INTERNET READY

OPEN a new, blank workbook.

In this lesson you applied formatting styles that are preset in Excel. You also created a custom style. Open Excel Help and key **create style** in the Excel Help Search box. Open the *Apply, create, or remove a cell style* link. Click **Create a custom cell style**.

Merge four cells in an open worksheet and key **your name** in the cell. Follow the steps provided and create a custom style. Use your first name as the style name. Include the following formats in the style:

- Alignment   Horizontal Center
                     Vertical Center
- Font   CG Omega, 16 point, Italic
- Border   Broken line (your choice)
                     Green line color
                     Outline Preset
- Fill   Yellow Pattern Color
                     Thin Vertical Stripe Pattern Style

Key your name in cell A1 of a new blank workbook. Apply the style to your name. Save the workbook as *My Style*.

CLOSE Excel.

4 Worksheet Formatting

LESSON SKILL MATRIX

Skills	Matrix Skill	Skill Number
Working with Rows and Columns		
Inserting or Deleting a Row or Column	Insert and delete cells, rows, and columns	2.2.1
Modifying Row Height and Column Width	Modify row height and column width	2.2.4
Formatting an Entire Row or Column	Format rows and columns	2.2.2
Hiding and Unhiding a Row or Column	Hide and unhide rows and columns	2.2.3
Using Themes	Use themes to format workbooks	2.1.1
Modifying a Worksheet's On-Screen and Printed Appearance		
Formatting a Sheet Background	Format worksheet backgrounds	2.1.4
Changing the Color of a Worksheet Tab	Add color to worksheet tabs	2.1.3
Viewing and Printing a Worksheet's Gridlines	Show and hide gridlines and headers	2.1.2
Viewing and Printing Column and Row Headings	Show and hide gridlines and headers	2.1.2
Inserting Headers and Footers	Add and modify headers and footers	5.5.4
Preparing a Document for Printing		
Adding and Moving a Page Break	Insert and move a page break	5.5.2
Setting Margins	Set margins	5.5.3
Setting a Worksheet's Orientation on the Page	Change the orientation of a worksheet	5.5.5
Scaling a Worksheet to Fit on a Printed Page	Scale worksheet content to fit a printed page	5.5.6

KEY TERMS

boundary
column heading
column width
document theme
footer
gridlines
header
orientation
page break
Page Break Preview
Print Preview
row heading
row height
scaling

A travel agency sells travel-related products and services to clients on behalf of third parties such as airlines, hotels, and cruise lines. Margie's Travel custom designs corporate and leisure travel packages for its clients. The owner, Margie Shoop, specializes in creative, detailed, and personalized service to assure clients they will have an enjoyable and trouble-free travel experience. She employs experienced and knowledgeable travel consultants whose goal is to save the client time, effort, and money. The company maintains a 24/7 emergency service hotline and nationwide toll-free accessibility for business travelers and tourists.

■ SOFTWARE ORIENTATION

Page Layout Commands

One of the easiest ways to share information in a worksheet or workbook is to print copies for others to review. You will continue to use some of the Home tab command groups as you format worksheets, but you will primarily use the Page Layout command groups shown in Figure 4-1 to prepare worksheets for printing and distribution. Applying formatting techniques from these command groups will ensure that your printed worksheets are more useful, more readable, and more attractive.

Figure 4-1

Use Page Layout command groups to prepare worksheets for printing

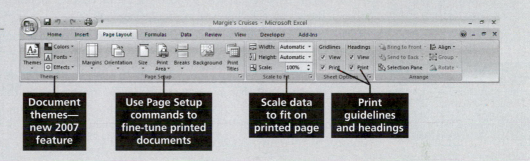

■ Working with Rows and Columns

↓ THE BOTTOM LINE When you open a new worksheet, columns and rows are uniform. However, uniformity rarely fits the data you want to include in a worksheet or workbook. For some columns, you need only two or three characters; for others, you need to increase the *column width* to accommodate more data than will fit in the default column width of 8.43 characters.

Inserting or Deleting a Row or Column

After some data has been entered, you often need to insert additional rows or columns. To insert a row, select the row or a cell in the row below which you want the new row to appear. The new row is inserted above the selected cell or row. For example, to insert a row above row 10, click any cell in row 10. To insert multiple rows, select the same number of rows as you want to insert.

Inserting columns works the same way. If you want to insert a column to the left of column D, click any cell in column D. Columns are inserted to the left of the selected cell, and by default, the inserted column is formatted the same as the column to the left.

The same principles apply when you need to delete a row or column. In the following exercise, you will delete an entire row from a worksheet.

TAKE NOTE ✱ It does not matter which column you use to select cells when you want to insert rows or which row you select when you want to insert columns.

⊙ INSERT OR DELETE A ROW OR COLUMN

GET READY. Place the CD that accompanies this text in your computer.

1. **OPEN** *Margie's Cruises* from the data files for this lesson. The Home tab should be active.
2. Select any cell in row 12; press Ctrl and select a cell in row 17. Click the arrow next to **Insert** in the Cells group and click **Insert Sheet Rows**.
3. Select any cell in column A. Click the arrow next to **Insert** and then click **Insert Sheet Columns**.
4. In A5, key **Destination**.
5. Select **A6:A11**. Click **Merge & Center** in the Alignment group.
6. Select **A13:17**. Click **Merge & Center**.
7. Select **A19:23**. Click **Merge & Center**.
8. Label the merged cells **Mexico**, **Hawaii**, and **Alaska**.
9. Select **A6:A23**. Click **Center** and **Middle Align** in the Alignment group and **Bold** in the Font group.
10. Select any cell in row 2. Click the arrow next to **Delete** and click **Delete Sheet Rows**. Repeat this process in the new row 2.

   PAUSE. LEAVE the workbook open to use in the next exercise.

○ CD

The *Margie's Cruises* workbook is available on the companion CD-ROM.

⬥ ANOTHER WAY

After you insert a row or column, you can select the location where you want to insert another row or column and press Ctrl+Y.

CERTIFICATION READY?
How do you insert rows or columns into a worksheet?
2.2.1

An associate at Margie's Travel prepared the workbook you opened in the previous exercise for a corporate client that rewards its top sales representatives with a cruise. The workbook contains cruise data for dates and locations specified by the client. In the following exercises, you will continue to apply formatting tools to make the workbook easier to understand and improve the presentation of the data to the client.

Modifying Row Height and Column Width

By default, all columns in a new worksheet are the same width and all rows are the same height. In most worksheets, you will want to change some column or row defaults to accommodate more or less data. Changes can be made using the Format commands in the Cells group on the Home tab.

Modifying row height and column width can make a worksheet's contents easier to read and increase its visual appeal. You can set a row or column to a specific height or width, change the height or width to fit the contents, or change the height or width by dragging the *boundary*, the line between rows or columns.

⊙ MODIFY ROW HEIGHT AND COLUMN WIDTH

USE the workbook from the previous exercise.

1. Click the column **D** heading. Press and hold the mouse button and drag to select column **E**.
2. Click **Format** in the Cells group.
3. Under Cell Size, click **Column Width** on the options list shown in Figure 4-2.

Figure 4-2

Cell Size options

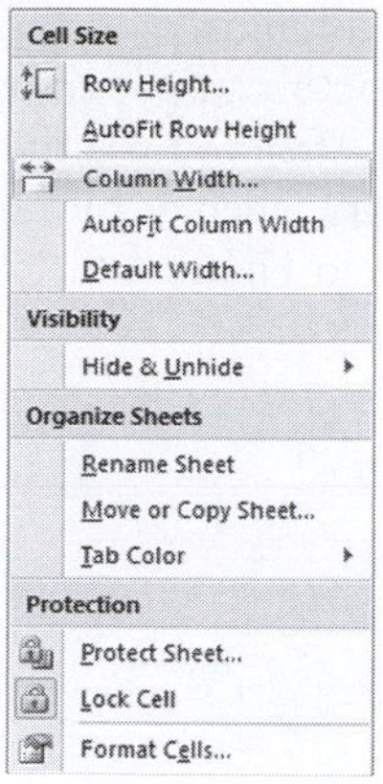

4. In the Column Width dialog box shown in Figure 4-3, key **15**. Click **OK**.

Figure 4-3

Key a column width number in the box

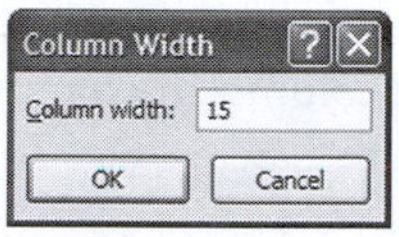

XREF

In previous lessons, when you double-clicked the right column boundary, you utilized the AutoFit Column Width option.

5. Select column **C**. Click **Format** and click **AutoFit Column Width**. This command adjusts the column width to fit the longest entry in the column.

6. Click the column **G** right boundary and drag to the right until the ScreenTip says *Width: 17.00*.

7. Click any cell in column A. Click **Format** in the Cells group.

8. Under Cell Size, click **Column Width**.

9. In the Column Width dialog box, key **16**. Click **OK**.

10. Set the width for column B to 30 characters.

11. Select row **3** and click **Format**. Click **Row Height** and key **25** in the Row Height dialog box. Click **OK**.

PAUSE. LEAVE the workbook open to use in the next exercise.

CERTIFICATION READY?

How do you modify row height and column width in a worksheet?

2.2.4

Looking Ahead

You will hide rows and columns later in this lesson.

Row height, the top-to-bottom height, is measured in points; one point is equal to 1/72 inch. The default row height is 15 points, but you can specify a row height of 0 to 409 points. Although you can specify a column width of 0 to 255 characters, the default column width is 8.43 characters (based on the default font and font size). If the column width or row height is set to 0, the column or row is hidden.

As you learned in Lesson 2, when the text you enter exceeds the column width, the text overflows to the next column or it is truncated when the next cell contains data. If the value entered in a column exceeds the column width, a series of #### symbols, shown in Figure 4-4, indicate the number is larger than the cell width.

Figure 4-4

Number is larger than column width

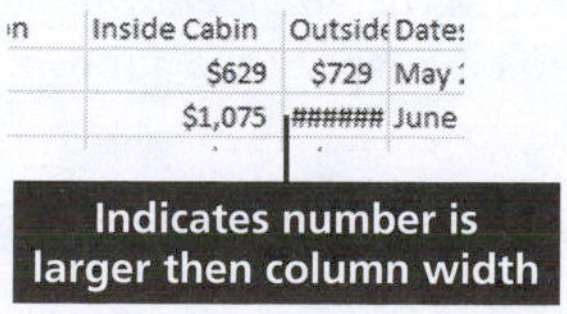

	Inside Cabin	Outside	Date:
	$629	$729	May
	$1,075	######	June

Indicates number is larger then column width

To quickly autofit the entries in all rows on the worksheet, click Select All and then double-click one of the column boundaries.

Depending upon the alignment of data within columns, worksheet data may appear crowded when you use the AutoFit Column Width option because it adjusts column width to the exact width of the longest entry in the column. After you use the option, you may want to use the mouse to drag the right column boundary when a column with right-aligned data is adjacent to one with left-aligned data, as shown in Figure 4-5.

Figure 4-5

Drag column boundary to separate right-aligned and left-aligned columns

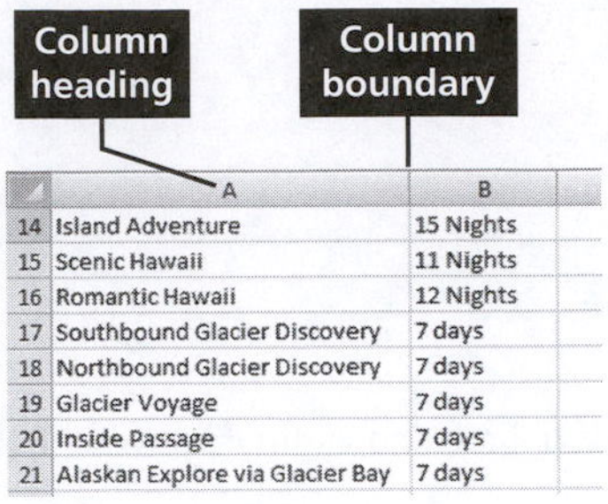

When you drag the boundary, the width of the column in characters and pixels appears in a ScreenTip above the column headings. See Figure 4-6.

Figure 4-6

Column width shown as you drag boundary

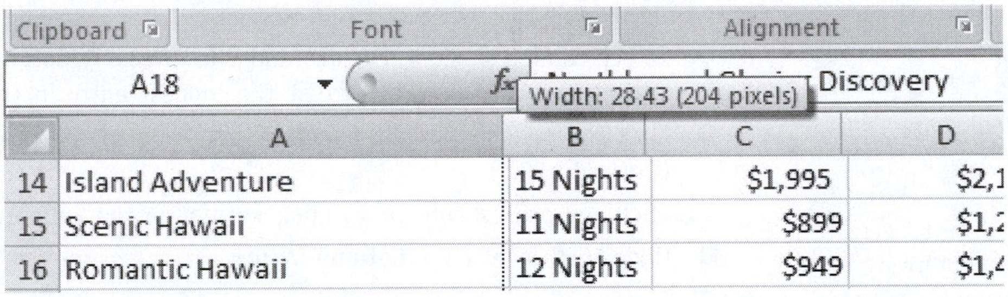

ANOTHER WAY

You can also use the Format Painter to copy the width of one column to other columns. Select the heading of the first column, click Format Painter, and then click the heading of the column or columns to which you want to apply the column width.

You can change the default width for all columns on a worksheet or a workbook. Click Format and under Cell Size, click Default Width. In the Standard Width dialog box, key a new default column measurement. If you change the default column width for a worksheet that contains data, only empty columns will be changed. Columns that contain data or that have been previously formatted retain their formatting.

TAKE NOTE

When you are more familiar with the ways to modify rows and columns, you will likely use one method consistently.

Formatting an Entire Row or Column

To save time, to achieve a consistent appearance, and to align cell contents in a consistent manner, you often want to apply the same format to an entire row or column. To apply formatting to a row or column, click the *row heading* or *column heading* (its identifying letter or number) to select it. Then apply the appropriate format or format style.

⊙ **FORMAT AN ENTIRE ROW OR COLUMN**

USE the workbook from the previous exercise.

1. Select **A1:G1**, and then click **Merge & Center**. With A1 selected, click **Cell Styles** in the Styles group and click **Heading 1** under Titles and Headings.

2. Key **Margie's Travel** and press **Enter**.

3. With A1 selected, click **Increase Font Size** until the font size is **20** points. Notice that the height of row 1 increased to accommodate the larger font size.

TROUBLESHOOTING If you select row 1 rather than the data range and apply the style, the bottom border style effect will extend to the end of the row (cell XFD1).

4. Merge and center A2:G2. Apply the Heading 2 style.

5. Key **Cruise Options, Prepared for Fabrikam, Inc**. Increase the font size to 16 points.

6. Select **A3:G3** and apply Heading 3 style to the column labels. Increase font size to 12 points.

7. Select row 3. Click **Middle Align** and **Center** in the Alignment group.

8. Select columns **D** and **E**. Click the **Number Format** box and click **Accounting**.

TAKE NOTE * Accounting format will be applied to any number you enter in column C or D, even if, for example, you enter the number as currency.

9. Select rows **4-9** and click the **Font Color** arrow in the Font group.

10. Click **Green** under Standard Colors.

11. Select rows **11-15**. Click the **Font Color** arrow and click **Purple** under Standard Colors.

12. Select rows **17-21**. Click the **Font Color** arrow and click **Red** under Standard Colors.

    PAUSE. LEAVE the workbook open to use in the next exercise.

CERTIFICATION READY?
How do you format entire rows and columns?
2.2.2

Formatting rows and columns rather than applying formatting to the range of cells containing data has an advantage. When you insert rows or columns or add additional data to a worksheet, it will be formatted correctly.

Hiding and Unhiding a Row or Column

You may not want or need all rows and columns to be visible all the time, particularly if a worksheet contains a large number of rows or columns. You can hide a row or a column by using the Hide command or by setting the row height or column width to zero. When rows are hidden, they do not appear on the screen or in printouts.

⊕ HIDE AND UNHIDE A ROW OR COLUMN

USE the workbook from the previous exercise.

1. Click the column **D** heading to select the entire column. Click **Format** in the Cells group.

2. Point to **Hide & Unhide** and click **Hide Columns**.

3. Click the row **11** heading, press [Shift], and click the row **15** heading. Click **Format** in the Cells group.

4. Point to **Hide & Unhide** and click **Hide Rows**.

5. Click **Quick Print** on the Quick Access Toolbar. The boundary line in the row or column heading displays as a thicker line than normal when rows or columns are hidden. As you can see in Figure 4-7, you also recognize when rows or columns are hidden because numbers are skipped in the row headings or letters are skipped in the column headings.

Figure 4-7

Hidden rows marked by thicker boundary and missing headings

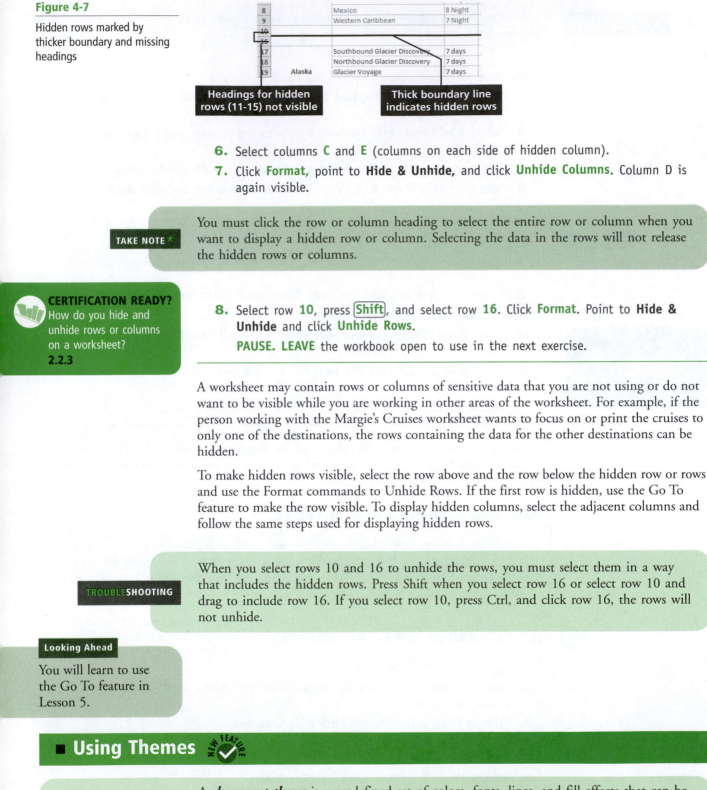

Headings for hidden rows (11-15) not visible

Thick boundary line indicates hidden rows

6. Select columns **C** and **E** (columns on each side of hidden column).
7. Click **Format**, point to **Hide & Unhide**, and click **Unhide Columns**. Column D is again visible.

TAKE NOTE *

You must click the row or column heading to select the entire row or column when you want to display a hidden row or column. Selecting the data in the rows will not release the hidden rows or columns.

CERTIFICATION READY?
How do you hide and unhide rows or columns on a worksheet?
2.2.3

8. Select row **10**, press Shift, and select row **16**. Click **Format**. Point to **Hide & Unhide** and click **Unhide Rows**.

   PAUSE. LEAVE the workbook open to use in the next exercise.

A worksheet may contain rows or columns of sensitive data that you are not using or do not want to be visible while you are working in other areas of the worksheet. For example, if the person working with the Margie's Cruises worksheet wants to focus on or print the cruises to only one of the destinations, the rows containing the data for the other destinations can be hidden.

To make hidden rows visible, select the row above and the row below the hidden row or rows and use the Format commands to Unhide Rows. If the first row is hidden, use the Go To feature to make the row visible. To display hidden columns, select the adjacent columns and follow the same steps used for displaying hidden rows.

TROUBLESHOOTING

When you select rows 10 and 16 to unhide the rows, you must select them in a way that includes the hidden rows. Press Shift when you select row 16 or select row 10 and drag to include row 16. If you select row 10, press Ctrl, and click row 16, the rows will not unhide.

Looking Ahead

You will learn to use the Go To feature in Lesson 5.

■ Using Themes

THE BOTTOM LINE

A *document theme* is a predefined set of colors, fonts, lines, and fill effects that can be applied to an entire workbook or to specific items within a workbook, such as charts or tables. In Excel 2007, you can use document themes to quickly and easily format an entire document, giving it a fresh, professional look.

Themes can be shared across other Office 2007 applications such as Microsoft Office Word and Microsoft Office PowerPoint. Because document themes can be shared, this feature enables you to give all your Office documents a uniform look in terms of colors, fonts, and effects. Effects, such as shadows or bevels, modify the appearance of an object.

Choosing a Theme for a Worksheet *NEW FEATURE*

Excel has several predefined document themes. When you apply a theme to a worksheet or workbook, the colors, fonts, and effects contained within that theme replace any styles that were applied to cells or ranges.

TROUBLESHOOTING

If you or another user has customized one or more document themes, those themes will appear at the top of the list and you may have to scroll down to see all built-in themes.

⊕ CHOOSE A THEME FOR A WORKSHEET

USE the workbook from the previous exercise.

1. Click the **Page Layout** tab to make it active.
2. Click **Themes**. The 20 built-in themes are displayed in a preview window (see Figure 4-8). Point to each theme and observe the changes in the title lines of your worksheet.

Figure 4-8

Excel's built-in document themes

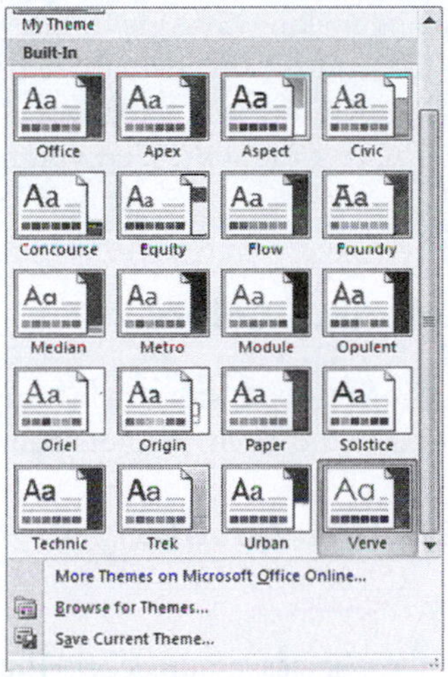

3. Click **Verve** (last theme listed) to apply it to your worksheet.
4. Click **Save As** and create a Lesson 4 folder. Name your workbook *Verve Theme* and save it in the Lesson 4 folder. You changed the default document theme by selecting another predefined document theme. As you can see, document themes that you apply immediately affect the styles that have been applied in your document.

TAKE NOTE *

Because you increased the font size after you applied Heading 1 to the title, the font size remains at 20 points. If you had changed the font size before applying the heading style, the title would be displayed in points, because that is the default font size for themes.

5. Click **Themes** and click **Opulent**. The appearance of your document is significantly changed.
6. Click **Save As** and save the workbook in the Lesson 4 folder. Name your workbook *Opulent Theme*.

   PAUSE. LEAVE the workbook open to use in the next exercise.

Figure 4-8 shows the 20 built-in themes for Excel 2007. The styles that you applied in the previous exercises were the styles associated with the default Office theme. When you opened the styles gallery, the colors, fonts, and effects that were displayed were those that make up the Office theme.

Remember that styles are used to format specific cells or ranges within a worksheet; document themes are used to apply sets of styles (colors, fonts, lines, and fill effects) to an entire document. All of the default Office theme styles you applied to the titles in a previous exercise were changed when you applied a different theme.

In this exercise, you applied two document themes so that the owner of Margie's Travel can select the one that will be used on all company documents. Because themes are consistent in Microsoft Office 2007 programs, all of Margie's Travel company documents can have a uniform appearance.

Many companies create a customized document theme and use it consistently. You can experiment by applying various predefined themes until you decide on the "look" that appeals to you, or you can design a customized theme, as you will do in the next exercise.

CERTIFICATION READY?
How do you use themes to format a worksheet?
2.1.1

Customizing a Theme

> You can create a customized theme by making changes to one or more of the theme components—theme colors, fonts, or line and fill effects that are used. You can customize one of the existing themes to create your own theme. Changes you make to one or more of the theme components immediately affect the styles that you have applied in the active document.

Customizing a Theme by Selecting Colors

> When you change any of the colors to create a customized theme, the colors that are shown in the Theme Colors button and next to the Theme Colors name change accordingly.

⊕ CUSTOMIZE A THEME BY SELECTING COLORS

USE the workbook from the previous exercise.

1. On the Page Layout tab, in the Themes group, click **Theme Colors**. Figure 4-9 illustrates the color array for each of the built-in themes.

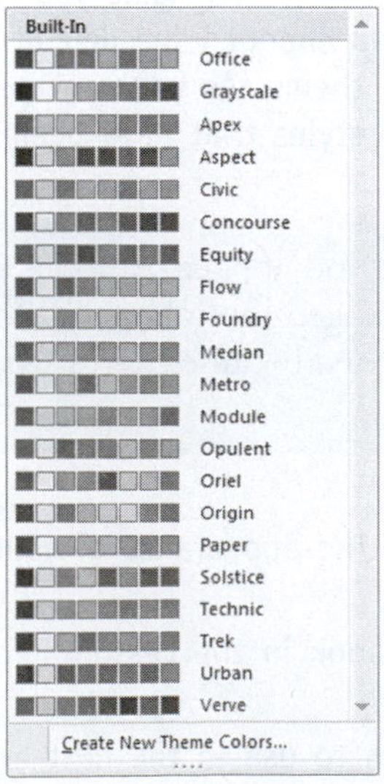

Figure 4-9

Accent and hyperlink colors for built-in document themes

Built-In
Office
Grayscale
Apex
Aspect
Civic
Concourse
Equity
Flow
Foundry
Median
Metro
Module
Opulent
Oriel
Origin
Paper
Solstice
Technic
Trek
Urban
Verve
Create New Theme Colors...

2. Click **Create New Theme Colors**. The Create New Theme Colors dialog box opens (see Figure 4-10), showing the colors used in the Opulent theme that is currently applied to the worksheet. Move the dialog box so that you can see the worksheet titles and column labels.

Figure 4-10

Create New Theme Colors dialog box

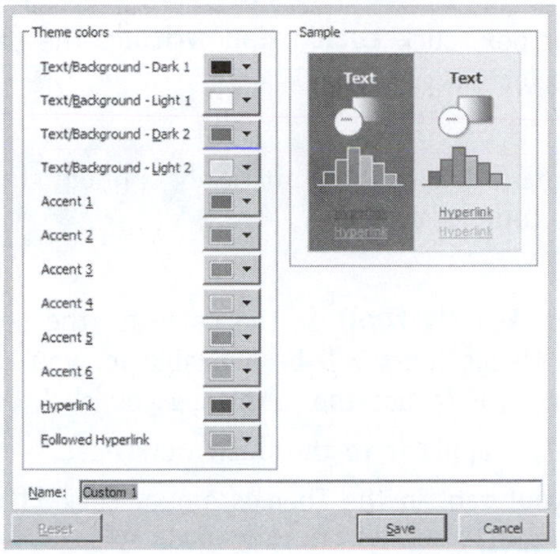

3. Click the **Text/Background – Dark 2** arrow. The current color is highlighted under Theme Colors. Click **Accent 6** to change the color to orange.

4. Click the arrow next to **Accent 1** in the dialog box and click **Accent 6** under Theme Colors. In the Name box, key **My Colors**. Click **Save**. The font and line color in the worksheet titles reflect the customized theme colors.

PAUSE. LEAVE the workbook open to use in the next exercise.

TAKE NOTE To return all theme color elements to their original theme colors, you can click Reset before you click Save.

In the Create New Theme Colors dialog box, click the button next to the theme color element that you want to change. The theme colors are presented in every color gallery with a set of lines and shades based on those colors. By selecting colors from this expanded matched set, you can make formatting choices for individual pieces of content that will still follow the themes. When the theme colors change, the gallery of colors changes and so does all document content using them.

It is easy to create your own theme that can be applied to all of your Excel workbooks and other Office 2007 documents. You can choose any of the color combinations you see in Figure 4-9, which represent the built-in themes, or you can create your own combination of colors.

When you clicked Create New Theme Colors, the dialog box shown in Figure 4-10 opened. Theme colors contain four text and background colors, six accent colors, and two hyperlink colors. You can change any or all of these when you customize a theme.

Customizing a Theme by Selecting a Font and Effects

Now that you have customized the color of your themes, you are ready to choose the font for your theme. Use fonts and effects that create a unique image for your documents. Themes contain a heading font and a body font. When you click the Theme Fonts button, you see the name of the heading font and body text font that is used for each theme font below the Theme Fonts name.

CUSTOMIZE A THEME BY SELECTING A FONT AND EFFECTS

USE the workbook from the previous exercise.

1. On the Page Layout tab, click **Fonts** in the Themes group.
2. Click **Create New Theme Fonts**. In the Heading font box, click **Lucida Calligraphy**.
3. In the Body font box, click **Lucida Handwriting**. The sample is updated with the fonts that you selected.

> **TROUBLESHOOTING**
>
> If your customized theme font is not automatically applied, click Cell Styles and click the customized heading font to apply it.

4. In the Name box, key **My Fonts** as the name for the new theme fonts. Click **Save**. Your customized theme fonts will be available for you to use to customize any of the built-in themes or to use the next time you click Cell Styles on the Home tab.
5. Click your theme to apply it to the open worksheet.
6. On the Page Layout tab, in the Themes group, click **Effects**.
7. Click the **Aspect** effect.
8. In the Themes group, click **Themes**. Click **Save Current Theme**.
9. In the File name box, key **My Theme**. Click **Save**. Your customized document theme is saved in the Document Themes folder, and it is automatically added to the list of custom themes that now appears at the top of the themes preview window.

   PAUSE. LEAVE the workbook open to use in the next exercise.

> **CERTIFICATION READY?**
> How do you use themes to format worksheets?
> **2.1.1**

You can customize the built-in themes by the manner in which you apply the attributes of the theme. For example, you like the colors in the Verve theme, but you want to use a different font. Apply the Verve theme, and then click Theme Fonts and apply the font of your choice. You can then save that theme and apply it to other documents. You cannot customize theme effects, but you can apply a different built-in effect to modify appearance by changing the shading, beveling, or other effects.

■ Modifying a Worksheet's On-Screen and Printed Appearance

> **↓**
> **THE BOTTOM LINE**
>
> You can add interest to a worksheet's on-screen appearance by displaying a background picture. You can also add color to worksheet tabs. Gridlines, row headings, and column headings are displayed by default, but they are not printed automatically. *Gridlines* are the lines that display around the worksheet cells.

Formatting a Sheet Background

> You can use a picture as a sheet background for display purposes only. A sheet background is saved with your worksheet, but it is not printed and it is not retained in a worksheet or as an item that you save as a web page. Because a sheet background is not printed, it cannot be used as a watermark.

FORMAT A SHEET BACKGROUND

> **CD**
> The *Sunset* image and the *Open Sea* image are available on the companion CD-ROM.

USE the workbook from the previous exercise.

1. On the Page Layout tab, in the Page Setup group, click **Background**.
2. Click the *Sunset* image on the companion CD, and then click **Insert**. The selected picture is displayed behind the text and fills the sheet.
3. In the Sheet Options group, click **View** to remove the gridlines.

4. Select **A1:G21**, click the **Home** tab, and click the **Fill Color** arrow. To improve readability, click **Lavender Background 2** to add solid color shading to cells that contain data.

5. Click in the worksheet. Click the **Page Layout** tab. In the Page Setup group, click **Delete Background**. The background is removed; the shading applied to the data range remains.

6. On the Page Layout tab, in the Page Setup group, click **Background** and click the *Open Sea* image on the companion CD. Click **Insert**.

7. **SAVE** the file in the Lesson 4 folder as *Background*. The background will be saved with the worksheet.

8. Click **Delete Background** in preparation for the next exercise.

9. Select **A1:G21**. Click the **Home** tab, click the **Fill Color** arrow, and click **No Fill**.
   PAUSE. LEAVE the workbook open to use in the next exercise.

CERTIFICATION READY?
How do you insert and format a picture as a worksheet background?
2.1.4

The owner of Margie's Travel often uses worksheets in presentations to clients as well as providing the client with printed copies. You can increase the effectiveness of the worksheet presentation by adding an appropriate background picture and adding color to worksheet tabs. It is best to remove gridlines when a sheet background is used, but printing gridlines makes printed worksheets easier to read. Printing column and row headings can help to identify the location of data during discussions.

Changing the Color of a Worksheet Tab

By default, a new workbook contains three blank worksheets identified as Sheet1, Sheet2, and Sheet3. You often use more than one worksheet to enter related data because it is easier to move between sheets than to scroll up and down through large amounts of data. Adding color to the worksheet tabs makes it easy to locate needed information.

→ CHANGE THE COLOR OF A WORKSHEET TAB

USE the workbook from the previous exercise.

1. Right-click the **Sheet1** tab and click **Tab Color**. Under Standard Colors, click **Green**.

2. Right-click the **Sheet2** tab and click **Tab Color**. Click **Purple**.

3. Right-click the **Sheet3** tab and click **Tab Color**. Click **Red**.

4. Click the **Sheet1** tab. Click the **Home** tab in the Ribbon. Select **A1:A3**. Click **Copy**.

5. Click **Sheet2**. Select **A1** and click **Paste**.

6. Click the **Paste Options** button and click **Keep Source Column Widths**.

7. Click **Sheet3**. Select **A1** and click **Paste**.

8. Click the **Paste Options** button and click **Keep Source Column Widths**.

9. On the Sheet1 worksheet, select **A11:G15** and click **Cut**.

10. On the Sheet2 worksheet, select **A4** and click **Paste**.

11. Cut the Alaska data from Sheet1 and paste it to A4 on Sheet3.
    PAUSE. LEAVE the workbook open to use in the next exercise.

Looking Ahead

You will rename worksheets in Lesson 5.

CERTIFICATION READY?
How do you change the tab color of a worksheet?
2.1.3

The workbook contained data about cruises to three destinations in one worksheet. In this exercise, you separated the data so that data related to each destination is on a separate worksheet in the workbook.

Viewing and Printing a Worksheet's Gridlines

You can have gridlines visible on your work surface or work without them. By default, gridlines are present when you open a worksheet. You can also choose whether gridlines are printed. A printed worksheet is easier to read when gridlines are included.

→ VIEW AND PRINT A WORKSHEET'S GRIDLINES

USE the workbook from the previous exercise.

1. Click the **Sheet1** tab. On the Page Layout tab, in the Sheet Options group, remove the checkmark from the **View** option in the Gridlines section if necessary.

2. In the Page Setup group, click **Orientation** and click **Landscape**. In the Scale to Fit group, click **1 page** in the Width box.

3. Click **Quick Print** on the Quick Access Toolbar. Gridlines are not present on the work surface or in the printout.

4. Click the **Sheet2** tab to make it the active worksheet. Click the **Print** checkbox under Gridlines. Click **Orientation** and click **Landscape**.

5. In the Scale to Fit group, click **1 page** in the Width box. Click **Quick Print**. Although gridlines are not present on the work surface, they are included on the printout.

6. With Sheet3 as the active worksheet, check **View** and **Print** under Gridlines. Click **Orientation** and **Landscape**.

7. Click **Quick Print**. Gridlines are present on the work surface and in the printout.

PAUSE. LEAVE the workbook open to use in the next exercise.

CERTIFICATION READY?
How do you show and hide gridlines?
2.1.2

Viewing and Printing Column and Row Headings

Column and row headings are displayed by default, but they are not printed automatically. Displaying row and column headings makes it easier to identify data in a printout.

→ VIEW AND PRINT COLUMN AND ROW HEADINGS

USE the workbook from the previous exercise.

1. Click **Sheet1**. On the Page Layout tab, in the Sheet Options group under Headings, click **View** to remove the check. Column and row headings are removed from the display.

2. Check the **View** box again. Headings are restored. Click the **Print** check box under Headings.

3. Click the **View** tab and click **Page Layout** in the Workbook Views group. Column and row headings appear in the worksheet as it will be printed. Page Layout View allows you to see the worksheet exactly as it will appear on a printed page. You can use this view to see where pages begin and end.

PAUSE. LEAVE the workbook open to use in the next exercise.

CERTIFICATION READY?
How do you show and print column and row headings?
2.1.2

■ Inserting Headers and Footers

↓ THE BOTTOM LINE

You can add headers or footers to your worksheets to provide useful information about the worksheet, such as who prepared it, the date it was created or last modified, the page number, and so on. Headers and footers are visible in Page Layout View and they are printed on printouts.

A *header* is a line of text that appears at the top of each page of a printed worksheet. *Footers* appear at the bottom of each page. You can add predefined header or footer information; insert elements such as page numbers, the date and time, and the file name; or add your own content to a header or footer.

Adding Page Numbers to a Worksheet

To add or to change a header or footer, click the Insert tab and click Header & Footer in the Text group. The worksheet displays in Page Layout View, a Design tab as shown in Figure 4-11 is added to the Ribbon, and the Header & Footer Tools command groups are displayed.

Figure 4-11

Design tab added to Ribbon

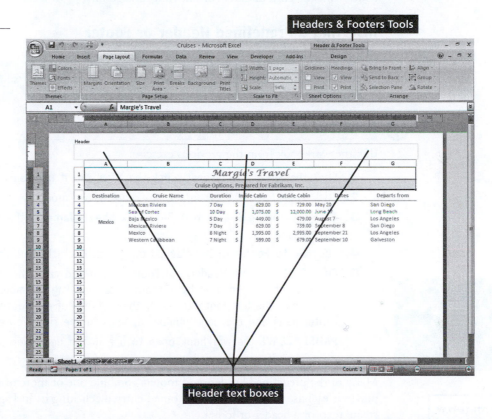

The addition of the Design tab illustrates an advantage of Excel's Ribbon interface. Instead of every command being available all the time, some commands appear only in response to an action you take.

TAKE NOTE*

⊙ ADD PAGE NUMBERS TO A WORKSHEET

USE the workbook from the previous exercise.

1. Click the **Sheet1** tab if necessary. Click the **Insert** tab, and click **Header & Footer**. The worksheet is displayed in Page Layout View. The Center Header text box is active. The Design tab is added to the Ribbon. Header & Footer Tools command groups are available for you to use in the worksheet.

2. Press Tab to move to the right text box in the Header section of the worksheet.

3. Click **Page Number** in the Header & Footer Elements group. The code &[Page] appears in the text box. This symbol indicates that the appropriate page number will be added to each page of the printed worksheet.

4. Click **Go to Footer** in the Navigation group.

5. Click the left text box in the footer and click **Sheet Name** in the Header & Footer Elements group. Press `Tab` twice.

6. Click **Current Date** in the Header & Footer Elements group. Click anywhere in the worksheet outside the header and footer to close the Design tab.

7. **SAVE** the workbook in the Lesson 4 folder as *Cruises*.

PAUSE. LEAVE the workbook open to use in the next exercise.

You can create headers and footers by keying the text that you want to appear or, as you practiced in this exercise, you can click one of the predefined elements to insert codes for headers or footers that Excel provides. When the workbook is printed, Excel replaces the codes with the current date, current time, and so on.

Inserting a Predefined Header or Footer

On the Design tab, the Header & Footer group contains predefined headers and footers that allow you to automatically add text to the header or footer such as the date, page number, number of pages, the name of the sheet, and so on.

➜ INSERT A PREDEFINED HEADER OR FOOTER

USE the workbook from the previous exercise.

1. Click the **Sheet3** worksheet. Click the **View** tab if necessary.

2. Click **Page Layout View** in the Workbook Views group.

3. Click the center **Header** text box. Click **Sheet Name** in the Header and Footer Elements group.

4. Click **Go to Footer** in the Navigation group. Click the left **Footer** box.

5. Click **Footer** in the Header and Footer group and click the last option in the list, which combines Prepared by, Current Date, and Page Number. Because the footer is wider than the left footnote pane, the majority of the footnote is moved to the center pane and the page number appears in the right footer pane.

PAUSE. LEAVE the workbook open to use in the next exercise.

Many of the predefined headers and footers combine one or more of the elements. In the previous exercise, you inserted a combined entry by clicking it. In Page Layout view, you can create text for a header or footer.

Adding Content to a Header or Footer

The content of the header and footer elements or the predefined headers and footers will not always meet your needs. In that case, simply key any text into one of the header or footer text boxes.

You may be familiar with the watermark functionality that is available in Microsoft Word. You cannot insert a watermark in Excel, but you can mimic one by displaying a graphic in a header or footer. The graphic will appear behind the text and it will display and print like a watermark.

➜ ADD CONTENT TO A HEADER OR FOOTER

USE the workbook from the previous exercise.

1. Click **Sheet3.** Click the center **Header** text box and delete the existing header.

2. Key **For Presentation to Client**. Press `Tab` to move to the right Header text box.

CERTIFICATION READY?
How do you add content to a header and footer?
5.5.4.

3. Click **Picture** in the Header and Footer Elements group. Click the *Sailing* image from the companion CD and click **Insert**.

4. Click **Format Picture**.

5. On the Format Picture dialog box, under Size & Rotate, set height to **8.5"** and accept the default width. Click **OK**. The image appears behind the text once you click in the worksheet. You can resize or scale the graphic to fill the page, to appear below the text, or to appear as a graphic image in one of the header or footer boxes.

6. **SAVE** and **CLOSE** the workbook.

LEAVE Excel open for the next exercise.

You can create header or footer content by entering text that is not available in the predefined headers and footers. To enter text, click the header or footer text box where you want the text to appear and key the text that you want.

TAKE NOTE✳ If you want to create a multi-line header or footer, press Enter and key text or add a predefined element.

■ Preparing a Document for Printing

THE BOTTOM LINE

When worksheet data prints on more than one page, you can use the Page Break Preview command on the View tab to control where the page breaks occur. This allows you to break data where it is most logical, so that printed documents are well-organized and easy to read.

The Page Layout view is new in Excel 2007. Figure 4-12 illustrates that when you click Page Layout View on the View tab, you can view headers and footers, view (but not change) page breaks, and change page margins at the top, sides, and bottom of the worksheet.

Figure 4-12

Page Layout View

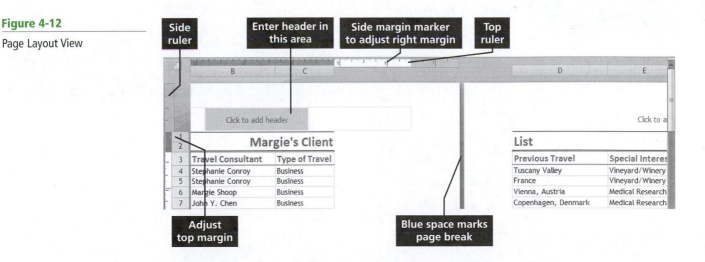

Adding and Moving a Page Break

The *Print Preview* window displays a full-page view of the worksheet just as it will be printed. You can check the format and overall layout before actually printing. You cannot make changes to the document in print preview. A *page break* is a divider that breaks a worksheet into separate pages for printing. Excel inserts automatic vertical page breaks (broken line) based on the paper size, margin settings, scaling options, and the positions of any manual page breaks (solid line) that you insert. In the *Page Break Preview* window, shown in Figure 4-13, you can quickly adjust automatic page breaks to achieve a more desirable printed document.

Figure 4-13

Page Break Preview window

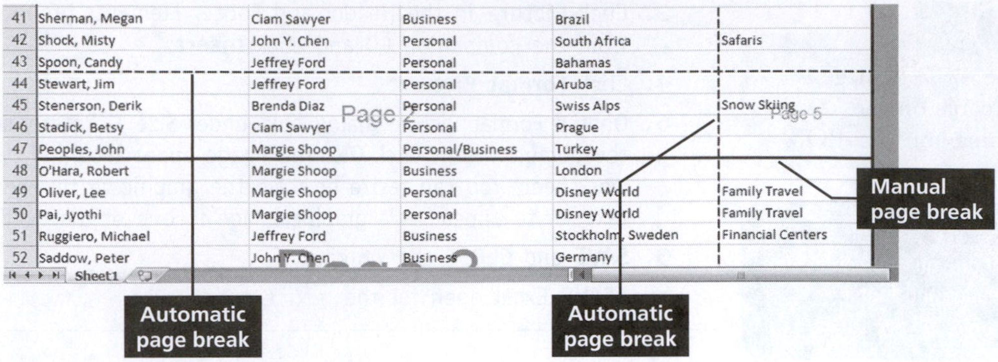

41	Sherman, Megan	Ciam Sawyer	Business	Brazil	
42	Shock, Misty	John Y. Chen	Personal	South Africa	Safaris
43	Spoon, Candy	Jeffrey Ford	Personal	Bahamas	
44	Stewart, Jim	Jeffrey Ford	Personal	Aruba	
45	Stenerson, Derik	Brenda Diaz	Personal	Swiss Alps	Snow Skiing
46	Stadick, Betsy	Ciam Sawyer	Personal	Prague	
47	Peoples, John	Margie Shoop	Personal/Business	Turkey	
48	O'Hara, Robert	Margie Shoop	Business	London	
49	Oliver, Lee	Margie Shoop	Personal	Disney World	Family Travel
50	Pai, Jyothi	Margie Shoop	Personal	Disney World	Family Travel
51	Ruggiero, Michael	Jeffrey Ford	Business	Stockholm, Sweden	Financial Centers
52	Saddow, Peter	John Y. Chen	Business	Germany	

Page 2   Page 5

Manual page break

Automatic page break   **Automatic page break**

ADD AND MOVE A PAGE BREAK

The *Margie's Client List* workbook is available on the companion CD-ROM.

TAKE NOTE*

When you move an automatic page break, it becomes a manual page break.

CERTIFICATION READY?
How do you insert or move a page break?
5.5.2

OPEN *Margie's Client List* from the companion CD.

1. On the View tab, click **Page Break Preview** if necessary. If a dialog box welcoming you to the view is displayed, click **OK**. The worksheet will print on four pages. An automatic page break occurs after row 45 and another automatic page break occurs between columns D and E.

2. Click the horizontal page break and drag it below row 40. The automatic page break is now a manual page break represented by a solid blue line.

3. Click row A22. Click the Page Layout tab. In the Page Setup group, click Breaks and click Insert Page Break. A horizontal page break is added above row 22. Press [Ctrl] + [Home] to move to cell A1.

PAUSE. LEAVE the workbook open to use in the next exercise.

Use manual page breaks to control the page break locations. Drag the automatic page break to a new location to convert an automatic page break to a manual page break.

Setting Margins

Margins are an effective way to manage and optimize the white space on a printed worksheet. Achieving balance between data and white space adds significantly to the readability and appearance of a worksheet. You can choose one of three built-in margin sets shown in Figure 4-14 or create customized margins using the Page Setup dialog box.

Figure 4-14

Built-in margin sets

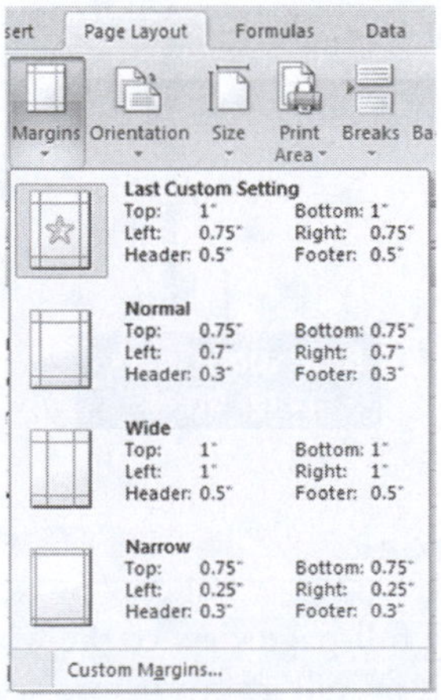

| | Page Layout | Formulas | Data |

Margins Orientation Size Print Area Breaks Ba

Last Custom Setting
Top: 1" Bottom: 1"
Left: 0.75" Right: 0.75"
Header: 0.5" Footer: 0.5"

Normal
Top: 0.75" Bottom: 0.75"
Left: 0.7" Right: 0.7"
Header: 0.3" Footer: 0.3"

Wide
Top: 1" Bottom: 1"
Left: 1" Right: 1"
Header: 0.5" Footer: 0.5"

Narrow
Top: 0.75" Bottom: 0.75"
Left: 0.25" Right: 0.25"
Header: 0.3" Footer: 0.3"

Custom Margins...

SET MARGINS

USE the workbook from the previous exercise.

1. Click the **View** tab. In the Workbook Views group, click **Page Layout**.

2. Click the **Page Layout** tab. In the Page Setup group, click **Margins** and click **Narrow**.

3. Click **Zoom In** on the status bar and increase the zoom to **100%** if necessary.

4. Click Page Break Preview on the **Status** bar. The margin adjustment has moved the vertical page break to between **Columns E and F**.

5. Click **Margins** and click **Custom Margins**. On the Page Setup dialog box, change the left and right margins to 0.5. Click **OK**.

6. Click cell A22, click Breaks in the Page Setup group, and click Remove Page Break.

7. Click the vertical **page break line** and drag it to the right of column E.

8. Click the **Microsoft Office Button.** Point to **Print** and click **Print Preview**. The worksheet will now print on two pages, with all columns fitting to one page wide.

9. **Print** the worksheet or CLOSE the Print Preview window without printing.
   PAUSE. CLOSE the workbook without saving any changes.

CERTIFICATION READY?
How do you set margins?
5.5.3

The Normal margin setting is the default for a new workbook. The custom margins shown in Figure 4-14 were set in the workbook you used in the exercise. Narrower margins allow more area for data when you print the workbook. You can change the margin settings to fit the needs of each workbook. When you click Custom Margins at the bottom of the Margins list, the Page Setup dialog box will open with the settings that have been applied to the open worksheet. You can change any of the settings to create a custom margin setting. Header and footer margins automatically adjust when you change the page margins.

Worksheets that do not fill the entire page can be centered vertically and horizontally, thereby evenly distributing the page's white space. Use the Margins tab of the Page Setup dialog box for this function.

⊕ ANOTHER WAY

You can also alter the margins in Page Layout View by clicking the top or bottom border on the margin area in the ruler. When a vertical two-headed arrow appears, drag the margin to the size you want.

Setting a Worksheet's Orientation on the Page

Printed worksheets are easiest to read and analyze when all of the data appears on one piece of paper. Excel's orientation and scaling features give you control over the number of printed pages of worksheet data. You can change the *orientation* of a worksheet so that it prints either vertically or horizontally on a page. A worksheet printed vertically uses the Portrait orientation and looks like the document shown in Figure 4-15. Portrait orientation is the default setting. A worksheet printed horizontally uses the Landscape orientation, also shown in Figure 4-15.

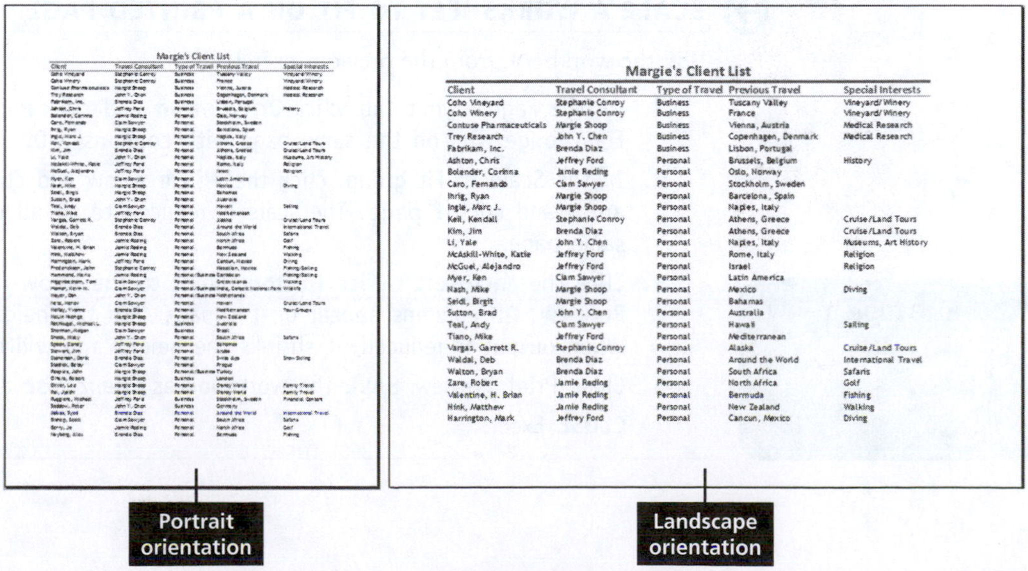

Figure 4-15

Portrait and landscape orientation

SET A WORKSHEET'S ORIENTATION ON THE PAGE

OPEN *Margie's Client List* again from the companion CD.

1. Click the **Page Layout** tab.
2. Click **Orientation** in the Page Setup group and click **Landscape**. Scroll through the document to see that it will now print on two pages with each page containing all columns.
3. In the Page Setup group, click **Print Titles**. The Page Setup dialog box opens. Click the Collapse dialog box next to *Rows to repeat at top*.
4. Click row **3** (the column labels). Row 3 data is identified in the dialog box. Press Enter. Click **OK** to close the dialog box.
5. Click the **Microsoft Office Button**, point to **Print**, and click **Print Preview**. Press Page Down. Notice that the column labels appear on page 2 of the document.
6. **CLOSE** the Print Preview.

   PAUSE. LEAVE the workbook open to use in the next exercise.

> **CERTIFICATION READY?**
> How do you change the orientation of a worksheet?
> 5.5.5

Use the Landscape orientation when the width of the area you want to print is greater than the height. Data is easier to read when all the columns fit on one page. This can be accomplished by changing the orientation to landscape. When you can't fit all of the data on one printed page by changing the orientation, you can shrink or reduce it by using Excel's scaling options described in the next exercise.

Scaling a Worksheet to Fit on a Printed Page

> *Scaling* refers to shrinking or stretching the printed output to a percentage of its actual size. Before attempting to change the scaling for a worksheet's output, the maximum width and height must be set to "Automatic" to use the scaling feature. See Figure 4-16.

Figure 4-16

Scaling a worksheet to fit

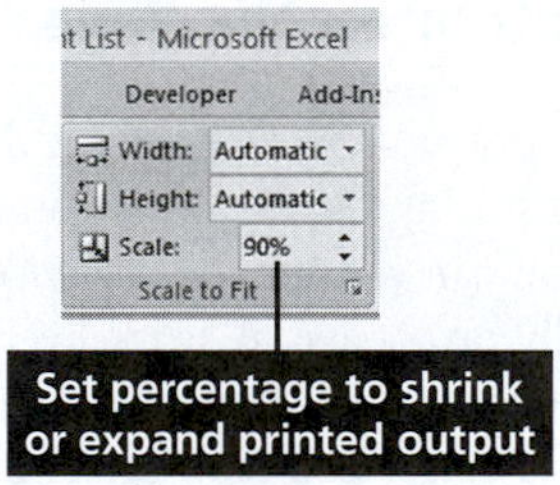

Set percentage to shrink or expand printed output

 SCALE A WORKSHEET TO FIT ON A PRINTED PAGE

USE the workbook from the previous exercise.

1. On the Page Layout Tab, click **Orientation** and click **Portrait**. Notice that column E no longer fits on the same page with columns A-D.
2. In the Scale to Fit group, click the **Width** arrow and click **1 page**. Click the **Height** arrow and click **1 page**. The scale is reduced to fit all columns and rows on the same page.
3. Click the **Microsoft Office Button**. Point to the arrow next to **Print** and click **Print Preview**. All columns appear on the page, and the height is one page as well. When output is reduced, it shrinks the height and width proportionally.
4. Close Print Preview. **SAVE** the workbook as *Client List* and **CLOSE** the workbook.

   CLOSE Excel.

> **CERTIFICATION READY?**
> How do you scale a worksheet to fit on a printed page?
> 5.5.6

The most common reason for scaling a worksheet is to shrink it so that you can print it on one page. You can also enlarge the sheet so that data appears bigger and fills up more of the printed page. When the Width and Height boxes are set to automatic, you can click the arrows in the Scale box to increase or decrease scaling of the printout. Each time you click the arrow, the scaling changes by 5%.

TAKE NOTE *

Remember that width and height must be set to automatic if you want to specify a scale, such as 75%.

SUMMARY SKILL MATRIX

IN THIS LESSON YOU LEARNED	MATRIX SKILL	SKILL NUMBER
To work with rows and columns		
To insert and delete rows and columns	Insert and delete cells, rows, and columns	2.2.1
To modify row height and column width	Modify row height and column width	2.2.4
To apply formatting to an entire row or column	Format rows and columns	2.2.2
To hide and unhide rows and columns	Hide and unhide rows and columns	2.2.3
To apply and customize worksheet themes	Use themes to format workbooks	2.1.1
To modify a worksheet's on-screen and printed appearance		
To insert and format a worksheet background	Format worksheet backgrounds	2.1.4
To change the color of a worksheet's tab	Add color to worksheet tabs	2.1.3
To view and print a worksheet's gridlines	Show and hide gridlines and headers	2.1.2
To view and print a worksheet's row and column headers	Show and hide gridlines and headers	2.1.2
To insert and modify headers and footers	Add and modify headers and footers	5.5.4
To prepare a document for printing		
To add and move page breaks in a worksheet	Insert and move a page break	5.5.2
To set worksheet margins	Set margins	5.5.3
To set a worksheet's orientation on a page	Change the orientation of a worksheet	5.5.5
To scale a worksheet to fit on a printed page	Scale worksheet content to fit a printed page	5.5.6

■ Knowledge Assessment

True / False

Circle T if the statement is true or F if the statement is false.

T F **1.** You can insert a graphic in the header or footer of a worksheet.

T F **2.** Column width and row height can be changed.

T F **3.** After you enter a manual page break, you cannot remove it.

T F **4.** You can center a worksheet's data horizontally, but not vertically.

T F **5.** You can hide a column by setting the column width to zero.

T F **6.** Hidden rows are not displayed on the screen but they will appear when the page is printed.

T F **7.** You can change page endings in the Page Break Preview.

T F **8.** You can use one of Excel's predefined Header & Footer elements to enter the worksheet author's name.

T F **9.** You cannot make changes to a worksheet in the Print Preview window.

T F **10.** By default, gridlines will print in an Excel worksheet.

Fill in the Blank

Complete the following sentences by writing the correct word or words in the blanks provided.

1. The _____ option allows you to enlarge or shrink worksheet data to achieve a more logical fit on the printed page.

2. There are _____ header and footer text boxes on a workbook page where you can enter information.

3. You can manually adjust page breaks in the _____ view.

4. You can mimic a watermark on printouts by adding a(n) _____ as a header or footer.

5. Applying a(n) _____ will override any formatting styles that have been applied to a data range.

6. To format an entire row or column, you must select its _____.

7. A(n) _____ is a line of text that appears at the top of each printed page.

8. The row _____ will automatically expand to accommodate increased font size.

9. Document themes are used to apply sets of styles including colors, fonts, and _____.

10. _____ is a setting that specifies the direction a worksheet appears on the printed page.

■ Competency Assessment

Project 4-1: Work with Rows and Columns

The School of Fine Art has developed a workbook to track enrollment for the academic year. Enrollments for courses in two departments have been entered. You will apply formatting techniques learned in Lesson 4 to enhance the appearance of the two worksheets in the workbook.

GET READY. Launch Excel if it is not already running.

1. **OPEN** *SFA Enrollment* from the data files for this lesson. Sheet1 should be active and the Home tab should be displayed.
2. Select **A1,** click the **Insert** arrow in the Cells group, and click **Insert Sheet Rows**.
3. Select **A1:C1** and click **Merge & Center** in the Alignment group.
4. Select **A1** and key **School of Fine Art**.
5. Select **A2:C2** and click **Merge & Center**. Key **Fine Arts Department**, replacing the existing text.
6. Merge and center **A3:C3** and key **Enrollment**, replacing the existing text.
7. Click the row 4 heading, click the **Insert** arrow, and click **Insert Sheet Rows**.
8. In A5, key **Call No**.
9. In B5, key **Course**.
10. In C5, key **Fall**, replacing the existing text.
11. Select row **5**. Click **Bold** and **Italic** in the Font group. Click **Center** in the Alignment group.
12. Select row **1**. Click **Format** in the Cells group and click **Row Height** under Cell Size.
13. Key **20** in the Row Height dialog box and click **OK**.
14. Click the bottom boundary for row 2 and drag down until the ScreenTip says the height is 18 points.
15. Click the **Sheet2** tab and repeat steps 2-14. If necessary, double-click the boundary between columns to adjust the column width to display all of the text.
16. In A2, key **Media Studies Department**.
17. **SAVE** the workbook in your Lesson 4 folder. Name the workbook *SFA Enrollment 4-1*.

    CLOSE the workbook. **LEAVE** Excel open for the next project.

Project 4-2: **Work with Rows and Columns**

Insert columns and rows to add additional data to the client list for Margie's Travel. Apply styles and a document theme to add visual appeal.

Open *Client Update* from the CD data files for this lesson.

1. Select column **E**. Click the **Insert** arrow in the Cells group and click **Insert Sheet Columns**.
2. In E3, key **Anticipated Travel**.
3. Insert a row above row 3.
4. Select columns **C** and **D**. Click **Format** in the Cells group. Under Visibility, point to **Hide & Unhide** and click **Hide Columns**.
5. Open the **Page Layout** tab and click **Themes** in the Themes group. Click **Metro**.
6. Select A1. Open the **Home** tab and click **Middle Align** in the Alignment group.
7. Select **A4:F4**. Click **Cell Styles**. Apply Heading 3 to the column labels.
8. Enter the following anticipated travel for the listed clients:

Kiel, Kendall	**Romantic Hawaii Cruise**
Nash, Mike	**Aruba**
Li, Yale	**Paris**

9. **SAVE** the workbook as *Client Update 4-2*.

    LEAVE the workbook open for the next project.

■ **Proficiency Assessment**

Project 4-3: Modify a Worksheet's On-Screen Appearance

Create a customized theme for Margie's Travel. Prepare the document for printing on two pages.

USE the workbook from Project 4-2.

1. Click the **Home** tab.
2. Select **A1**. Increase the font size to 20.
3. Select row **4**. Increase the font size to 14.
4. Click the **Page Layout** tab.
5. Click **Theme Colors** and click **Create New Theme Colors**.
6. Change the third Text/Background to Purple.
7. Key your name in the Name box. Click **Save**.
8. Set gridlines to print.
9. Insert a footer that prints the File Name in the Left Footer text box.
10. Insert a footer that prints the Page Number in the Right Footer text box.
11. Click **Print** under Headings on the Page Layout tab. Set the column headings to print on the second page. Click **Page Break Preview**. Move the horizontal automatic page break to the bottom of row 40 and move the vertical page break to the right of column F.
12. **PRINT** the worksheet.
13. **SAVE** the workbook in your Lesson 4 folder as *Client Update 4-3*.

    CLOSE the workbook. **LEAVE** Excel open for the next project.

Project 4-4: Prepare a Worksheet for Printing

Apply styles and a theme to a School of Fine Art worksheet. Create and apply a custom margin setting, and print the worksheet with gridlines and headings.

OPEN *SFA Enrollment Update* from the CD data files for this lesson.

○ **CD**

The *SFA Enrollment Update* workbook is available on the companion CD-ROM.

1. **OPEN** Sheet1. Apply Heading 1 to A1.
2. Apply Heading 2 to A2.
3. Apply Heading 3 to A3.
4. Apply the Oriel theme to the worksheets.
5. Click **Margins** and **Custom Margins** to open the Page Setup dialog box.
6. For Sheet1, set top, bottom, left, and right margins to 1.5.
7. Center the data horizontally and vertically.
8. Print Sheet2 with gridlines.
9. Print Sheet1 with headings.
10. Add Blue color to the Sheet1 tab and Green to the Sheet2 tab.
11. **SAVE** the workbook as *SFA Enrollment 4-4*.

    LEAVE the workbook open for the next project.

■ Mastery Assessment

Project 4-5: Updating and Printing a Workbook

Add additional data to an existing workbook and prepare the workbook for printing. **USE** the workbook from Project 4-4.

1. On Sheet1, select **A1:C5**. Copy the heading to Sheet3.
2. Click the **Paste Options** button. Click **Keep Source Column Widths**.
3. Enter the data for the Biomedical Art Department enrollments.

MED114	Principles of Biology	463
MED115	Human Forms	236
MED116	Biomedical Art Methods	365
MED351	Traditional and Digital Color	446
MED352	3D Modeling	234
MED353	Advanced Problem in Biomedical Art	778
MED354	3D Texture	567
ILL302	Digital Imaging and Illustration	643
ILL303	Storyboarding	234
ILL304	Drawing Beyond Observation	123
DRG333	Visual Editor	434

4. Color the Sheet3 tab Orange.
5. Insert a footer in the center text box that reads **Academic Year 20XX** (with XX being the current year).
6. In the Left Footer text box, key **Current as of** and click **Current Date**.
7. Center Sheet3 vertically and horizontally.
8. Print the sheet with gridlines.
9. **SAVE** the workbook as *SFA Enrollment 4-5*.

   CLOSE the workbook; **LEAVE** Excel open for the next project.

Project 4-6: Page Layout—Challenge

The owner of Margie's Travel plans to meet with each travel consultant to discuss his or her client list. Insert manual page breaks in a worksheet so that each consultant's data prints on a separate page.

OPEN *Anticipated Travel* from the CD data files for this lesson.

1. Remove all existing headers and footers.
2. In the right Header box, insert the *Lighthouse* image from the CD data files for this lesson. Click **Format Picture**. Set the scale to 10% of its original size, so that it appears only in the header.
3. In the center Footer box, click **Footer** and click the last option in the predefined footers.
4. Unhide columns C and D.
5. Set the orientation to landscape.
6. Open the Page Break Preview and move and add page breaks so that each consultant's client list appears on a different page.
7. Titles and column labels should print on each page.
8. Scale the data so that it is only one page wide.
9. Print the complete worksheet with gridlines. You should have a page for each consultant.
10. **SAVE** the workbook as *Anticipated Travel 4-6*. **CLOSE** the workbook.

    LEAVE Excel open for the next project.

The *Anticipated Travel* workbook and the *Lighthouse* image are available on the companion CD-ROM.

INTERNET READY

GET READY: Use the *Anticipated Travel 4-6* workbook from the previous project.

You and two friends from your class have an appointment with Stephanie Conroy, a travel consultant with Margie's Travel, to plan your next vacation.

Add your name and your friends' names to the client list. Identify Stephanie as your consultant. List at least one special interest for each of you.

Go online and find an ideal vacation spot that will fulfill the special interests for all of you. For example, if the three interests were golfing, theater, and swimming, where could you vacation that would satisfy the three interests?

SAVE the revised workbook as *My Vacation*. When you have finished, **CLOSE** Excel.

Circling Back

Cross Cultural Solutions is a nonprofit organization that is recognized by the United Nations as an expert in the field of international volunteering. Whereas well-known programs such as the Peace Corps and Volunteer Service Overseas (VSO) require a two-year commitment, Cross Cultural Solutions provides volunteer opportunities ranging from 1 to 12 weeks. The organization offers a choice of three programs with year-round start dates. The goal is to provide a balance of volunteer work, cultural activities, and learning activities with time to explore the host country.

As an employee in the organization's home office, you create, edit, and format workbooks related to the programs and the individuals who volunteer.

Project 1: Create and Format a Workbook

The 2- to 12-week **Volunteer Abroad** program is Cross Cultural Solutions' most popular program because it offers the greatest flexibility of locations and start dates. Volunteer work is personalized to the volunteer's skills and interests. Create a worksheet that contains details about this program.

GET READY. Launch Excel if it is not already running.

1. Click the **Microsoft Office Button** and click **New** if necessary. Click the **Create** button. The Home tab should be active.
2. Select **A2** and key **Volunteer Abroad**.
3. In row 4, key the column labels:

   Country

   Location

   Language
4. **SAVE** the document as *Volunteer Abroad*.
5. Select columns **A** and **C**. Click **Format**, click **Column Width**, and change the column width to 20 characters.
6. Change the width of column B to 25 characters.
7. Enter data for the countries and locations where the Volunteer Abroad program is available.

   Ghana, Volta Region

   Tanzania, Arusha

   Tanzania, Kilimanjaro

   China, Xi'an

   Thailand, Bangkok

   Thailand, Trang

   India, New Delhi

   India, Dharamsala (Himalayas)

   Brazil, Salvador

   Costa Rica, San Carlos

   Costa Rica, Cartago

   Guatemala, Guatemala City

   Peru, Lima

   Peru, Ayacucho

   Russia, Yaroslavl

8. Click any cell in column A. Click the **Insert** arrow and click **Insert Sheet Columns**.

9. Select **A4** and key **Continent**.

10. Select **A5:A7**. Click **Merge & Center** and key **Africa**.

11. Select **A8:A12**. Click **Merge & Center** and key **Asia**.

12. Select **A13:A18**. Click **Merge & Center**. Key **Latin America**. Click **Wrap Text**.

13. Select **A19** and key **Europe**. Click **Center** in the Alignment group.

14. Format column A as follows:

    Click **Middle Align**.

    Increase the font size to 14.

    Set the Font Color to Blue.

    Double-click the column A boundary to autofit the contents.

15. Select a continent and the three columns associated with that continent. Click **Format** and click **Format Cells**. Click the **Border** tab. Place an outline around each continent's data.

16. Merge and center A2:D2. Click **Cell Styles** and apply Heading 2 style.

17. With A1 active, click **Insert** and click **Insert Sheet Rows**.

18. In A1, key **Cross Cultural Solutions**. Merge and center the title above the columns and apply Heading 1 style.

19. Merge and center A2:D2; then merge and center A4:D4.

20. Apply Heading 3 style to the column labels and a light blue fill color.

21. Click the **Microsoft Office Button**, point to **Print**, and click **Print Preview**.

22. Click **Page Setup** and make the following selections.

    Portrait Orientation

    Center Vertically and Horizontally

23. **PRINT** the worksheet.

24. **SAVE** the changes. **CLOSE** the workbook.

    LEAVE Excel open for the next project.

Project 2: Format Cells and Ranges

In addition to the Volunteer Abroad program, the organization offers a 2- to 12-week **Intern Abroad** program for students interested in an international internship or academic credit and a 1-week **Insight Abroad** program. You have prepared a workbook with data related to volunteers who will depart for their assignments within the next two months. After preparing the workbook, you learned that assignments are made by the on-site coordinators. You need to edit and format the worksheet.

OPEN *Cross Cultural Volunteers* from the data files.

1. With Sheet1 active and the Home tab displayed, delete column E.

2. Click the row **18** heading to select the entire row. Press Ctrl and select row **23**. Continue to scroll through the worksheet, selecting the blank rows.

TROUBLESHOOTING

If you hold down Ctrl before you select the first row to delete, you will receive an error message when you attempt to delete the rows. Select the first row and then press Ctrl.

3. Click **Delete** and click **Delete Sheet Rows**.

CD

The *Cross Cultural Volunteers* workbook is available on the companion CD-ROM.

4. On the Insert tab, click **Header & Footer**. Key **July and August Departures** in the center Header pane.

5. Click **Go to Footer** and key **Prepared by (your name)** in the left Footer pane.

6. Move to the center Footer pane and click the **Current Date** button.

7. Move to the right Footer pane and click the **Page Number** button.

8. Right-click the **Sheet1** tab and change the tab color to purple.

9. Right-click **Sheet2** and change the tab color to green.

10. With Sheet1 active, select column **E**, click the **Home** tab, and display the Number dialog box. Format dates to display as day-month (i.e., 20-Jul).

11. Click the **Sheet2** tab to make it the active worksheet. Format columns B and C as Currency and decrease the decimals to zero.

12. **SAVE** the workbook as *Volunteers Project 2*.

   LEAVE the workbook open for the next project.

Project 3: Prepare Workbook for Printing and Display

USE the *Volunteers Project 2* workbook from the previous project.

1. With Sheet1 active, set a Wide Margin.

2. Click **Page Break Preview** and move the page breaks so that page 1 ends with row 30 and page 2 ends with row 60.

3. Prepare the workbook for printing.

   Use Landscape Orientation.

   Print the gridlines.

   Print the titles (row 4) at the top of all pages.

4. Examine the Print Preview to verify that the printout will be in landscape orientation, that column labels print on pages 2 and 3, and that only cells that contain data are included in the printout.

5. Print the entire workbook.

6. Prepare Sheet1 for display at a meeting. On the Page Layout tab, click **Background**. Select the *Blue Hills* image from the data files and click **Insert**.

   Remove gridlines and headings from the viewed worksheet.

   Double-click the **Ribbon** tab to minimize the Ribbon.

   Zoom in until the worksheet data fills the screen.

7. **SAVE** the workbook as *Volunteers Project 3*.

   CLOSE Excel.

The *Blue Hills* image file is available on the companion CD-ROM.

Managing Worksheets

LESSON SKILL MATRIX

SKILLS	MATRIX SKILL	SKILL NUMBER
Organizing Worksheets		
Copying a Worksheet	Copy worksheets	1.5.1
Renaming a Worksheet	Rename worksheets	1.5.3
Repositioning the Worksheets in a Workbook	Reposition worksheets within workbooks	1.5.2
Hiding and Unhiding a Worksheet	Hide and unhide worksheets	1.5.4
Inserting a New Worksheet into a Workbook	Insert and delete worksheets	1.5.5
Deleting a Worksheet from a Workbook	Insert and delete worksheets	1.5.5
Working with Multiple Worksheets		
Finding and Replacing Data		

The School of Fine Art (SFA) is a private college that is recognized as a leader in art education. More than 2,500 students are enrolled in its four-year programs of study. Admission requires an audition and/or portfolio presentation. Students pursue a BA degree in one of six majors: Fine Arts, Media Studies, Biomedical Art, Dramatic Arts, Interior Design, and Advertising and Graphic Arts. The school also offers a degree program for students who wish to combine major areas of concentration. In addition to its degree programs, SFA offers continuing education courses and Saturday and summer courses for children, teens, and adults who hope to pursue a career in the creative arts or who have exceptional artistic talent.

KEY TERMS
freeze
group worksheets
hide
string
unhide
zoom

■ SOFTWARE ORIENTATION

Worksheet Management

An Excel workbook should contain information about a unique subject. For example, SFA might have a workbook for enrollment data, one for faculty course assignments, and one for summer workshop course offerings. Each worksheet within a workbook contains a subset of information about that subject. The number of worksheets that a workbook can contain is limited only by the available memory of your computer. In this lesson, you will learn to move between worksheets, manage and reorganize sheets, and use Excel's search tools to find and replace information in a worksheet or workbook. To accomplish these tasks, you will use commands in the Home tab's Cells and Editing groups.

Figure 5-1

Commands to organize worksheets

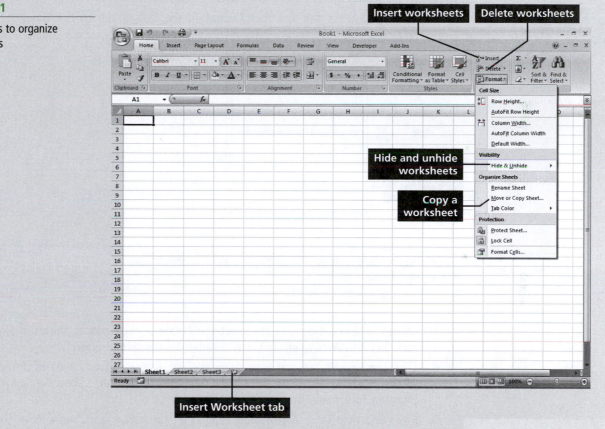

■ Organizing Worksheets

↓ THE BOTTOM LINE

A new, blank Excel workbook has three worksheets. You can add to, delete from, and move and copy worksheets as desired. You can also rename worksheets and hide and unhide worksheets when you need to do so. The flexibility to organize worksheets with similar subject matter together in one file enables you to effectively and efficiently manage related data.

Copying a Worksheet

Just as you can copy data from one cell or range in a worksheet to another cell or range, you can copy data from one worksheet to another within a workbook. For example, when a new worksheet will contain similar information to that contained in an existing worksheet, you can copy the worksheet and delete cell contents or overwrite existing data with new data. When you copy a worksheet, you retain the structure and formatting of the original worksheet so that you don't need to rebuild it from scratch. You can copy a worksheet using the Home tab's Format commands, the mouse, or the shortcut menu.

⊕ COPY A WORKSHEET

GET READY. Before you begin these steps, launch Microsoft Excel.

1. **OPEN** *School of Fine Art* from the data files for this lesson.
2. Click the **Sheet1** tab and click **Format** in the Cells group on the Home tab.
3. Click **Move or Copy Sheet**. The dialog box shown in Figure 5-2 opens.

CD

The *School of Fine Art* workbook is available on the companion CD-ROM.

Figure 5-2

Move or Copy dialog box

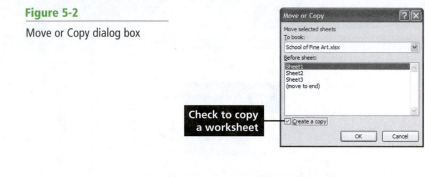

Check to copy a worksheet

⊕ ANOTHER WAY

You can right-click a sheet tab to display the shortcut menu. Click Move or Copy to display the dialog box.

4. Sheet1 is selected by default. Select the **Create a copy** box as shown in Figure 5-2 and click **OK**. A copy of Sheet1 is inserted to the left of Sheet1.
5. Click the **Sheet3** tab and hold down the left mouse button. A down arrow appears at the boundary between Sheet2 and Sheet3 and the cursor becomes an arrow pointing to a blank document symbol.
6. Press and hold **Ctrl**. A plus sign appears in the cursor document. Move the cursor to the right until the down arrow appears on the right side of Sheet3. Release the mouse button. The new sheet is named Sheet3 (2).
7. With Sheet3 (2) active, select **A2** and key **Dramatic Arts Department**.
8. Select **A6:C18** and press **Delete**.

⊕ ANOTHER WAY

Rather than delete the existing data, you can overwrite it. Select A6 and begin keying new data. Press Tab and key the data for B6. Press Tab and key the data for C6 and press Enter, etc. As you move to the next cell, the existing text is selected and it will be deleted when you enter new text.

9. Enter the data for the Dramatic Arts Department, beginning in A6.

DRAM321	Acting Studio I: Discover the Actor	106
DRAM322	Naturalism and Realism Techniques	95
DRAM326	Acting Studio: Improvisation	87
DRAM302	Acting Studio: Comedy	69
DRAM301	Fundamentals of Dance	110
DRAM312	Acting Studio: Shakespeare	95
DRAM315	Acting Studio: Iconoclastic Voices	95
DRAM400	Dialects and Accents	95
DRAM401	Advanced Voice and Diction	75
DRAM420	Theatre History	125
DRAM435	Acting for Film and TV	76
DRAM460	Auditioning Techniques	95

CERTIFICATION READY?
How do you copy a worksheet within a workbook?
1.5.1

10. If necessary, adjust column widths to display all data.

11. Click the **Microsoft Office Button** and click **Save As**. Create a Lesson 5 folder. **SAVE** the workbook as *Department Enrollments*. **PAUSE. LEAVE** the workbook open to use in the next exercise.

When an existing worksheet contains the formatting that you want to use in a new worksheet, it is more efficient to copy the existing worksheet rather than start the new worksheet from scratch. You can then delete or overwrite the data with new data. You will not need to format the new worksheet—the formatting is copied with the data. You can be assured that formatting is consistent among the worksheets within the workbook.

In the preceding exercise, you used two methods to copy a worksheet, and the workbook now has five worksheets. When you copy a worksheet, the new sheet is identified as a copy by a number in parentheses following the worksheet name. When you click and hold the left mouse button on the worksheet tab, the cursor becomes a new workbook icon and an arrow appears next to the active worksheet tab as shown in Figure 5-3.

Figure 5-3

Copy a worksheet using the mouse

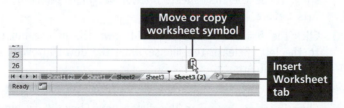

TAKE NOTE * Notice that when a worksheet is copied, the tab color is copied as well as the worksheet contents and formatting.

When you use the Format command or the shortcut menu to copy a worksheet, the Move or Copy dialog box shown in Figure 5-2 lets you identify the worksheet you want to copy. The copied worksheet is inserted before the sheet you select in the dialog box.

Renaming a Worksheet

When a workbook contains multiple worksheets with data, it is helpful to replace the generic Sheet1, Sheet2, etc. names with names that identify the data contained in the sheet. Each of the worksheets contains information about one department within the School of Fine Art. Renaming the tabs with department names will allow you to quickly locate needed enrollment data.

➡ RENAME A WORKSHEET

USE the workbook you saved in the previous exercise.

1. Double-click the **Sheet1 (2)** tab to select the tab name.
2. Key **Interior Design** and press ⌅Enter. The new name appears on the worksheet tab.
3. Key **Interior Design Department** in A2 of the sheet. Select **A6:C19** and press ⌅Delete. You will enter data for this department in a later exercise.
4. Click the **Sheet1** tab. Click **Format** and click **Rename Sheet**. Key **Fine Arts** and press ⌅Enter.
5. Click the **Sheet2** tab. Rename the sheet **Media Studies** and press ⌅Enter.
6. Click the **Sheet3** tab. Rename the sheet **Biomedical Arts** and press ⌅Enter.
7. Click **Sheet3 (2)**. Rename the sheet **Dramatic Arts** and press ⌅Enter.
8. Check each worksheet to ensure that the shortened name on the sheet tab matches the department name in A2.

   PAUSE. LEAVE the workbook open to use in the next exercise.

CERTIFICATION READY?
How do you rename a worksheet?
1.5.3

By naming the worksheets, it will be much easier to locate enrollment data for any course within a department. Each worksheet name indicates the type of data contained in the sheet.

Repositioning the Worksheets in a Workbook

> Now that the worksheets in the Department Enrollments workbook are appropriately named, you can rearrange them in any way you wish. An alphabetical arrangement is a logical way to organize the worksheets in this workbook. In the following exercise, click the tab for the sheet you want to move.

➡ REPOSITION THE WORKSHEETS IN A WORKBOOK

USE the workbook from the previous exercise.

1. Click the **Biomedical Arts** tab. Click **Format** in the Cells group.
2. Click **Move or Copy Sheet**. The Move or Copy dialog box opens. You want this sheet to be the first sheet. *Interior Design* is selected. Click **OK** to move Biomedical Arts **before** Interior Design.
3. Click the **Dramatic Arts** tab. Hold down the mouse button and move the worksheet to the left. Release the mouse when the down arrow is on the right side of the Biomedical Arts tab.
4. Click the **Fine Arts** tab. Click **Format** and click **Move or Copy Sheet**.
5. Click **Interior Design** in the dialog box. Click **OK** to move Fine Arts before Interior Design. The Fine Arts sheet is moved to the third position and the sheets are now in alphabetic order.
6. Click the **Dramatic Arts** tab. Click **Format** and click **Tab Color**. Click **Red** under Standard Colors. As noted previously, when you copied worksheets, the tab color was copied as well as the contents and formatting. Changing the tab color for the copied worksheets ensures that each tab has a different color.
7. Right-click the **Interior Design** tab, click **Tab Color**, and click **Purple** under Standard Colors.
8. **SAVE** the workbook with the same name.

   PAUSE. LEAVE the workbook open to use in the next exercise.

CERTIFICATION READY?
How do you reposition worksheets in a workbook?
1.5.2

Hiding and Unhiding a Worksheet

In Lesson 4, you hid columns and rows when you wanted to exclude particular columns or rows from a printout or when you wanted to hide sensitive or confidential information while you worked with other data in the worksheet. You can apply the same procedure to **hide** (make a worksheet invisible) and **unhide** (make visible again) worksheets. For example, because the Interior Design worksheet does not contain data at this time, you would hide that sheet if you wanted to print the entire workbook.

HIDE AND UNHIDE A WORKSHEET

USE the workbook from the previous exercise.

1. Select the **Interior Design** worksheet. Click **Format** in the Cells group.
2. Click **Hide & Unhide** and click **Hide Sheet**. The Interior Design worksheet is no longer visible. Click the **Fine Arts** tab.

TAKE NOTE * Right-click any worksheet tab. If worksheets are hidden, the Unhide option will be active on the shortcut menu.

3. Click **Format**, click **Hide & Unhide**, and click **Unhide Sheet**. The Unhide dialog box shown in Figure 5-4 opens.

Figure 5-4

Unhide dialog box

4. Click **OK** to unhide the Interior Design worksheet. Enter the following enrollment information.

ID201	Elements of Design I	103
ID205	Interior Design I	106
ID207	History of Interiors	110
ID232	Drawing and Composition	121
ID320	Interior Design II	86
ID322	Architectural Drafting	98
ID325	Elements of Design II	95
ID330	Color Theory	89
ID335	Textiles	121
ID405	CAD I	82
ID432	CAD II	75
ID430	Perspectives in Design	63
ID461	Furniture Design	59
ID465	Lighting Design	49

CERTIFICATION READY?
How do you hide and unhide a worksheet in a workbook?
1.5.4

5. **SAVE** your workbook.

PAUSE. LEAVE the workbook open to use in the next exercise.

You can hide several worksheets at the same time. Hold down Ctrl and click the tab of the sheets you want to hide. You cannot, however, select multiple worksheets in the Unhide dialog box; you must unhide worksheets individually.

Inserting a New Worksheet into a Workbook

You can insert one or multiple worksheets into an existing workbook. The Insert Worksheet tab (Figure 5-5) at the bottom of a worksheet is a new Excel 2007 feature that allows you to quickly insert a new worksheet at the end of the existing worksheets. To insert a new worksheet before an existing worksheet, select the worksheet tab before which you want the new sheet and use the Cells group Insert command.

Figure 5-5

Insert Worksheet tab

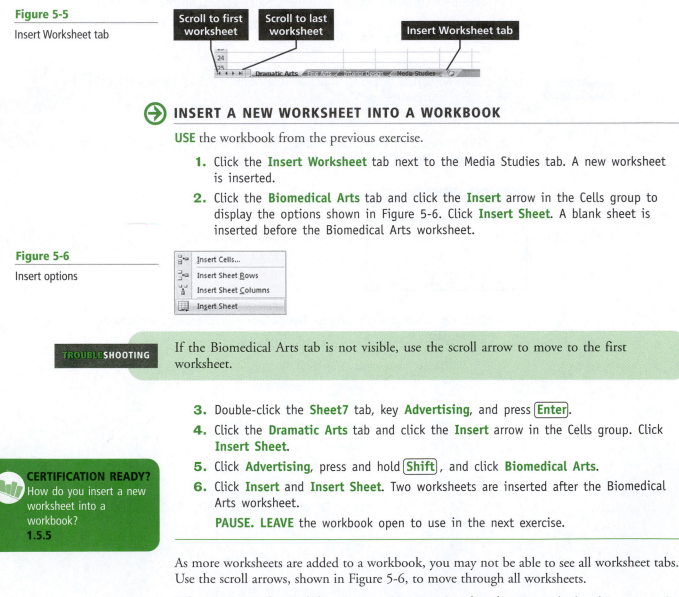

➜ INSERT A NEW WORKSHEET INTO A WORKBOOK

USE the workbook from the previous exercise.

1. Click the **Insert Worksheet** tab next to the Media Studies tab. A new worksheet is inserted.

2. Click the **Biomedical Arts** tab and click the **Insert** arrow in the Cells group to display the options shown in Figure 5-6. Click **Insert Sheet**. A blank sheet is inserted before the Biomedical Arts worksheet.

Figure 5-6

Insert options

> **TROUBLESHOOTING** If the Biomedical Arts tab is not visible, use the scroll arrow to move to the first worksheet.

3. Double-click the **Sheet7** tab, key **Advertising**, and press **Enter**.
4. Click the **Dramatic Arts** tab and click the **Insert** arrow in the Cells group. Click **Insert Sheet**.
5. Click **Advertising**, press and hold **Shift**, and click **Biomedical Arts**.
6. Click **Insert** and **Insert Sheet**. Two worksheets are inserted after the Biomedical Arts worksheet.

   PAUSE. LEAVE the workbook open to use in the next exercise.

CERTIFICATION READY?
How do you insert a new worksheet into a workbook?
1.5.5

As more worksheets are added to a workbook, you may not be able to see all worksheet tabs. Use the scroll arrows, shown in Figure 5-6, to move through all worksheets.

When you copied a worksheet in a previous exercise, the tab name and tab color were copied with the worksheet's contents and formatting. When you insert a new worksheet, it is blank and has the generic Sheet1 title. When you inserted a worksheet before the existing sheets were named, the new sheet was given the next consecutive number, such as Sheet6.

You can right-click a worksheet tab and click Insert on the shortcut menu to insert a worksheet. The Insert dialog box shown in Figure 5-7 opens and you can insert a blank worksheet from the General tab, insert a worksheet based on a template from the Spreadsheet Solutions tab, or insert an online template if you are connected to the Internet.

Figure 5-7

Insert dialog box

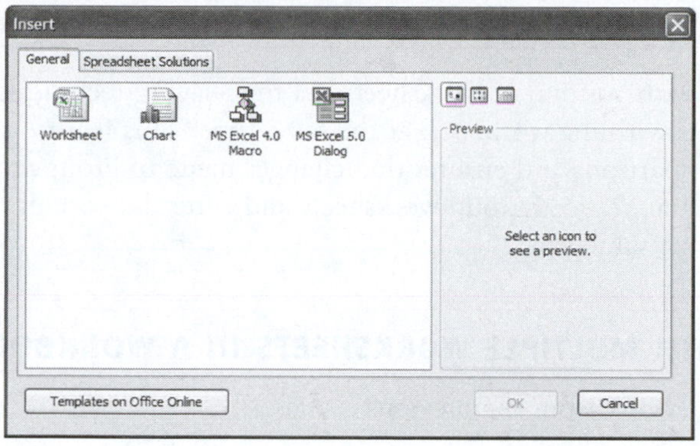

When you open the Insert dialog box, multiple Excel files may be shown on the General tab. The listed files represent templates that have been downloaded, created by you, or created by another user.

To insert multiple worksheets at the same time, press and hold Shift, and then select the same number of worksheet tabs that you want to insert in the open workbook. In the exercise, when you selected the tabs of two existing worksheets, clicked Insert, and clicked Insert Sheet, two new worksheets were inserted.

Deleting a Worksheet from a Workbook

If a workbook contains blank worksheets or worksheets that contain data that is no longer needed, you can delete the unnecessary sheets.

→ DELETE A WORKSHEET FROM A WORKBOOK

USE the workbook from the previous exercise.

1. Click **Sheet6** and click the **Delete** arrow in the Cells group.
2. Click **Delete Sheet**.
3. Click the **Sheet8** tab, press and hold [Shift], and click the **Sheet9** tab. The selection should include Sheet10 as well as Sheet8 and Sheet9.
4. Click the **Delete** arrow and click **Delete Sheet**.
5. **SAVE** the workbook.

   PAUSE. LEAVE the workbook open to use in the next exercise.

CERTIFICATION READY?
How do you delete a worksheet from a workbook?
1.5.5

You can right-click the tab of a worksheet you do not need and click Delete. The worksheet will be deleted.

■ Working with Multiple Worksheets

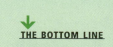

THE BOTTOM LINE

You can *group worksheets*, a feature that allows you to enter and edit data on several worksheets at the same time or apply formatting to multiple worksheets. When sheets are grouped, you can enter data in one worksheet and have it appear in multiple worksheets in a workbook. When multiple worksheets are selected, [*Group*] appears in the title bar at the top of the worksheet. Be cautious. When you change data in grouped sheets, you may accidentally replace data on other sheets.

Working with Multiple Worksheets in a Workbook

Working with a group of worksheets is a time-saving technique. You can view several worksheets within a workbook at the same time. This feature allows you to make quick visual comparisons and ensures that changes made to grouped sheets will not overwrite existing data. You can group worksheets and enter data on all worksheets within the group at the same time.

WORK WITH MULTIPLE WORKSHEETS IN A WORKBOOK

USE the workbook from the previous exercise.

1. Right-click a worksheet tab and click **Select All Sheets**. The title bar reads *Departmental Enrollments [Group]*.

ANOTHER WAY If you want to group some but not all worksheets within a workbook, press Ctrl and click the tab of each worksheet you want to include in the group.

2. In B20, key **Total Enrollment**.

TAKE NOTE * If you copy a data range from a worksheet to grouped worksheets, the Paste Options button does not appear. Some formatting, such as column width, is not copied.

3. Right-click a worksheet tab and click **Ungroup Sheets**.
4. Click the **View** tab if necessary. With Biomedical Arts data displayed, click **New Window** in the Windows group.
5. Click the **Dramatic Arts** tab and click **New Window**.
6. Click the **Fine Arts** tab to make the sheet active and click **Arrange All** in the Windows group. The Arrange Windows dialog box opens. Click **Vertical** as shown in Figure 5-8. Click **Windows of active workbook**.

Figure 5-8

Arrange Windows dialog box

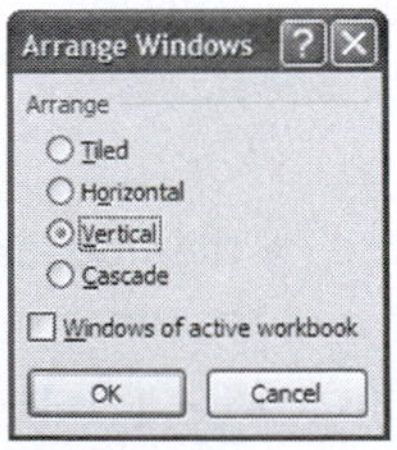

TAKE NOTE * Data that you copy or cut in grouped sheets cannot be pasted on another sheet because the size of the copy area includes all layers of the selected sheets and is therefore different from the paste area in a single sheet. Make sure that only one sheet is selected before you attempt to copy or move data to another worksheet.

7. Click **OK**. Your screen should look like Figure 5-9 with the three worksheets displayed side by side.

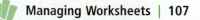

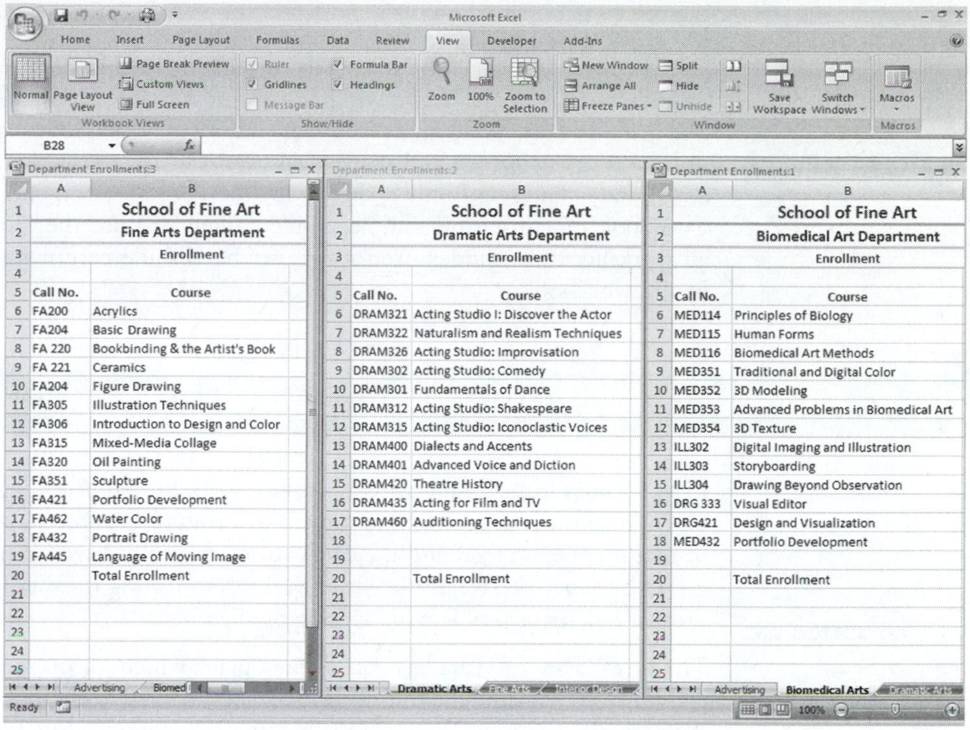

Figure 5-9

Vertically tiled worksheets

PAUSE. LEAVE the workbook open to use in the next exercise.

The New Window and Arrange All options enable you to display worksheets side by side for a quick visual comparison. You can enter and edit data, scroll, and move around in the individual windows just as you would in a normal-view window. You can click a cell in any of the displayed worksheets to make changes or to select cells or ranges.

Hiding and Unhiding Worksheets in a Workbook

You can replace any worksheet in the view by clicking the tab of another worksheet. You can also hide and unhide worksheets or an entire workbook in this view.

HIDE AND UNHIDE WORKSHEETS IN A WORKBOOK

USE the workbook from the previous exercise.

1. Click any cell in the Fine Arts window.
2. Click **Hide Window** in the Window group of the View tab. The Fine Arts window is closed; the Dramatic Arts and Biomedical windows remain visible.
3. Click **Unhide Window**. Select the sheet you want to unhide and click **OK**.
4. Click the **Close** button in the upper-right corner of the Fine Arts and Dramatic Arts windows. Restore the Biomedical Arts window to full-screen view.
5. **SAVE** and **CLOSE** the workbook.

PAUSE. LEAVE Excel open to use in the next exercise

If you click Hide in the Window group with one worksheet window open, the entire workbook is hidden. Excel remains open, but the Taskbar no long displays the worksheet name. This feature allows you to quickly mask confidential data from view. In a later exercise, you will group worksheets and enter data on all of them at one time.

TROUBLESHOOTING

Do not confuse the Hide and Unhide commands you used in this lesson with those you used in Lesson 4. The View tab commands in this lesson are used to hide and unhide what is in the active window—in most cases a complete worksheet. The Hide and Unhide commands in the Format options on the Home tab are used to hide and unhide rows, columns, and worksheets. You can hide a worksheet with either Hide command. When you hide a sheet with the Format command, other worksheets in the workbook remain visible and accessible. When you use the Hide Window command, all worksheets are hidden. You must use the Unhide command to access any worksheet in the workbook.

Using Zoom and Scroll to Change Onscreen View

THE BOTTOM LINE

Excel's *Zoom* feature allows you to make a worksheet appear bigger (zoom in) or smaller (zoom out) on your screen. You can use this feature to zoom in on a portion of a worksheet so that it appears larger and the data is easier to read. Or you can zoom out to get a better perspective of the entire worksheet, making it easier to identify formatting inconsistencies or problematic spacing or alignment.

The Freeze Panes feature lets you *freeze* a pane, which means that you keep rows or columns visible while the rest of the worksheet scrolls. You often want to freeze the row that contains column labels and the column that contains row headings so that it is always clear what the data you see represents.

USE ZOOM AND SCROLL TO CHANGE ONSCREEN VIEW

OPEN *SFA Staff Directory* from the data files for this lesson.

CD

The *SFA Staff Directory* workbook is available on the companion CD-ROM.

1. Select a data cell in the **SFA Staff Directory** worksheet. Click **Zoom to Selection** on the View tab. Zoom is increased to 400%.
2. Click **Undo** on the Quick Access Toolbar to return to 100% zoom.
3. Click **Zoom** on the View tab. In the Zoom dialog box, under Magnification, click **200%**. Click **OK**.
4. Click **Zoom** and under Magnification, click **Custom**. Key **150** in the percentage box and click **OK**.
5. Click **100%** in the Zoom group.
6. Select **A5**. Click **Freeze Panes** in the Window group on the View tab. Click **Freeze Panes** in the dropdown list.
7. Press ⌜Ctrl⌟ + ⌜End⌟. Row 4 with the column labels appears at the top of the screen to let you know what each column represents, even when the active cell is the last cell in the data range.

   PAUSE. LEAVE the workbook open to use in the next exercise.

You can use the Zoom scale on the Status bar to customize magnification. To zoom in (magnify), select a size greater than 100%; to zoom out (shrink), select a size less than 100%.

Some mouse devices have built-in zooming capabilities. If your mouse has a wheel, hold down Ctrl while you rotate the wheel forward or back to increase and decrease zoom.

If the SFA Staff Directory worksheet contained more columns than you could view at one time, you can freeze column A and the row containing the column labels. The Freeze First Column and Freeze First Row commands shown in Figure 5-10 are quick and easy to use if your worksheet begins with column headings, but when the data is preceded by a title and subtitle, you must tell Excel where you want the "freeze" to be located. That is why you need to select the cell below the line that you want to be visible as you move through the worksheet.

Figure 5-10

Freeze Panes options

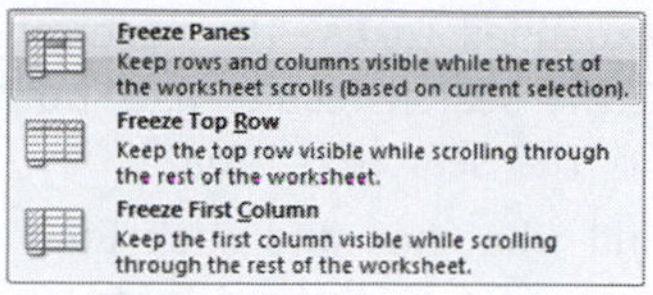

> **Freeze Panes**
> Keep rows and columns visible while the rest of the worksheet scrolls (based on current selection).
>
> **Freeze Top Row**
> Keep the top row visible while scrolling through the rest of the worksheet.
>
> **Freeze First Column**
> Keep the first column visible while scrolling through the rest of the worksheet.

The column labels will be visible as you make changes to the worksheet in the next exercises.

TAKE NOTE ✳ The Freeze First Row and Freeze First Column commands do not work together. When you want to freeze the first row and first column at the same time, locate the "freeze point" and use the Freeze Panes command.

■ Finding and Replacing Data

THE BOTTOM LINE The Find and Replace options let you locate specific data quickly and, if necessary, replace it with new data. These features are most effective in large worksheets in which all of the data is not visible on the screen, thus saving you the time of scanning through vast amounts of data to find the information you need.

Locating Data with the Find Command

Excel's Find feature lets you look for specific data. If you want to locate a particular item of data that isn't immediately visible, you can scan the worksheet visually to look for the needed data. A much easier and quicker way is to use the Find & Select commands shown in Figure 5-11.

Figure 5-11

Find & Select commands

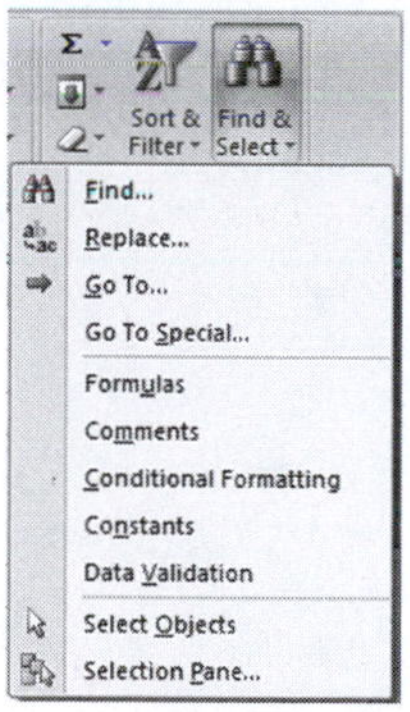

> Σ ▾
> ▦ ▾   Sort &   Find &
> ◇ ▾   Filter ▾ Select ▾
>
> 🔍 Find...
> 🔄 Replace...
> ➡   Go To...
>   Go To Special...
>   Formulas
>   Comments
>   Conditional Formatting
>   Constants
>   Data Validation
> ▯   Select Objects
> ▥   Selection Pane...

ANOTHER WAY

You can open the Find and Replace dialog box with the keyboard shortcut Ctrl+F.

⊙ LOCATE DATA WITH THE FIND COMMAND

USE the workbook from the previous exercise.

1. Select **Find & Select** in the Editing group on the Home tab.
2. Click **Find**. The **Find and Replace** dialog box opens with the Find tab displayed.
3. Key **tutor** in the *Find what* box. It does not matter whether you key the text in uppercase or lowercase—Excel will find it.

TAKE NOTE ✳ It does not matter which cell is currently the active cell when you enter a search string. If you do not select a range of cells, Excel will search the entire worksheet.

4. Click **Find All**. The box is expanded to list the occurrences of *tutor* in the worksheet and you see that the search results lists both academic and writing tutors, so you need to refine the search criteria.

5. Key **writing tutor** in the Find what box and click **Find All**. The worksheet contains data for two individuals whose title is Writing Tutor.

6. Click **Options** on the dialog box to view the default settings for the **Find** feature.

7. **CLOSE** the dialog box.

   PAUSE. LEAVE the workbook open to use in the next exercise.

When you enter the text or number that you want to find and click Find All, Excel locates all occurrences of the search string and lists them at the bottom of the dialog box, as shown in Figure 5-12. A *string* is any sequence of letters or numbers in a field.

Figure 5-12

Results of Find All search

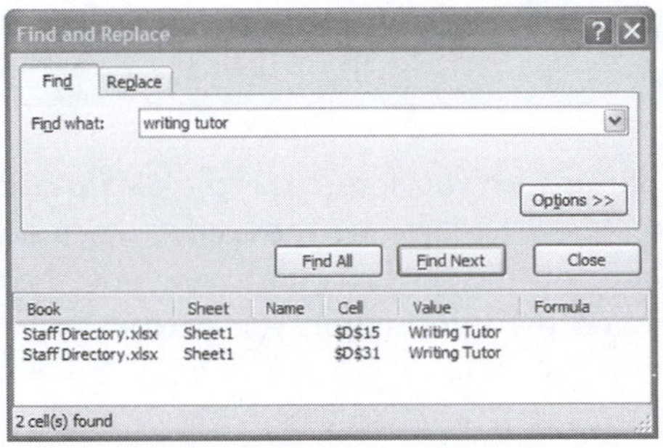

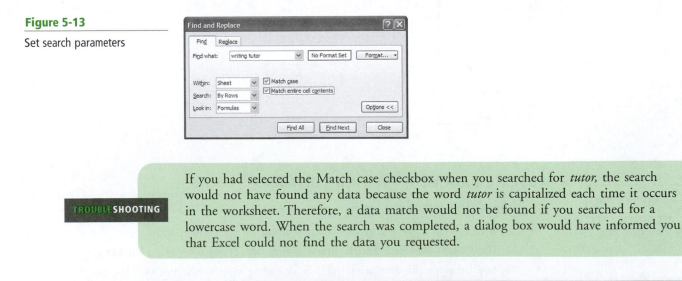

If you click Find Next after you key the search string, Excel selects the cell in which the first occurrence of the string is found. You can edit the cell or click Find Next and continue to browse through the worksheet. The cursor will stop at each cell where the search string is located.

The Options button on the Find tab allows you to set additional parameters for the search. As shown in Figure 5-13, the default is to search the active worksheet, but you can also search an entire workbook. You can locate instances in which only the case (capitals or lower case) matches the search string you key or the entire cell contents match the search string—more precise search strings create more concise search results.

Figure 5-13

Set search parameters

TROUBLESHOOTING

If you had selected the Match case checkbox when you searched for *tutor,* the search would not have found any data because the word *tutor* is capitalized each time it occurs in the worksheet. Therefore, a data match would not be found if you searched for a lowercase word. When the search was completed, a dialog box would have informed you that Excel could not find the data you requested.

Looking Ahead

The Look in box on the Find and Replace dialog box lets you look for data in formulas, values, or comments. You will work with formulas in Lesson 7 and with comments in Lesson 11.

Replacing Data with the Replace Command

To look for specific data and replace it with other data, you will use the Replace tab on the Find and Replace dialog box. You can quickly find and replace all or some occurrences of a character string in a worksheet. Replacing data with the click of a button can save you the time of finding occurrences of the data and repeatedly keying replacement data.

→ REPLACE DATA WITH THE REPLACE COMMAND

USE the workbook from the previous exercise.

1. Click **Find & Select** in the Editing group.
2. Click **Replace**. The Find and Replace dialog box opens with the Replace tab displayed.
3. In the Find what box, key **Johnson**.
4. In the Replace with box, key **Johnston** as shown in Figure 5-14.

Figure 5-14

Replace tab of Find and Replace dialog box

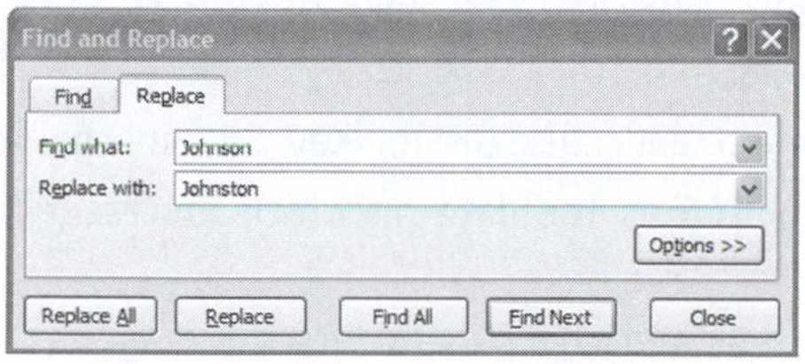

5. Click **Options** to expand the dialog box. In the Search box, click **By Columns** and click **Find Next**. The first occurrence of Johnson is not the one you are looking for, so click **Find Next** until you locate the entry for Tamara Johnson.

TROUBLESHOOTING If the Find and Replace dialog box obstructs your view of column A where the search data will be located, click the title bar and drag the box to the right so that you have a clear view of columns A and B.

6. Click **Replace** and click **Close**.
7. Click **Find & Select** and then click **Replace**. Key **Advertising** in the Find what field and key **Advertising and Graphic Arts** in the Replace with field.
8. Click **Replace All**. A dialog box tells you that Excel made 9 replacements. Click **OK** and then click **Close** to close the dialog box.

TROUBLESHOOTING Use discretion when deciding whether to use Replace All or Find Next when looking for specific data. When you needed to correct the spelling of a last name, you did not know whether there were other entries with the last name Johnson. Therefore, as a precaution, you needed to find the entry and decide whether to replace it with the corrected spelling. If you had chosen Replace All, you would have incorrectly changed two other last names in the directory.

9. **SAVE** your workbook in the Lesson 5 folder. Name the file *Staff Directory*.
   PAUSE. LEAVE the workbook open to use in the next exercise.

As you have seen in this exercise, the Replace All command allows you to quickly change the contents of multiple cells. When the staff directory was created, it was easier to key *Advertising* rather than the complete name, *Advertising and Graphic Arts*. You corrected all nine occurrences of the department name, however, by clicking Replace All.

Navigating a Worksheet with the Go To Command

As you learned in an earlier lesson, you can key a cell location in the Name box, press Enter, and Excel makes the designated cell active. Another method of moving to a specific cell is to use the Go To feature. In the following exercise, you will use the Go To feature to navigate the worksheet and enter new data and to unhide the first worksheet row.

→ NAVIGATE A WORKSHEET WITH THE GO TO COMMAND

USE the workbook you saved in the previous exercise.

1. On the View tab, click **Freeze Panes** and click **Unfreeze Panes**. This removes the freeze so you can display the hidden row 1.
2. Click the **Home** tab. Click **Find & Select** and then click **Go To**. The Go To dialog box is displayed.
3. Key **A1** in the Reference box and click **OK**. Column headers A through E become highlighted. A1 is still hidden.
4. In the Cells group, click **Format**, click **Hide & Unhide**, and click **Unhide Rows**. Row 1 is displayed.
5. Click **Find & Select** and click **Go To**. Key **E67** in the Reference box and click **OK**.
6. Key **5/15/06** in **B46** as the date on which Professor Young was hired. Press [Enter].
7. Click **Find & Select** and click **Go To Special**.
8. On the Go To Special dialog box, click **Blanks** and click **OK**. The blank cells within the data range are highlighted.
9. Press [Tab] three times until E13, the first blank cell in the Date Hired column, is the active cell. Enter **6/8/87** and press [Tab] to move to the next blank cell. Enter the following dates. Press [Tab] after each entry.

Gronchi	12/8/05
Hasselberg	10/20/00
Kahn	11/2/03
Liu	6/5/07
Male	7/10/00
Vande Velde	3/1/01
Wadia	6/1/02
Yang	6/1/02

10. **SAVE** the *Staff Directory* workbook and **CLOSE** the workbook.
    CLOSE Excel.

ANOTHER WAY

Ctrl+G is the keyboard command to display the Go To dialog box.

TROUBLESHOOTING

The reason you needed to tab three times to reach E13 is the blank cells in the heading rows. Remember that when cells are merged, entries in the merged cells are considered to be in the upper-left cell. Therefore, Excel considers the remaining cells in the merge to be blank.

As you experienced in the preceding exercises, the Find & Select features allow you to find and, if necessary, quickly replace existing data. The Go To feature is a fast way to move to specific cell references, especially in a large worksheet.

When you opened the worksheet, row 1 was hidden. By using the Go To feature, you were able to make row 1 visible. In Lesson 4 you learned to select the row before and after the hidden row to unhide a row. However, to unhide the first row or column, you need to use the Go To feature before you click Format, click Hide & Unhide, and click Unhide Rows to unhide the first row or first column.

You used one of several Go To Special commands, shown in Figure 5-15, when you located and filled blank cells in the worksheet. You will use the Special commands to go to conditional formatting in Lesson 6 and to go to formulas in Lesson 7.

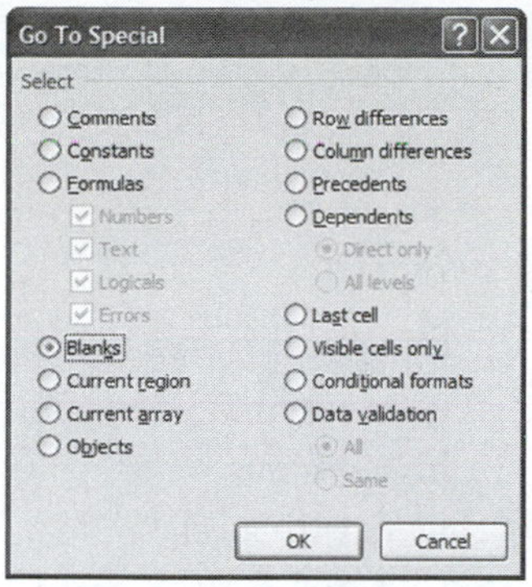

Figure 5-15

Go to Special dialog box

In the exercises you completed as you learned new Excel features, you worked with relatively small amounts of data. In the business world, you often work with worksheets that contain massive amounts of data. The Find & Select and Go To features are most effective in large worksheets where it can take a significant amount of time to scan numerous rows and/or columns to find the data you need.

SUMMARY SKILL MATRIX

In This Lesson You Learned	Matrix Skill	Skill Number
To organize worksheets		
To copy data from one worksheet to another worksheet in the same workbook	Copy worksheets	1.5.1
To rename a worksheet to identify the sheet's content	Rename worksheets	1.5.3
To move worksheets within a workbook to organize the worksheets logically	Reposition worksheets within workbooks	1.5.2
To hide worksheets temporarily and then make them visible again	Hide and unhide worksheets	1.5.4
To insert a worksheet into an existing workbook	Insert and delete worksheets	1.5.5
To delete a worksheet from a workbook	Insert and delete worksheets	1.5.5
To work with multiple worksheets		
To hide a worksheet and then make it visible again		
To use the zoom and scroll features to change the on-screen view of a worksheet		
To find and replace data		

■ Knowledge Assessment

Matching

Match each vocabulary term with its definition.

a. Hide command   f. Unhide command
b. freeze   g. zoom in
c. group worksheets   h. zoom out
d. string   i. Go To Special
e. search and replace   j. Arrange All command

_____ 1. To make a hidden workbook or worksheet visible.

_____ 2. To make certain rows or columns remain visible on your screen even when you scroll your worksheet.

_____ 3. To make a worksheet appear larger on the screen.

_____ 4. To make a workbook or worksheet invisible.

_____ 5. Any sequence of letters or numbers that you type.

_____ 6. To make a worksheet appear smaller on the screen.

_____ 7. Selecting multiple worksheets to enter and edit data on them.

_____ 8. A command you can use to locate blank cells in a worksheet.

_____ 9. A feature you can use to locate and replace specific data in a worksheet.

_____ 10. A feature that allows you to visually compare worksheets.

Multiple Choice

Circle the choice that best completes or responds to the following statements.

1. To find data using the Find and Replace dialog box, you must enter a sequence of characters called a
   a. range.
   b. string.
   c. cell address.
   d. menu.

2. You can tell that worksheets are grouped by
   a. a bracket around the grouped sheets.
   b. the word *group* on the sheet tabs.
   c. the word *group* in the title bar.
   d. the words *grouped sheets* on the Status bar.

3. When Sheet1 has been copied, the new worksheet title says
   a. copy of Sheet1.
   b. Sheet1 (2).
   c. Sheet1 Copy.
   d. Sheet2.

4. Which of the following is **not** a way to insert a new worksheet into a workbook?
   a. On the Home tab, click Insert and click Insert Sheet.
   b. Right-click a sheet tab, click Insert, and click Insert Worksheet.

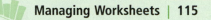

   c. On the Insert tab, click New Sheet.

   d. On the Home tab, click Format, click Move or Copy Sheet, and click Create a Copy.

5. To insert multiple worksheets at one time, what action is needed in addition to selecting the same number of tabs as the number of sheets to insert?

   a. Press and hold Shift as you select the tabs.

   b. Press and hold Ctrl as you select the tabs.

   c. Press Shift after you select the tabs.

   d. Press Ctrl after you select the tabs.

6. To enter data in multiple worksheets at one time, you must

   a. use the Arrange command in the Window group on the View tab.

   b. use the Freeze command in the Window group on the View tab.

   c. use the Format command in the Cells group on the Home tab.

   d. group all worksheets and enter data in the open worksheet.

7. If you want to magnify data on the screen,

   a. decrease zoom to less than 100%.

   b. increase zoom to 100%.

   c. increase zoom to more than 100%.

   d. increase the font size in the data range.

8. When a worksheet is hidden,

   a. Unhide is active on the shortcut menu.

   b. a bold line appears where the sheet is hidden.

   c. the word Hidden appears on the Status bar.

   d. the word Hidden appears in the title bar.

9. To hide a workbook that has multiple worksheets,

   a. click Format and click Hide in the Cells group on the Home tab.

   b. click Hide in the Window group on the View tab.

   c. right-click a sheet tab and click Hide.

   d. group all worksheets and click Format, click Hide & Unhide, and click Hide Sheet.

10. When you use the Freeze command,

   a. data cannot be entered in the worksheet.

   b. you cannot scroll through the worksheet.

   c. you cannot change the worksheet view.

   d. the column and/or row headings remain visible as you scroll through the worksheet.

■ Competency Assessment

Project 5-1: School of Fine Art

You will move and copy worksheets, rename worksheets, change the tab color, and rearrange worksheets within a workbook.

GET READY. Launch Excel if it is not already running.

The *SFA Enrollments* workbook is available on the companion CD-ROM.

   1. OPEN *SFA Enrollments* from the data files for this lesson.

   2. Click **Advertising** to make it the active worksheet. If the tab is not visible, click the scroll arrow to take you to the first worksheet.

3. Click **Format** in the Cells group on the Home tab. Click **Move or Copy Sheet**.

4. In the Move or Copy dialog box, click the **Create a copy** box and click **OK**.

5. On the Advertising (2) worksheet, select **A2** and key **Foundational Studies**. Press [Enter].

6. Select **A6:C20** and press [Delete].

7. Click **Format**, click **Rename Sheet**, and key **Foundations**. Press [Enter].

8. Click **Format**, click **Tab Color**, and click **Dark Red**.

9. Click **Format** and click **Move or Copy Sheet**. In the Before sheet box, click **(move to end)** and click **OK**.

10. **SAVE** the workbook as *SFA Enrollments 5-1* and then **CLOSE** the file.

    LEAVE Excel open for the next project.

Project 5-2: Graphic Design Institute

You will rename worksheets, hide and unhide worksheets, and insert and delete worksheets from a workbook.

The *Training Expenditures* workbook is available on the companion CD-ROM.

1. **OPEN** *Training Expenditures* from the data files for this lesson.

2. Right-click **Sheet1**. Click **Rename** and key **Budget**. Press [Enter].

3. Double-click the **Sheet2** tab. Key **January**. Press [Enter].

4. Rename Sheet3 **March** and press [Enter].

5. Rename Sheet4 **Previous Qtr** and press [Enter].

6. Click the **Insert Worksheet** tab. Rename the new sheet **Summary**.

7. Click the **March** tab and click the **Insert** arrow in the Cells group on the Home tab. Click **Insert Sheet**.

8. Name the new worksheet **February**.

9. Click the **Previous Qtr** tab. Click **Format**, click **Hide & Unhide**, and click **Hide Sheet**.

10. Click **Format**, click **Hide & Unhide**, and click **Unhide Sheet**. In the Unhide dialog box, click **OK**.

11. Click the **Previous Qtr** tab. Click the arrow next to **Delete** and click **Delete Sheet**. Click **Delete** on the dialog box to confirm that you want to delete the Previous Qtr sheet.

12. **SAVE** the workbook as *Training Expenditures 5-2*.

    LEAVE the workbook open for the next project.

■ Proficiency Assessment

Project 5-3: Graphic Design Institute

You will move between worksheets, change the workbook view, and group worksheets to enter data on multiple sheets.

USE the workbook from the previous project.

1. Click the **View** tab to make it active.

2. On the Budget worksheet, select **E18** and click **Zoom to Selection** in the Zoom group.

3. Click **100%** in the Zoom group.

4. Click **Zoom In** on the Status bar and increase magnification to 150%.

5. Click the **January** tab and click **Select All**. Click **Copy**.

6. Click the **Summary** sheet tab, select **A1**, and click **Paste**.

7. On the February worksheet, select **A1**, right-click, and click **Paste**. Click the **Paste Options** button and click **Keep Source Formatting**.

If the formatting is not copied, make the January worksheet active and select the text containing the formatting. Double-click the Format Painter and apply the formatting to the necessary cells.

8. Double-click **A2** to put it in Edit mode (noted on Status bar). Select **January**, key **February**, and press **Enter**.

9. Select **C4** and key **February**.

10. Delete the January expenditures from C5:C17. Then enter the February expenditures for the items listed below. (Not all items have February expenditures; leave those cells blank.)

Courseware development	$2,500
Courseware purchase	400
Certification	250
Train-the-trainer	1,200
Hardware purchases	10,500
Consulting fees	150
Instructor fees	4,000
Travel	600
Per diem	400

11. Select **A2** on the **Summary** worksheet and key **Quarterly Expenditures**.

12. Copy **C4:C18** from the **February** worksheet to the **Summary** sheet. Paste the data next to the January data.

13. Copy **C4:C18** from the March worksheet to the Summary sheet. Paste the data next to the February data.

14. Select **A1:E1** and click **Merge & Center** two times.

15. Click **Merge & Center** two times for cells **A2:E2**.

16. **SAVE** the workbook as *Training Expenditures 5-3*. **CLOSE** the workbook.

LEAVE Excel open for the next project.

Project 5-4: School of Fine Art

Update the school's staff directory.

OPEN *Updated Directory* from the data files for this lesson.

The *Updated Directory* workbook is available on the companion CD-ROM.

1. At the bottom of the worksheet, add information for three new staff members.

DeGrasse, Kirk	**Media Studies**	**Associate Professor**	**2/15/07**
Sheperdigian, Janet	**Student Services**	**Academic Advisor**	**3/1/07**
Playstead, Craig	**Administration**	**Associate Dean**	**4/1/07**

2. Gail Erickson has been promoted to Professor. Click **Find & Select**. Change her title.

3. Use the Find & Select feature to replace BioMedical with **Biomedical Art**.

4. Use Find & Select to go to **A33**. Sidney Higa's title should be **Vice President**.

5. Click **Format** and change the name of Sheet1 to **Directory**.

6. Click **Sheet2**. Press **Ctrl** and click **Sheet3**. Click **Format** and hide the blank worksheets.

7. Name the workbook *Staff Directory 5-4*.

8. **SAVE** and **CLOSE** the workbook.

LEAVE Excel open for the next project.

■ Mastery Assessment

The *Advisor Recommendations* workbook is available on the companion CD-ROM.

Project 5-5: School of Fine Art

Debra Core, an academic advisor, has asked you to search the enrollment data and highlight courses for some of the continuing education students with whom she is working.

1. **OPEN** *Advisor Recommendations* from the data files for this lesson.
2. Identify the courses that investigate various aspects of color.
   a. Use the **Find & Select** options to search the entire workbook.
   b. Use **color** as the search string.
   c. In the Within field, click **Workbook**.
   d. Find all courses that have color as part of the course name.
3. Your search should return a list of six courses. Add Yellow fill color to highlight each course.
   a. Click the first course (Biomedical Arts). Click **Fill Color**.
   b. Click the second course and click **Fill Color** in the Fonts group.
   c. Continue until the six courses have been highlighted.
4. Identify the available painting courses.
   a. Use **painting** as the search string.
   b. Search the workbook and mark painting courses with a Light Blue fill.
5. Mark photography courses with a Light Green fill.
6. **SAVE** the workbook as *Advisor Recommendations 5-5*. **CLOSE** the file.
   LEAVE Excel open for the next project.

Project 5-6: Contoso, Ltd.

Use the Find & Select command to locate specific information and fill blank spaces in a worksheet. Freeze the column headings so they remain visible as you scroll through the list of Contoso employees.

The *Contoso Employees* workbook is available on the companion CD-ROM.

1. **OPEN** *Contoso Employees* from the data files for this lesson.
2. Use the Freeze Panes command so that the column headings in row 4 remain visible as you scroll to the end the data range.
3. Find and Replace all occurrences of Billing Clerk with **Accounts Receivable Clerk**.
4. Use Find and Replace options to find all blank cells on the worksheet. Key **Records Management** in each blank in column C.
5. **SAVE** the workbook as *Contoso Employees 5-6*.
   LEAVE Excel open for the next project.

INTERNET READY

The *College Comparisons* workbook is available on the companion CD-ROM.

OPEN *College Comparisons* in the data files for this lesson.

In this lesson you worked with data files for the School of Fine Art. Go online and investigate colleges that offer degrees in your career interest. Use the College Comparisons worksheet to record information about three colleges that offer a degree program in your area of interest.

Fill in as much information as you can locate about each college. Based on your limited research, indicate which college would be your choice to pursue the degree you investigated. **SAVE** the file and **CLOSE** excel.

Working with Data

6

KEY TERMS
ascending order
AutoFilter
comparison operator
criteria
descending order
duplicate value
filter
grouping
outline symbols

An employee's name is added to the list of Contoso, Ltd.'s employees when he or she joins the company. However, viewing the employee list according to the employees' positions would be more useful to the office manager when he develops the work schedule. Reorganizing the data enables the office manager to ensure that the office is fully staffed when it is open. The office manager also needs to update employee data files with additional data. Because other employees often need to access the files, he plans to restrict the data that can be entered in some files to ensure that valid results are obtained when data entry is complete and the data is analyzed for decision making.

■ SOFTWARE ORIENTATION

Excel's Data Tab

Excel is primarily a tool for organizing, analyzing, and presenting numerical information. Sorting data from highest to lowest or smallest to largest, for example, lets you quickly and easily identify trends and generate forecasts or probabilities. In this lesson you will learn to use commands on Excel's Data tab, shown in Figure 6-1, to sort, filter, and display data needed for specific purposes.

Figure 6-1

Data tab

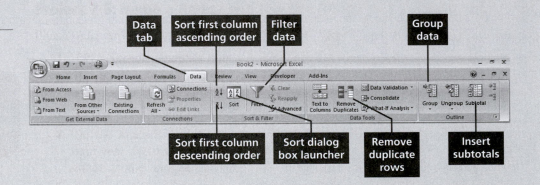

The commands on this tab enable you to sort and filter data, convert text to columns, ensure valid data entry, conduct what-if analysis, and outline data. You can also get external data into Excel by using Data commands. Use Figure 6-1 throughout this lesson as a guide to various commands.

■ Ensuring Your Data's Integrity

THE BOTTOM LINE

In many worksheets that you create, other users may enter data to get desired calculations and results. Ensuring valid data entry is an important task. Restricting the type of data that can be entered in a cell is one way to ensure data integrity. You may want to restrict data entry to a certain range of dates, limit choices by using a dropdown list, or make sure that only positive whole numbers are entered.

Restricting Cell Entries to Certain Data Types

Once you decide what validation you want to use on a worksheet, you are ready to set up the validation *criteria*, which is the test that Excel uses to filter data that is to be entered or displayed. When data entry is restricted, it is necessary for you to provide immediate feedback to instruct users about the data that is permitted in a cell. You can provide an input message when a restricted cell is selected or provide an instructive message when an invalid entry is made. Clear feedback to users assures a smooth, trouble-free data entry experience.

➔ RESTRICT CELL ENTRIES TO CERTAIN DATA TYPES

The *Employee Data* workbook is available on the companion CD-ROM.

GET READY. Before you begin these steps, be sure to launch Microsoft Excel.

1. **OPEN** *Employee Data* from the data files for this lesson.
2. Select **D3:D50**.
3. On the Data tab, in the Data Tools group, click **Data Validation**.
4. On the Settings tab of the Data Validation dialog box, select **Whole number** in the Allow box.
5. Key **15** in the Minimum box and **40** in the Maximum box. The Data Validation dialog box should look like Figure 6-2.

Figure 6-2

Restrict data entry using the Data Validation dialog box

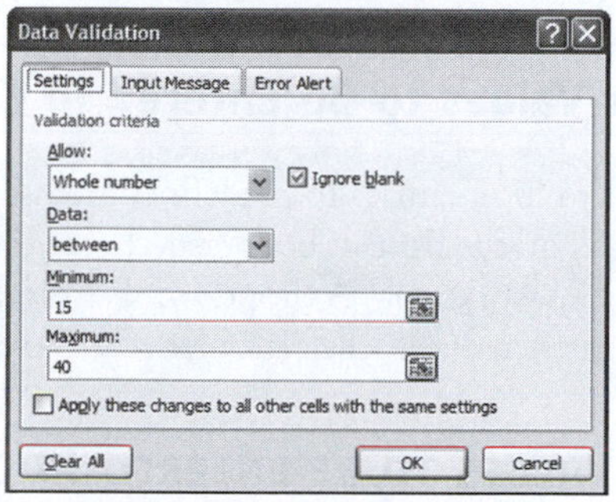

6. Click the **Error Alert** tab. Be sure the *Show error alert after invalid data is entered* checkbox is selected. Key **Invalid Entry** in the Title box.
7. Key **Only whole numbers can be entered** in the error message box as shown in Figure 6-3.

Figure 6-3

Error Alert message

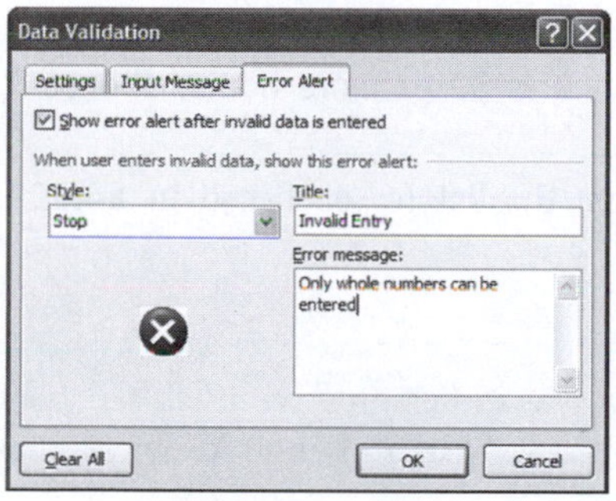

8. Click the **Input Message** tab and key **Enter a whole number between 15 and 40**. Click **OK**.
9. Select cell **D6**, key **35.5**, and press Enter. The Invalid Entry dialog box (Figure 6-4) opens, displaying the error message you created.

Figure 6-4

Invalid Entry message

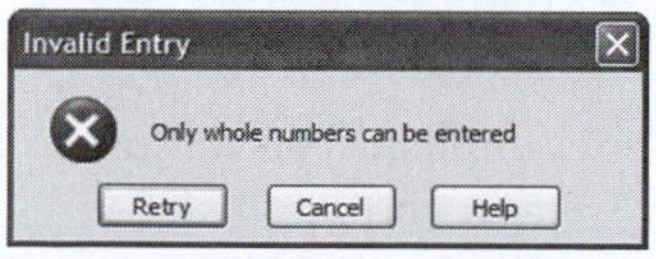

10. Click **Retry**; key **36**, and press Enter.
11. Use the following employee information to key values in row 29.

    Patricia Doyle was hired today as a receptionist. She will work 20 hours each week.
12. Create a Lesson 6 folder and **SAVE** the file as *Contoso Data*.

    PAUSE. LEAVE the workbook open to use in the next exercise.

CERTIFICATION READY?
How do you restrict cells to accept only one type of data?
1.2.1

You have just taken the first step toward ensuring the integrity of data entered in the *Contoso Data* workbook. An employee cannot inadvertently enter text or values that are outside the parameters you set in the validation criteria. By extending the range beyond the current data, when new employee data is entered, the validation criteria will be applied.

You can specify how you want Excel to respond when invalid data is entered. In the preceding exercise, you accepted the default value, Stop, in the Style box on the Error Alert tab (Figure 6-3). If you select Warning in the Style box, you will be warned that you have made an entry that is not in the defined range, but you can choose to ignore the warning and enter the invalid data.

 TAKE NOTE If you do not enter an Error Alert title or text, the Excel default message will be displayed: *The value you entered is not valid. A user has restricted values that can be entered in this cell.*

Allowing Only Specific Values to Be Entered in Cells

To make data entry easier, or to limit entries to predefined items, you can create a dropdown list of valid entries. The entries on the list can be forced-choice (i.e., yes, no) or can be compiled from cells elsewhere in the workbook. A dropdown list displays as an arrow in the cell. To enter information in the restricted cell, click the arrow and then click the entry you want.

→ ALLOW ONLY SPECIFIC VALUES TO BE ENTERED IN CELLS

USE the workbook from the previous exercise.

1. Select **E3:E29**. Click **Data Validation**.
2. On the Settings tab, in the Allow box, select **List**. The *In-cell dropdown* checkbox is selected by default.
3. In the Source box, key **Yes, No**. Click **OK**.
4. Select **E3**. Click the arrow to the right of the cell.
5. If the value in column D is 30 or more hours, choose **Yes**. If it is less than 30 hours, select **No**.
6. Continue to select from the list for each cell in **E4:E29**.
7. **SAVE** the workbook.

 CERTIFICATION READY?
How do you allow only specific values to be entered in cells?
1.2.1

Looking Ahead When you learn to create formulas in Lesson 7, you will be able to create a formula that will analyze the number of hours worked and enter Yes or No based on the analysis.

PAUSE. LEAVE the workbook open to use in the next exercise.

In the previous exercise, Contoso, Ltd. provided health insurance benefits to those employees who work 30 or more hours each week. By applying a Yes, No list validation, the office manager can quickly identify employees who are entitled to insurance benefits. You restricted the input for column E to two choices, but a list can include multiple choices. As you did in the exercise, the choices can be defined in the Source box on the Settings tab.

Use a comma to separate choices. For example, if you wanted to rate a vendor's performance, you might have three choices: Low, Average, and High.

There are a variety of other ways to limit data that can be entered into a cell range. You can base a list on criteria contained in the active worksheet, within the active workbook, or in another workbook. Enter the range of cells in the Source box on the Settings tab or key the cell range for the criteria. You can calculate what will be allowed based on the content of another cell. For example, you can create a data validation formula that enters yes or no in column E based on the value in column D. You will learn to create formulas in the next lesson.

Data validation can be based on a decimal with limits, a date within a timeframe, or a time within a timeframe. You can also specify the length of the text that can be entered within a cell.

Always test the data validation to make sure that it works correctly. Try entering both valid and invalid data in the cells to make sure that your settings work as you intend and that the expected message appears when invalid data is entered.

Removing Duplicate Cells, Rows, or Columns from a Worksheet

A *duplicate value* occurs when all values in the row are an exact match of all the values in another row. In a very large worksheet, data may be inadvertently entered more than once. This is even more likely to happen when more than one individual enters data into a worksheet. Duplicate rows or duplicate columns need to be removed before data is analyzed. When you remove duplicate values, only the values in the selection are affected. Values outside the range of cells are not altered or removed.

➔ REMOVE DUPLICATE CELLS, ROWS, OR COLUMNS FROM A WORKSHEET

USE the workbook from the previous exercise.

1. Select **A3:E29**. In the Data Tools group, click **Remove Duplicates**. The Remove Duplicates dialog box shown in Figure 6-5 opens.

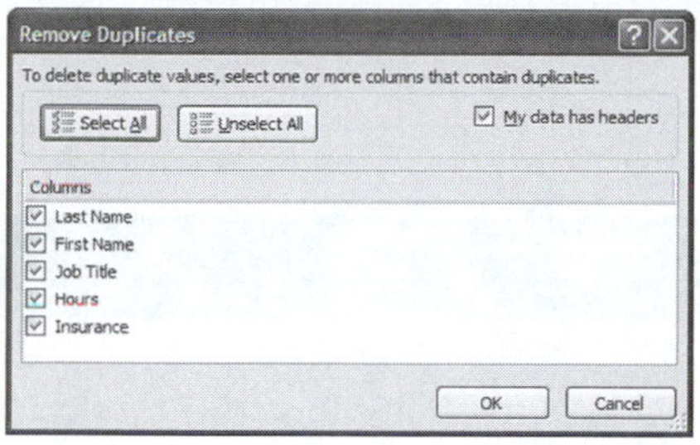

Figure 6-5

Identify duplicate values to be removed

2. Remove the check from **Hours** and **Insurance**. You want to identify duplicate employee data based on last name, first name, and job title.

3. *My data has headers* is selected by default. Click **OK**. Duplicate rows are removed and the confirmation box shown in Figure 6-6 appears informing you that two duplicate values were found and removed.

Figure 6-6

Duplicate values removed

Because you are permanently deleting data, it is a good idea to copy the original range of cells to another worksheet or workbook before removing duplicate values. You saved the file at the end of the previous exercise; therefore, you have a backup if you inadvertently remove data that you do not intend to remove.

Later in this lesson you will to learn to filter data. You can filter for unique values first to confirm that the results of removing duplicate values will return the result you want.

CERTIFICATION READY?
How do you remove duplicate rows from worksheets?
1.2.2

PAUSE. LEAVE the workbook open to use in the next exercise.

You are working with a relatively small amount of data in the practice exercises, and it would not take a great deal of time to review the data and identify duplicate entries. However, if a company has hundreds of employees, you can see the benefit of this Excel feature.

You can specify which columns should be checked for duplicates. When the Remove Duplicates dialog box (Figure 6-5) opens, all columns are selected by default. If the range of cells contains many columns and you want to select only a few columns, you can quickly clear all columns by clicking Unselect All and then selecting the columns you want to check for duplicates. In the data used for this exercise, it is possible that an employee had been entered twice, but the number of hours was different. If you accepted the default and left all columns selected, that employee would not have been removed.

Regardless of the format applied to and displayed in a cell, the cell's true value is displayed in the Formula bar. Duplicate values are determined by the value displayed in the cell and not necessarily the true value stored in the cell. This is an important distinction when dates are entered in different formats. For example, if Aug 5, 2008 is entered in one row and 08/05/2008 is entered in another row, the values are considered unique—not duplicate. It is a good idea to check formatting before removing duplicate values.

■ Sorting Data

THE BOTTOM LINE Excel's most important function is its ability to perform calculations. However, it also includes database functions that allow you to sort by text, numbers, dates, and times in one or more columns, that is, on a single criterion or on multiple criteria. Sorting data enables you to quickly visualize and understand the data better. You can rearrange and locate the data that you need to make more effective decisions.

Sorting Data on a Single Criterion

Data can be sorted on a single criterion (one column) in ascending or descending order. In *ascending order*, alphabetic data appears A to Z, numeric data appears from lowest to highest or smallest to largest, and dates appear from oldest to most recent. In *descending order*, the opposite is true—alphabetic data appears Z to A, numeric data appears from highest to lowest or largest to smallest, and dates appear from most recent to oldest.

→ SORT DATA ON A SINGLE CRITERION

USE the workbook from the previous exercise.

1. Select **D2:D27** (column heading and data in column D).
2. On the Data tab, click **Sort Smallest to Largest**.
3. A Sort Warning message prompts you to expand the data selection. With only one column selected, the data will not be sorted properly. With the *Expand the selection* option selected, click **Sort**. The data is sorted by Hours.
4. Select any cell in column A and click **Sort A to Z**. Data is sorted by last name.
5. Select **A2:E27** and click **Sort** to launch the Sort dialog box shown in Figure 6-7.

Figure 6-7

Specify sort criterion in the Sort dialog box

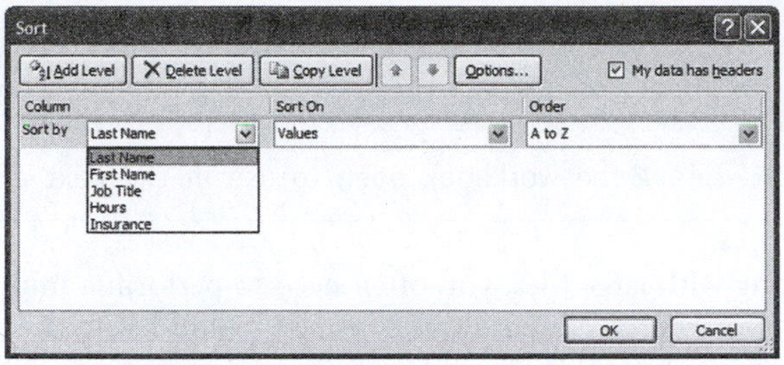

6. The first column is the default in the *Sort by* box. Click the arrow and select **Job Title**. Click **OK**.

7. Click **Sort**. The data range is automatically selected and the Sort dialog box opens. Select **Hours** in the *Sort by* box. In the Order box, select **Largest to Smallest**. Click **OK**.

   PAUSE. LEAVE the workbook open to use in the next exercise.

CERTIFICATION READY?

How do you sort data using one criterion?

4.6.1

TAKE NOTE*

Sort and Filter commands are in the Editing group on the Home tab as well as the Sort & Filter group on the Data tab.

In this exercise, you sorted data on one criterion. Unless the worksheet contains multiple merged cells, you do not need to select data to use the Sort commands. The Sort A to Z and Sort Z to A commands automatically sort the data range on the column that contains the active cell.

It is best to have column headings that have a different format than the data when you sort a data range. By default, the heading is not included in the sort operation. In your worksheet, a heading style was applied to the column headings. Therefore, Excel recognized the header row and *My data has headers* was selected by default on the Sort dialog box.

Sorting Data on Multiple Criteria

You can sort data by more than one column. For example, in the following exercise, you will sort the Contoso employee data by job title and then sort the names alphabetically within each job category. In the Sort dialog box, identify each criterion by which you want to sort.

⊕ **SORT DATA ON MULTIPLE CRITERIA**

USE the workbook from the previous exercise.

1. Select the range **A2:E27** if necessary.

2. Click **Sort** to open the dialog box.

3. Select **Job Title** in the *Sort by* box and **A to Z** in the Order box.

4. Click **Add Level** to identify the second sort criteria. A new criterion line is added to the dialog box.

5. Select **Last Name** as the second criterion. A to Z should be the default in the Order box as shown in Figure 6-8. Click **OK**.

Figure 6-8

Create a multiple-criteria sort

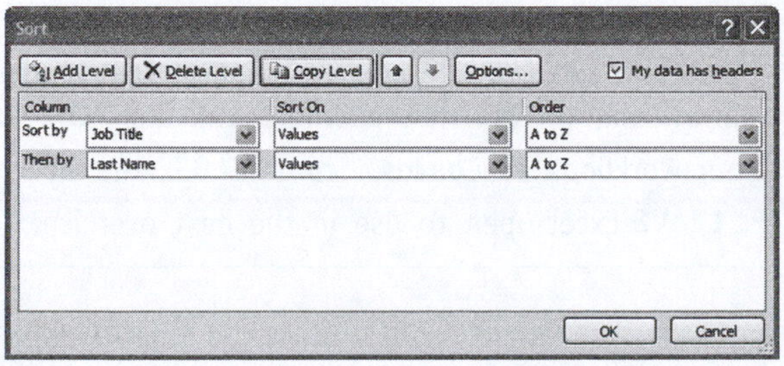

CERTIFICATION READY?

How do you sort data using multiple criteria?

4.6.1

6. **SAVE** the workbook.

TAKE NOTE ∗ You can sort by up to 64 columns. For best results, the range of cells that you sort should have column headings.

PAUSE. LEAVE the workbook open to use in the next exercise.

When working with large files, you often need to perform a multiple-criteria sort. Figure 6-8 illustrates a two-criteria sort. You can continue to add levels as well as delete or copy a criterion level. To change the sort order, select the criterion and click the up or down arrow. Entries higher in the list are sorted before entries lower in the list. To sort by case sensitivity, click the Options button to open the Sort Options dialog box shown in Figure 6-9. If Case sensitive is activated, lowercase entries will be sorted before uppercase entries.

Figure 6-9

Use case-sensitive criteria to sort data

Sorting Data by Using Conditional Formatting

If you have conditionally formatted a range of cells with an icon set, you can sort by the icon. As you learned in Lesson 3, an icon set can be used to annotate and classify data into categories. Each icon represents a range of values. For example, in a three-color arrow set, the green up arrow represents the highest values, the yellow sideways arrow represents the middle values, and the red down arrow represents the lower values.

⊙ SORT DATA BY USING CONDITIONAL FORMATTING

USE the workbook from the previous exercise.

1. On the Home tab, click **Find & Select** and click **Conditional Formatting**. A message is returned that no cells in the worksheet contain conditional formatting. Click **OK** to close the dialog box.
2. Select **D3:D27**. Click **Conditional Formatting** and then click **Icon Sets**.
3. Click **3 Arrows (Colored)**. Each value in the column now has an arrow that represents whether the value falls within the high, middle, or low range.
4. Select **A3:E27**. On the Home tab, click **Sort & Filter** and then click **Custom Sort**.
5. Select **Hours** in the *Sort by* box. Select **Cell Icon** under Sort On. Click the green arrow under Order.

TROUBLESHOOTING This sort will result in the green arrows (highest values) on top. However, the medium and low range values are not sorted. You need to implement a multiple-criteria sort.

CERTIFICATION READY?
How do you sort data by using conditional formatting?
4.6.3

6. Select **Hours** in the *Then by* box. Select **Cell Icon** under Sort On and accept the yellow arrow and **On top** in the Order field. Click **OK**. Data is sorted by icon set.
7. **SAVE** your workbook as *Contoso Icons*. **CLOSE** the workbook.

PAUSE. LEAVE Excel open to use in the next exercise.

The first time you perform a sort, you must select the entire range of cells, including the column header row. When you want to sort the data using different criteria, select any cell within the data range and the entire range will be selected for the sort. You need to select the data only if you want to use a different range for a sort.

Sorting Data by Using Cell Attributes

If you have formatted a range of cells by cell color or by font color, you can create a custom sort to sort by colors. To sort by cell attribute, use the Sort dialog box to select the order in which you want the colors sorted.

SORT DATA BY USING CELL ATTRIBUTES

CD

The *MA Assignments* workbook is available on the companion CD-ROM.

1. **OPEN** ***MA Assignments*** from the data files for this lesson.
2. Select the data range (including the column headings). On the Data tab, click **Sort**.
3. On the Sort dialog box, accept **Last Name** in the *Sort by* box. Under Sort On, select **Cell Color**.
4. Under Order, select **Pink** and **On Top**.
5. Click **Add Level** and select **Last Name** in the *Sort by* box. Under Sort On, select **Cell Color**. Select **Yellow** and **On Top**.
6. Add a level for Green and then add a level for Blue. You should have a criterion for each color as illustrated in Figure 6-10. Click **OK**.

Figure 6-10

Multiple cell attribute sort

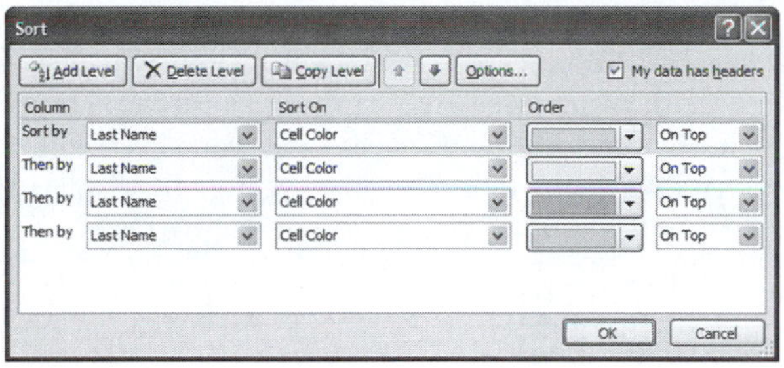

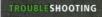

CERTIFICATION READY?
How do you sort data using cell attributes?
4.6.4

7. **SAVE** the workbook in your Lesson 6 folder as ***MA Assignments***.

PAUSE. LEAVE the workbook open to use in the next exercise.

TROUBLESHOOTING

When a worksheet contains unevenly sized merged cells, if you do not select data before you open the Sort dialog box, you will receive an error message that tells you a sort requires merged cells to be identically sized. The *MA Assignments* worksheet contained two rows with merged cells. Therefore, you had to select the data range (including column labels) the first time you sorted the worksheet. If you performed additional sorts, Excel would remember the data range and you would not need to select it again.

At Contoso, Ltd., each medical assistant is assigned to work with a specific physician. To assist with scheduling, the office manager created the *MA Assignments* worksheet with the physician/medical assistant assignments color coded. The color coding is a reminder that the two must be scheduled for the same days and hours when the weekly schedule is created. The color coding enabled you to sort the data so that the physician and his or her medical assistant were grouped.

Most sort operations are by columns, but you can custom sort by rows. Create a custom sort by clicking Options on the Sort dialog box. You can then choose *Sort left to right* under Orientation (see Figure 6-9).

Sort criteria are saved with the workbook so that you can reapply the sort each time the workbook is opened. Table 6-1 summarizes Excel's default ascending sort orders. The order is reversed for a descending sort.

Table 6-1

Default ascending sort order

VALUE	ASCENDING SORT ORDER
Numbers	Smallest negative number to largest positive number
Dates	Earliest date to most recent date
Text	Alphanumeric data is sorted left to right, character by character. For example, A5, A501, A51 are correctly sorted.
	Numbers and symbols are sorted before text.
	If the Case sensitive option is active, lowercase text is sorted before uppercase text.
Logical values	False is placed before true.
Blank cells	In both ascending and descending sorts, blank cells are placed last.

■ Filtering Data

THE BOTTOM LINE

Worksheets can hold as much data as you need, but you may not want to work with all of the data at the same time. You can temporarily isolate specific data in a worksheet by placing a restriction, called a *filter*, on the worksheet. Filtering data enables you to focus on the data pertinent to a particular analysis by displaying only the rows that meet specified criteria and hiding rows you do not want to see.

Using AutoFilter

See *Setting Up Data in a Table Format* later in this lesson.

AutoFilter is a built-in set of filtering capabilities. Using AutoFilter to isolate data is a quick and easy way to find and work with a subset of data in a specified range of cells or table columns. You can use AutoFilter to create three types of filters: list value, format, or criteria. Each is mutually exclusive. For example, you can filter by list value or format, but not both.

⊕ USE AUTOFILTER

USE the workbook from the previous exercise.

1. Select **A3:E28**. Click **Filter** on the Data tab in the Sort & Filter group. A down arrow is added to each column heading.
2. Click the arrow in the **Job Title** column. The AutoFilter menu shown in Figure 6-11 is displayed.

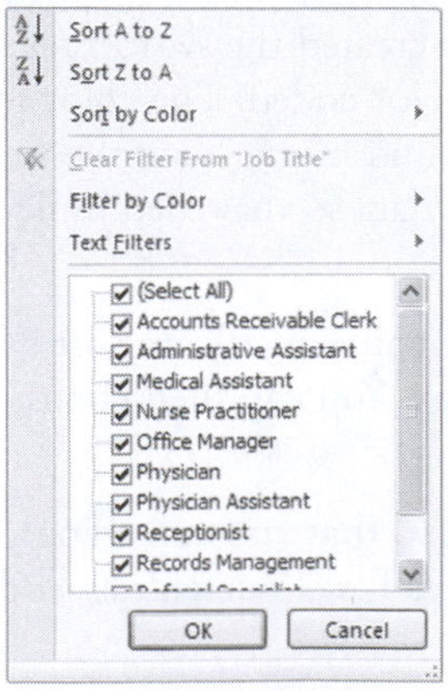

Figure 6-11

Select text values to filter

A↓	Sort A to Z
Z↓	Sort Z to A
	Sort by Color ▸
⫧	Clear Filter From "Job Title"
	Filter by Color ▸
	Text Filters ▸
	☑ (Select All)
	☑ Accounts Receivable Clerk
	☑ Administrative Assistant
	☑ Medical Assistant
	☑ Nurse Practitioner
	☑ Office Manager
	☑ Physician
	☑ Physician Assistant
	☑ Receptionist
	☑ Records Management
	OK Cancel

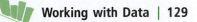

TAKE NOTE * To make the AutoFilter menu wider or longer, click and drag the grip handle at the bottom.

3. Currently the data is not filtered, so all job titles are selected. Click **Select All** to deselect all titles.

4. Click **Accounts Receivable Clerk** and **Receptionist**. Click **OK**. Data for six employees is displayed. All other employees are filtered out.

   PAUSE. LEAVE the workbook open with the filtered data displayed to use in the next exercise.

CERTIFICATION READY?
How do you use AutoFilter to isolate specific data?
4.6.2

In this exercise, you used two text filters to display only the receptionists and accounts receivables clerks. This information is especially useful when the office manager is creating a work schedule. This feature allows him to isolate relevant data quickly.

Creating a Custom AutoFilter

You can create a custom AutoFilter to further filter data by two comparison operators. A *comparison operator* is a sign that is used in criteria to compare two values. For example, you might create a filter to identify values *greater than* 50 but *less than* 100. Greater than and less than are comparison operators. Such a filter would display values from 51 to 99.

➔ **CREATE A CUSTOM AUTOFILTER**

USE the workbook from the previous exercise.

1. With the filtered list displayed, click the arrow in column D. Point to **Number Filters**. As shown in Figure 6-12, the menu expands to allow you to customize the filter.

Figure 6-12

Numeric comparison criteria

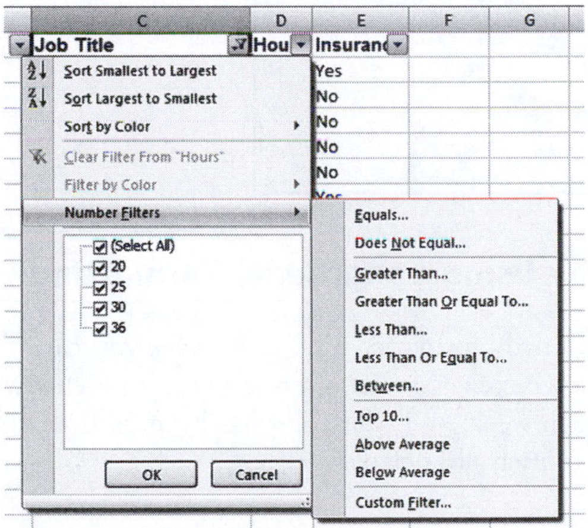

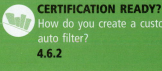

2. Select **Less Than** on the expanded menu and key **30** in the amount box. Click **OK**. The filtered list is reduced to four employees.

3. Click **Filter** to display all data. Select the data range and click **Filter**.

4. Click the arrow in column D. Point to **Number Filters** and select **Greater Than**. Key **15** and press ⌈Tab⌉ twice.

5. Click the arrow and select **is less than** as the second comparison operator and press ⌈Tab⌉. Key **30** and click **OK**. The list should be filtered to six employees.

6. Click **Filter** to display all data.

7. **SAVE** and **CLOSE** the workbook.

   PAUSE. LEAVE Excel open to use in the next exercise.

CERTIFICATION READY?
How do you create a custom auto filter?
4.6.2

Comparison operators are used to create a formula that Excel uses to filter numeric data. The operators are identified in Table 6-2.

Table 6-2

Comparison operators

Operator	Meaning
=	Equal to
>	Greater than
<	Less than
>=	Greater than or equal to
<=	Less than or equal to
<>	Not equal to

Equal to and *Less than* are options for creating custom text filters. Text Filter options also allow you to filter text that begins with a specific letter (Begins With option) or text that has a specific letter anywhere in the text (Contains option).

As illustrated in Figure 6-13, you can design a two-criterion custom filter that selects data that contains both criteria (*And* option) or selects data that contains one or the other of the criteria (*Or* option). If you select *Or*, less data will be filtered out.

Figure 6-13

Two-criterion custom filter

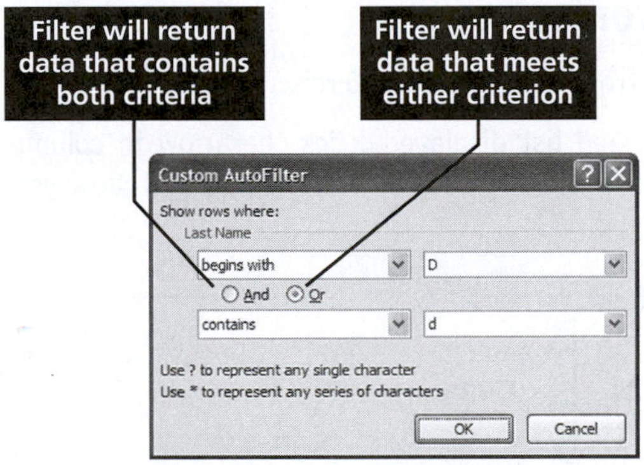

Filtering Data by Using Conditional Formatting

If you have conditionally formatted a range of cells, you can filter the data by that format. In the following exercise, icon sets are used to identify the number of hours employees work each week, and font color has been used to identify the medical assistant assigned to each physician.

FILTER DATA BY USING CONDITIONAL FORMATTING

OPEN ***Conditional Format*** from the data files for this lesson.

1. Select **A3:E32**. On the Data tab, click **Filter**.
2. Click the arrow in column D. Point to **Filter by Color**. Click the **green flag** under *Filter by Cell Icon*. Data formatted with a green flag (highest number of work hours) is displayed.
3. Click the filter arrow in column D. Point to **Filter by Color**. Click the **red flag** under *Filter by Cell Icon*. The data formatted by a green flag is replaced by data formatted with a red flag (lowest number of work hours).
4. Click **Filter** to remove the filter arrows.

PAUSE. LEAVE the workbook open to use in the next exercise.

CD

The ***Conditional Format*** workbook is available on the companion CD-ROM.

As you learned in Lesson 3, a conditional format is a visual guide that helps you quickly understand variation in a worksheet's data. By using conditional formatting as a filter, you can easily highlight interesting cells or ranges in order to emphasize the values based on one or more criteria.

CERTIFICATION READY?
How do you filter data by using conditional formatting?
4.6.3

Filtering Data by Using Cell Attributes

If you have formatted a range of cells with fill color or font color, you can filter on those attributes. It is not necessary to select the data range to filter using cell attributes. Excel will search for any cell that contains either background or font color.

→ FILTER DATA BY USING CELL ATTRIBUTES

USE the workbook from the previous exercise.

1. Select any cell in the data range and click Filter.
2. Click the arrow next to the title and point to **Filter by Color**. Click More Font Colors. A dialog box opens that displays the font colors used in the worksheet.
3. As in Figure 6-14, the first color appears in the *Selected* field. Click OK. The heading rows are displayed. These are the colors in the Oriel theme that was applied to this worksheet.

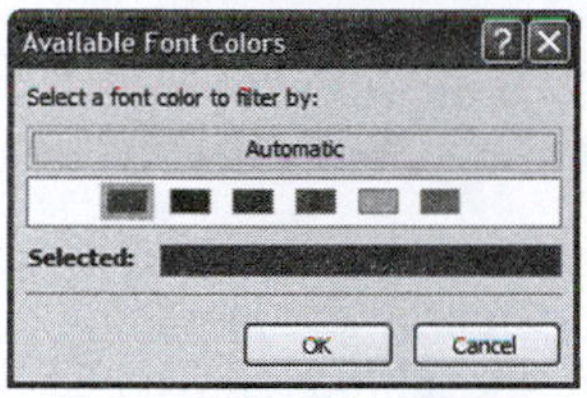

Figure 6-14

Colors used in worksheet displayed in dialog box

4. Click the **filter** arrow at the top of the worksheet and click Clear Filter From "(Column A)".
5. Click the **filter** arrow and point to **Filter by Color**. Select Purple. Data for Dr. Blythe (new physician) and his two medical assistants is displayed.
6. Click Filter to clear the filter arrows.
7. **CLOSE** the file. You have not made changes to the data, so it is not necessary to save the file.

   PAUSE. LEAVE Excel open to use in the next exercise.

CERTIFICATION READY?
How do you filter data using cell attributes?
4.6.4

In the preceding exercises, you used Excel's Sort and Filter features to group data using a variety of criteria. Both Sort and Filter allow you to select and analyze specific data. The two functions have a great deal in common. In both instances, you can focus on data that meets specific criteria. Unrelated data is displayed when you sort; it is hidden when you use the filter command.

■ Subtotaling Data

THE BOTTOM LINE

Excel provides a number of features that enable you to organize large groups of data into more manageable groups. Data in a list can be summarized by inserting a subtotal. Before you can subtotal, however, you must first sort the list by the field on which you want the list subtotaled.

Grouping and Ungrouping Data for Subtotaling

If you have a list of data that you want to group and summarize, you can create an outline. *Grouping* refers to organizing data so that it can be viewed as a collapsible and expandable outline. To group data, each column must have a label in the first row and the column must contain similar facts. The data must be sorted by the column or columns for that group.

GROUP AND UNGROUP DATA FOR SUBTOTALING

OPEN *Salary* from the data files for this lesson.

1. Select any cell in the data. Click **Sort** on the Data tab.
2. On the Sort dialog box, sort first by Job Category in ascending order.
3. Add a sort level, sort by Job Title in ascending order, and click **OK**.
4. Select row **14**, press Ctrl, and select row **27**. On the Home tab, click the **Insert** arrow and click **Insert Sheet Rows**. This step inserts rows to separate the job categories.
5. In C14, key **Subtotal**. Select **F14** and click **Sum**. The values above F14 are selected. Press Enter and the category is subtotaled.
6. In C28, key **Subtotal**. Select **F28** and click **Sum**. Press Enter.
7. In C36, key **Subtotal**. Select **F36** and click **Sum**. Press Enter.
8. In C37, key **Grand Total**. Select **F37** and click **Sum**. The three subtotals are selected. Press Enter.
9. Select a cell in the data range. On the Data tab, click the arrow below **Group**, and then click **Auto Outline**. A three-level outline is created.

PAUSE. LEAVE the workbook open to use in the next exercise.

CERTIFICATION READY?
How do you group and ungroup data?
4.5.1

In the preceding exercises, you manually grouped and subtotaled salary data for Contoso, Ltd. You will use Excel's automatic subtotal feature in the next exercise.

To outline data by rows, you must have summary rows that contain formulas that reference cells in each of the detail rows for that group. In the preceding exercise, your outline contained three levels: the grand total level, the subtotals level, and the detail rows level. You can create an outline of up to eight levels.

Each inner level displays detail data for the preceding outer level. Inner levels are represented by a higher number in the **outline symbols**, which are symbols that you use to change the view of an outlined worksheet. You can show or hide detailed data by pressing the plus sign, minus sign, and the numbers 1, 2, or 3 that indicate the outline level.

Subtotaling Data in a List

You can automatically calculate subtotals and grand totals for a column by using the Subtotal command in the Outline group on the Data tab. You can display more than one type of summary function for each column. The Subtotal command outlines the list so that you can display and hide the detail rows for each subtotal.

SUBTOTAL DATA IN A LIST

USE the worksheet from the previous exercise.

1. In the Outline group on the Data tab, click the **Ungroup** arrow and then click **Clear Outline.**
2. Select rows 14, 28, 36, and 37 and delete all selected rows.
3. Select the data range. Include the column labels in the selection.
4. Click **Subtotal** in the Outline group on the Data tab. The Subtotal dialog box is displayed.
5. Select **Job Category** in the *At each change in* box.
6. Under *Add subtotal to*, click **Salary**. Click **OK** to accept the remaining defaults. Figure 6-15 illustrates the appropriate selections. Subtotals are inserted for each of the three job categories and a grand total is calculated at the bottom of the list.

Figure 6-15

Subtotal a data range.

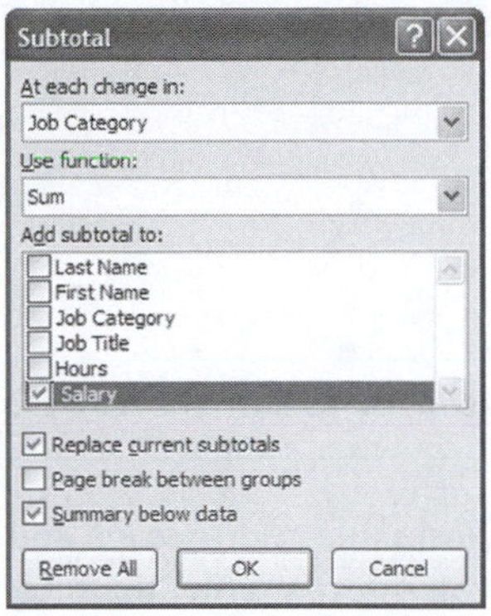

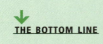

CERTIFICATION READY?

How do you insert subtotals in a list?

4.5.2

TAKE NOTE*

If the workbook is set to automatically calculate formulas, the Subtotal command recalculates subtotal values automatically as you edit the detail data.

7. **SAVE** the workbook as *Salaries*.

CLOSE the workbook but **LEAVE** Excel open for the next exercise.

When the data you want to subtotal can be grouped according to a category, such as Job Category in this exercise, the Subtotal command is the best choice. However, when data is not categorized, you can manually insert subtotals as you did in the previous exercise.

You can subtotal groups within categories. For example, you could subtotal the salaries for the accounts receivable clerks or the records management employees as well as find a total for the entire office staff.

■ Setting Up Data in a Table Format

THE BOTTOM LINE

When you create a table in Excel, you can manage and analyze data in the table independently of data outside the table. For example, you can filter table columns, add a row for totals, apply table formatting, and publish a table to a server that is running Microsoft SharePoint Services 3.0.

Formatting a Table with a Quick Style

When you create a table, Table Tools become available, and a Design tab appears on the Ribbon. You can use the tools on the Design tab to customize or edit the table. Four table styles are displayed in the Table Styles group. Click the arrows to the right of the styles to display additional styles.

→ **FORMAT A TABLE WITH A QUICK STYLE**

OPEN *Salary* from the data files for this lesson.

CD

The *Salary* workbook is available on the companion CD-ROM.

1. Select any cell in the data. Click **Sort** on the Data tab.
2. On the Sort dialog box, sort first by Job Category in ascending order.
3. Add a sort level and sort by Job Title in ascending order. Click **OK**.
4. On the Home tab, click **Format as Table** in the Styles Group.
5. Click **Table Style Medium 5** from the format gallery. The Format as Table dialog box opens.
6. Click the arrow in *Where is the data for your table?* The dialog box collapses.
7. Select **A27:F32** as shown in Figure 6-16 and press [Enter]. Your table does not have headers, so click **OK**. The banded rows style format is applied and filtering column headers are inserted.

CERTIFICATION READY?

How do you apply Quick Styles to tables?

2.4.1

Figure 6-16

Identify data to include in table

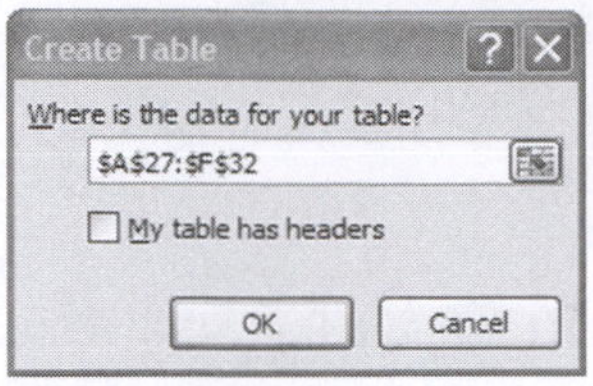

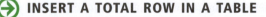

TAKE NOTE*

Because the data selected for the table did not have headers, default names (i.e., Column1) are displayed above the table.

PAUSE. LEAVE the workbook open to use in the next exercise.

You can turn a range of cells into an Excel table and manage and analyze a group of related data independently. By default, when you insert a table, the table has filtering enabled in the header row so that you can filter or sort your table quickly. As you will see in the next exercise, you can add a Totals row that provides a dropdown list of functions for each cell in the total row. You can insert more than one table in the same worksheet.

Inserting a Total Row in a Table

You could insert a new row at the end of the table, but it is faster to total the data in an Excel table by using the Total Row command in the Table Styles Options group on the Design tab.

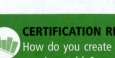

INSERT A TOTAL ROW IN A TABLE

ANOTHER WAY

You can also right-click on a table row or column to open the shortcut menu. Point to Insert and options to insert rows or columns appear.

USE the workbook from the previous exercise.

1. Select a cell in the table and click **Total Row** in the Table Style Options on the Design tab. A row is inserted below the table and the salaries in column F of the table are totaled.
2. Click a blank cell to deselect the table. Adjust the column width to display the total amount if necessary.

PAUSE. LEAVE the workbook open to use in the next exercise.

If you press Tab in the last cell of the last row of the table, a blank row will be added at the end of the table, which would allow you to add new data to the table. Once a Totals row has been added to the table, however, pressing Tab will not add a new row.

CERTIFICATION READY?
How do you create a total row in a table?
2.4.2

Adding and Removing Rows or Columns in a Table

After you create a table in your worksheet, you can easily add rows or columns. You can add adjacent rows to the table by using the mouse to drag the resize handle down to select rows or drag to the right to select columns. You can enter text or values in an adjacent row or column that you want to include in the table. You can add a blank row at the end of the table, or insert table rows or columns anywhere in the table.

ADD AND REMOVE ROWS OR COLUMNS IN A TABLE

USE the workbook from the previous exercise.

1. On the Design tab, in the Properties group, click **Resize Table**.
2. Collapse the Resize Table dialog box, and select **A27:F35**. Press **Enter**. Click **OK**. The physician assistant data is moved above the total line and the total is recalculated.
3. Select **C28**. On the Home tab, click the **Delete** arrow and click **Delete Table Columns**. Column C is deleted.
4. Click the **Column1** heading and key **Last Name**. Press **Tab**. Key **First Name** and press **Tab**. Key **Job Title** and press **Tab**.

5. Key **Hours** in column 5. Press [Tab]. Click **Yes** to continue when the Invalid Entry dialog box opens. Key **Salary** in the column 6 heading.

6. Adjust the column E width to display the total salary amount.

7. In the Properties group on the Design tab, select the text in the Table Name box and key **Schedule**. This table represents the individuals with whom patients schedule appointments.

8. **SAVE** the file as *Table* and then **CLOSE** the file.

   CLOSE Excel.

CERTIFICATION READY?
How do you add and remove rows and columns in a table?
2.4.3

When you resize a table, the table headers must remain in the same row, and the revised table range must overlap the original table range. In the exercise, you added a row from below to the table, but you would not be able to add a row from above the table. You can click the resizing handle in the lower-right corner of the table and drag it to the right to add a column.

When you finish working with table, you can click Convert to Range in the Tools group and convert the table to a data range. The formatting, column headers, and table total remain.

In a previous exercise, you restricted column E to whole numbers. When you keyed the column heading, the Invalid Entry dialog box opened, allowing you to override the data restriction. The text was accepted when you clicked Yes to continue.

SUMMARY SKILL MATRIX

IN THIS LESSON YOU LEARNED	MATRIX SKILL	SKILL NUMBER
To ensure your data's integrity		
To restrict the type of data that can be entered into specific cells	Restrict data using data validation	1.2.1
To allow only specific values to be entered in cells	Restrict data using data validation	1.2.1
To remove duplicate rows of data from a worksheet	Remove duplicate rows from spreadsheets	1.2.2
To sort data		
To sort data on a single criterion and on multiple criteria	Sort data using single or multiple criteria	4.6.1
To sort data by using conditional formatting icon sets	Filter and sort data by using conditional formatting	4.6.3
To sort data using cell and font color	Filter and sort data using cell attributes	4.6.4
To filter data		
To use AutoFilter to isolate specific data	Filter data using AutoFilter	4.6.2
To use icon sets to isolate specific data	Filter and sort data by using conditional formatting	4.6.3
To filter data by using cell and font color	Filter and sort data using cell attributes	4.6.4
To subtotal data		
To group and ungroup data to insert subtotals	Group and ungroup data	4.5.1
To automatically total rows of related data by inserting subtotals	Subtotal data	4.5.2
To set up data in a table format		
To apply a Quick Style to format a table	Apply Quick Styles to tables	2.4.1
To increase the size of an inserted table by inserting row(s) below the table	Add rows to tables	2.4.2
To insert blank rows in a table and delete rows from a table	Insert and delete rows and columns in tables	2.4.3

✴ Workplace Ready

Using a Template with Built-in Formulas

Microsoft Excel provides numerous templates that can be downloaded and used to start new worksheets. Templates are time-saving tools that eliminate the need for you to spend time setting up the structure of a worksheet and applying complex formatting and formulas. All you need to do is enter the raw data, because the template has built-in formatting and formulas.

When you click the Microsoft Office Button and click New, the New Workbook window opens, as shown in the following figure. Recently used templates are shown in the window's middle pane. The Templates pane lists categories of templates that can be downloaded from Microsoft Office Online. Although some are personal-use templates, the majority are business templates. You can browse templates by category and select and download a template of your choice. You can then use it as the basis for a new workbook

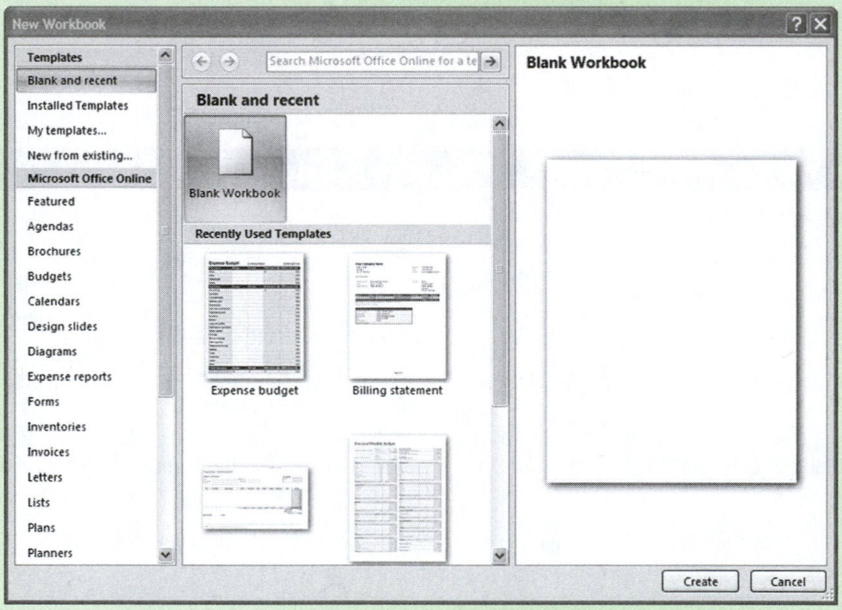

The Expense Budget template can be downloaded from Microsoft Office Online. Download the *Expense Budget* file and explore this template that could be used in a business setting. This template, shown in the following figure, makes it easy for you to perform calculations because formulas and other worksheet features are already set up for you.

Placeholders mark cells in which to enter your company's name and the date. Categories of expenses are identified in column A. You can insert cells and rows if necessary. The existing cells and rows can be deleted or moved and the labels can be edited to reflect the line items in your company's budget.

You can key the data for your company's budget amounts and actual expenditures in columns B and C. The data cells in columns D and E contain formulas to calculate the difference between budget and actual expenditures as values and percentages. When you enter data, both calculations are completed automatically. When you scroll to the bottom of the worksheet, you see that formulas have been created to total each column.

You can easily see that using this template to create a company expense budget would take far less time than creating the worksheet from scratch. With a template you just enter the data—Excel provides the formulas and performs all the calculations.

Knowledge Assessment

Fill in the Blank

Complete the following sentences by writing the correct word or words in the blanks provided.

1. The process of organizing data so that it can be viewed as a collapsible and expandable outline is _____.

2. Values in the row that are an exact match of all the values in another row are referred to as _____.

3. Excel uses _____ rules to determine which worksheet rows to display.

4. In _____, sorted values appear Z to A or highest to lowest.

5. The _____ are conditions specified to limit which records to include in the result of a sort or filter.

6. A sign used in criteria to compare two values is a(n) _____.

7. Using a(n) _____ allows you to apply a built-in set of filtering capabilities.

8. In _____ sort order, values appear A to Z or smallest to largest.

9. You can use outline _____ to change the view of an outlined worksheet.

10. You can quickly rearrange the data sequence when you use Excel's _____ feature.

True / False

Circle T if the statement is true or F if the statement is false.

T F **1.** You can sort a data range using conditional formatting.

T F **2.** When numbers are sorted in ascending order, the largest number is on top.

T F **3.** You can create a custom AutoFilter that will isolate data that falls between a high and low number.

T F **4.** You can filter data to display all cells with a specific background color and cells that contain specific text.

T F **5.** In a case-sensitive sort, lowercase letters will be sorted before uppercase letters.

T F **6.** To temporarily isolate a specific list of rows in a worksheet containing data, use the Sort feature.

T F **7.** The Data Validation command enables you to locate and remove duplicate values in a worksheet.

T F **8.** To outline data, the data must have a blank line that includes a formula that references all the cells in the detail rows for that group.

T F **9.** When a table is inserted in a worksheet, the Design tab is added to the Ribbon and Table tools are available.

T F **10.** Data validation enables you to allow only specific values to be entered in cells.

■ Competency Assessment

Project 6-1: Analyze Semiannual Sales Data

Litware, Inc. has divided its sales representatives into two teams that are in competition for sales rewards. The sales report worksheet has been color coded to identify team members.

GET READY. Launch Excel if it is not already running.

CD

The *Semiannual Sales* workbook is available on the companion CD-ROM.

1. **OPEN** *Semiannual Sales* from the data files for Lesson 6.

2. Click the **Data** tab to make it active.

3. Select **A4:H12**. The data range should include the column headings but not the monthly totals.

4. Click **Sort** in the Sort & Filter group. *My data has headers* should be selected by default. If not, select it.

5. On the Sort dialog box, select **Total** (or Column H) in the *Sort by* field. In the Sort On field, select **Values**. Select **Largest to Smallest** (descending) in the Order field. Click **OK**. The sales representative with the highest total sales is listed first. The rest are listed in descending order.

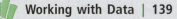

6. With the data still selected, click **Sort**. Sort by Sales Representative. Sort on Font Color. In the Order fields, select **Red** and **On Top**. Click **OK**. The red team is listed first. Within the red team, representatives are listed in descending order in terms of sales.

7. **SAVE** the workbook as *Semiannual Sales 6-1*. **CLOSE** the file.

   LEAVE Excel open for the next project.

Project 6-2: Ensuring Data Integrity

Create a workbook that you will use to collect survey responses from a random sample of students at your college. Your survey will consist of ten questions, and you will survey ten students.

1. Click the **Microsoft Office Button** and open a new blank workbook.

2. Select **A2**, key **Survey Questions**, and press [Tab].

3. Key **Student 1** and press [Tab]. Key **Student 2** and press [Tab].

4. Select **B2:C2**. Use the fill handle to complete the series to Student 10 (Cell K2).

5. Select **A3** and key **In what year did you begin college?** Press [Enter].

6. Key **Have you met with an advisor this year?** Press [Enter].

7. Key **How many hours per week do you study?** Press [Enter].

8. Select **B3:K3**. On the Data tab, click **Data Validation**.

9. On the Settings tab, in the Allow box, select **Whole number**. In the Data box, select **less than or equal to**. In the Maximum field, enter the current year in 20XX format.

10. Click the **Input Message** tab. In the *Input message* box, key **Enter year in 20XX format**. Click **OK**. The input message should be displayed when you close the dialog box.

11. Select **B4:K4**. Click **Data Validation**.

12. Click the **Settings** tab if necessary. In the Allow box, select **List**. In the Source box, key **Yes, No**. Click **OK**. A dropdown arrow should be displayed next to the active cell.

13. Resize the columns if necessary.

14. **SAVE** the workbook as *Survey 6-2* and then **CLOSE** the file.

    LEAVE Excel open for the next project.

■ Proficiency Assessment

Project 6-3: Filter Data on Multiple Criteria

The Litware sales manager needs to filter the sales report data in a variety of ways that he can use in team meetings to acknowledge those who have achieved sales objectives and to motivate the teams. Create the filters for the sales manager.

The *Sales Teams* workbook is available on the companion CD-ROM.

1. **OPEN** *Sales Teams* from the data files for this lesson.

2. Select **A4:H12**. Click **Filter**. Click the arrow in the Total column.

3. Click **Number Filters** and then click **Greater Than**. Key **100,000** on the dialog box. Click **OK**. Four sales representatives are displayed.

4. Click **Filter** to display all data. Select any cell that contains data and create a filter to display the Red Team's statistics. (Hint: Because entire rows are color coded, you do not have to select the data. Data does not have to be sorted when you filter for color.)

5. **SAVE** the workbook as *Red Team*.

6. Click **Filter** to display all data. Click **Filter** again to display the filter arrows.

7. Click a filter arrow and display the Blue Team's statistics.

8. **SAVE** the workbook as *Blue Team*. **CLOSE** the workbook.

   LEAVE Excel open for the next project.

Project 6-4: Sort and Filter Using Conditional Formatting

Each year *Fortune Magazine* surveys employees and publishes a list of the ten best employers based on employee ranking. The Top Ten worksheet contains additional information about the top ten companies in terms of their size (number of employees), percentage of minorities, and percentage of women.

1. **OPEN** *Top Ten* from the data files for this lesson.

2. Select the data range, including the column headings. Click **Sort** on the Data tab.

3. Sort the data by % Minorities. Click **Cell Icon** in the Sort On field.

4. Under Order, place the green flagged data (highest) on top. Click **OK**. Because you sorted by one criterion, the highest is on top, but the Red and Yellow are intermixed.

5. Click **Sort** to add a second criterion to sort on yellow flags, which represent the middle range.

6. With the data range selected, click **Filter**. Arrows are added to the column headings.

7. Click the filter arrow in the % Women column. Choose to filter by color.

8. Select the green arrow. Women comprise more than 60 percent of the workforce in two of the top ten companies.

9. **SAVE** the workbook as *Top Ten 6-4*. **CLOSE** the workbook.

   LEAVE Excel open for the next project.

■ Mastery Assessment

Project 6-5: Subtotal Data

As a motivational tool, Litware's sales manager wants to group the teams and enter a subtotal as well as the grand total.

1. **OPEN** *Semiannual Sales* from the data files for this lesson.

2. Select the data range only and sort by font color with the Blue Team on top.

3. Clear contents and formatting from the Totals row.

4. Select the Blue Team and group the rows. Group the Red Team.

5. Insert a column to the left of column A. Merge and center the title and subtitle to include the new column.

6. Key **Team** in A4. Select **B4:B14**.

7. Click the **Format Painter** and format column A. In column A, key **Red** or **Blue** to identify the salesperson's team.

8. Create team subtotals in the Total column.

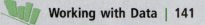

9. Collapse the outline to Level 2 so that only the team totals and grand total are displayed.

10. **SAVE** the workbook as *Teams 6-5*, and then **CLOSE** the file.

   LEAVE Excel open for the next project.

Project 6-6: Create a Table in a Worksheet

The Records Management Director at Contoso has asked you to create a table within the Salary workbook.

The *Salary* workbook is available on the companion CD-ROM.

1. **OPEN** *Salary* from the data files for this lesson.

2. Sort the data by Job Category and then by Job Title.

3. Click **Format as Table** on the Home tab. Select **Table Style Light 10** on the Quick Styles list.

4. In the Format As Table dialog box, select the records management personnel data as the data for the table.

5. Apply Table Style 10.

6. Add a Total Row to the table.

7. Rename the table column labels to match those in the worksheet (Last Name, First Name, Job Category, Job Title, Hours, and Salary).

8. **SAVE** the workbook as *Records Management Table*. **CLOSE** the workbook.

   LEAVE Excel open for the next project.

INTERNET READY

In this lesson, you worked with salary data for a medical facility. The salary figures were based on average earnings for employees in medical care facilities in the Midwest. Go online and research salary data for your chosen profession. Identify three positions in which you might like to work. Conduct research into the average salary in those professions in three different cities in different parts of the country. For example, you might find earnings information for accountants in New York City; St. Louis, Missouri; and Seattle, Washington.

Create a worksheet to report your research findings. Format all data appropriately. **SAVE** your worksheet as *Salary Research*. **CLOSE** Excel.

7 Using Basic Formulas and Functions

LESSON SKILL MATRIX

Skills	Matrix Skill	Skill Number
Building Basic Formulas	Create formulas that use absolute and relative cell references	3.1.1
Using Cell References in Formulas		
Using Relative Cell References in a Formula	Create formulas that use absolute and relative cell references	3.1.1
Using Absolute Cell References in a Formula	Create formulas that use absolute and relative cell references	3.1.1
Referring to Data in Another Worksheet	Create formulas that reference data from other worksheets or workbooks	3.1.2
Referring to Data in Another Workbook	Create formulas that reference data from other worksheets or workbooks	3.1.2
Using Cell Ranges in Formulas	Manage named ranges	3.1.3
Creating a Formula that Operates on a Named Range	Use named ranges in formulas	3.1.4
Summarizing Data with Functions	Use SUM, COUNT, COUNTA, AVERAGE, MIN, and MAX	3.2.1
Using Formulas to Create Subtotals	Create and modify list ranges	3.3.1
Controlling the Appearance of Formulas	Display and print formulas	3.8

Most people agree that it is vitally important for a business to have a realistic budget. It is equally important for an individual to have a personal budget—a plan for managing income and expenses.

Katie Jordan has been managing, or more accurately, spending her money without a formal budget. In fact, the only budget she prepared was one she scribbled on the back of her résumé immediately after being offered what she considered to be her dream job. Since that time, Katie has changed jobs several times. Now, she wants to purchase a condominium, and she

KEY TERMS
absolute cell reference
constant
external reference
formula
function
mathematical operator
mixed reference
name
operand
reference
relative cell reference
scope

142

realizes that she needs to create a comprehensive personal budget that will enable her to real-
ize her goal of home ownership.

Katie uses Excel in her job as a marketing analyst at Tailspin Toys. She plans to use Excel to
track her expenditures and to develop a realistic budget. She has conducted online research
and developed a preliminary budget. This is her first step toward financial independence.

■ SOFTWARE ORIENTATION

The Formulas Tab

Formulas make Excel a powerful tool. In this lesson, you will learn to write simple formulas
and use many of Excel's functions that have built-in formulas that enable you to perform many
types of calculations by clicking a command on the Formulas tab illustrated in Figure 7-1.

Figure 7-1

Formulas tab

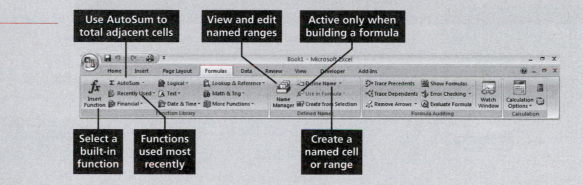

Use this illustration as a reference throughout this lesson as you become familiar with the
command groups on the Formulas tab and use them to create formulas.

■ Building Basic Formulas

THE BOTTOM LINE

The real strength of Excel is its ability to perform common and complex calculations. In
the following exercises, you will learn how to perform basic Excel calculations with formulas. A *formula* is an equation that performs calculations on values in a worksheet. When
you enter a formula in a cell, the formula is stored internally and the results are displayed
in the cell. Formulas give results and solutions that help you assess and analyze data.

Creating a Formula that Performs Addition

A formula consists of two elements: operands and mathematical operators. *Operands*
identify the values to be used in the calculation. An operand can be a constant value, a
cell reference, a range of cells, or another formula. A *constant* is a number or text value
that is entered directly into a formula. *Mathematical operators* specify the calculations
to be performed. In the following exercises, you will create basic formulas using different
methods to enter the formulas.

⊕ CREATE A FORMULA THAT PERFORMS ADDITION

GET READY. Before you begin these steps, launch Microsoft Excel and open a blank workbook.

1. Select **A1** and key **=25+15**. Press `Tab`. The value in A1 is 40.

2. In B1, key **+18+35**. Press `Tab`. The sum of the two numbers is 53.

TAKE NOTE* Formulas should be keyed without spaces, but if you key spaces, Excel eliminates them when you press Enter.

3. Select **B1**. As illustrated in Figure 7-2, although you entered + to begin the formula, when you pressed Enter, Excel replaced the + with = as the beginning mathematical operator.

Figure 7-2

Equal sign marks the beginning of a formula

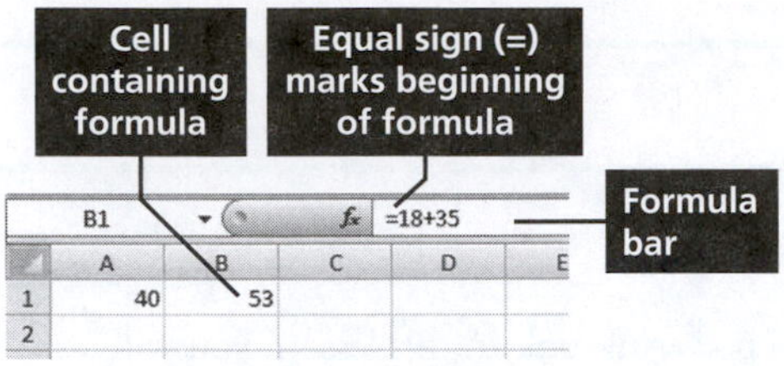

TAKE NOTE*

When you click the formula bar, you are automatically in Edit mode.

CERTIFICATION READY?
How do you create a formula that performs addition?
3.1.1

4. Select **A3**. Click the **formula bar** and key **=94+89+35**. Press [Enter]. The sum of the three numbers is 218.
5. Select **A3** and click the **formula bar**. Select **89** and key **98**. Press [Enter].
   PAUSE. LEAVE the workbook open to use in the next exercise.

To begin creating a formula, select the cell in which you want the formula to appear. To allow Excel to distinguish formulas from data, all formulas begin with an equal sign (=).

TAKE NOTE* You can begin a formula with a + or − as the beginning mathematical operator, but Excel changes it to = when you press Enter.

When you build a formula, it appears in the formula bar and in the cell itself. As illustrated in Figure 7-2, when you complete the formula and press Enter, the value displays in the cell and the formula displays in the formula bar. As you practiced in this exercise, you can edit a formula in the cell or in the formula bar the same as you can edit a data entry.

Creating a Formula that Performs Subtraction

The same methods you used to create a formula to perform addition can be used to create a formula to perform subtraction. When you create a subtraction formula, enter = followed by the positive number and then enter a minus sign to indicate subtraction.

⊕ CREATE A FORMULA THAT PERFORMS SUBTRACTION

USE the workbook from the previous exercise.

1. Select **A5**. Key **=456−98**. Press [Enter]. The value in A5 should be 358.
2. Select **A6** and key **=45−13−8**. Press [Enter]. The value in A6 should be 24.
3. In A8, create a formula to subtract 125 from 189. The value in A8 should be 64.

TROUBLESHOOTING If your formula returned a negative value (i.e., −64), you reversed the order in which the numbers should have been entered.

PAUSE. LEAVE the workbook open to use in the next exercise.

CERTIFICATION READY?
How do you create a formula that performs subtraction?
3.1.1

When you create a subtraction formula, the minus sign must precede the number to be subtracted. When you entered a formula to subtract 125 from 189, you could have entered =189−125 or = −125+189. Either formula would yield a positive 64. If the positive number is entered first, it is not necessary to enter a plus sign.

Creating a Formula that Performs Multiplication

The formula to multiply 33 times 6 is =33*6. If a formula contains two or more operators, operations are not necessarily performed in the order in which you read the formula. The order is determined by the rules of mathematics, but you can override standard operator priorities by using parentheses. Operations contained in parentheses are completed before those outside parentheses.

 CREATE A FORMULA THAT PERFORMS MULTIPLICATION

USE the workbook from the previous exercise.

1. Select **D1**. Key **=125*4** and press **Enter**. The value should be 500.
2. Select **D3** and key **=2*7.50*2**. Press **Enter**. The value should be 30.
3. Select **D5** and key **=5*3**. Press **Enter**. The value should be 15.
4. Select **D7** and key **=5+2*8**. The value should be 21.
5. Select **D9** and key **=(5+2)*8**. The value should be 56.

   PAUSE. LEAVE the workbook open to use in the next exercise.

CERTIFICATION READY?
How do you create a formula that performs multiplication?
3.1.1

When you added parentheses to the last formula you entered in this exercise, you changed the order of the calculations. When you entered the formula without parentheses, Excel multiplied 2 times 8 and added 5 for a value of 21. When you entered (5+2)*8, Excel performed the addition first and returned a value of 56. The order of calculations will be further illustrated in the next exercise.

Creating a Formula that Performs Division

The forward slash is the mathematical operator for division. When a calculation includes multiple values, use parentheses to indicate the part of the calculation that should be performed first.

 CREATE A FORMULA THAT PERFORMS DIVISION

USE the workbook from the previous exercise.

1. Select **D7** and create the formula **=795/45**. Press **Enter**. The value in D7 is 17.66667.
2. Select **D7**. The Number format has been applied to D7. Click the **Accounting Number Format ($)** button. Accounting format is applied and the number is rounded to $17.67 because two decimal places is the default format for the Accounting format.
3. Select **D9** and create the formula **=65−29*8+97/5**. Press **Enter**. The value in D9 is −147.6.
4. Select **D9**. Click in the formula bar and place parentheses around 65−29. Press **Enter**. The value in D9 is 307.4.
5. **CLOSE** but do not save the workbook.

   PAUSE. LEAVE Excel open to use in the next exercise.

CERTIFICATION READY?
How do you create a formula that performs division?
3.1.1

Because the cells in this worksheet were not formatted before you entered data, the default General format was applied to the numbers you entered. When you created the formula =795/45, Excel returned a value of 17.66667 and the Number format was applied to cell D7. The results of the formula calculation rounded the value after the seventh digit (eighth character) because the standard column width is 8.43. In other words, the value was rounded at that number of places only because of the column width.

When you inserted parentheses into the formula, the results were different than when there were no parentheses. Excel does not necessarily perform the operations in the same order that you enter or read them in a formula, which is left to right. Excel uses the rules of mathematics to determine which operations to perform first when a formula contains multiple operators. The order is:

- negative number (−)
- percents (%)
- exponentiation (^)
- multiplication (∗) and division (/)
- addition (+) and subtraction (−)

For example, consider the following equation.

$$5 + 6 * 15 / 3 - 1 = 34$$

Following mathematical operator priorities, the first operation would be 6 multiplied by 15 and that result would be divided by 3. Then 5 would be added and finally, 1 would be subtracted. Figure 7-3 illustrates the formula entered into Excel.

Figure 7-3

Structure of a formula

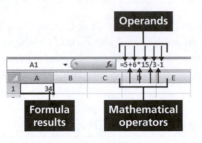

When you use parentheses in a formula, you indicate which calculation to perform first, which overrides the standard operator priorities. Therefore, the result of the following equation would be significantly different from the previous one. Figure 7-4 illustrates the Excel formula. Here is the mathematical formula.

$$(5 + 6) * 15 / (3 - 1) = 83$$

Figure 7-4

Use parentheses to control the order of operations

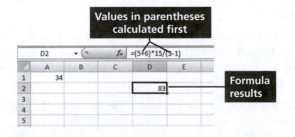

Using Cell References in Formulas

THE BOTTOM LINE

A *reference* identifies a cell or a range of cells on a worksheet and tells Excel where to look for the values you want to use in a formula. With references, you can use values contained in different parts of a worksheet in one formula or use the value from one cell in several formulas. You can also refer to cells on another worksheet in the same workbook and to other workbooks.

Using Relative Cell References in a Formula

Using cell references in formulas rather than constant amounts enables you to copy formulas without having to manually change cell references. When you include a cell reference in a formula and copy that formula, Excel changes the reference to match the column or row to which the formula is copied. A *relative cell reference* is, therefore, one whose references change "relative" to the location where it is copied or moved.

⊙ USE RELATIVE CELL REFERENCES IN A FORMULA

GET READY. Launch Microsoft Excel if it is not already open.

1. **OPEN** *Personal Budget* from the data files for this lesson.
2. Select **B7** and key **=sum(B4:** (colon). As shown in Figure 7-5, cell B4 is outlined in blue, and the reference to B4 in the formula is also blue. The ScreenTip below the formula identifies B4 as the first number in the formula.

Figure 7-5

Color-coordinated cell references

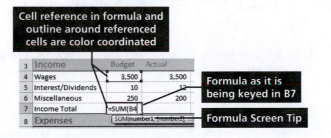

3. Key **B6** and press **Enter**. The total of the cells (3,760) appears in B7.
4. Select **B15**. Key **=sum(** and click **B10**. As shown in Figure 7-6, B10 appears in the formula bar and a flashing marquee appears around B10.

Figure 7-6

Selecting a cell to include in a formula

8	Expenses	Budget	Actual	Diff
9	Home			
10	Mortgage/Rent	950	950	
11	Utilities	236	230	
12	Telephone	56	67	
13	Home Repairs	100	75	
14	Home Security	35	35	
15	Home Total	=Sum(B10		
16	Daily Living	SUM(number1, [number2], ...)		

Select first cell to include in formula

TAKE NOTE*

You can use either uppercase or lowercase when you key a cell reference in a formula. For example, it would not matter whether you keyed B4 or b4 in the formula you entered.

5. Drag the flashing marquee to B14. As shown in Figure 7-7, the formula bar reveals that values within the B10:B14 range will be summed (added).

Figure 7-7

Extend the cell range for a formula

	SUM	▼ X ✓ fx	=Sum(B10:B14)	
	A	B	C	D
1	**Personal Budget**			
2				
3	Income	Budget	Actual	Differe
4	Wages	3,500	3,500	
5	Interest/Dividends	10	12	
6	Miscellaneous	250	200	
7	Income Total	3,760		
8	Expenses	Budget	Actual	Differe
9	Home			
10	Mortgage/Rent	950	950	
11	Utilities	236	230	
12	Telephone	56	67	
13	Home Repairs	100	75	
14	Home Security	35	35	
15	Home Total	=Sum(B10:B14)		
16	Daily Living			

6. Press [Enter] to accept the formula. Select **B15**. As illustrated in Figure 7-8, the value is displayed in B15 and the formula is displayed in the formula bar.

Figure 7-8

Formula always displayed in the formula bar

B15	fx =SUM(B10:B14)

	A	B	C	D	
1	**Personal Budget**				← Formula
2					
3	Income	Budget	Actual	Differen	
4	Wages	3,500	3,500		
5	Interest/Dividends	10	12		
6	Miscellaneous	250	200		
7	Income Total	3,760			
8	Expenses	Budget	Actual	Differen	
9	Home				
10	Mortgage/Rent	950	950		
11	Utilities	236	230		
12	Telephone	56	67		
13	Home Repairs	100	75		
14	Home Security	35	35		
15	Home Total	1,377			← Value returned by formula

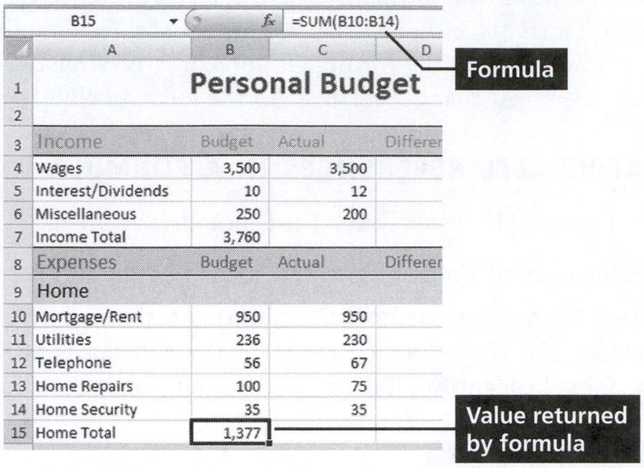

7. Select **D4** and key **=**. Click **B4** and key **−**. Click **C4** and press [Enter]. By default, when a subtraction formula yields no difference, Excel enters a hyphen.

TAKE NOTE*

Open the Format Cells dialog box to change the way Excel displays "no difference" results. On the Numbers tab, you can choose to display 0, for example.

8. Select **D4**. Click and drag the fill handle to D7.
9. Use the fill handle to copy the formula in B7 to C7. Notice that the amount in D7 changes when the formula is copied.
10. Select **D7** and click **Copy**. Select **D10:D15** and click **Paste**.
11. Select **D17:D21** and click **Paste**.
12. Create a Lesson 7 folder and **SAVE** your worksheet as *Budget*.

   PAUSE. LEAVE the workbook open to use in the next exercise.

CERTIFICATION READY?

How do you create formulas that use relative cell references?

3.1.1

ANOTHER WAY

You can select a cell and click the formula bar to key a formula.

In this exercise, you copied formulas rather than entering a formula repeatedly. You saved a considerable amount of time by copying a cell with a completed formula and pasting it in a destination cell.

To understand a relative cell reference, let's examine the formula in B7, which is =sum(B4:B6). The reference to B4 is based on its relative position to B7, the cell that contains the formula. When you copied the formula to C7, the position of the cell containing the formula changed, so the reference changed to C7. You use relative cell references when you want the reference to automatically adjust when you copy or fill the formula across rows or down columns. By default, new formulas use relative references.

In this exercise, you used two methods to create formulas using relative references:

- Key an equal sign to mark the entry as a formula. Then, key the formula, including cell references, constant values, and mathematical operators directly into the cell.
- Key an equal sign and click a cell or the range of cells included in the formula instead of keying cell references.

The second method is usually quicker and eliminates the possibility of typing an incorrect cell or range reference. Cell references and the borders around the corresponding cells are color coded to make it easier to verify that you selected the desired cell.

As you saw in Figure 7-8, when you build a formula, it appears in the formula bar and in the cell. When you complete the formula and press Enter, the value displays in the cell and the formula displays in the formula bar.

Using Absolute Cell References in a Formula

Sometimes you do not want a cell reference to change when you move or copy it. For example, when you review your personal budget, you might want to know what percentage of your income is budgeted for each category of expenses. Each formula you create to calculate those percentages will refer to the cell that contains the total income amount. The reference to the income cell is an *absolute cell reference*—a reference that does not change when the formula is copied or moved.

→ USE ABSOLUTE CELL REFERENCES IN A FORMULA

USE the workbook from the previous exercise.

1. Select **B15**. Use the fill handle to copy the formula to C15.
2. Select **B21**. Key **=sum(** and select **B17:B20**. Press **Enter**.

TAKE NOTE* It is not necessary to key the closing parenthesis when you complete the selection for a formula. Excel supplies it when you press Enter.

3. Select **B21** and drag the fill handle to C21.
4. Select **E10**. Key **=** and click **B10**. Key **/** and click **B7**. Press **Enter**.
5. Select **E10**. Click the **formula bar** and edit the formula to make B7 an absolute reference. The edited formula should read =B10/$B$7. Press **Enter**.

TROUBLESHOOTING When you enter a formula that will yield a result less than a whole number, be sure the cell is formatted for decimals. If the cell is formatted for whole numbers, the cell will display 0 or 1 rather than the expected value.

6. Select **E10** and drag the fill handle to E15.
7. With E10:E15 selected, click the **Percent Style** button (**%**) in the Numbers group. Click **Increase Decimal**. The values should display with one decimal place and a %.
8. **SAVE** your workbook.

   PAUSE. LEAVE the workbook open to use in the next exercise.

CERTIFICATION READY?
How do you create a formula that contains an absolute cell reference?
3.1.1

You can recognize an absolute cell reference by the inclusion of one or more dollar signs in the formula. The absolute cell reference $B$7 in the preceding exercise will always refer to cell B7 because both column B ($B) and row 7 ($7) have been made absolute. When you copy or fill the formula across rows or down columns, the absolute reference will not adjust to the destination cells. By default, new formulas use relative references, and you must edit them if you want them to be absolute references.

You can also create a mixed reference in which either a column or a row is absolute and the other is relative. For example, if the cell reference in the formula were $B7 or B$7, you would have a *mixed reference* in which one component is absolute and one is relative. The column is absolute and the row is relative if the reference is $B7.

If you copy or fill a formula across rows or down columns, the relative reference automatically adjusts, and the absolute reference does not adjust. For example, if you copied or filled a formula containing the mixed reference $B7 to a cell in column C, the formula in the destination cell would be =$B8. The column reference would be the same because that portion of the formula is absolute. The row reference would adjust because it is relative.

Referring to Data in Another Worksheet

You can refer to the contents of cells in another worksheet within the same workbook. This strategy is often used to create a summary of data contained in several worksheets. The formula-building principles operate the same as for building formulas from data within a worksheet.

→ REFER TO DATA IN ANOTHER WORKSHEET

USE the workbook you saved in the previous exercise.

1. Click **Sheet2** to make it the active sheet.
2. Select **B4**. Key = to indicate the beginning of a formula. Click **Sheet1** and select **B7**. Press **Enter**. The value of cell B7 on Sheet1 is displayed in cell B4 of Sheet2. The formula bar displays =Sheet1!B7.
3. Select **B4** and drag the fill handle to D4. The values from Sheet1 row 4 are copied to Sheet2 row 4.
4. On the Home tab, click **Format** and click **Rename Sheet**.
5. Key **Summary** and press **Enter**.
6. Make Sheet1 active. Click **Format** and click **Rename Sheet**.
7. Key **Expenses** and press **Enter**.
8. Make Summary active and select **B4**. The formula bar now shows the formula as =Expenses!B7.
9. **SAVE** your workbook.

   PAUSE. LEAVE the workbook open to use in the next exercise.

CERTIFICATION READY?
How do you create a formula that refers to data in another worksheet?
3.1.2

In this exercise, you referenced data in another worksheet within the Budget workbook. In the next exercise, you will reference data in another workbook. By renaming the worksheets within this workbook, you have prepared it for the next exercise.

Referring to Data in Another Workbook

An *external reference* refers to a cell or range on a worksheet in another Excel workbook, or to a defined name in another workbook. External references are useful when it is not practical to keep large worksheets together in the same workbook.

→ REFER TO DATA IN ANOTHER WORKBOOK

USE the workbook you saved in the previous exercise.

1. Click the **Microsoft Office Button** and click **Excel Options**.
2. On the Excel Options window, click **Advanced**.
3. Click **Show all windows in the Taskbar** if necessary, and click **OK**.

Looking Ahead

You will name a range of cells later in this lesson.

If your system administrator has disabled the *Show all windows in the Taskbar* option, you will need to use the Switch Windows command in the Windows group on the View tab to move between the two workbooks.

TROUBLESHOOTING

CD

The *Financial Obligations* workbook is available on the companion CD-ROM.

4. Make the Summary worksheet active. In A10, key **Other Expenses** and press **Tab**.
5. **OPEN** *Financial Obligations* from the data files for this lesson. This is the source workbook. The *Budget* workbook is the destination workbook.
6. Switch to the destination workbook, and select **B10** on the Summary worksheet.
7. Key = to indicate the beginning of a formula. Select **B8** in the source workbook. A flashing marquee identifies the cell reference.

CERTIFICATION READY?
How do you create a formula that refers to data in another workbook?
3.1.2

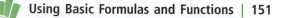

8. Press **Enter** to complete the external reference formula. The formula bar displays square brackets around the name of the source workbook, indicating that the workbook is open.
9. **CLOSE** the source workbook. The formula bar now displays the entire path for the source workbook.
10. **SAVE** the destination workbook.

    PAUSE. LEAVE the workbook open to use in the next exercise.

Although external references are similar to cell references, there are important differences. You normally use external references when working with large amounts of data and complex formulas that encompass several workbooks.

When you create external references, the workbook or workbooks must be open. In a previous exercise, you created a reference to another worksheet within the same workbook. An exclamation point in the formula for that reference indicated that the source was in the same workbook.

Formulas with external references are displayed in two ways, depending upon whether the workbook that contains the referenced data is open or closed. When the source is open, the external reference encloses the workbook name in square brackets, followed by the worksheet name, an exclamation point (!), and the cell range on which the formula depends. When the source workbook is closed, the brackets are removed and the entire file path is shown in the formula.

Using Cell Ranges in Formulas

THE BOTTOM LINE

You can simplify formula building by naming ranges of data so that you can easily identify their content and specify the name when making selections or building formulas rather than keying or selecting the cell range each time you use it in a formula. By default, a named range becomes an absolute reference in a formula.

Naming a Range

A ***name*** is a meaningful shorthand that makes it easier to understand the purpose of a cell reference, constant, formula, or table. You can create your own names to represent cells, ranges of cells, formulas, constant values, or Excel tables. Naming a range clarifies the purpose of the data within the range of cells. A named range in a formula is easily understood, whereas a reference to a cell range is difficult to comprehend at first glance, especially when the referenced range is not visible.

NAME A RANGE

USE the workbook you saved in the previous exercise.

1. Select **B7** on the Expenses worksheet and click **Define Name** in the Defined Names group on the Formulas tab. The New Name dialog box shown in Figure 7-9 opens with Excel's suggested name for the range.

Figure 7-9

Accept default name or create a name

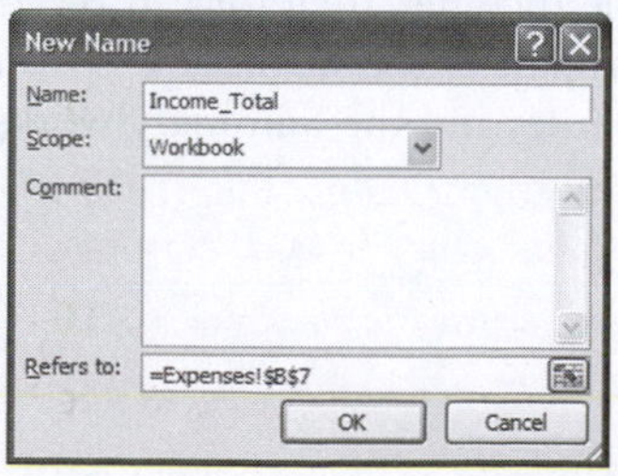

New Name
Name:
Income_Total
Scope:
Workbook
Comment:
Refers to:
=Expenses!$B$7
OK
Cancel

2. Click **OK** to accept Income_Total as the name for B7.

> **TAKE NOTE** ★
> There are several syntax rules for creating names. For example, the first character must be a letter, an underscore character (_), or a backslash (\). You cannot use a C, c, R, or r as a defined name, and you must use the underscore or period as word separators rather than spaces.

3. Select **B36**. Click **Define Name**. Click the **Name** box and key **Expenses**. Accept the default in the Scope box.

4. Click **Collapse Dialog** to select the range that makes up total expenses.

> **TAKE NOTE** ★
> You can name a range using the shortcut menu. Select the range and right-click. Click Name a Range to open the New Name dialog box.

5. Select and delete the text in the *Refers to* box. Press Ctrl and click **B15**, **B21**, **B28**, and **B33**, and then click **Expand Dialog**. Click **OK** to close the New Name dialog box. Some of the selected cells are blank. In the following exercises, you will use the names you create to fill them.

> **TROUBLESHOOTING**
> If, in the process of naming a range, you receive a message that the name already exists, display the Name Manager (discussed later in this lesson) and edit the existing name or delete it and begin again.

6. Select **B23:B27** and select the text in the **Name box** to the left of the formula bar. Key **Transportation** and press Enter.

7. Select **B30:B32** and click **Define Name**. Key **Entertainment** in the Name box on the dialog box. Click **OK**.

8. Select **A15:B15**. Click **Create from Selection**. Click **Left column**, if necessary, on the dialog box that opens (shown in Figure 7-10). Click **OK**. The dialog box closes and it appears that nothing has happened, but a range has been named, as you will see in a later exercise.

Figure 7-10

Create a name from a row or column label

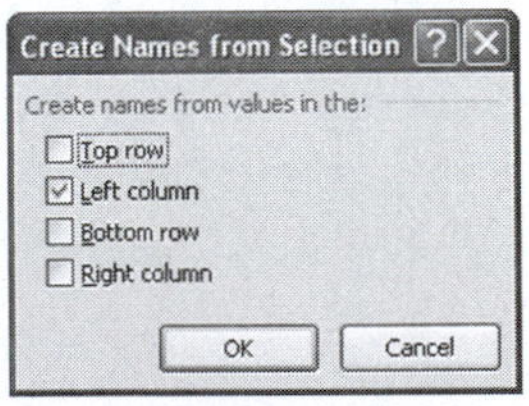

PAUSE. LEAVE the workbook open to use in the next exercise.

> **CERTIFICATION READY?**
> How do you manage named ranges?
> 3.1.3

All names have a scope, either to a specific worksheet or to the entire workbook. The *scope* of a name is the location within which the name is recognized without qualification. For example, when you created the name Income_Total for cell B7, the New Name box, shown in Figure 7-9, identified the scope as part of the workbook. This means the named cell can be used in formulas on the Expenses and the Summary worksheets in this workbook.

In this exercise, you used three methods to name cells and ranges of cells. You created names by

- clicking Define Name on the Formulas tab and selecting the cell or range to be included in the name.
- selecting a cell or range and entering a name in the Name box next to the formula bar.
- selecting a cell or range that included a label and clicking the Create from Selection button on the Formulas tab.

TROUBLESHOOTING

You must select the range of cells you want to name before you use the Name box to create a named range. When you create a name using the Define Name command, you have the opportunity to select the range after you enter the name. This option is not available when you use the Name box.

Naming ranges or an individual cell according to the data they contain is a time-saving technique, even though it may not seem so when you work with limited data files in practice exercises. In the business environment, you will often use a worksheet that contains data in hundreds of rows and columns. After you name a range, you can select it from the Name box and then perform a variety of functions, such as cutting and pasting it to a different workbook as well as using it in a formula.

Changing the Size of a Range

If you need to change the parameters of a named range, you can easily redefine the range by using the Name Manager on the Formulas tab. In the following exercise you will edit the range for Home_Total.

→ CHANGE THE SIZE OF A RANGE

USE the workbook from the previous exercise.

1. Click **Name Manager** on the Formulas tab. Select **Home_Total** and click **Edit**. The Edit Name dialog box opens. You want to change the range rather than the name.

X REF

This is the range you named in an earlier exercise using the Create from Selection command. Although it appeared that nothing happened when you created the named range, it was created, and now you can edit it.

2. The Home_Total range is identified in the *Refers to* box at the bottom of the dialog box. Click **Collapse Dialog** and select **B10:B14**.
3. Click **Expand Dialog** to view the dialog box as shown in Figure 7-11. Click **OK** to close the dialog box.

Figure 7-11

Edit the size of a range

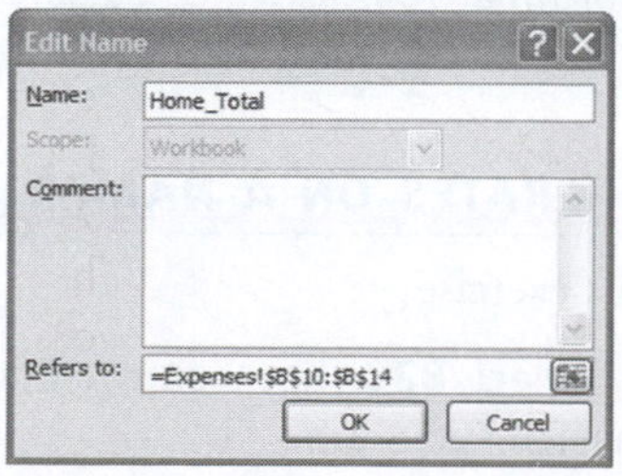

4. Click **Close** to close the Name Manager dialog box.

   PAUSE. LEAVE the workbook open to use in the next exercise.

In the previous exercise, you used the Name Manager dialog box to extend the reference for a named range. You can also rename a range, or use the Filter function to display names that meet a specific criterion, such as names scoped to the worksheet or names scoped to the workbook.

Keeping Track of Ranges

Use the Name Manager dialog box to work with all of the defined names in the workbook. From this dialog box you can also add, change, or delete names. You can use the Name Manager as a convenient way to confirm the value and reference of a named reference or to determine its scope.

⊕ KEEP TRACK OF RANGES

USE the workbook from the previous exercise.

1. Click **Name Manager** on the Defined Names group on the Formulas tab.

2. Select **Income_Total** and click **Edit**.

3. Select **_Total** in the Name field and press ⟦Delete⟧. Click **OK** to close the dialog box.

4. Click **New**. Key **Short\Over** in the Name box. Be sure to use the backslash.

TROUBLESHOOTING You will receive an error message if you use the forward slash in a name. Although the forward slash is used in the Short/Over label on the worksheets, you can use only the underscore or the backslash as a word divider in a named range.

5. In the *Refers to* box, key **=Income-Expenses**. Click **OK**.

6. Click **Close** to close the Name Manager dialog box.

   PAUSE. LEAVE the workbook open to use in the next exercise.

If you defined a named reference after you entered a cell reference in a formula, you may want to update the existing cell reference to the defined name. Select an empty cell, click the arrow next to Define Name, and click Apply Names. On the Apply Names dialog box, click one or more names, and click OK.

You can create a list of defined names in a workbook. Select an area of a worksheet with two empty columns, one for the name and one for a description. Select the upper-left cell of the list. Click Use in Formula and click Paste Names. Click Paste List.

Creating a Formula that Operates on a Named Range

You can use a named range in a formula. You have created several named ranges, which you can now use to fill cells on the worksheets in your Budget workbook.

⊕ CREATE A FORMULA THAT OPERATES ON A NAMED RANGE

USE the workbook from the previous exercise.

1. On the Expenses worksheet, select **B28.** Key **=sum(**. Click **Use in Formula** in the Defined Names group on the Formulas tab.

2. Click **Transportation** on the dropdown list. Key the closing parenthesis and press ⟦Enter⟧.

CERTIFICATION READY?
How do you create a formula that operates on a named range?
3.1.4

3. Select **B33**. Click **Use in Formula**. Select **Entertainment.** Click the **formula bar**. Enter the rest of the formula, **=sum(Entertainment)**, and press Enter.

4. Select **B36**. Key the formula **=sum(** and click **Use in Formula**. Select **Expenses** from the list of named cells and ranges. Press Enter.

   PAUSE. LEAVE the workbook open to use in the next exercise.

Use the Name Manager dialog box to work with all of the defined names in the workbook. You can view or edit the scope or sort and filter the list of names.

■ Summarizing Data with Functions

↓
THE BOTTOM LINE

A *function* is a predefined formula that performs a calculation. Excel's built-in functions are designed to perform all sorts of calculations—from simple to complex. When you apply a function to specific data, you eliminate the time involved in manually constructing a formula. Using functions ensures the accuracy of the formula's results.

Using SUM

Adding a range of cells is one of the most common calculations performed on worksheet data. You can use the SUM function to easily and accurately select the cells to be included in a calculation. The AutoSum function makes that even easier.

⊙ **USE SUM**

USE the workbook from the previous exercise.

1. On the Expenses worksheet, select **C28**. Click **Insert Function** in the Function Library group on the Formulas tab. The Insert Function dialog box shown in Figure 7-12 opens.

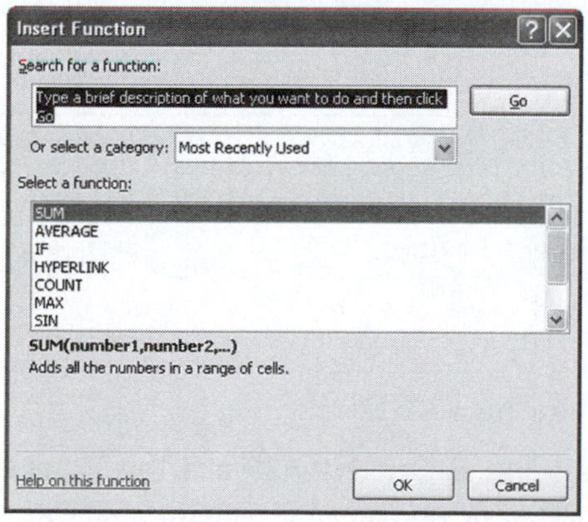

Figure 7-12

Accept default name or create a name

2. Select SUM if necessary. Click **OK**.

3. On the Function Arguments box, illustrated in Figure 7-13, the default range is C26:C27. Click **Collapse Dialog** in the Number1 field and select **C23:C27**.

Figure 7-13

Accept default range or select a new range

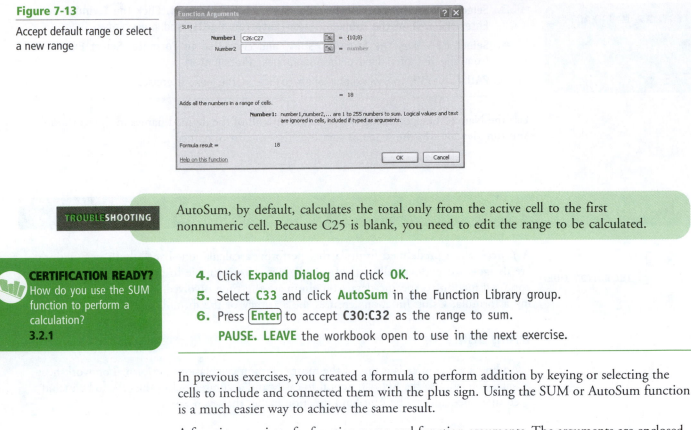

AutoSum, by default, calculates the total only from the active cell to the first nonnumeric cell. Because C25 is blank, you need to edit the range to be calculated.

CERTIFICATION READY?
How do you use the SUM function to perform a calculation?
3.2.1

4. Click **Expand Dialog** and click **OK**.
5. Select **C33** and click **AutoSum** in the Function Library group.
6. Press **Enter** to accept **C30:C32** as the range to sum.

    PAUSE. LEAVE the workbook open to use in the next exercise.

In previous exercises, you created a formula to perform addition by keying or selecting the cells to include and connected them with the plus sign. Using the SUM or AutoSum function is a much easier way to achieve the same result.

A function consists of a function name and function arguments. The arguments are enclosed in parentheses in the formula. Depending upon the function, an argument can be a constant value, a single-cell reference, a range of cells, or even another function. If a function contains multiple arguments, the arguments are separated by commas.

TAKE NOTE *

Because it is used so frequently, AutoSum is available on the Formulas tab in the Function Library group and on the Home tab in the Editing group.

Using COUNT

Statistical functions, such as SUM and COUNT, are used to compile and classify data to present significant information. Use the COUNT function to count the number of numeric entries in a range.

⊕ USE COUNT

USE the workbook from the previous exercise.

1. On the Expenses worksheet, select **A39** and key **Expense Categories**. Press **Tab**.
2. Click **Insert Function** in the Function Library group on the Formulas tab.
3. On the Insert Function dialog box, select **COUNT** and click **OK**. You want to count only the expenses in each category and not include the category totals.
4. Click **Collapse Dialog** for Value1.
5. Select **B10:B14** and press **Enter**.
6. Click **Collapse Dialog** for Value2 and select **B17:20**. Press **Enter**.

TAKE NOTE *

As you add arguments, the Value fields on the Function Arguments dialog box expand to allow you to enter multiple arguments.

7. Collapse the dialog box for Value3. Select **B23:B27** and press [Enter]. The identified range is one you named in a previous exercise. That name (Transportation) appears in the Value3 box rather than the cell range, and the values of the cells in the Transportation and Entertainment named ranges appear to the right of the value boxes.

8. In the Value4 box, key **Entertainment**. See Figure 7-14.

Figure 7-14

Include named ranges in function

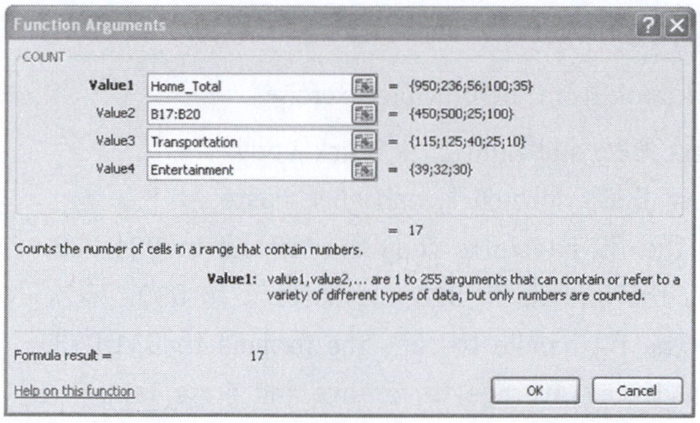

Function Arguments	? X
COUNT	

Value1	Home_Total	[📷]	= {950;236;56;100;35}
Value2	B17:B20	[📷]	= {450;500;25;100}
Value3	Transportation	[📷]	= {115;125;40;25;10}
Value4	Entertainment	[📷]	= {39;32;30}

= 17

Counts the number of cells in a range that contain numbers.

Value1: value1,value2,... are 1 to 255 arguments that can contain or refer to a variety of different types of data, but only numbers are counted.

Formula result =   17

Help on this function   [OK] [Cancel]

9. Click **OK** to accept the function arguments.

PAUSE. LEAVE the workbook open to use in the next exercise.

Text or blank cells are ignored in a COUNT formula. If a cell contains a value of 0 (zero), the COUNT function will count it as a cell with a number.

Using COUNTA

Use the COUNTA function to count the number of cells in a range that are not empty. COUNTA counts both text and values in a selected data range.

➔ USE COUNTA

USE the workbook from the previous exercise.

1. On the Expenses worksheet, select **A40** and key **Cells Containing Data.** Press [Tab].
2. Click **Insert Function** in the Function Library group on the Formulas tab.
3. On the Insert Function dialog box, select **COUNTA**. If COUNTA does not appear in your list, key **COUNTA** in the *Search for a function* box and click **Go**. The function will appear at the top of the function list and be selected by default. Click **OK**.

 **ANOTHER WAY**   By default the most recently used functions are displayed when the Insert Function dialog box opens. You can click the arrow in the category field and select All to display a list of all functions.

CERTIFICATION READY?
How do you create a COUNTA formula?
3.2.1

4. Select **B4:B33** in the Value1 box. Click **OK**. The formula returns a value of 26.
PAUSE. LEAVE the workbook open to use in the next exercise.

COUNTA returns a value that indicates the number of cells that contain data. Empty cells within the data ranges are ignored.

CERTIFICATION READY?
How do you create a COUNT formula?
3.2.1

Using AVERAGE

> The AVERAGE function adds a range of cells and then divides by the number of cell entries. It might be interesting to know the average difference between what you budgeted for expenses and the amount you actually spent during the month. Before you can calculate the average, however, you will need to finish calculating the differences.

⊕ USE AVERAGE

USE the workbook from the previous exercise.

1. Select **D21** and right-click. Click **Copy**.
2. Select **D23**, right-click, and click **Paste**.
3. Use the fill handle to copy the formula to D24:D28.
4. Copy the formula in D28 and paste it to D30.
5. Use the fill handle to copy the formula to D31:D33.
6. In A41, key **Average Difference** and press Tab.
7. Click **Recently Used** in the Function Library group and click **AVERAGE**.
8. Click **Collapse Dialog** in Value1. Press Ctrl and select the category totals (**D15**, **D21**, **D28**, and **D33**). Notice that the arguments are separated by a comma.
9. Click **Expand Dialog**. Click **OK**. There is a $38 average difference between the amount budgeted and the amount you spent in each category.
10. **SAVE** and **CLOSE** the *Budgets* workbook.

    PAUSE. LEAVE Excel open to use in the next exercise.

CERTIFICATION READY?
How do you find the average of a range of cells?
3.2.1

Although you entered the numbers (cell references) as one number, if you open the Function Arguments dialog box after the formula has been entered, each cell reference is in a separate Number box.

The exact value returned for the AVERAGE formula was 38.25. Because column B is formatted for zero decimals, the value returned by the formula is 38.

Using MIN

> The MIN formula returns the smallest number in a set of values. For example, a professor would use the MIN function to determine the lowest test score; a sales organization would determine which sales representative earned the lowest commission or which employee earns the lowest salary. Maximum values are usually calculated for the same set of data.

⊕ USE MIN

CD

The *Personnel* workbook is available on the companion CD-ROM.

OPEN *Personnel* from the data files for Lesson 7.

1. Select **A22** and key **Minimum Salary**. Press Tab.
2. Click **Recently Used** in the Function Library group on the Formulas tab. The MIN function is not available. Key **=min** in **B22** and click **MIN** when it appears on the popup list. Press Tab. An opening parenthesis is added to your formula.

◆ **ANOTHER WAY**   You can display the Insert Function dialog box by clicking the Insert Function button on the formula bar.

3. Select **E6:E19** and press Enter.

4. SAVE the workbook as *Analysis*.

PAUSE. LEAVE the workbook open to use in the next exercise.

CERTIFICATION READY?
How do you create a formula that returns the lowest number in a data range?
3.2.1

In this exercise, you calculated the lowest (minimum) value in a data range. The arguments typed into the Function Arguments dialog box can be cell references, a named range, or a number. If the arguments contain no number, MIN returns 0.

Using MAX

The MAX function returns the largest value in a set of values. Minimum values are usually calculated for the same set of data.

⊙ USE MAX

USE the workbook from the previous exercise.

1. In A23, key **Maximum Salary** and press [Tab].
2. Click **Insert Function** in the Function Library group and click **MAX**. Click **OK**.
3. Click **Collapse Dialog** in Value1 and select **E6:E19**.
4. Click **Expand Dialog**. Click **OK**. The maximum salary is $89,000.
5. SAVE and **CLOSE** the workbook.

PAUSE. LEAVE Excel open to use in the next exercise.

CERTIFICATION READY?
How do you find the highest value in a range of cells?
3.2.1

The arguments for the MAX function can be numbers, names, or references that contain numbers. Empty cells within the range are ignored.

■ Using Formulas to Create Subtotals

THE BOTTOM LINE

You can calculate subtotals using the SUBTOTAL function, but it is generally easier to create a list by using the Subtotal command in the Outline group on the Data tab. After the subtotal list has been created, you can edit it in the SUBTOTAL function.

Selecting Ranges for Subtotaling

Groups are created for subtotaling by sorting the data. Data must be sorted by groups to insert a subtotal function. Subtotals are calculated with a summary function, and you can use the SUBTOTAL function to display more than one type of summary function for each column.

CD

The *Personnel* workbook is available on the companion CD-ROM.

⊙ SELECT RANGES FOR SUBTOTALING

1. OPEN *Personnel* from the data files for this lesson.
2. Select **A5:F19** (the data range and the column labels). Click **Sort** in the Sort & Filter group on the Data tab.

TROUBLESHOOTING

If you do not include the labels in the data selection, Excel will prompt you to include the labels so that you can sort by label rather than the column heading.

3. On the Sort dialog box, select **Department** as the sort by criterion. Select the *My data has headers* checkbox if it is not selected. Click **OK**. The list is sorted by department.

4. Select the data range (**A5:F19**) and click **Subtotal** in the Outline group on the Data tab. The Subtotal dialog box opens.

5. Select **Department** in the *At each change in* box. Sum is the default in the Use function box.

6. Select **Salary** in the *Add subtotal to* box. Deselect any other column labels. Select **Summary below data** if it is not selected. Click **OK**. Subtotals are inserted below each department with a grand total at the bottom.

7. With the data selected, click **Subtotal**. On the dialog box, click **Average** in the *Use function* box.

8. Click **Replace current subtotals** to deactivate it. Click **OK**.

9. **SAVE** the workbook as *Dept Subtotals*.

   PAUSE. LEAVE the workbook open to use in the next exercise.

CERTIFICATION READY?
How do you create subtotals within a worksheet?
3.3.1

Subtotals are calculated with a summary function, such as Sum, Count, or Average. You can display more than one type of summary function for each column. Grand totals, on the other hand, are derived from the detail data, not from the values in the subtotals. Therefore, when you used the Average summary function, the grand total row displays an average of all detail rows in the list, not an average of the values in the subtotal rows.

SUBTOTAL function numbers specify which subtotal function to use in calculating subtotals within your list. When you use the Subtotal command on the Data tab, you choose the summary function from a dropdown list and the function number is automatically included in the subtotal formula. When you use the SUBTOTAL function, you will need to enter the function number. Table 7-1 lists the function numbers.

Table 7-1

SUBTOTAL function numbers

FUNCTION_NUM (INCLUDES HIDDEN VALUES)	FUNCTION_NUM (IGNORES HIDDEN VALUES)	FUNCTION
1	101	AVERAGE
2	102	COUNT
3	103	COUNTA
4	104	MAX
5	105	MIN
6	106	PRODUCT
7	107	STDEV
8	108	STDEVP
9	109	SUM
10	110	VAR
11	111	VARP

Modifying a Range in a Subtotal

You can change the way data is grouped and subtotaled by modifying the subtotal range using the SUBTOTAL function. This option is not available when you create subtotals from the Data tab commands.

→ MODIFY A RANGE IN A SUBTOTAL

USE the workbook you saved in the previous exercise.

1. Insert a row above the Grand Total row.
2. Key **Sales/Marketing Total** in B29.
3. Copy the subtotal formula from E27 to E29.
4. In the formula bar, change the function to 109 to exclude subtotals within the data range.
5. Replace the range in the formula bar with E15:E25 and press [Enter]. The salaries for the sales and marketing departments combined are $310,000.
6. **SAVE** the workbook as *Dept Subtotals Revised*. **CLOSE** the workbook.

   PAUSE. LEAVE Excel open to use in the next exercise.

CERTIFICATION READY?
How do you create and modify subtotals within a worksheet?
3.3.1

When you modified the function number (changed 9 to 109) in the exercise, you excluded the sum and average subtotals for the individual departments. If you had not changed the function number to 109, the formula result would have included the average salary and the total salaries as well as the salaries for the individual employees.

Building Formulas to Subtotal and Total

In the previous exercise, you copied and modified a formula to create a subtotal for a combined group. You can accomplish the same result by using the SUBTOTAL function to build a formula and add subtotals to data that you cannot or do not want to sort into one category in order to use the built-in function in the Data tab's subtotal function.

→ BUILD FORMULAS TO SUBTOTAL AND TOTAL

CD

The *Personnel* workbook is available on the companion CD-ROM.

1. **OPEN** *Personnel* from the data files for this lesson.
2. Insert a row above row 11.
3. Select **E11** and click **Recently Used** in the Formula Library group on the Formulas tab. Click **SUBTOTAL**.
4. Key **9** in the Function_num box on the Function Arguments dialog box.
5. Click **Collapse Dialog** in Ref1 and select **E6:E10**.
6. Click **Expand Dialog** and click **OK** to close the dialog box.
7. Select **B11** and key **Support Staff Total**.
8. Select **B21** and key **Sales and Marketing Total**.
9. Select **E21** and click **Recently Used**. Click **SUBTOTAL**. Create a subtotal for the values in E12:E20. Format the subtotal for currency.
10. Press [Ctrl] and select row **11** and row **21**. Click **Bold** on the Home tab to emphasize the subtotals.
11. **SAVE** the workbook as *Combined Depts*.

    PAUSE. LEAVE the workbook open to use in the next exercise.

When you use the Subtotal command on the Data tab, subtotal entries have a predefined format, and you can create multiple subtotals, as you did in a previous exercise. When you use the SUBTOTAL function, you must build the formula and label and format the subtotal entries manually.

TAKE NOTE* If the workbook is set to automatically calculate formulas, the Subtotal command recalculates subtotal and grand total values automatically when you edit the detail data.

■ Controlling the Appearance of Formulas

THE BOTTOM LINE When you work with extremely large worksheets that contain numerous formulas, you sometimes need to see all formulas to audit the calculations in the worksheet. You can display and print the worksheet with all formulas visible.

Displaying Formulas on the Screen

When you create a formula, the result of the calculation is displayed in the cell and the formula is displayed in the formula bar. You may need to see all formulas on the screen in order to audit them. You can click the Show Formulas command to display the formula in each cell instead of the resulting value.

⊙ DISPLAY FORMULAS ON THE SCREEN

USE the workbook from the previous exercise.

1. Click **Show Formulas** in the Formula Auditing group on the Formulas tab. All worksheet formulas are displayed.
2. Click **Show Formulas**. Values are displayed.
3. **SAVE** and **CLOSE** the workbook. When you open the workbook again, it will open with values displayed.

ANOTHER WAY You can also press Ctrl+` (grave accent) to switch between formulas and their values. The accent is located to the left of the number 1 key on most keyboards.

Looking Ahead For security reasons, you may want to hide formulas from other workbook users. This and other security issues will be presented in Lesson 11.

PAUSE. LEAVE Excel open to use in the next exercise.

CERTIFICATION READY?
How do you display formulas in a worksheet?
3.8

If you work with dates and times, you will find it useful to understand Excel's date and time system. Although you normally do not have to be concerned with serial numbers, when you displayed the worksheet formulas in the preceding exercise, you probably wondered what happened to the numbers in your worksheet. Excel stores dates as sequential serial numbers. By default, January 1, 1900, is serial number 1, and January 2, 1900, is serial number 2, and so on. This serial number date system allows you to use dates in formulas. For example, you can enter a formula to calculate the number of days you have lived by creating a formula to subtract your birth date from today's date.

Printing Formulas

When you audit the formulas in a large worksheet, you may find it useful to print the worksheet with the formulas displayed. To gain maximum benefit from the printed copy, print gridlines and row and column headers.

➜ PRINT FORMULAS

1. **OPEN** *Budget* from your Lesson 7 folder. This is the exercise you saved earlier.
2. Click **Show Formulas** in the Formula Auditing group on the Formulas tab.
3. Click the **Page Layout** tab and click **Print Gridlines** and **Print Headings** in the Sheet Options group.
4. Click **Orientation** in the Page Setup group and click **Landscape**.
5. Click the **Microsoft Office Button**. Point to **Print** and click **Print Preview**.
6. On the Print Preview tab, click **Page Setup**.
7. On the Page tab, click **Fit to 1 page wide**.
8. Click the **Header/Footer** tab. Click **Custom Header** and key your name in the left section. Click **OK**. Close the Page Setup dialog box.
9. Click **Print** on the Print Preview tab. Click **OK** to print the document.
10. **SAVE** the workbook with the same name. **CLOSE** the workbook. **CLOSE** Excel.

 CERTIFICATION READY?
How do you print a worksheet with formulas displayed?
3.8

SUMMARY SKILL MATRIX

IN THIS LESSON YOU LEARNED	MATRIX SKILL	SKILL NUMBER
To build formulas to perform basic mathematical functions	Create formulas that use absolute and relative cell references	3.1.1
To use cell references in formulas		
To create formulas containing cell references that change relative to the location of the referenced cells	Create formulas that use absolute and relative cell references	3.1.1
To create cell references that do not change when the formula is copied to other cells	Create formulas that use absolute and relative cell references	3.1.1
To create formulas that refer to data in another worksheet in the same workbook	Create formulas that reference data from other worksheets or workbooks	3.1.2
To create formulas that refer to data in another workbook	Create formulas that reference data from other worksheets or workbooks	3.1.2
To create and use named cell ranges in formulas		
To use the Name Manager to keep track of ranges	Manage named ranges	3.1.3
To create formulas that operate on named ranges	Use named ranges in formulas	3.1.4
To summarize data with functions	Use SUM, COUNT, COUNTA, AVERAGE, MIN, and MAX	3.2.1
To use formulas to create subtotals	Create and modify list ranges	3.3.1
To control the appearance of formulas	Display and print formulas	3.8

■ Knowledge Assessment

Matching

a. absolute cell reference   f. operand
b. constant   g. mathematical operator
c. external reference   h. relative cell reference
d. formula   i. mixed reference
e. function   j. scope

_____ 1. In formulas, cell references that change in relation to the location where they are moved or copied.

_____ 2. A predefined formula that performs calculations on values in a worksheet.

_____ 3. The components of a formula that identify the values to be used in the calculation.

_____ 4. Numbers or text values entered directly into a formula. These values are not calculated.

_____ 5. In a formula, a reference to a specific cell that does not change when the formula is copied or moved.

_____ 6. A reference to a cell or range on a worksheet in another Excel workbook.

_____ 7. An equation that performs calculations on values in a worksheet.

_____ 8. The formula component that specifies what calculations are to be performed.

_____ 9. A cell reference in which the column is absolute and the row is relative or vice versa.

_____ 10. The location within which a name is recognized without qualification.

Multiple Choice

Circle the choice that best completes the following statements.

1. Which of the following is not a mathematical operator?
   a. ×
   b. +
   c. −
   d. *

2. Which function automatically totals cells directly above or to the left of the cell containing the formula?
   a. COUNT
   b. AutoFill
   c. AutoSum
   d. SUM

3. Which of the following shows a formula for an external reference?
   a. =Sum(Expenses)
   b. =Sum(B6:b10)
   c. =Expenses!B7
   d. ='[Financial Obligations.xlsx]Sheet1'!$B$2

4. Which of the following shows a formula for a reference to another worksheet in the same workbook?

   a. =Sum(Expenses)

   b. =Sum(B6:b10)

   c. =Expenses!B7

   d. ='[Financial Obligations.xlsx]Sheet1'!$B$2

5. Which of the following shows a formula that references a named range?

   a. =Sum(Expenses)

   b. =Sum(B6:b10)

   c. =Expenses!B7

   d. ='[Financial Obligations.xlsx]Sheet1'!$B$2

6. Which character designates a cell reference as absolute?

   a. ^

   b. @

   c. $

   d. #

7. The COUNTA function

   a. counts the number of cells in a range that contain values.

   b. counts all cells in the range.

   c. counts the number of cells that are not empty.

   d. counts the text entries in the range.

8. The COUNT function is an example of a _____ function.

   a. logical

   b. financial

   c. statistical

   d. text

9. Which of the following is an acceptable name for a named range?

   a. C

   b. C_Contracts

   c. C/Contracts

   d. C Contracts

10. Which of the following statements accurately describes the default selection for AutoSum?

    a. By default, AutoSum totals all entries above the cell in which the formula is located.

    b. By default, AutoSum calculates the total from the active cell to the first nonnumeric cell.

    c. AutoSum does not have a default selection.

    d. You must make the selection before clicking AutoSum.

▪ Competency Assessment

Project 7-1: Create Formulas to Calculate Income and Expenses

An employee at Tailspin Toys has entered second quarter income and expense data into a worksheet. You will enter formulas to calculate monthly and quarterly totals.

The *Tailspin Toys*
workbook is available
on the companion
CD-ROM.

GET READY. Launch Excel if it is not already running.

1. **OPEN** *Tailspin Toys* from the data files for this lesson.
2. Select **E4** and key **=B4+C4+D4** and press Enter.
3. Select **B6**. On the Formulas tab, in the Function Library group, click **Insert Function**.
4. On the Insert Function dialog box, select **SUM** and click **OK**.
5. On the Function Arguments dialog box, click **Collapse Dialog** and click **B4**. Key - and click **B5**.
6. Expand Dialog and click **OK** to close the dialog box.
7. Select **B6** and use the fill handle to copy the formula to C6:D6.
8. Click **B11** and click **AutoSum** in the Function Library group. Press Enter to accept B8:B10 as the cells to total.
9. Select **B11** and use the fill handle to copy the formula to C11:D11.
10. Select **B13** and click **Insert Function** in the Function Library group. On the Insert Function dialog box, select **SUM** and click **OK**.
11. Click **Collapse Dialog** for Number1 and click **B6**, key - and click **B11**. Press Enter and click **OK** to close the dialog box.
12. Select **B13** and use the fill handle to copy the formula to C13:D13.
13. Select **E4**. Click **AutoSum** in the Function Library group. Press Enter to accept the range as B4:D4. Copy the formula to E5:E14. Then delete the data in cells E7 and E12.
14. Select **B15**, key **=B13-B14,** and press Enter Copy the formula to C15:E15.
15. **SAVE** the workbook as *Tailspin Toys 7-1* and then **CLOSE** the file.
    LEAVE Excel open to use in the next project.

Project 7-2: Use AutoSum to Total Sales; Calculate Percentage of Increase

Blue Yonder Airlines has created a workbook to analyze sales for its first four years of operation. Enter formulas to determine the total sales for each division and the percentage increase/decrease each year.

The *Blue Yonder*
workbook is available
on the companion
CD-ROM.

1. **OPEN** *Blue Yonder* from the data files for this lesson.
2. Select **F4** and click **AutoSum** in the Function Library group on the Formulas tab.
3. Press Enter to accept B4:E4 as the range to add.
4. Use the fill handle to copy the formula in F4 to F5:F8.
5. Select **B12** and key **=(C4-B4)/B4**. Press Enter. This formula calculates the percentage increase in sales from 2005 to 2006. The numbers in parentheses yield the amount of the increase. The increase is then divided by the 2006 sales.
6. Select **B12**. Use the fill handle to copy the formula to B13:B15.
7. Select **B12:B15**. Use the fill handle to copy the formulas in the selected range to C12:D15.
8. Select **F12**. Key **=(E4-B4)/B4** and press Enter. This enters a formula to calculate the percentage increase from the first year (2005) to the most recent (2008).
9. Copy the formula in F12 to F13:F15.
10. **SAVE** the workbook as *Blue Yonder 7-2* and then **CLOSE** the file.
    LEAVE Excel open for the next project.

■ Proficiency Assessment

Project 7-3: Calculate Totals and Percentages

In the previous project, you calculated total sales for Blue Yonder's first four years of operation. You also calculated the percentage of increase or decrease in sales for each year. In this project, you will calculate expense totals and percentage increase or decrease.

The *Blue Yonder Expenses* workbook is available on the companion CD-ROM.

1. **OPEN** *Blue Yonder Expenses* from the data files for this lesson. Expense History should be the active worksheet.
2. Select **B8** and click **AutoSum** to total the 2005 expenses.
3. Copy the formula in B8 to C8:F8.
4. Select **F4** and click **AutoSum** to total Corporate Contracts expenses for the four-year period.
5. Copy the formula in F4 to F5:F7.
6. In B12, create a formula to calculate the percentage increase in Corporate Contracts expenses from 2005 to 2006. Begin with 2006 expenses minus 2005 expenses, divided by 2005. Use parentheses to instruct Excel which function to perform first.
7. Copy the formula from B12 to B13:B15 and to C12:D15.
8. In F12, create a formula to calculate the percentage increase in expenses from 2005 to 2008. Remember to construct the formula to subtract and then divide.
9. Click **Percentage Style** (%) in the Number group. If necessary, click **Increase Decimal** to display one position after the decimal point.
10. Copy the formula in F12 to F13:F15.
11. **SAVE** the workbook as *Blue Yonder Expenses 7-3* and then **CLOSE** the file.
    LEAVE Excel open for the next project.

Project 7-4: Create Formulas in a Template Worksheet

Tailspin Toys wants to project income and expenses for the third quarter based on its performance in the second quarter. A template has been created for the projections. In this project, you will create formulas for the calculations that affect only this worksheet. In the next exercise, you will create formulas that refer to data in another worksheet in this workbook. You are creating a template, so the values returned by your formulas will be $0 until you use the template in the next exercise.

The *Tailspin Projections* workbook is available on the companion CD-ROM.

1. **OPEN** *Tailspin Projections* from the data files for this lesson.
2. In the Third Qtr worksheet, key **0** (zero) as a placeholder in B4 and in B5.
3. Select **B6** and enter a formula to subtract the cost of goods sold from sales. The value returned will be $0.
4. Key **0** as a placeholder in B8:B10.
5. Select **B11** and click **AutoSum** to calculate total expenses.
6. Select **B13** and enter a formula to subtract total expenses from the gross margin.
7. Federal taxes are estimated to be 34% net income. Select **B14** and enter a formula to multiply net income before taxes by 34%.
8. In B15, enter a formula to calculate net income after taxes.
9. **SAVE** the workbook as *Tailspin Projections 7-4*.
    LEAVE the workbook open for the next project.

■ Mastery Assessment

Project 7-5: Refer to Data in Another Worksheet

Tailspin Toys wants to set goals for the third quarter based on its performance in the second quarter. Its goal is to increase sales by 10% while keeping costs and expenses to 5%. You will create formulas to calculate the projections.

1. **USE** the workbook you saved in Project 7-4.

2. Make Third Qtr the active sheet and display the Formulas tab. The formula to establish the sales goal for third quarter will be second quarter total sales + (second quarter total sales *10%).

3. Select **B4**, click **Recently Used** in the Function Library group, and click **Sum**. Select **Second Qtr E4** as the Number1 function argument. Click **Expand Dialog**.

4. In the Number2 argument box, key **+(** and click **Second Qtr**. Select **E4**.

5. In the Number2 argument box, key ***10%)** and press **Enter**. Your completed formula should read =SUM('SecondQtr'!E4, + ('Second Qtr'!E4*10%)).

6. On the Third Quarter worksheet, select **B5**. Click **Recently Used** in the Function Library group and click **Sum**. Select **Second Qtr E5** as the Number1 function argument.

7. In the Number2 argument box, key **+(** and click **Second Qtr**. Select **E5**.

8. In the Number2 argument box, key ***5%)** and press **Enter**.

9. Copy the formula in **B5** to **B8:B10**.

10. **SAVE** the workbook as *Tailspin Projections 7-5* and then **CLOSE** the file.

    LEAVE Excel open for the next project.

Project 7-6: Name a Range and Use the Range in a Formula

Blue Yonder Airlines wants to analyze the sales and expense data from its four-year history.

CD

The *Income Analysis* workbook is available on the companion CD-ROM.

1. **OPEN** *Income Analysis* from the data files for this lesson.

2. On the Expenses worksheet, select **B4:E4** and click **Define Name** on the Formulas tab. Accept the defaults on the dialog box and click **OK**.

3. Repeat Step 2 and name the other three expenses sources.

4. On the Analysis worksheet, select **B5** and create a formula to calculate the four-year average for corporate contract sales. Use the Corporate Contracts named range in the formula.

5. Create a formula using the appropriately named range in B6, B7, and B8.

6. In column C, create a formula to calculate the maximum sales for each division.

7. Show the formulas on the screen. Adjust column width, if necessary, to display the entire formulas.

8. Print the Analysis worksheet in landscape orientation with gridlines and column headings included.

9. **SAVE** the workbook as *Income Analysis 7-6* and then **CLOSE** the file.

   LEAVE Excel open for the next project.

INTERNET READY

As mentioned at the beginning of this lesson, a personal budget helps you make sound financial decisions and enables you to reach financial goals. Various governmental organizations and private financial counselors recommend percentages of your income to allocate for housing, transportation, etc. Use Web search tools to find recommended guidelines for the percentage of income you should allocate in various spending categories. Be sure to use "personal budget guidelines" to avoid business and government budget sites.

From your research, create a worksheet that lists the categories and percentages that you think are reasonable for your personal or family budget. **SAVE** the workbook as *My Budget*. **CLOSE** Excel.

Using More Advanced Formulas

LESSON SKILL MATRIX

SKILLS	MATRIX SKILL	SKILL NUMBER
Using Formulas to Conditionally Summarize Data	Use SUMIF, SUMIFS, COUNTIF, COUNTIFS, AVERAGEIF, and AVERAGEIFS	3.4.1
Using Formulas to Look Up Data in a Workbook	Use VLOOKUP and HLOOKUP	3.5.1
Adding Conditional Logic Functions to Formulas	Use IF, AND, OR, NOT, IFERROR	3.6.1
Using Formulas to Format Text	Use PROPER, UPPER, LOWER, SUBSTITUTE	3.7.1
Using Formulas to Modify Text		
Using SUBSTITUTE	Use PROPER, UPPER, LOWER, SUBSTITUTE	3.7.1
Converting Text to Columns	Convert text to columns	3.7.2, 2.3.5

Fabrikam, Inc. uses several of Excel's analytical tools to review sales data during its strategic planning activities. The owners have created a standard bonus program as a part of its employee-retention efforts and as a performance award to recognize sales agents who have been instrumental in achieving the company's strategic goals. The standard bonus program is based on years of service to Fabrikam. The performance bonus is awarded when an agent reaches his or her sales goal for the year. Fabrikam's accountants will create formulas to analyze Fabrikam's sales data.

KEY TERMS
arguments
array
conditional formula
lookup functions
table

■ SOFTWARE ORIENTATION

The Formulas Tab

In previous lessons you applied formatting to cells based on Excel's predefined conditional formats, such as greater than and less than. The predefined conditional formats enable you to specify that cells be formatted in a different manner if the values stored in them meet a certain condition. Conditional formatting can make the data more understandable to viewers by highlighting significant aspects of the data.

In this lesson, you will use commands on the Formulas tab shown in Figure 8-1 to create formulas to conditionally summarize data, to look up data, to apply conditional logic, and to format and modify text. Use this illustration as a reference throughout this lesson as you become familiar with more of the commands on the Formulas tab and use them to create formulas.

Figure 8-1

Formulas tab

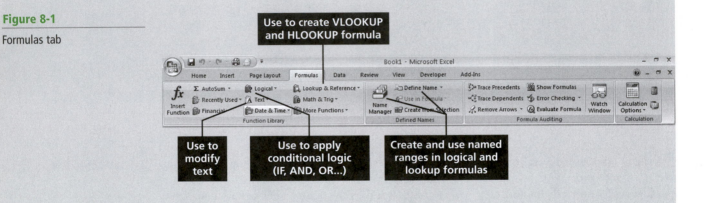

■ Using Formulas to Conditionally Summarize Data

↓ **THE BOTTOM LINE**

As you learned in an earlier lesson, you can use a conditional format to help you analyze data, detect critical issues, identify patterns, and visually explore trends. A conditional format changes the appearance of a cell range based on a criterion. Conditional formulas add another dimension to data analysis by summarizing data that meets one or more criteria. A ***conditional formula*** is one in which the result is determined by the presence or absence of a particular condition.

Using SUMIF

The SUMIF function calculates the total of only those cells that meet a given criterion or condition. The syntax for the SUMIF function is SUMIF(range, criteria, sum_range). The values that a function uses to perform operations or calculations in a formula are ***arguments***. Thus, the arguments of the SUMIF function are range, criteria, and sum range which, when used together, create a conditional formula in which cells that meet a stated criterion are added. Cells within the criterion range that do not meet the criterion are not included in the total.

⊕ USE SUMIF

GET READY. Before you begin these steps, launch Microsoft Excel.

The *Fabrikam Sales* workbook is available on the companion CD-ROM.

1. **OPEN** *Fabrikam Sales* from the data files for this lesson.
2. Select **A20** and key **Sum of sales over $200,000**. Press Enter. If necessary, select **A20** and click **Wrap Text** in the Alignment group on the Home tab.
3. Select **C20** and click **Insert Function** in the Function Library group on the Formulas tab. Select **SUMIF**.
4. Click **OK** to close the dialog box.

TROUBLESHOOTING If the SUMIF function is not visible, key SUMIF in the *Search for a function* box and click Go. Click SUMIF when it appears in the Function box.

5. On the Function Arguments dialog box, click **Collapse Dialog** and select **C5:C16**. Press Enter.
6. In the Criteria box, key **>200000** as shown in Figure 8-2. You do not have to enter the range in the Sum_range box. If you leave the range blank, Excel sums the cells you enter in the Range box.

Figure 8-2

Function Arguments dialog box guides you in building SUMIF formulas

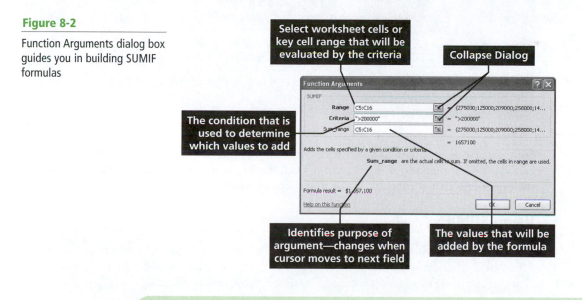

TROUBLESHOOTING It is not necessary to key the dollar sign or the comma. If you key them, Excel removes them from the formula and returns an accurate value.

7. Click **OK** to close the dialog box. You see that $1,657,100 of Fabrikam's December revenue came from properties valued in excess of $200,000.

TAKE NOTE* The result of the SUMIF formula in C20 does not include the property value in C15 because the formula specified values greater than $200,000. To include this value, the criterion would have to be >= (greater than or equal to).

8. In C21, click **Recently Used** in the Function Library group and click **SUMIF** to open the Function Arguments dialog box. The insertion point should be in the Range box.

When you click Recently Used, the last function used appears at the top of the list. When you click Insert Function, the Insert Function dialog box opens with the last-used function highlighted.

9. Select **E5:E16** in the Range field and press Enter.
10. Key **<3%** in the Criteria box and press Tab.
11. Select **C5:C16** in the Sum_range field. Click **OK** to close the dialog box.
12. Click the **Microsoft Office Button** and select **Save As**. Create a Lesson 8 folder.
13. **SAVE** the workbook as *December Sales*.

    PAUSE. LEAVE the workbook open to use in the next exercise.

CERTIFICATION READY?
How do you use a SUMIF formula to conditionally summarize data?
3.4.1

Table 8-1 explains the meaning of each argument in the SUMIF syntax. If sum_range is omitted from the formula, as you did in the first calculation in the preceding exercise, the cells in the range are evaluated and added if they match the criterion.

Table 8-1

Arguments in the SUMIF syntax

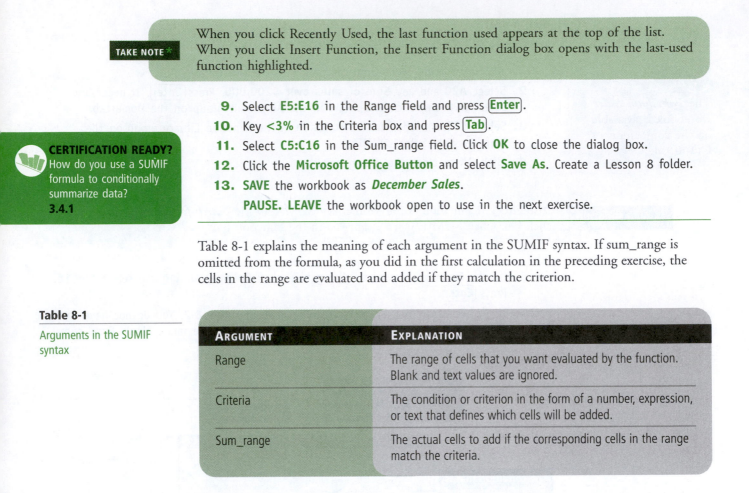

ARGUMENT	EXPLANATION
Range	The range of cells that you want evaluated by the function. Blank and text values are ignored.
Criteria	The condition or criterion in the form of a number, expression, or text that defines which cells will be added.
Sum_range	The actual cells to add if the corresponding cells in the range match the criteria.

Sum_range does not have to be the same size and shape as range. The actual cells that are added are determined by using the top-left cell in sum_range as the beginning cell, and then including cells that correspond in size and shape to range.

Using SUMIFS

SUMIFS adds cells in a range that meet multiple criteria. It is important to note that the order of arguments is different from SUMIF. In a SUMIF formula, the sum_range argument is the third argument; in SUMIFS, it is the first argument.

USE SUMIFS

USE the workbook from the previous exercise.

1. Select **C22**. Click **Insert Function** in the Function Library group on the Formulas tab.
2. Key **SUMIFS** in the *Search for a function* box and click **Go**. SUMIFS will be highlighted in the Function box.
3. Click **OK** to accept the function and close the dialog box.
4. On the Function Arguments dialog box, select **C5:C16** in the Sum_range box.
5. In the Criteria_range1 box, select **F5:F16**. In the Criteria1 box key **<=60.**
6. In the Criteria_range2 box, select **C5:C16**.
7. In the Criteria2 box, key **>200000**. Click **OK**.
8. Select **C23** and click **Recently Used** in the Function Library group.
9. Select **SUMIFS**. In the Sum_range box, select **C5:C16**.

10. In the Criteria_range1 box, select **F5:F16**. Key **<60** in the Criteria1 box.

11. In the Criteria_range2 box, select **E5:E16**. Key **<3%** in the Criteria2 box. Your Function Arguments dialog box should look like Figure 8-3. Click **OK**.

Figure 8-3

SUMIFS formula applies two or more criteria

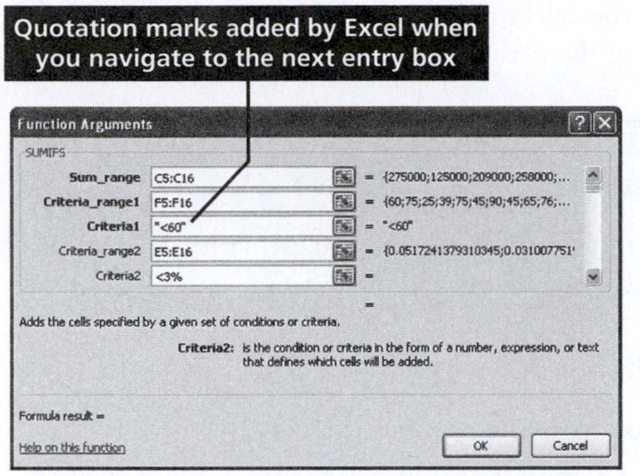

Quotation marks added by Excel when you navigate to the next entry box

12. **SAVE** the workbook

PAUSE. LEAVE the workbook open to use in the next exercise.

CERTIFICATION READY?
How do you create a formula that sums values that meet multiple criteria?
3.4.1

A SUMIFS formula allows you to specify multiple criteria to conditionally summarize data. The first SUMIFS formula you created added the selling price of properties that sold for more than $200,000, which were on the market 60 days or less. The second formula added the properties that sold at 98% (<3%) of their listed price within 60 days. These formulas analyzed the data on two criteria. You can continue to add up to 127 criteria on which data can be evaluated.

Because the order of arguments is different in SUMIF and SUMIFS, if you want to copy and edit these similar functions, be sure to put the arguments in the correct order.

Using COUNTIF

The COUNTIF function counts the number of cells in a given range that meet a specific condition. The syntax for the COUNTIF function is COUNTIF(range, criteria). The range is the range of cells to be counted. The condition can be a number, expression, or text.

USE COUNTIF

USE the workbook from the previous exercise.

1. Select **C24**. Click **Insert Function** in the Function Library group.

2. Key **COUNTIF** in the Search for a function box and click **Go**. COUNTIF will be highlighted in the Function box.

3. Click **OK** to accept the function and close the dialog box.

4. On the Function Arguments dialog box, select **B5:B16** in the Range box.

5. In the Criteria box, key **>=200000**. Click **OK**.

6. Select **C25** and click **Recently Used** in the Function Library group.

7. Select **COUNTIF**. In the Range box, select **C5:C16**.

8. In the Criteria box, key **>=200000**. Click **OK**.

CERTIFICATION READY?
How do you create a formula that counts the number of cells in a range that meet a specified condition?
3.4.1

9. **SAVE** the workbook.

PAUSE. LEAVE the workbook open to use in the next exercise.

The range is the range of cells to be counted. The criteria are the conditions than must be met in order for the cells to be counted. In the exercise, the range was the selling price of homes sold during the period. The criterion was homes that sold for $200,000 or more.

Using COUNTIFS

The COUNTIFS formula counts the number of cells within a range that meet multiple criteria. The syntax is COUNTIFS(range1, criteria1, range2, criteria2 . . .). You can create up to 127 ranges and criteria.

→ **USE COUNTIFS**

USE the workbook from the previous exercise.

1. Select **C26**. Click **Insert Function** in the Function Library group.
2. Key **COUNTIFS** in the *Search for a function* box and click **Go**. COUNTIFS will be highlighted in the Function box.
3. Click **OK** to accept the function and close the dialog box.
4. On the Function Arguments dialog box, select **F5:F16** in the Criteria_range1 box.
5. In the Criteria1 box, key **>=60**.
6. In the Criteria_range2 box, select **E5:E16**.
7. In the Criteria2 box, key **>=5%**. Click **OK**.
8. **SAVE** the workbook.

PAUSE. LEAVE the workbook open to use in the next exercise.

CERTIFICATION READY?
How do you create a formula that counts the number of cells within a range that meet multiple criteria?
3.4.1

A cell in the range you identify in the Function Arguments box is counted only if all of the corresponding criteria specified are true for that cell. If a criterion refers to an empty cell, COUNTIFS treats it as a 0 value. As illustrated in Figure 8-4, the tips for each box on the Function Arguments dialog box are replaced with the value when you navigate to the next argument box. The formula result is also displayed, enabling you to review and make corrections if an error message occurs or an unexpected result is returned.

Figure 8-4

Arguments and results for COUNTIFS formula

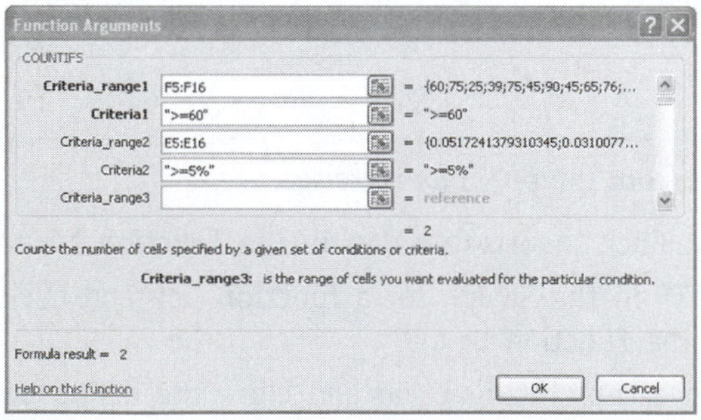

When you create formulas, you can use the wildcard characters question mark (?) and asterisk (*) in the criteria. A question mark matches any single character; an asterisk matches any sequence of characters. If you want to find an actual question mark or asterisk, type a grave accent (`) preceding the character.

Using AVERAGEIF

AVERAGEIF returns the arithmetic mean of all the cells in a range that meet a given criteria. The syntax is AVERAGEIF(range, criteria, average_range).

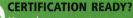 **USE AVERAGEIF**

USE the workbook from the previous exercise.

1. Select **C27** and click **Recently Used** in the Function Library group.
2. Click **AVERAGE**. Select **B5:B16** in the Number1 box and click **OK**. A mathematical average is returned.
3. Select **C28** and click **Insert Function** in the Function Library group.
4. Select **AVERAGEIF** from the function list or use the function search box to locate and accept the AVERAGEIF function.
5. On the Function Arguments dialog box, select **B5:B16** in the Range box.
6. In the Criteria box, key **>=200000**.
7. In the Average_range box, select **F5:F16**. Click **OK** to close the dialog box.
   PAUSE. LEAVE the workbook open to use in the next exercise.

In the AVERAGEIf syntax, range is the set of cells you want to average. For example, in this exercise, you wanted to know the average number of days a property valued at $200,000 or more was on the market before it sold. The range is B5:B16, the listed value of the homes that were sold. The criteria is the condition against which you want the cells to be evaluated, that is, >=200000. Average_range is the actual set of cells to average—the number of days each home was on the market before it was sold.

Using AVERAGEIFS

An AVERAGEIFS formula returns the average (arithmetic mean) of all cells that meet multiple criteria. The syntax is AVERAGEIFS(average_range,criteria_range1,criteria1, criteria_range2,criteria2 . . .).

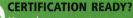 **USE AVERAGEIFS**

USE the workbook from the previous exercise.

1. Select **C29**. Click **Insert Function** in the Function Library group.
2. Key **AVERAGEIFS** in the *Search for a function* box and click **Go**. AVERAGEIFS will be highlighted in the Function box.
3. Click **OK** to accept the function and close the dialog box.
4. On the Function Arguments dialog box, select **F5:F16** in the Average_range box. Press [Tab].
5. In the Criteria_range1 box, select **B5:B16** and press [Tab].
6. In the Criteria1 box, key **<200000**.
7. In the Criteria_range2 box, select **E5:E16** and press [Tab].
8. In the Criteria2 box, key **<=5%**. Click **OK**.
9. **SAVE** the workbook. **CLOSE** the workbook.
   PAUSE. LEAVE Excel open to use in the next exercise.

TAKE NOTE*

You can reference another worksheet in the same workbook in a conditional formula, but you cannot use references to another workbook.

You entered only two criteria for the SUMIFS, COUNTIFS, and AVERAGEIFS formulas you created in the previous exercises. However, in very large worksheets, you often need to use multiple criteria for the formula to return the value that is meaningful for your analysis. You can enter up to 127 conditions that data must match in order for a cell to be included in the conditional summary that results from a SUMIFS, COUNTIFS, or AVERAGEIFS formula.

The following statements summarize how values are treated when you enter an AVERAGEIF or AVERAGEIFS formula.

- If Average_range is omitted from the function arguments, the range is used.
- If a cell in Average_range is an empty cell, AVERAGEIF ignores it.
- If a range is blank or contains a text value, AVERAGEIF returns the #DIV0! error value.
- If a cell in a criterion is empty, AVERAGEIF treats it as a 0 value.
- If no cells in the range meet the criteria, AVERAGEIF returns the #DIV/0! error value.

■ Using Formulas to Look Up Data in a Workbook

↓
THE BOTTOM LINE

When worksheets contain long, and sometimes cumbersome, lists of data, you need a way to find specific information within the list. Excel's *lookup functions* are used to find information stored in a table in an Excel worksheet. Lookup functions are an efficient way to search for and insert a value in a cell when the desired value is stored elsewhere in the workbook or in a different workbook. A *table* refers to a range of cells in a worksheet that can be used by a lookup function. These functions can return cell references identifying where the information is found, or they can return the actual contents of the found cell.

Using VLOOKUP

The V in VLOOKUP stands for vertical. This formula is used when the comparison values are located in a column to the left of the data that you want to find. The VLOOKUP function searches for a value in the first column of a table array on the worksheet and then returns a value from a specific column, in the same row as the value it found, into a different location in the worksheet.

→ **USE VLOOKUP**

GET READY. Launch Microsoft Excel if it is not already open.

The *Fabrikam Bonus* workbook is available on the companion CD-ROM.

1. **OPEN** *Fabrikam Bonus* from the CD data files for this lesson.
2. Click the **Bonus** tab and select **C15:F24**. Click **Define Name** in the Defined Names group on the Formulas tab.
3. Key **Bonus** in the Name box on the New Name dialog box. Click **OK** to close the dialog box.

TAKE NOTE*

Arguments used in VLOOKUP or HLOOKUP are not case-sensitive, so you can key them in uppercase, lowercase, or any combination of uppercase and lowercase characters. Also, the VLOOKUP and HLOOKUP function names are not case-sensitive.

4. Select **E5** and click **Insert Function**.
5. Select **VLOOKUP** in the *Select a function* box and click **OK**. The Function Arguments dialog box opens with the cursor in the Lookup_value box.
6. Select **D5** and press **Tab**.

TAKE NOTE *

TRUE in the range lookup box will return the closest value. False returns only an exact value. If you leave the Range_lookup box empty, Excel will enter TRUE when you click OK.

CERTIFICATION READY
How do you create a VLOOKUP formula that retrieves a value from a table?
3.5.1

7. In Table_array, click **Use in Formula** in the Defined Names group and select **Bonus**. Press [Tab].
8. In the Col_index_num box, key **2,** the column containing the standard bonus amounts. Press [Tab].
9. In the Range_lookup box, key **True** and click **OK**.
10. Copy the formula in E5 to E6:E11. Bonuses for the other sales agents are calculated. The N/A error message appears in E11 because a value is not available for agents who have been employed less than one year. Agents become eligible for a bonus after a full year of service. You will change this error message in another exercise.

PAUSE. LEAVE the workbook open to use in the next exercise.

The VLOOKUP function syntax is LOOKUP(lookup_value,table_array,col_index_num). The argument components used in lookup formulas are shown in Figure 8-5 and described in Table 8-2, which applies to VLOOKUP and HLOOKUP formulas.

Figure 8-5

Function arguments for VLOOKUP formula

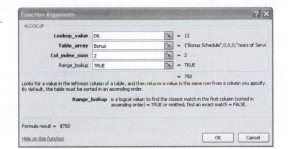

Table 8-2

Function syntax for VLOOKUP

ARGUMENT	DESCRIPTION
Lookup_value	The value to be found in the column or row; the lookup value can be a constant value, a text contact enclosed in quotation marks, or the address or name of a cell that contains a numeric or text constant.
Table_array	Two or more columns of data. Use a reference to a range or a range name. The values in the first column of table_array are the values searched by lookup_value.
Row_index_num	The numeric position of the row that is to be searched for HLOOKUP.
Col_index_num	The numeric position of the column that is to be searched for VLOOKUP.
	The column number in table_array from which the matching value must be returned. A col_index_num of 1 returns the value in the first column in table_array; a col_index_num of 2 returns the value in the second column in table_array, and so on.
Range_lookup	A logical value that specifies whether you want VLOOKUP to find an exact match or an approximate match. If the function is to return the nearest value, even when there is no match, this value should be set to TRUE; if an exact match is required, this value should be set to FALSE; if this argument is not included, the function assumes the value to be TRUE.

Review the following key points related to VLOOKUP and HLOOKUP functions and arguments.

- An *array* is used to build single formulas that produce multiple results or that operate on a group of arguments. The data in a table array must be arranged in rows and columns. It can be a constant or a formula.

- If lookup_value is smaller than the smallest value in the first column of table_array, VLOOKUP returns the #N/A error value, as you saw in E11 in the preceding exercise.

- Table_array values can be text, numbers, or logical values. Uppercase and lowercase text is equivalent.

- The values in the first column of table_array must be placed in ascending sort order, otherwise VLOOKUP may not give the correct value. The lookup table you used in the exercise listed years of service in ascending order.

- If Range_lookup is TRUE or omitted, an exact or approximate match is returned. If an exact match is not found, the next largest value that is less than lookup_value is returned.

- If Range_lookup is FALSE, VLOOKUP will find only an exact match. If an exact match is not found, the error value #N/A is returned. In the exercise, the same bonus is paid for a range of years, so you entered TRUE in the Range_lookup box so that a value would be returned for all agents who have been with the company more than one year.

Using HLOOKUP

HLOOKUP searches for a value in the top row of a table or an array and then returns a value in the same column from a row you specify in the table or array. Use HLOOKUP when the comparison values are located in a row across the top of a table of data, and you want to look down a specified number of rows, as you will do in the following exercise.

⊙ USE HLOOKUP

USE the workbook from the previous exercise.

1. Select **F5** and click **Insert Function** in the Function Library group.
2. Select **HLOOKUP** and click **OK**.
3. Enter the HLOOKUP formula **=HLOOKUP("performance award",F16:F24,7,true)** in the argument boxes as shown in Figure 8-6. Click **OK**.

Figure 8-6

Use an HLOOKUP formula to lookup and retrieve a value

Function Arguments	?×
HLOOKUP	
Lookup_value	"Performance Award" = "Performance Award"
Table_array	F16:F24 = {"Performance Award";200;300;400;...
Row_index_num	7 = 7
Range_lookup	TRUE = TRUE
	= 3000

Looks for a value in the top row of a table or array of values and returns the value in the same column from a row you specify.

Range_lookup is a logical value: to find the closest match in the top row (sorted in ascending order) = TRUE or omitted; find an exact match = FALSE.

Formula result = 3000

Help on this function   OK   Cancel

4. **SAVE** the workbook in your Lesson 8 folder. Name the workbook *Employee Bonus*.
   PAUSE. LEAVE the workbook open to use in the next exercise.

CERTIFICATION READY?
How do you create an HLOOKUP formula that retrieves a value from a specific row in a table?

3.5.1

It may be difficult to remember the syntax for an HLOOKUP or VLOOKUP function. Use the Function Arguments dialog box to help you remember the order of the arguments. When you click in each field, review the tips that appear on the right side of each box as well as the explanation below the argument boxes that tells the purpose of each argument in the formula.

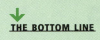

■ Adding Conditional Logic Functions to Formulas

THE BOTTOM LINE

You can use the AND, OR, and NOT functions to create conditional formulas that result in a logical value, that is, TRUE or FALSE. Such formulas test whether conditions are true or false and make logical comparisons. You can use the IF, AND, and OR functions to create a conditional formula that results in another calculation or in values other than TRUE or FALSE.

Using IF

The result of a conditional formula is determined by the state of a specific condition or the answer to a logical question. An IF formula returns one value if a condition you specify is true and another value if it is false. The IF function requires the following syntax: IF(logical_test, value_if_true, value if false).

➔ USE IF

USE the workbook you saved in the previous exercise.

1. Click the **Performance** tab to make it the active worksheet.
2. Select **D5**. Click **Logical** in the Function Library group and click **IF**.
3. Key **C5>=B5** in the Logical_test box. This component of the formula determines whether the agent has met his or her sales goal.
4. Key **Yes** in the Value_if_true box. This is the value returned if the agent met his or her goal.
5. Key **No** in the Value_if_false box and click **OK**.
6. Select **D5**. Use the fill handle to copy the formula to D6:D11. Four agents have earned the performance award.

   PAUSE. LEAVE the workbook open to use in the next exercise.

CERTIFICATION READY?
How do you create a formula that returns one value if a condition exists and a different value if the condition does not exist?
3.6.1

An IF function sets up a conditional statement to test data. If the condition exists, one value will be returned. If the condition does not exist, another value is returned.

Using AND

The AND function returns TRUE if all its arguments are TRUE and returns FALSE if one or more arguments are FALSE. The Syntax is AND(logical1,logical2,. . .). You will use the AND function to determine whether Fabrikam's total annual sales met the strategic goal **and** whether the sales goal exceeded the previous year's sales by 5 percent.

➔ USE AND

USE the workbook from the previous exercise.

1. Click the **Annual Sales** tab.
2. Select **B5**. Click **Logical** in the Function Library group and click the **AND** option. The Function Arguments dialog box opens with the cursor in the Logical1 box.
3. Select **B3**, key **<=**, select **B16**, and press ⏎**Enter**. This argument represents the first condition: Did actual sales exceed the sales goal? Because this is the first year, only one logical test will be entered.
4. Select **C5**, click **Recently Used**, and click **AND**. In the Logical1 box, key **C3<=C16**.
5. In the Logical2 box, key **C16>=B16*1.05**. Click **OK**. The formula returns True, which means that both conditions in the formula have been met. The arguments are illustrated in Figure 8-7.

Figure 8-7

AND function arguments

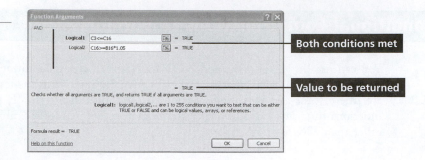

Both conditions met

Value to be returned

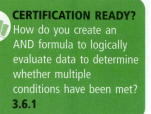
6. Select **C5** and copy the formula to D5:F5.

PAUSE. LEAVE the workbook open to use in the next exercise.

The AND function returns a TRUE result only when both conditions in the formula have been met. Let's examine the results you achieved in the preceding exercise. Sales in the second year exceeded sales for the previous year; therefore, the first condition has been met. Year 2 sales also exceeded Year 1 Sales by 5 percent. Because both conditions were met, the formula returns a TRUE result.

Consider the arguments for the logical tests for year 3 (formula in D5). Sales did not exceed the sales goal; therefore, the first argument returns a FALSE value. However, sales did exceed the previous year's sales by 5 percent. When only one condition has been met, the formula returns FALSE.

Using OR

> The syntax for an OR formula is similar to AND; however, OR returns TRUE if any argument is TRUE, and returns FALSE only when all arguments are FALSE.
>
> The arguments must evaluate to logical values such as TRUE or FALSE, or arrays or references that contain logical values. In the following exercise, you will create a formula that evaluates whether sales increased each year during the data period. The OR formula will return True if any of the periods increased.

⊕ USE OR

USE the workbook from the previous exercise.

1. If necessary, select the **Annual Sales** worksheet. Select **A18** and click **Logical** in the Function Library group.

2. Click **OR**. The Function Arguments dialog box opens. You will create a formula that answers the question *Did Carey's sales increase by 3% in year 3 or year 4?*

3. In the Logical1 box, key **D9>=C9*1.03** and press [Tab].

4. In the Logical2 box, key **E9>=D9*1.03**.

5. Click **OK** to close the dialog box. The formula returns TRUE, indicating that Carey's sales increased by 3 percent in at least one of the identified years. A FALSE finding is returned only when both logical arguments are false. In this case, Mr. Carey's sales increased less than 3 percent from year 2 to year 3 and increased by more than 3 percent from year 3 to year 4. Because OR returns a FALSE result only if all conditions are false, at least one of the arguments in this case equates to true.

TAKE NOTE ∗

As you add arguments, the Value fields on the Function Arguments dialog box expand to allow you to enter multiple arguments.

PAUSE. LEAVE the workbook open to use in the next exercise.

In the first OR formula you entered in this exercise, both logical tests returned a TRUE value. Mr. Carey's sales in year 3 were at least 3 percent more than in year 2. His year 4 sales were also at least 3 percent more than his year 3 sales. If one of the tests had resulted in a TRUE value and the other in a FALSE value, the formula would still have returned a TRUE value in A18.

Using NOT

> The NOT function reverses the value of its arguments. Use NOT when you want to make sure a value is not equal to one particular value. If the logical value is false, NOT returns true. In the following exercise, you will answer the question: Did Calafato's year 5 sales exceed his year 4 sales by 3 percent?

→ USE NOT

USE the workbook from the previous exercise.

1. On the Annual Sales worksheet, select **A19** and click **Logical** in the Function Library group.
2. Select **NOT** from the list of logical formulas.
3. On the Function Arguments dialog box, key **F11>=E11*3%** and click **OK**. False is returned by the formula. Calafato's year 5 sales were at least 3 percent greater than his year 4 sales. The NOT formula returns the opposite response.
4. **SAVE** the workbook.

PAUSE. LEAVE the workbook open to use in the next exercise.

In this exercise, you want to be sure that in year 5, Calafato's sales increased by at least 3 percent over the previous year. The NOT conditional formula results in a logical value (True or False) and can be used for this logical test—returning the opposite value of what would be returned by an IF formula.

Using IFERROR

> An error message is returned when a formula does not contain sufficient arguments to return a value. Use the IFERROR function to trap and handle errors in a formula. The function returns a value you specify if a formula evaluates to an error; otherwise, it returns the result of the formula. The syntax is IFERROR(value,value_if_error).

→ USE IFERROR

USE the workbook you saved in the previous exercise.

1. Click the **Bonus** worksheet tab. Select **E11** and click after the = in the formula bar to edit the formula.
2. Key **IFERROR(** before VLOOKUP. Leave the existing formula intact. Press **End**.
3. At the end of the original formula, key,**"Not Eligible")**. As shown in Figure 8-8, the complete formula is =IFERROR(VLOOKUP(D11,Bonus,2, TRUE) "Not Eligible").

Figure 8-8

Edit formula to specify error message

`=IFERROR(VLOOKUP(D11,Bonus,2,TRUE),"Not Eligible")`

4. Click **OK**. The #N/A error message is replaced with the message that the agent is not eligible for the bonus.

   PAUSE. LEAVE the workbook open to use in the next exercise.

CERTIFICATION READY?
How do you replace an error message with specific text when the formula equates to an error?
3.6.1

Value is the argument that is checked for an error. If you select E11 and click the Insert Function button next to the formula bar, you will see that the original VLOOKUP formula appears in the Value box (first argument) in the IFERROR formula. As illustrated in Figure 8-9, that argument returned a #N/A error. The Value_if_error box contains the text to replace the error message.

Figure 8-9

IFERROR function arguments

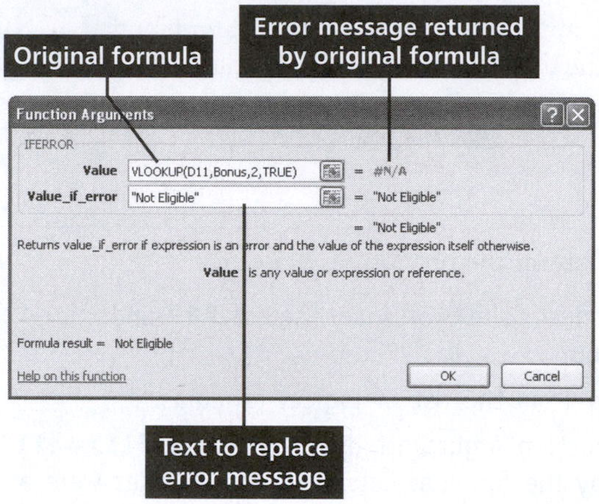

The following error types are evaluated by IFERROR: #N/A, #VALUE!, #REF!, #DIV/0!, #NUM!, #NAME?, or #NULL!. In the exercise, you replaced the error message with text that explained why one of the sales agents did not receive a bonus when the VLOOKUP formula was applied.

■ Using Formulas to Format Text

↓
THE BOTTOM LINE

You may be familiar with Microsoft Word's convert text command that enables you to change the capitalization of text. You can use PROPER, UPPER, and LOWER formulas to capitalize the first letter in a text string or to convert uppercase to lowercase or vice versa.

Using PROPER

The PROPER function capitalizes the first letter in a text string and any other letters in text that follow any character other than a letter. All other letters are converted to lowercase. In the PROPER(text) syntax, text can be enclosed in quotation marks, a formula that returns text, or a reference to a cell containing the text you want to capitalize. You can use PROPER to change uppercase or lowercase text to title case text.

⊙ USE PROPER

USE the workbook from the previous exercise.

1. Click the **Performance** worksheet tab. Select **A17** and click **Text** in the Function Library group on the Formulas tab.

2. Scroll down the list and click **PROPER**. The Function Arguments dialog box opens.

3. Select **A16** and click **OK**. The uppercase text in A16 is entered in A17 in title case.

4. Select **A17** and click **Copy** in the Clipboard group on the Home tab.

TAKE NOTE*

Notice that the s letters following the apostrophe in Fabrikam's and Agent's are capitalized. Text that follows any character other than a letter is capitalized when you use the PROPER formula. You will need to proofread carefully when you convert capitalization.

CERTIFICATION READY?
How do you modify text using a PROPER formula?
3.7.1

5. Select **A14** and click the arrow under **Paste** in the Clipboard group.
6. Click **Paste Values**. The text appears in A14. Click **A14** and change the letters following the apostrophes to lowercase text.
7. Select **A16:A17** and press Delete. The duplicate lines of text are removed.
   PAUSE. LEAVE the workbook open to use in the next exercise.

The PROPER function capitalizes the first letter in each word in a text string. All other letters are converted to lowercase letters. That is why you edited the text after it was converted in the previous exercise. Because Excel recognized the apostrophe as a break, it capitalized the next letter. In the PROPER(text) syntax, text can be enclosed in quotation marks or cell references can be selected as you selected them in the previous exercise.

When you created the formula to convert the uppercase text to title case, you had two lines of text. If you deleted the original text in A16, the converted text in A17 would have been deleted as well. When you used the Paste Values option, the contents of A17 were pasted to A14 rather than the formula, which would be dependent on the text remaining in A16. After you pasted the results rather than the formula, you were able to remove the duplicate lines of text.

Using UPPER

The UPPER function allows you to convert text to uppercase (all capital letters). The syntax is UPPER(text), with text referring to the text you want converted to uppercase. Text can be a reference or a text string.

USE UPPER

USE the workbook you saved in the previous exercise.

1. Click the **Performance** worksheet tab. Select **A13** and click **Text** in the Function Library group.
2. Scroll down the list of functions, if necessary, and select **UPPER.** The Function Arguments dialog box opens.
3. Select **A14** as the text to convert and click **OK.** The text from A14 is entered in A13 in uppercase letters.
4. Click the **Home** tab. Select **A13** and click **Copy** in the Clipboard group.
5. With A13 still selected, click the arrow under **Paste**. Click **Paste Values**. With this action, you replaced the UPPER function in A13 with the actual result (value) of the function.
6. Select A14 and press Delete. **SAVE** the workbook.
   PAUSE. LEAVE the workbook open to use in the next exercise.

CERTIFICATION READY?
How do you use UPPER to convert text to uppercase using a formula?
3.7.1

Converting capitalization in text is a two-step process. You cannot enter the formula in the text's present location, so after the text has been converted, you will want to cut and paste the text to the desired location. The Paste Values command pastes the contents without the formula so that you can remove the duplicate data.

Using LOWER

The LOWER function converts all uppercase letters in a text string to lowercase. LOWER does not change characters in text that are not letters.

USE LOWER

USE the workbook from the previous exercise.

1. Click the **Annual Sales** worksheet tab. Select **B20** and click **Text** in the Function Library group.
2. Scroll down the list of functions, if necessary, and select **LOWER**.
3. Select **B19** as the text to convert and click **OK**. The text from B19 is converted to lowercase and it is displayed in B20 below the original uppercase text in B19.
4. **SAVE** the workbook.

   PAUSE. LEAVE the workbook open to use in the next exercise.

CERTIFICATION READY?
How do you use LOWER to convert text to lowercase using a formula?
3.7.1

It is important that you review text after you have changed the case. For example, the agent's name in B20 should be capitalized as well as the first word in the sentence. If you replace the text in B19 with the lowercase text in B20, you will need to edit the text.

■ Using Formulas to Modify Text

↓ THE BOTTOM LINE

The SUBSTITUTE function allows you to edit data and substitute new text for existing text. Formulas can also be used to convert text to columns.

Using SUBSTITUTE

Excel's SUBSTITUTE function is especially useful when you need to edit data and you want to substitute new text for existing text in a text string. Use SUBSTITUTE when you want to replace specific text in a text string; use REPLACE when you want to replace any text that occurs in a specific location in a text string, such as when a name change occurs.

USE SUBSTITUTE

USE the workbook from the previous exercise.

1. Click the **Annual Sales** worksheet tab if necessary. Select **B22**, click **Text** in the Function Library, and click **SUBSTITUTE**.
2. Select **B18** in the Text box.
3. Key **3** in the Old_text box. This is the text you want to replace.
4. Key **5** in the New_text box.
5. Key **1** in the Instance_num box and click **OK**.
6. **SAVE** the workbook.

   PAUSE. LEAVE the workbook open to use in the next exercise.

CERTIFICATION READY?
How do you use SUBSTITUTE to replace existing text with new text using a formula?
3.7.1

When you want to use existing text with small changes, you can use the SUBSTITUTE function. On the Function Arguments dialog box, Text can be the actual text you want to substitute, or it can be a cell reference. You wanted to use the text in B18 with one change. Figure 8-10 illustrates the function arguments that result in changing 3% to 5% in the new text. The number 3 occurs three times in the original text. The last function argument indicates which occurrence should be replaced.

Figure 8-10

SUBSTITUTE function
arguments

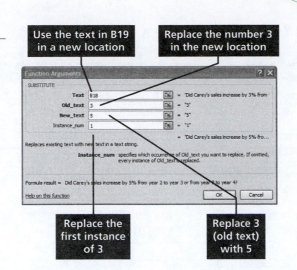

Use the text in B19
in a new location

Replace the number 3
in the new location

Replace the
first instance
of 3

Replace 3
(old text)
with 5

Converting Text to Columns

You can use the Convert Text to Columns Wizard to separate simple cell content, such as
first names and last names, into different columns. Depending upon how your data is
organized, you can split the cell contents based on a delimiter, such as a space or a
comma, or based on a specific column break location within your data. In the following
exercise, you will convert the data in column A to two columns.

⊕ CONVERT TEXT TO COLUMNS

USE the workbook from the previous exercise.

1. Click the **Performance** worksheet tab if necessary. Select any cell in column B. Right-
   click to open the shortcut menu. Click **Insert** and click **Entire Column**. Click **OK**.
2. Select **A5:A11**. Click the **Data** tab and click **Text to Columns** in the Data Tools
   group.
3. The Text Wizard opens with Delimited checked as the default because Excel recognized that the data in the selected range is separated by a comma. Click **Next** to
   move to the next step in the wizard.
4. Select **Comma** as the delimiter. If other delimiters are checked, deselect them and
   click **Next**.
5. Select **Text** as the Column data format and click **Finish**. First names of the agents
   are moved to column B.
6. Select **A4**, key **Last Name**, and press `Tab`.
7. Select **B4**, key **First Name**, and press `Tab`.
8. **SAVE** the workbook with the same name. **CLOSE** the workbook.
   CLOSE Excel.

 CERTIFICATION READY?
How do you convert text to
columns?
3.7.2, 2.3.5

◆ **ANOTHER WAY** You can also use text functions such as LEFT, MID, and RIGHT to convert text data
from one column to multiple columns.

SUMMARY SKILL MATRIX

In This Lesson You Learned	Matrix Skill	Skill Number
To create formulas to summarize data that meets specified criteria	Use SUMIF, SUMIFS, COUNTIF, COUNTIFS, AVERAGEIF, and AVERAGEIFS	3.4.1
To create formulas to look up data in a workbook	Use VLOOKUP and HLOOKUP	3.5.1
To create formulas that test whether conditions are present	Use IF, AND, OR, NOT, IFERROR	3.6.1
To create formulas to change the case of text	Use PROPER, UPPER, LOWER, SUBSTITUTE	3.7.1
To use formulas to modify text		
To substitute new text for existing text	Use PROPER, UPPER, LOWER, SUBSTITUTE	3.7.1
To separate cell content into different columns	Convert text to columns	3.7.2, 2.3.5

■ Knowledge Assessment

Matching

a. AND function	**f.** OR function
b. arguments	**g.** SUMIF
c. array	**h.** SUMIFS
d. conditional formula	**i.** Table
e. HLOOKUP	**j.** VLOOKUP

_____ **1.** A function used to look up information stored in the first column of an Excel table in the worksheet.

_____ **2.** A function in which a TRUE result is returned if data meets any condition specified in the formula.

_____ **3.** The values that a function uses to perform operations or calculations.

_____ **4.** A function in which a TRUE result is returned if data meets all conditions specified in the formula.

_____ **5.** In a worksheet, a range of cells that can be used by a lookup formula.

_____ **6.** A formula component used to build single formulas that produce multiple results.

_____ **7.** A function in which the result is determined by the state of multiple criteria.

_____ **8.** A function that references the first row of an Excel table in the worksheet in order to look up information stored in the same column.

_____ **9.** A function that returns the total of cells that meet one condition.

_____ **10.** A function in which the result is determined by the state of a particular condition.

Multiple Choice

Circle the choice that best completes the following statements or answers the questions.

1. Which of the following functions would you use to convert text from uppercase to title case?
   a. UPPER
   b. PROPER
   c. LOWER
   d. SUBSTITUTE

2. Which function automatically counts cells that meet multiple conditions?
   a. COUNTIF
   b. COUNT
   c. COUNTIFS
   d. SUMIFS

3. Which function automatically counts cells that meet a specific condition?
   a. COUNTIF
   b. COUNT
   c. COUNTIFS
   d. SUMIFS

4. In the formula =SUMIFS(C5:C16,F5:F16,"<=60," B5:B16,">200000"), the range of cells to be added is
   a. =C5:C16.
   b. =F5:F16.
   c. =B5:B16.
   d. =C5:F16.

5. In the formula =SUMIFS(C5:C16,F5:F16,"<=60,"B5:B16,">200000"), >=60 means
   a. if the value in C5:C16 is greater than or equal to 60, the value in C5:16 will be included in the total.
   b. if the value in F5:F16 is greater than or equal to 60, the value in C5:16 will be included in the total.
   c. if the value in B5:BF16 is less than or equal to 60, the value in C5:16 will be included in the total.
   d. if the value in F5:F16 is less than or equal to 60, the value in C5:16 will be included in the total.

6. Criteria range in a formula refers to
   a. the worksheet data to be included in the formula's results.
   b. the range containing a condition that must be met in order for data to be included in the result.
   c. the type of formula being used for the calculation.
   d. the type of data contained in the cells to be included in the formula.

7. Which function returns one value if a condition is true and a different value when the condition is not true?
   a. AND
   b. OR
   c. IF
   d. IFERROR

8. Which function returns a value if all conditions are met?

   a. AND

   b. OR

   c. IF

   d. IFERROR

9. Which function specifies the result that will be returned if no values meet the specified condition(s)?

   a. AND

   b. OR

   c. NOT

   d. IFERROR

10. Which function reverses the value of the function arguments?

   a. AND

   b. NOT

   c. IF

   d. IFERROR

■ Competency Assessment

Project 8-1: Create SUMIF and SUMIFS Formulas to Conditionally Summarize Data

Salary information for Contoso, Ltd. has been entered in a workbook so the office manager can analyze and summarize the data.

GET READY. Launch Excel.

The *Salaries* workbook is available on the companion CD-ROM.

1. **OPEN** *Salaries* from the data files for this lesson.
2. Select **F4** and click **Insert Function** in the Function Library group.
3. If the SUMIF function is not visible, key **SUMIF** in the *Search for a function* box and click **Go**. Select **SUMIF** from the *Select a function* list. Click **OK**.
4. On the Function Arguments dialog box, select **C4:C33** in the Range field.
5. In the Criteria box, key **>100000**.
6. Click **OK**. Because the range and sum range are the same, it is not necessary to enter a sum range.
7. Select **F5** and click **Insert Function**. Select **SUMIFS** and click **OK**.
8. On the Function Arguments dialog box, select **C4:C33** as the sum range.
9. Select **D4:D33** as the first criteria range.
10. Key **>=10** as the first criteria.
11. Select **C4:C33** as the second criteria range.
12. Key **>60000** as the second criteria. Click **OK** to finish the formula.
13. **SAVE** the workbook as *Salaries 8-1*. **CLOSE** the file.

   LEAVE Excel open to use in the next project.

Project 8-2: Create COUNTIF and AVERAGEIF Formulas

Enter COUNTIF and AVERAGEIF formulas to analyze and summarize grades for a course at the School of Fine Arts.

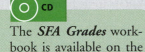

The **SFA Grades** workbook is available on the companion CD-ROM.

1. **OPEN** *SFA Grades* from the data files for this lesson.
2. Select **N4** and click **Insert Function** in the Function Library group on the Formulas tab.
3. If the COUNT function is not visible, key **COUNT** in the *Search for a function* box and click **Go**. Select **COUNT** from the *Select a function* list. Click **OK**.
4. Select **L4:L41** in the Value1 field. Click **OK**.
5. Select **N5** and click **Insert Function**.
6. Select **COUNTIF** and click **OK**.
7. In the Range field, key **$M$4:$M$41**. This is an absolute reference.
8. Key **A** in the Criteria field and click **OK**.
9. Copy the formula in N5 to N6:N8.
10. Select **N6**. In the formula bar, select **A** (the criteria) and key **B**. Press Enter.
11. Select **N7**. In the formula bar, select **A** (the criteria) and key **C**. Press Enter.
12. Select **N8**. In the formula bar, select **A** (the criteria) and key **D**. Press Enter.
13. Select **N10**, click **Insert Function**, and select **AVERAGEIF**.
14. Select **M4:M41** as the range to evaluate.
15. Key **A** as the criteria. Select **L4:L41** in the Average_range field. Click **OK**.
16. **SAVE** the workbook as *SFA Grades 8-2* and then **CLOSE** the file.
    LEAVE Excel open for the next project.

■ Proficiency Assessment

Project 8-3: Create LOOKUP Formulas

In this project you will use a lookup table to determine an employee's end-of-year bonus.

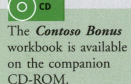

The **Contoso Bonus** workbook is available on the companion CD-ROM.

1. **OPEN** *Contoso Bonus* from the data files for this lesson.
2. Select **B36:C44** and click **Define Name**.
3. Key **Bonus** in the Name box and click **OK**.
4. Select **E4** and click **Lookup & Reference** in the Function Library group. Click **VLOOKUP**.
5. Select **D4** in the Lookup_value field.
6. Key **Bonus** in the Table_array field.
7. Key **2** in the Col_index_num field.
8. Key **TRUE** in the Range_lookup field. Click **OK**.
9. Use the fill handle to copy the formula from E4 to E5:E33.
10. **SAVE** the workbook as *Contoso Bonus 8-3* and then **CLOSE** the file.
    LEAVE Excel open for the next project.

Project 8-4: Separate Text Into Columns

In this project, you will separate student names into two columns rather than one.

1. **OPEN** *SFA Grades 8-2* that you saved in Project 8-2.
2. Select any cell in column B; right-click to open the shortcut menu. Click **Insert** and **Entire Column**. Click **OK**.

3. Select **A4:A41**. Click the **Data** tab and click **Text to Columns** in the Data Tools group.

4. The Convert Text to Columns Wizard opens with Delimited checked as the default because Excel recognized that the data in the selected range is separated. Click **Next**.

5. Select **Comma** as the delimiter. If other delimiters are checked, deselect them and click **Next**.

6. Select **Text** as the Column data format and click **Finish**.

7. Select **A3**, key **Last Name**, and press Tab.

8. Select **B4**, key **First Name**, and press Tab.

9. **SAVE** the workbook as *SFA Grades 8-4*. **CLOSE** the workbook.

   LEAVE Excel open for the next project.

■ Mastery Assessment

Project 8-5: **Create Conditional Logic Formulas**

Professor Garrett Young has asked you to create formulas to identify the highest and lowest achieving students in one of his classes.

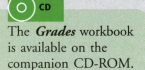

The *Grades* workbook is available on the companion CD-ROM.

1. **OPEN** *Grades* from the data files for this lesson.

2. Select **M4** and click **Logical** in the Function Library group.

3. Select **IF** on the function list.

4. Key **L4>=90%**.

5. In the Value_if_true box, key **High**.

6. In the Value_if_false box, press **Spacebar**. (Pressing the spacebar will insert a space so that the cells that do not meet the criterion will be blank.) Click **OK**.

7. Copy the formula in M4 to M5:M27.

8. Select **N4**, click **Logical**, and click **IF**.

9. Key **L4<70%**.

10. In the Value_if_true box, key **Low**.

11. In the Value_if_false box, press **Spacebar**. Click **OK**.

12. Copy the formula in N4 to N5:N27.

13. **SAVE** the workbook as *Grades 8-5* and then **CLOSE** the file.

    LEAVE Excel open for the next project.

Project 8-6: **Use Formulas to Format Text**

The *Financing* workbook is available on the companion CD-ROM.

1. **OPEN** *Financing* from the data files for this lesson.

2. On the Investments worksheet, select **A12** and click **Text** on the Formulas tab. Enter a formula to convent the text in A4 to title case (i.e., **PROPER(A4)**).

3. Select **A12** and drag the fill handle to A18.

4. Select **A12:18** and click **Copy** in the Clipboard group on the Home tab.

5. Select **A4** and click the arrow under **Paste** in the Clipboard group.

6. Click **Paste Values**. The text appears in A4:A10.

7. Select **A12:A18** and press **Delete**. The duplicate lines of text are removed.

8. **SAVE** the workbook as *Financing 8-6* and then **CLOSE** the file.

   LEAVE Excel open for the next project.

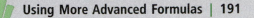

INTERNET READY

If you are employed, does your employer provide a seniority-based bonus similar to the one offered by Fabrikam in the practice exercises? If your employer offers a bonus program, create a lookup table similar to the ones you used in this chapter that could be used to assign bonus amounts to employees.

Go online and research a company where you would like to seek employment when you complete your coursework. What salary and benefits are provided? If you can locate data related to a bonus or profit-sharing program, create a lookup table with the information. Create only the lookup table that could be added to a salary worksheet. For example, Payscale.com, a private research group, reported in 2006 that the average annual bonus for an administrative assistant was $800. Such a bonus might be tied to years of service or to an employee's performance ranking.

Create a worksheet to report your research findings. Format all data appropriately. **SAVE** your worksheet as *Bonus and Incentives*.

CLOSE Excel.

↻ Circling Back

Cross-Cultural Solutions, a nonprofit organization, offers three short-term international volunteer programs. Volunteers can choose from ten countries, with year-round start dates and programs that are 1–12 weeks long.

As international volunteers with Cross-Cultural Solutions, individuals work side-by-side with local people on locally designed and locally driven projects, allowing them to see and learn about a country through the eyes of its people. The organization sends more than 1000 volunteers abroad each year. Excel is a valuable tool for organizing data related to volunteers, the programs they choose, and the start date and duration of their volunteer activity.

➔ Project 1: Sort and Filter Data

Sort and filter the list of volunteers who are scheduled to begin their volunteer experience in July and August.

GET READY. Launch Excel if it is not already running.

CD

The *Volunteers* file is available on the companion CD-ROM.

1. **OPEN** *Volunteers* from the data files.
2. With the Data tab active, select any cell in column D. Click **Sort** in the Sort & Filter group.
3. The Sort dialog box opens. In the *Sort by* field, select **Program**.
4. Click **Add Level**. In the *Then by* box, select **Location**.
5. Click **Add Level**. In the *Then by* box, select **Start Date**. Click **OK**.
6. **SAVE** the document as *Volunteers Project 1*.
7. Click **Filter** in the Sort & Filter group.
8. Click the arrow in the **Duration** column. On the dropdown list, click the **(Select All)** checkbox to deselect all filters. Click the **6 weeks** checkbox and click **OK**.
9. Click the arrow in the **Start Date** column and deselect **August**. Click **OK**.
10. Click **Quick Print** to print the list of volunteers who will depart in July and remain on location for six weeks.
11. Select any cell in the data range. Click **Remove Duplicates** in the Data Tools group.
12. On the Remove Duplicates dialog box, click **Select All** and click **OK**. A dialog box indicates that one duplicate entry was removed.
13. Click **Filter** to display all data.
14. **SAVE** the workbook.

    LEAVE the workbook open for the next project.

➔ Project 2: Manage Worksheets in a Workbook

Data can be accessed easily if you organize the data and create a worksheet for each program.

GET READY. Use the workbook from the previous project.

1. Select **A1:F19** and click **Copy** in the Clipboard group on the Home tab.
2. Select **Sheet2**, click **A1**, and click **Paste** in the Clipboard group.
3. Click the **Paste Options** button and click **Keep Source Column Widths**.
4. With Sheet2 active, click **Format** on the Home tab and click **Move or Copy Sheet**. On the Move or Copy dialog box, in the Before Sheet list, select **Sheet3**. Click **Create a Copy** and click **OK**.

5. Click the **Insert Worksheet** icon. This creates Sheet5.

6. With Sheet1 active, click **Format** and click **Rename Sheet**. Key **Summary** and press [Enter]. Click the **Sheet2** tab and rename it **Insight Abroad**.

7. Click the **Sheet2(2)** tab and rename the worksheet **Intern Abroad**. Click the **Sheet3** tab and rename the worksheet **Volunteer Abroad**.

8. On the Summary worksheet, select **A20:F45** (Intern Abroad volunteers) and click **Copy**. Click the **Intern Abroad** tab and select **A5**. Click **Paste**. This replaces data on the worksheet.

9. On the Summary worksheet, select **A1:F4** and click **Copy**. Click the **Volunteer Abroad** tab, select **A1**, and click **Paste**.

10. Click the **Paste Options** button and click **Keep Source Column Widths**.

11. Select **A46:F87** on the Summary worksheet and click **Copy**. Select **A5** on the Volunteer Abroad worksheet and click **Paste**.

12. With the Summary worksheet active, press [Ctrl] and click the **Sheet5** tab to group the two worksheets.

13. Click **Format**, point to **Hide & Unhide**, and click **Hide Sheet**. Three worksheets remain visible.

14. Click the **Microsoft Office Button** and click **Print**. On the Print dialog box, click **Entire workbook**.

15. Click **Format**. Point to **Hide & Unhide** and click **Unhide Sheet**. Select **Summary** and click **OK**. Select **Format** and unhide Sheet5.

16. With Sheet5 active, click the **Delete** arrow, and click **Delete Sheet**.

17. Click the **Summary** tab and click **Format**. Click **Move or Copy Sheet**. On the Move or Copy dialog box, click **(move to end)**. Click **OK**.

18. **SAVE** the workbook as *Volunteers Project 2* and **CLOSE** the file.

    LEAVE Excel open for the next project.

➔ Project 3: **Sort and Subtotal Data**

Cross-Cultural Solutions is supported in part by individual and corporate tax-deductible contributions. Contributors are asked to select a fund to which their contribution will apply.

1. **OPEN** *Contributions* from the data files.

2. Click the **Data** tab.

3. Select any data cell. Click **Sort** in the Sort & Filter group on the Data tab.

4. On the Sort dialog box, select **Fund** and click **OK**.

5. Click **Subtotal** in the Outline group on the Data tab. The Subtotal dialog box opens.

6. In the *At each change in* box, select **Fund**. Select or accept **Sum** in the *Use function* box and **Amount** in the *Add subtotal to* box. Click **OK**.

7. Adjust column widths if necessary to display all data.

8. **SAVE** the workbook as *Contributions Project 3* and **CLOSE** the file.

    LEAVE Excel open for the next project.

CD

The *Contributions* file is available on the companion CD-ROM.

→ Project 4: Use Formulas and Functions

In Project 3, you determined the amount contributed to each fund. Use formulas and functions to perform additional analyses in preparation for Cross-Cultural Solutions' annual fundraising drive.

OPEN *Contributions* from the data files.

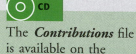

The *Contributions* file is available on the companion CD-ROM.

1. Click the **Formulas** tab. Select **A36**. Key **Total Contributions**.
2. Select **C36** and click **AutoSum** in the Function Library group. C5:C35 should be selected by default. Press [Enter].
3. Select **A36:C36**. Click **Cell Styles** on the Home tab. Click **Total** under Titles and Headings.
4. Select **A38** and key **Count**. Press [Tab].
5. On the Formulas tab, click **Insert Function**. Select **Count** and click **OK**.
6. Select **C5:C35** in the Value1 box. Click **OK**.
7. In **A39**, key **Contributions <$1,000** and press [Tab].
8. Click **Insert Function** and select **SUMIF**. Click **OK**. Select **C5:C35** in the Range box.

TROUBLESHOOTING

If the function you want to use is not visible in the *Select a function* box on the Insert Function dialog box, key the function in the *Search for a function* box and click Go.

9. In the Criteria box, key **<1000**. Click **OK**.
10. Select **A40** and key **Average Individual**. Press [Tab].
11. Click **Insert Function** and click **AVERAGE**. Click **OK**. Select **C25:C35** in the Number1 box. Click **OK**. A triangle appears in the upper-left corner of B40 and an error message button is displayed. Click the arrow and click **Ignore Error**.
12. Select **A41**, key **Contributions >=5000**, and press [Tab].
13. Click **Recently Used** in the Function Library group and click **SUMIF**.
14. In the Range box, select **C5:C35** and press [Tab].
15. In the Criteria box, key **>=5000**. Click **OK**.
16. Select B39:B41 and click **Accounting Number Format** in the Number group on the Home tab.
17. Click **Decrease Decimal** twice.
18. **SAVE** the workbook as *Contributions Project 4* and **CLOSE** the file. **CLOSE** Excel.

Creating Charts from Your Data

9

Fourth Coffee owns espresso cafes in 15 major markets. Its primary income is generated from the sale of trademarked, freshly-brewed coffee and espresso drinks. The cafes also sell a variety of pastries, packaged coffees and teas, deli-style sandwiches, and coffee-related accessories and gift items. In preparation for an upcoming budget meeting, the corporate manager wants to create charts to show trends in each of the five revenue categories for a five-year period and to project those trends to future sales.

KEY TERMS
axis
chart
chart area
chart sheet
data labels
data marker
data series
embedded chart
legend
legend keys
plot area
title

■ SOFTWARE ORIENTATION

The Insert Tab

Excel 2007 makes it easy to create professional-looking charts. A *chart* is a graphical representation of numeric data in a worksheet. To create a basic chart in Excel that you can modify and format later, start by entering the data for the chart on a worksheet. Then, you can select that data and choose a chart type to graphically display the data. Simply by choosing a chart type, a chart layout, and a chart style—all of which are within easy reach on the Ribbon—you will have instant professional results every time you create a chart.

Figure 9-1

Insert tab

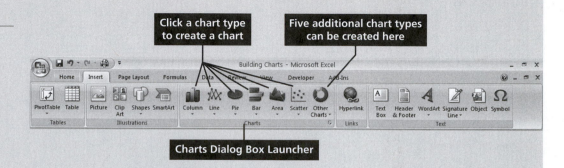

Use this illustration as a reference throughout this lesson as you become familiar with and use Excel's charting capabilities to create attention-getting illustrations that communicate an analysis of your data.

■ Building Charts

THE BOTTOM LINE

Because Excel allows you to track and work with substantial amounts of data, it is sometimes difficult to see the big picture by looking at the details in a worksheet. With Excel's charting capabilities, you can summarize and highlight data, reveal trends, and make comparisons that might not be obvious when looking at the raw data. Creating a chart is quick and easy, and Excel provides a variety of chart types from which to choose. In the following exercises, you will learn the types of charts available in Excel 2007 and how to create them. You will also learn how to modify, format, and move charts and chart elements.

Selecting Data to Include in a Chart

Excel's Ribbon interface makes it incredibly simple to create a chart. As you will see in the following exercise, you can create one of the common chart types by clicking its image on the Insert tab. More important than the chart type, however, is the selection of the data you want to display graphically. What aspects of the data do you want viewers to notice? The answer to that question is a major factor in selecting an appropriate chart type.

⊕ **SELECT DATA TO INCLUDE IN A CHART**

GET READY. Before you begin these steps, launch Microsoft Excel.

1. **OPEN** *Financial History* from the data files for this lesson.
2. Select **B4:B10** (the 2004 data) on the Sales History worksheet.
3. Click **Pie** in the Charts group on the Insert tab. Click the first **2-D Pie** chart. A pie chart is displayed.

The *Financial History* workbook is available on the companion CD-ROM.

TROUBLESHOOTING Notice that the chart is color-coded and the sections are identified by number. However, the pie has seven sections, and Fourth Coffee has only five sales categories that should be contrasted in the graphic. The pie chart includes the column label (2004) as the largest portion. The total sales amount is the second largest portion. These amounts should not be included in an analysis of sales for 2004.

4. Click in the chart's white space and press Delete.
5. Select **B5:B9**, click **Pie** in the Charts group, and click the first **2-D Pie** chart. The correct data is displayed, but the chart is difficult to interpret with only numbers to identify the parts of the pie.

TROUBLESHOOTING Use the Insert tab to create a chart. When a chart is inserted, the Ribbon displays the Format tab. You must select the Insert tab each time you want to insert a chart.

6. Click in the chart's white space and press Delete.
7. Select **A4:B9** and click **Pie** in the Charts group. Click the first **2-D Pie**. As illustrated in Figure 9-2, the data is clearly identified with a title and a label for each pie section.

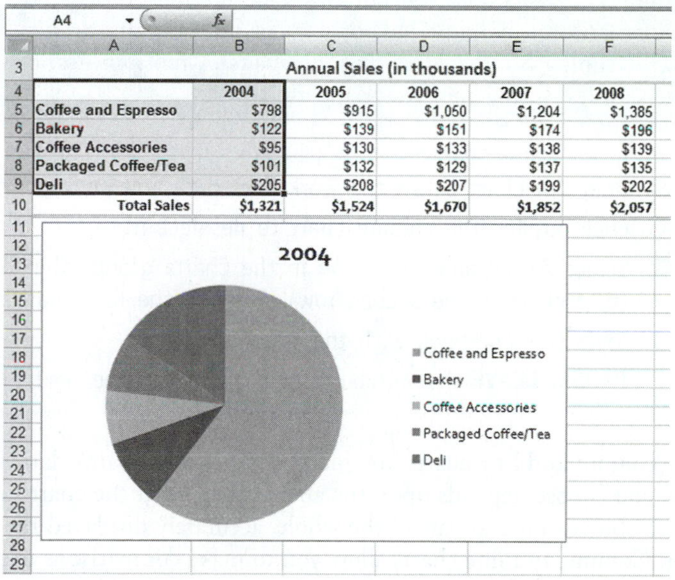

Figure 9-2

Accurate data selection is essential in building a chart

	A	B	C	D	E	F
3			Annual Sales (in thousands)			
4		2004	2005	2006	2007	2008
5	Coffee and Espresso	$798	$915	$1,050	$1,204	$1,385
6	Bakery	$122	$139	$151	$174	$196
7	Coffee Accessories	$95	$130	$133	$138	$139
8	Packaged Coffee/Tea	$101	$132	$129	$137	$135
9	Deli	$205	$208	$207	$199	$202
10	Total Sales	$1,321	$1,524	$1,670	$1,852	$2,057

2004

- Coffee and Espresso
- Bakery
- Coffee Accessories
- Packaged Coffee/Tea
- Deli

8. Create a Lesson 9 folder and **SAVE** the workbook as *Building Charts*.
   PAUSE. LEAVE the workbook open to use in the next exercise.

CERTIFICATION READY?
How do you select appropriate data sources for charts?
4.1.1

Excel did not distinguish between the column B label and its data when you selected only the data in column B. Although the label is formatted as text, because the column label was numeric, it was interpreted as data to be included in the graph. When you expanded the selection to include the row labels, 2004 was correctly recognized as a label and displayed as the title for the pie chart. This exercise illustrates that the chart's data selection must contain sufficient information to interpret the data at a glance. You will improve the display in subsequent exercises when you apply predefined layouts and styles.

When you selected data and created a pie chart, the chart was placed on the worksheet. This is referred to as an *embedded chart*, meaning it is placed on the worksheet rather than on a separate *chart sheet*, a sheet that contains only a chart.

Choosing the Right Chart for Your Data

Excel supports numerous types of charts to help you display data in ways that are meaningful to your audience. You can create most charts, such as column and bar charts, from data that you have arranged in rows or columns in a worksheet. Some charts, such as pie and bubble charts, require a specific data arrangement.

⊕ CHOOSE THE RIGHT CHART FOR YOUR DATA

USE the workbook from the previous exercise.

1. Delete the pie chart on the Sales History worksheet.

TROUBLESHOOTING To delete a chart, click in the white space. If you click on the graphic or another chart element and press Delete, only the selected element will be deleted.

2. Select **A4:F9** and click **Column** in the Charts group on the Insert tab. Click **3-D Clustered Column** on the dropdown list (first subtype under 3-D Column). The column chart illustrates the sales for each of the revenue categories for the five-year period.

TAKE NOTE* The pie chart was useful for displaying data in a single column, which illustrated the portion of total income generated by each revenue source. The pie chart cannot be used for comparisons across periods of time or for analyzing trends. The column chart works well for comparisons; in this case, it illustrates the significant increase in coffee and espresso sales during the five-year period.

3. Drag the chart below the worksheet data and position it at the far left.

4. Click outside the column chart to deselect it.

5. Select **A4:F9** and click **Line** in the Charts group. Click **2-D Line with Markers** (first chart in the second row). Position the line chart next to the column chart.

6. **SAVE** the workbook with the same name.

PAUSE. LEAVE the workbook open to use in the next exercise.

CERTIFICATION READY?
How do you select appropriate chart types to represent data sources?
4.1.2

The column and line charts provide two views of the same data, illustrating that the chart type you choose depends upon the analysis you want the chart to portray. The pie chart, which shows values as part of the whole, accurately displayed the distribution of sales for one year. Column and line charts allow you to make comparisons over a period of time as well as comparisons among items.

The line chart shown in Figure 9-3 includes data markers to indicate each year's sales. A *data marker* is a bar, area, dot, slice, or other symbol in a chart that represents a single data point or value that originates from a worksheet cell. Related data markers in a chart constitute a *data series*.

Figure 9-3

Line chart with data markers

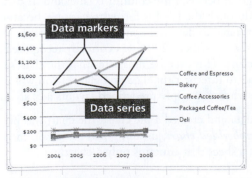

In a 2-D or 3-D column chart, each data marker is represented by a column. In a stacked column, data markers are stacked so that a column represents a data series.

The line chart is a good analysis tool. The chart you created illustrates not only the growth in coffee and espresso sales, but reveals a modest increase in bakery sales and static activity in the sale of packaged products.

When you want to create a chart or change an existing chart, you can choose from 11 chart types and subtypes within each chart type. Table 9-1 gives a brief description of each Excel chart type.

Table 9-1

Chart types

Icon	Chart Name	Function	Data Arrangement
	Column	Useful for showing data changes over a period of time or illustrating comparisons among data. Values are represented with vertical bars.	Columns or rows
	Line	Useful for showing trends in data at equal intervals. Displays continuous data over time set against a common scale. Values are represented as points along a line.	Columns or rows
	Pie	Useful for showing the size of items in one data series, proportional to the sum of the items. Data points are displayed as a percentage of a circular pie.	One column or row
	Bar	Useful for illustrating comparisons among individual items. Useful when axis labels are long or values are durations. Values are represented as horizontal rectangles.	Columns or rows
	Area	Useful for emphasizing magnitude of change over time; can be used to draw attention to the total value across a trend. Shows relationship of parts to the whole. Values represented as shaded areas.	Columns or rows
	XY (Scatter)	Useful for showing relationships among the numeric values in several data series or plotting two groups of numbers as one series of xy coordinates.	Columns or rows
	Stock	Useful for illustrating the fluctuation of stock prices or scientific data.	Columns or rows in a specific order
	Surface	Useful for finding optimum combinations between two sets of data. Use this chart when categories and data series are numeric values.	Columns or rows
	Donut	Useful for displaying relationship of parts to a whole; can contain more than one data series. Values represented as sections of a circular band.	Columns or rows
	Bubble	Useful for comparing three sets of values. The third value determines the size of the bubble marker.	Columns with x values in first column and y values in adjacent columns
	Radar	Useful for showing the trends of values relative to a center point; represent values as points that radiate from the center. Lines connect values in the series.	Columns or rows

Creating a Bar Chart

Bar charts are similar to column charts and can be used to illustrate comparisons among individual items. Data that is arranged in columns or rows on a worksheet can be plotted in a bar chart. Clustered bar charts compare values across categories. Stacked bar charts show the relationship of individual items to the whole of that item.

 CREATE A BAR CHART

USE the workbook from the previous exercise.

1. Click the **Expense History** tab.
2. Select **A4:F9**. Click **Bar** in the Charts Group on the Insert tab.
3. Click the **Clustered Bar in 3-D** subtype.

TAKE NOTE *

A ScreenTip displays the chart type name when you rest the mouse pointer over a chart type or chart subtype.

4. Position the clustered bar chart on the left below the worksheet data.
5. Deselect the chart and select **A4:F9**. Click **Bar** in the Charts group.
6. Click **Stacked Bar in 3-D**.
7. Position the stacked bar graph next to the 3-D bar graph.
8. **SAVE** and **CLOSE** the workbook.

   PAUSE. LEAVE Excel open to use in the next exercise.

TAKE NOTE *

The 3-D Bar graph displays the rectangles in 3-D but not the data.

CERTIFICATION READY?
How do you select appropriate chart types to represent data sources?
4.1.2

The side-by-side bar charts you created in this exercise illustrate two views of the same data. You can experiment with chart types and select the one that best portrays the message you want to convey to your target audience.

The Charts group on the Insert tab contains six of the eleven chart types. To create one of these charts, select the worksheet data and click the icon. You can insert one of the other five chart types by clicking the Charts Dialog Box Launcher to open the Insert Chart dialog box shown in Figure 9-4.

Figure 9-4

Insert Chart dialog box

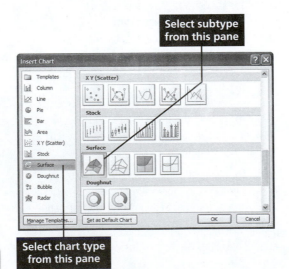

ANOTHER WAY

You can open the Insert Chart dialog box by clicking Other Charts and then clicking All Chart Types at the bottom of the dropdown list.

When you click a chart type in the left pane of the dialog box, the first chart of that type is selected in the right pane. You can also scroll through the right pane and select any chart subtype.

When you apply a predefined chart style, the chart is formatted based on the document theme that you have applied. The Metro theme was applied to the Financial History workbook. The Metro theme colors were therefore applied to the charts you created in the preceding exercises.

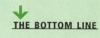

■ Formatting a Chart with a Quick Style

THE BOTTOM LINE

After you create a chart, you can instantly change its appearance by applying a predefined layout or style. Excel provides a variety of useful quick layouts and quick styles from which you can choose. As shown in Figure 9-5, when you create a chart, the chart tools become available and the Design, Layout, and Format tabs are added to the Ribbon.

Figure 9-5

Ribbon tabs added when chart is inserted

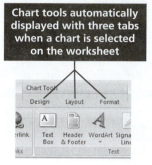

Chart tools automatically displayed with three tabs when a chart is selected on the worksheet

→ FORMAT A CHART WITH A QUICK STYLE

GET READY. Launch Microsoft Excel if it is not already open.

1. **OPEN** *Financial History* from the data files for this lesson.
2. On the Expense History worksheet, select **A4:A9**. Press **Ctrl** and select **F4:F9**.
3. Click **Pie** in the Charts group and click **Pie** under 2-D. The 2008 data is displayed and the Design tab is active.
4. In the Chart Layouts group on the Design tab, click **Layout 1**. The pie chart now displays the percentage that each sales category contributes to total sales.
5. In the Chart Styles group, click **Style 4**. The chart's color scheme is changed. Position the chart below the data.
6. On the Sales History worksheet, select **A4:A9**. Press **Ctrl** and select **F4:F9**.
7. Click **Bar** in the Charts group and click **Clustered Horizontal Cylinder** (third row).
8. Drag the chart below the worksheet data.
9. Click **Layout 2** in the Chart Layouts group on the Design tab. Click **Style 4** in the Chart Styles group.
10. **SAVE** the workbook as *Chart Styles*.

    PAUSE. LEAVE the workbook open to use in the next exercise.

 CD

The *Financial History* workbook is available on the companion CD-ROM.

TAKE NOTE*

To see all predefined styles, click More next to the last displayed style.

CERTIFICATION READY?
How do you format charts using Quick Styles?
4.1.3

When you applied Layout 1 and Style 4 to the expense chart, additional information was added to the chart and the appearance changed. Predefined layouts and styles are timesaving features that you can use to enhance the appearance of your charts.

■ Manually Formatting the Parts of a Chart

THE BOTTOM LINE

You can format individual chart elements. The following list defines some of the chart elements, which are illustrated in Figure 9-6. To format a chart element, click the chart element that you want to change

- *chart area*—the entire chart and all its elements.
- *plot area*—the area bounded by the axes.
- *axis*—a line bordering the chart plot area used as a frame of reference for measurement.
- *title*—descriptive text that is automatically aligned to an axis or centered at the top of a chart.
- *data labels*—text that provides additional information about a data marker, which represents a single data point or value that originates from a worksheet cell.
- *legend*—a box that identifies the patterns or colors that are assigned to the data series or categories in a chart.

Figure 9-6

Chart elements

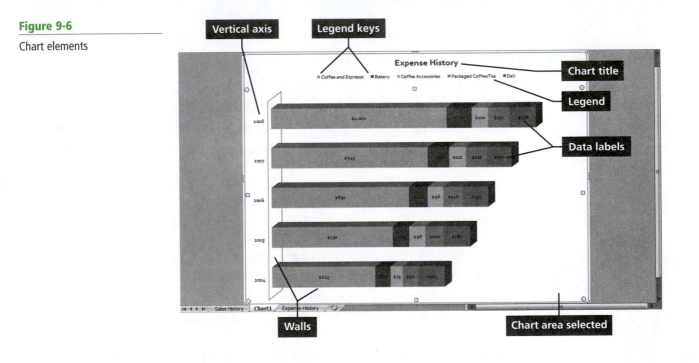

Changing the Chart's Fill Color or Pattern

Use commands on the Format tab to add or change fill colors or patterns applied to chart elements. When you select any chart element and click Format Selection, an element-specific dialog box opens. For example, if you click the data series, the Format Data Series dialog box opens. You also can use the Shape Fill command to fill any shape with color, gradient, or texture.

⊕ **CHANGE THE CHART'S FILL COLOR OR PATTERN**

USE the workbook from the previous exercise.

1. Click in the chart area of the **Clustered Horizontal Cylinder** chart on the Sales History worksheet to display the Chart Tools.

2. Click the **Format** tab and click **Format Selection**. The Format Chart Area dialog box opens.

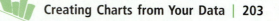
3. Click **Solid fill**. Click the **Color** arrow and click **Green, Accent 1, Lighter 80%**. A light green fill has been added to the entire chart area.

4. Click **Picture or texture fill**. Click the **Texture** arrow and click **Newsprint** (center of selection options). The textured format replaced the color fill in the chart area.

5. Click **Close** to close the dialog box.

6. Select **Plot Area** in the Current Selection group.

7. Click **More** next to the colored outlines in the Shape Styles group.

8. Click **Subtle Effect – Accent 1**.

9. Select **Legend** in the Current Selection group. Press [Delete].

> **TAKE NOTE** *Legend keys* appear to the left of legend entries and identify the color-coded data series. Because this chart contains only one data series, the legend is unnecessary.

10. **SAVE** your workbook.

   PAUSE. LEAVE the workbook open to use in the next exercise.

You can use the mouse to select a chart element to format. When you use the mouse to point to an element in the chart, the element name appears in a ScreenTip. You can also select the element you want to format by clicking the arrow next to the Chart Elements box in the Current Selection group on the Format tab. Figure 9-7 shows the list of chart elements in the bar chart on the Sales History worksheet. This list is chart specific. Legend is not listed because you deleted that element from the chart. When you click the arrow, the list will include all elements that you have included in the displayed chart.

Figure 9-7

Chart elements

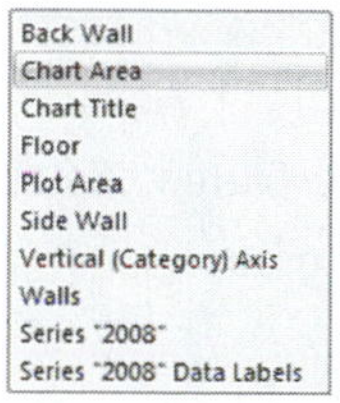

| Back Wall |
| Chart Area |
| Chart Title |
| Floor |
| Plot Area |
| Side Wall |
| Vertical (Category) Axis |
| Walls |
| Series "2008" |
| Series "2008" Data Labels |

The Format tab provides a variety of ways to format chart elements. Select the element to format and launch the Format dialog box or use the commands in the Shape Styles group on the Format tab, shown in Figure 9-8, to add fill color or a pattern to the selected chart element. The Shape Fill color choices are those associated with the theme applied to the worksheet.

Figure 9-8

Format tab with Chart Tools

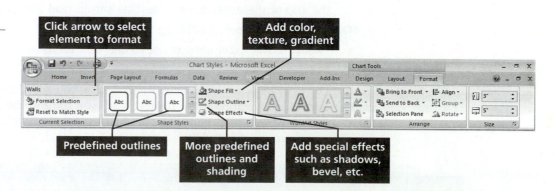

Changing the Chart's Border Line

You can apply a border around any chart element as well as around the entire chart. Select an element or the chart and use the colored outlines in the Shape Styles group or click Shape Outlines and choose a Theme or Standard color for the border.

➔ CHANGE THE CHART'S BORDER LINE

USE the workbook you saved in the previous exercise.

1. Click the arrow in the **Current Selection** group and click **Chart Area**.
2. Click **Colored Outline – Accent 1** in the Shape Styles group. The chart is outlined with a green border.
3. Click **Plot Area** in the Current Selection group and click **Colored Outline – Accent 2.** A red border is placed around the plot area.
4. Click **Walls** in the Current Selection group and click **Colored Outline – Dark 1.**
5. **SAVE** your workbook.

   PAUSE. LEAVE the workbook open to use in the next exercise.

TAKE NOTE＊

To display the Chart Tools, you must select the chart. If a worksheet cell is active, the Design, Layout, and Format tabs are not available.

You can outline any or all chart elements. Just select the element and apply one of the predefined outlines or click Shape Outline to format the shape of a selected chart element.

Formatting the Data Series

You can apply fill color to the data series, outline the series with a border, change the shape, or add special effects to the columns, bars, etc., that represent the data series.

➔ FORMAT THE DATA SERIES

USE the workbook you saved in the previous exercise.

1. Select the chart on the Sales History worksheet, then select **Series "2008"** in the Current Selection group on the Format tab.
2. Click **Shape Fill**.
3. Point to **Texture**. Click **Denim**.
4. Select **Series "2008" Data Labels** in the Current Selection.
5. Click **Shape Outline** in the Shape Styles group.
6. Click **Blue** under Standard Colors.
7. Select the data series for coffee and espresso. Drag the box above the bar so that the label is completely visible.
8. Click in the chart area to select it. Click **Print** in the Quick Access Toolbar. The Print dialog box opens with Selected Chart as the default print area. Click **Print**.
9. Click the **Expense History** worksheet tab. Select the **chart title**. Key **Expenses** at the end of the existing text. The title should read *2008 Expenses*.
10. **SAVE** the workbook. **CLOSE** the workbook.

    PAUSE. LEAVE Excel open to use in the next exercise.

The bar chart's content was easier to understand when you added the data series and formatted the series to call attention to the figures. When you clarified the chart title in the pie chart, you clarified the chart's contents. The chart is a communication tool. Use formatting to call attention to significant data.

TAKE NOTE＊ The data series is the most important element of the chart. Use formatting tools to call attention to the graphic and the label.

Modifying a Chart's Legend

You can modify the content of the legend, expand or collapse the legend box, edit the text that is displayed, and change character attributes. A finished chart should stand alone—that is, the chart should contain sufficient data to convey the intended data analysis.

The *Financial History* workbook is available on the companion CD-ROM.

→ MODIFY A CHART'S LEGEND

1. **OPEN Financial History** from the data files for this lesson.
2. On the Sales History worksheet, select **A4:F9**. Click **Column** on the Insert tab.
3. Select **Stacked Column in 3D** from the Column chart listing.
4. Click the down arrow next to the Chart Layouts group on the Design tab and click **Layout 4**. The legend appears below the plot area.
5. Select the legend and click **Colored Outline – Accent 1** in the Shape Styles on the Format tab to enclose the legend in a green border.
6. Select the **legend** and right-click to display the shortcut menu. Click **Font**.
7. On the Font dialog box, click **Small Caps** and click **OK**.
8. Select **Coffee and Espresso** in the legend, right-click to display the shortcut menu, and click **Font**.
9. Click **Font color** and click **Green**. Click **OK**.
10. Repeat step 9 for each legend item and apply the following font colors.

    Bakery – Red

    Coffee Accessories – Orange

    Packaged Coffee/Tea – Light Blue

    Deli - Blue

11. **SAVE** the file as *Chart 1*.

    PAUSE. LEAVE the workbook open to use in the next exercise.

Changing the font colors in the legend to match the blocks in the columns provides an additional visual aid that enables the viewer to quickly see the income contribution for each category. When you applied Layout 4 to the column chart, the legend was placed at the bottom of the chart. You can click the legend border and move it to any location on the chart. All other elements of the quick layout will remain the same.

■ Modifying a Chart

THE BOTTOM LINE

You can modify a chart by adding or deleting elements or by moving or resizing the chart. You can also change the chart type without having to delete the existing chart and create a new one.

Adding elements to a chart can provide additional information that was not available in the data you selected to create the chart. For example, the stacked column chart in the previous exercise does not have a title and it does not indicate that the sales amounts are in thousands.

Adding Elements to a Chart

Labels make it easy to understand chart data. You can display series names, category names, and percentages in data labels. To prevent data labels from overlapping and to make them easier to read, you can adjust their positions on the chart. Use the Layout tab commands to add chart labels.

→ ADD ELEMENTS TO A CHART

USE the workbook from the previous exercise.

1. Display the Layout tab.
2. Click **Axis Titles** and click **Primary Vertical Axis Title**.

3. Click **Vertical Title**. Key **(in Thousands)** in the title textbox.

4. Click **Chart Title** in the Labels group. Click **Above Chart**. A text box displaying *Chart Title* is inserted above the columns.

5. Select the text and key **Sales History**.

6. Click **Data Labels** in the Labels group. Click **Show**. Labels are added to each column showing the dollar amount of sales in each category.

Looking Ahead Because of the chart size, the data labels are difficult to read. You will correct this in a subsequent exercise.

7. Click **Gridlines** in the Axes group. Click **Primary Vertical Gridlines** and click **Major Gridlines**.

8. Click **Axis Titles** and click **Primary Horizontal Axis Title**.

9. Click **Title Below Axis**.

10. Key **Annual Sales** in the Axis Title textbox.

 **ANOTHER WAY** Rather than select and replace the text in the textboxes, you can key the new text in the formula bar. When you press Enter, the new text replaces the generic text in the title boxes.

11. **SAVE** the workbook with the same name.

PAUSE. LEAVE the workbook open to use in the next exercise.

CERTIFICATION READY?
How do you add chart elements?
4.2.1

Chart axes are used to measure and categorize data. A column or bar chart typically has two axes. The vertical axis (y axis) usually contains the data. In your chart, the y axis contains the amount of sales. It is important for the viewer to understand that sales amounts in this chart are expressed in thousands. Therefore, it was necessary to add a label to the y axis.

The horizontal axis (x axis) contains the categories. In your chart, the categories are self-explanatory. Thus, the x axis label is less critical.

Deleting Elements from a Chart

When a chart becomes too cluttered, you may need to delete nonessential elements. You can use the Layout tab commands to delete chart elements, or you can select an element on the chart and press the Delete key. You can also select an element in the Current Selection group and press Delete.

⊙ DELETE ELEMENTS FROM A CHART

USE the workbook from the previous exercise.

1. Display the Layout tab.

2. Click **Axis Titles** and click **Primary Horizontal Axis Title**. Click **None**.

3. Click Gridlines in the Axes group, click **Primary Vertical Gridlines,** and click **None**.

4. Click the **Design** tab and click **Switch Row/Column.** The data display is changed to have all sales for one category stacked.

5. Click **Undo**.

6. **SAVE** the workbook.

PAUSE. LEAVE the workbook open to use in the next exercise.

 CERTIFICATION READY?
How do you delete chart elements?
4.2.1

You can delete any element from a chart. Use the commands in the Labels group to add or remove a category of labels or select an element on the chart and press Delete. You can also right-click on a chart element and press Delete.

Moving a Chart

When you insert a chart, by default, it is embedded in the worksheet. You can click a corner of a chart or the midpoint of any side to display move handles (four-sided arrow). You can use the move handles to drag the chart to any location on the worksheet. Sometimes you want a chart to be on a chart sheet so that it can be reviewed without the worksheet data.

➔ MOVE A CHART

USE the workbook from the previous exercise.

1. Click a blank area in the Sales History chart.
2. Drag the chart so that it is centered in columns B to G.
3. With the chart selected, click the **Design** tab.
4. Click **Move Chart Location**. The Move Chart dialog box shown in Figure 9-9 opens, with the default setting—placing the chart as an object in the worksheet.

Figure 9-9

Choose where a chart is placed

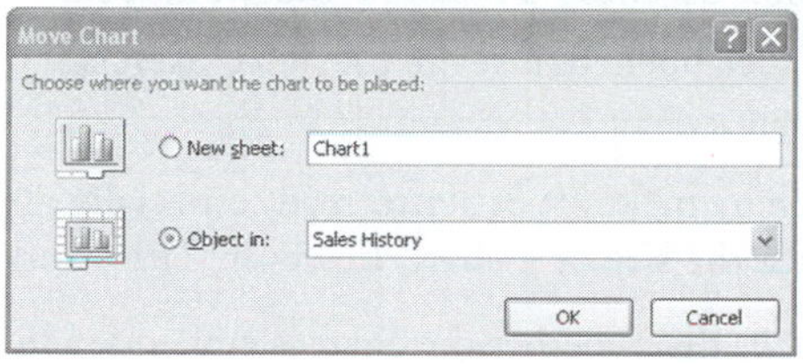

![Move Chart dialog box. Title "Choose where you want the chart to be placed:" with options New sheet: Chart1 and Object in: Sales History, with OK and Cancel buttons.]

5. Click **New Sheet** and key **Sales History Chart** in the text box. Click **OK**. A chart worksheet is inserted before the Sales History sheet.
6. Click **Legend** in Labels group on the Layout tab. Click **Show Legend at Right**.

TAKE NOTE ✱

The Chart Tools that you used on the Design, Layout, and Format tabs can be applied to the Chart Sheet. The data series amounts were difficult to read when you applied them to the embedded chart. They are easy to read and can be used for analysis when the chart is moved to a chart sheet.

7. **SAVE** and **CLOSE** the workbook.

PAUSE. LEAVE Excel open to use in the next exercise.

CERTIFICATION READY?
How do you move a chart from the worksheet to a chart sheet?
4.2.2

You can move chart elements or move the entire chart. In previous exercises, you moved an embedded chart by dragging it to a new location. When you move the chart to a new sheet, it becomes even more important for the chart to be self-explanatory. Moving the legend to the right makes it easier to identify the building blocks in the stacked columns.

Resizing a Chart

You can click a corner of a chart or the midpoint of any side to display sizing handles (two-sided arrow). Use the side handles to change chart height or width. Use the corner sizing handles to change both height and width.

RESIZE A CHART

GET READY. Launch Microsoft Excel if it is not already open.

1. **OPEN** *Financial History 2* from the data files for this lesson.
2. Click a blank area in the chart on the Expense History worksheet.
3. Click the **top-left sizing handle** and drag the left edge of the chart to the bottom of row 9 at the left edge of the worksheet.
4. Click the **top-right sizing handle** and align the right edge of the chart with the column G right boundary.
5. Click the **bottom-center sizing handle** and drag the chart boundary to the bottom of row 35.
6. Open the Sales History worksheet. Click a blank area in the chart. Click the **Format** tab.
7. In the Size group, click the **Shape Height** up arrow until the height is 3.5.
8. In the Size group, click the **Shape Width** down arrow until the width is 4.0.

ANOTHER WAY

You can click the Dialog Box Launcher in the Size group and enter the desired chart height and width.

The *Financial History 2* workbook is available on the companion CD-ROM.

9. **SAVE** the workbook as *Chart 2*. **CLOSE** the workbook.

PAUSE. LEAVE Excel open to use in the next exercise.

CERTIFICATION READY?
How do you change a chart size?
4.2.2

Increasing the size of a chart makes it easier to read, especially an embedded chart. Be cautious when you reduce the size of a chart, however. Titles and legends must be readable.

It is important to remember that whether the chart is embedded in the worksheet or located on a chart sheet, the chart is linked to the worksheet data. Any changes in the worksheet data will be reflected in the chart. Likewise, if the worksheet data is deleted, the chart will be deleted as well.

Choosing a Different Chart Type

For most 2-D charts, you can change the type of the entire chart and give it a completely different look. If a chart contains multiple data series, you can also select a different chart type for any single data series, creating a combined chart. You cannot combine a 2-D and a 3-D chart, however.

CHOOSE A DIFFERENT CHART TYPE

GET READY. Launch Microsoft Excel if it is not already open.

1. **OPEN** *Financial History* from the data files for this lesson.
2. On the Expense History worksheet, select **A4:F9**.
3. On the Insert tab, click **Bar** and click **Stacked Bar in 3-D**.
4. Click **Layout 2** on the Design tab.
5. Select the chart title text box and key **Expense History** in the formula bar. Press **Enter**.
6. On the Design tab, click **Change Chart Type**.
7. Click **Stacked Horizontal Cylinder** and click **OK**.
8. On the Sales History worksheet, select **A4:B9**. On the Insert tab, click **Pie**. Click **Pie**.
9. Click **Layout 1** on the Design tab.
10. Click **Change Chart Type** and click **Exploded pie in 3-D**. Click **OK**.
11. **SAVE** the workbook as *Chart 3*. **CLOSE** the workbook.

CLOSE Excel.

The *Financial History* workbook is available on the companion CD-ROM.

CERTIFICATION READY?
How do you change the chart type?
4.2.3

SUMMARY SKILL MATRIX

IN THIS LESSON YOU LEARNED	MATRIX SKILL	SKILL NUMBER
To build charts that summarize and highlight significant data		
To select suitable data to include in a chart	Select appropriate data sources for charts	4.1.1
To choose the best chart type to display the data	Select appropriate chart types to represent data sources	4.1.2
To change the appearance of a chart by applying a Quick Style	Format charts using Quick Styles	4.1.3
To modify and format parts of a chart		
To modify and move elements of a chart		
To add elements to a chart	Add and remove chart elements	4.2.1
To delete elements from a chart	Add and remove chart elements	4.2.1
To move an embedded chart to a chart sheet	Move and size charts	4.2.2
To move and resize an embedded chart	Move and size charts	4.2.2
To choose a different chart type to display selected data	Change chart types	4.2.3

Knowledge Assessment

Matching

a. axis
b. chart
c. chart area
d. chart sheet
e. data labels

f. data marker
g. data series
h. embedded chart
i. legend
j. title

_____ 1. A box that identifies the patterns or colors that are assigned to a data series or categories in a chart.

_____ 2. A graphical representation of numeric data in a worksheet.

_____ 3. A bar, area, dot, slice, or other symbol in a chart that represents a single data point or value that originates from a worksheet cell.

_____ 4. A chart that is placed on a worksheet rather than on a separate sheet.

_____ 5. A sheet in a workbook that contains only a chart.

_____ 6. The entire chart and all its elements.

_____ 7. Related data points that are plotted in a chart.

_____ 8. A line bordering the chart plot area used as a frame of reference for measurement.

_____ 9. Descriptive text that is automatically aligned to an axis or centered at the top of a chart.

_____ 10. A label that provides additional information about a data marker, which represents a single data point or value that originates from a worksheet cell.

Multiple Choice

Circle the choice that best completes the following statements.

1. Which chart type shows values as parts of a whole?
   a. column
   b. bar
   c. area
   d. pie

2. A(n) _____ chart appears on a worksheet with other data.
   a. chart sheet
   b. embedded
   c. Pivot chart
   d. mixed

3. What part of a chart do you click when you want to select the entire chart?
   a. chart area
   b. plot area
   c. chart title
   d. legend

4. What happens to a chart if the source data is deleted?

   a. Nothing.

   b. The chart will move to the area where the data was located.

   c. The data in the chart is deleted.

   d. You will be asked if you want the chart deleted.

5. What is the first step that should be taken when creating a chart?

   a. providing a name for the chart

   b. selecting the chart type

   c. selecting the range of cells that contain the data the chart will use

   d. choosing the data labels that will be used in the chart

6. If you want to print only the chart in a worksheet, what should you do before printing?

   a. click the chart to select it and then print

   b. select the *Print chart only* option in the Page Setup dialog box

   c. move the chart to a new sheet by itself and then print that sheet

   d. cannot print only the chart if it is part of a larger worksheet

7. To change the location of a legend on a chart, use the Legend command on this Ribbon tab.

   a. Insert

   b. Format

   c. Layout

   d. Design

8. A column chart represents values as

   a. horizontal bars.

   b. vertical bars.

   c. horizontal lines.

   d. vertical lines.

9. To move a chart from a worksheet to a chart sheet,

   a. use the move handles and drag it to the new location.

   b. use the Move Chart Location command on the Design tab.

   c. cut the chart from the worksheet and paste it to a new workbook sheet.

   d. You cannot move the chart after it has been created.

10. Which of the following statements is **not** true?

    a. You can change both the height and width of a chart with commands on the Format tab.

    b. You can use the sizing handles to change the height and width of a chart.

    c. You must delete an existing chart in order to have the data displayed in a different chart type.

    d. When a chart sheet is created it no longer appears on the worksheet containing the data series.

■ Competency Assessment

Project 9-1: Create a Pie Chart

Blue Yonder Airlines has created a workbook to analyze sales for its first four years of operation. The manager wants to create charts that reflect an analysis of the data.

GET READY. Launch Excel.

1. **OPEN** *BY Financials* from the data files for this lesson.
2. On the Income worksheet, select **A3:A7.** Press Ctrl and select **E3:E7.**
3. Click the **Insert** tab. Click **Pie** and click **Pie in 3-D.**
4. Click **Layout 1** in the Chart Layouts group on the Design tab.
5. Click **Move Chart Location**.
6. Select **New Sheet** and click **OK.**
7. Right-click the **Chart1** tab and click **Rename**.
8. Key **2008 Income Chart** and press Enter.
9. **SAVE** the workbook as *BY Financials 9-1.*
10. **CLOSE** the workbook.

LEAVE Excel open for the next project.

> **CD**
>
> The *BY Financials* workbook is available on the companion CD-ROM.

Project 9-2: Create a Bar Chart

Create a bar chart to analyze trends in Fourth Coffee's income before taxes.

1. **OPEN** *Financial History* from the data files for this lesson.
2. Make the Income worksheet active. Select **A4:F9** and click the **Insert** tab.
3. Click **Bar** in the Charts group and click **100% Stacked Horizontal Cylinder.**
4. Click in the **Chart Area** and click the **Layout** tab.
5. Click **Legend** and click **Show Legend at Bottom**.
6. Click the **Chart Area** to display the move handles. Move the chart so that the top-left corner is aligned with B12.
7. Click the bottom-right sizing handle and increase the size of the chart so that it fills B12:G29.
8. **SAVE** the workbook as *Financial History 9-2.*

LEAVE the workbook open to use in the next project.

> **CD**
>
> The *Financial History* workbook is available on the companion CD-ROM.

■ Proficiency Assessment

Project 9-3: Modify a Bar Chart

In the previous project, you created a bar chart to analyze trends in Fourth Coffee's income before taxes. Modify the chart by adding additional chart elements.

USE the workbook from the previous project.

1. Select the chart area and click **Chart Title** in the Labels group on the Layout tab.
2. Click **More Title Options** and click **Gradient fill**.
3. In the Preset colors box, click **Moss** and click **Close**. The Chart Title text box is selected.

4. In the formula bar, key **Income Before Taxes** and press **Enter**.

5. Click **Axis Titles** and click **Primary Vertical Axis Title**.

6. Click **Rotated Title**. The Axis Title text box is selected.

7. In the formula bar, key **in thousands** and press **Enter**.

8. Right-click the **axis title** text box and click **Font**.

9. Click **Font color** and click **Green**. Click **OK**.

10. **SAVE** the workbook as *Financial History 9-3*.

11. **CLOSE** the file.

  LEAVE Excel open for the next project.

Project 9-4: **Create a Line Chart**

CD

The *BY Financials* workbook is available on the companion CD-ROM.

1. **OPEN** *BY Financials* from the data files for this lesson.

2. On the Annual Sales worksheet, select **A3:E7**. Click **Line**.

3. Click **Stacked line with Markers**.

4. Apply **Layout 3**.

5. Click **Chart Title** and key **Blue Yonder Airlines** in the formula bar.

6. Click **Plot Area** and click **Format Selection**.

7. Click **Border Color** and click **Gradient line**.

8. Click **Preset Colors** and click **Day Break**.

9. Click **Direction** and click **Linear Diagonal**. Click **Close**.

10. Click **Chart Area**, click **Format Selection**, and click **Solid fill**.

11. Click **Color** and click **Blue, Accent 1, Lighter 80%**.

12. Click **Close**.

13. **SAVE** the workbook as *BY Financials 9-4*.

  LEAVE the workbook open for the next project.

■ Mastery Assessment

Project 9-5: **Create a Doughnut Chart**

1. **USE** the workbook from the previous project.

2. Click the **Annual Expenses** tab. Select **A3:E7** and click **Other Charts** on the Insert tab.

3. Click **Doughnut**.

4. Click **Layout 2**.

5. Click the **Size Dialog Box Launcher**. Set both height and width to 5 inches.

6. Key **Annual Expenses** as the chart title.

7. Print the chart only.

8. **SAVE** the workbook as *BY Financials 9-5*. **CLOSE** the workbook.

  LEAVE Excel open for the next project.

Project 9-6: Format Chart Elements

Fourth Coffee's corporate manager wants to change the chart type and some of the formatting in the chart prepared in a previous exercise.

1. **OPEN** *Income Chart* from the data files for this lesson.
2. Select the chart. Click the **Design** tab.
3. Click **Layout 3**.
4. On the Layout tab, click **Axis Titles** and key **Percentage of Income** below the axis.
5. Click **Data Labels** and add data labels to the bars.
6. Click **Chart Title**. Right-click and click **Font**. Click **Font color** and click **Pink – Accent 2** under Theme Colors.
7. Click **Small Caps** and click **OK**.
8. On the Layout tab, click **Legend** in the Current Selection group.
9. Click **Colored Outline – Accent 2** on the Format tab.
10. On the Design tab, click **Move Chart Location**. Click **New Sheet**.
11. **SAVE** the workbook as *Income Chart 9-6* and then **CLOSE** the file.

    LEAVE Excel open for the next project.

INTERNET READY

Customized chart styles cannot be saved and applied to other charts. However, you can save a customized chart as a template. Use Excel Help to learn how to save a chart as a template that can be used later. Open your Income Chart 9-6 workbook and save it as a template file. **SAVE** the workbook as *Chart Template.*
CLOSE Excel.

Adding Pictures and Shapes to a Worksheet

10

SKILLS	MATRIX SKILL	SKILL NUMBER
Inserting Pictures		
Inserting a Picture from a File	Insert and modify pictures from files	4.4.1
Using SmartArt Graphics	Insert and modify SmartArt graphics	4.4.2
Adding Shapes	Insert and modify shapes	4.4.3
Copying or Moving a Graphic		
Formatting Graphics		
Applying Styles to Shapes	Insert and modify SmartArt graphics	4.4.2
Applying Quick Styles to graphics	Insert and modify SmartArt graphics	4.4.2
Resizing a Graphic	Insert and modify SmartArt graphics	4.4.2
Rotating a Graphic	Insert and modify shapes	4.4.3
Resetting a Picture to Its Original State	Insert and modify pictures from files	4.4.1

Adding a chart, picture, or other illustration to a worksheet captures attention and immediately portrays an idea of what the worksheet is all about. The manager of Margie's Travel often inserts pictures, clip art, shapes and SmartArt graphics into the worksheets she sends to clients. Providing potential travelers with actual photos or other representations of highlights in vacation areas is an effective communication tool for a travel agency.

KEY TERMS
clip
clip art
Clip Organizer
connector
flowchart
organization chart
Quick Styles
SmartArt graphic
Text pane

■ SOFTWARE ORIENTATION

The Insert Tab

Microsoft Office includes a gallery of media images you can insert into worksheets such as pictures, clip art, shapes, and SmartArt graphics. You can also insert a text box that can be positioned anywhere on the worksheet or insert WordArt to call attention to a worksheet or chart's primary message. Use the Insert tab shown in Figure 10-1 to insert illustrations and special text.

Figure 10-1

Use Insert tab commands for illustrations and decorative text

Use this figure as a reference throughout this lesson as you become skilled in inserting and formatting illustrations within a worksheet.

■ Inserting Pictures

THE BOTTOM LINE

While the old adage *a picture is worth a thousand words* is perhaps an exaggeration, a visual adds interest and calls attention to statistical data presented in worksheets. Unlike a worksheet background that is displayed but does not print, pictures, clip art, shapes, and SmartArt graphics are included in worksheet printouts. Graphic objects can be used with charts to focus attention on relevant data.

Inserting a Picture from a File

Pictures can be an integral part of creating a compelling worksheet. You can insert or copy pictures into a worksheet from image providers or files on your computer, such as your favorite digital photographs. A well-chosen picture can portray a powerful message, or it can be used to enhance a chart or other Excel graphic display.

⊙ INSERT A PICTURE FROM A FILE

GET READY. Before you begin these steps, launch Microsoft Excel and open a blank workbook.

CD

The *Vernal Fall*, *El Capitan*, and *Sequoias* images are available on the companion CD-ROM.

1. Click the **Sheet1** tab. Click **Format** on the Home tab and click **Rename Sheet.** Key **Vernal Fall** and press `Enter`. Rename Sheet2 **El Capitan** and rename Sheet3 **Sequoias.**

2. Select **A1** on the Vernal Fall worksheet. On the Insert tab, click **Picture.** The Insert Picture dialog box opens.

3. Click *Vernal Fall* in the data files for this lesson. Click **Insert.** The picture is inserted and, as shown in Figure 10-2, the Format tab with Picture Tools is added to the Ribbon.

Figure 10-2

Picture Tools added to Ribbon on Format tab

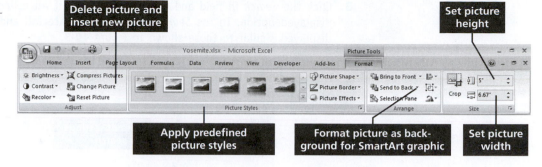

4. Select the number in the Shape Height field, key **5**, and press [Enter]. The picture portrays a view of Vernal Fall in Yosemite National Park.

5. Select **A1** on the El Capitan worksheet. Click the **Insert** tab and click **Picture**. Click *El Capitan* in the data files for this lesson. Click **Insert**.

6. Select the **Shape Height** value, key **5**, and press [Enter].

7. Select **A1** on the Sequoias worksheet. Click the **Insert** tab and click **Picture**. Click *Sequoias* in the data files for this lesson. Click **Insert**.

8. Select the **Shape Height** value, key **5**, and press [Enter].

9. Create a Lesson 10 folder and **SAVE** the workbook as *Yosemite*.

    PAUSE. LEAVE the workbook open to use in the next exercise.

The Insert Picture technique enables you to customize the presentation of worksheet data with selected photographs. The pictures you inserted in this exercise are digital photographs, demonstrating that you can take a picture of anything you want and insert it into a worksheet. The manager of Margie's Travel is preparing a worksheet with detailed travel arrangements for a client's annual sales meeting to be held at a hotel in Yosemite National Park. The client wants to combine the business travel with a family vacation package. The manager will use your worksheet with photos of the area and add the financial data related to the proposal. The visuals can be formatted to enhance the data and call attention to the most important aspects of the workbook.

Inserting a Clip Art Picture

You can insert a clip art image into a worksheet from Microsoft Office Online, other image providers, or files on your computer. A *clip art* image is a single piece of ready-made art, often appearing as a bitmap or a combination of drawn shapes. When you search for clip art in Excel, your search results can include clip art, photographs, movies, and sound files.

⊙ INSERT A CLIP ART PICTURE

USE the workbook from the previous exercise.

1. On the Home tab, click the **Insert** arrow and click **Insert Sheet**. Rename the sheet **Clip Art**.

2. On the Insert tab, click **Clip Art**. The Clip Art task pane opens.

If you are connected to the Internet, the search results can return numerous clip art images from Microsoft Office Online as well as the images in your clip art files. If you are not connected to the Internet, the search results will be limited to images stored in your clip art collections.

3. Click the *Search in* field and select **Everywhere** if All collections is not the displayed option. In the *Search for* field, key **waterfall** and click **Go**. Results are displayed similar to those shown in Figure 10-3.

Figure 10-3

Default settings for clip art search

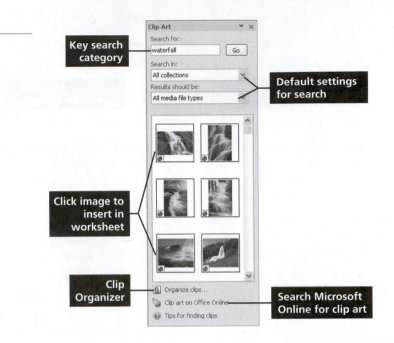

If waterfall images are not returned by your search, connect to the Internet to include search results from Microsoft Office Online or insert one of the waterfall images from the data files for this lesson.

TROUBLESHOOTING

4. Click an image in the search results to insert a waterfall into the Clip Art worksheet.

5. In the Clip Art task pane, click the arrow in the *Results should be* field. Deselect all media types except Clip Art. Click **Go**. The results include only clip art images.

6. Scroll through the list and click an image to insert a waterfall clip art image.

7. **SAVE** and **CLOSE** the workbook. **CLOSE** the Clip Art task pane.

PAUSE. LEAVE Excel open to use in the next exercise.

CERTIFICATION READY?
How do you insert a clip art image into a worksheet?
4.4.1

All media file types is the default for a clip art search. As shown in Figure 10-4, the results will include clip art, photographs, movies, and sounds. You can search for one type of file only or search for any combination of types.

Figure 10-4

Restrict search to clip art only

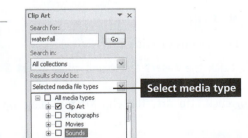

Whether you use your own photo or a clip art image, visuals add interest to financial data and help the audience focus on pertinent aspects of data that is often presented in management and sales meetings. The professional-quality photos returned by a clip art search are usually more appropriate in a business document than caricature-type artistic designs. Some of the photos in the clip art gallery have been sized to easily insert into a document, and you do not always need to adjust the size, as you did in the first exercise, to easily view the picture.

X REF

You will resize photographs later in this lesson.

If you frequently use illustrations in your worksheets, you can organize your favorites in the Microsoft Clip Organizer. The *Clip Organizer* is a way to gather and store your own clips so that you can easily locate and insert them into documents. A *clip* refers to a single media file including art, sound, animation, or movies.

You can access the Clip Organizer from the Clip Art task pane. The first time you open the Clip Organizer, you are asked if you want the organizer to scan your computer for photos and other media files and organize them into separate collections. Clip Organizer creates a shortcut to the files in their original location; it does not copy or move the files on your computer. The shortcuts let you preview, open, or insert a media file without going to its installed location. You can let the Clip Organizer decide which folders and hardware drives to scan for files, or you can specify where to search.

The folders in the Clip Organizer have the same names as the folders in which the original files are stored. Clip Organizer automatically adds keywords to media files. You can modify, delete, or add new keywords to ensure that you will find the clip when you want to insert it into a document. When you download or copy files from a clip art source such as Microsoft Online, the image will be stored in the Clip Organizer. Clips organized and saved in Excel can then be used in Microsoft Word and PowerPoint documents and on the company's Website.

Using SmartArt Graphics

A *SmartArt graphic*, new in Excel 2007, is a visual representation of information and ideas. The use of illustrations and graphics in presentations and printed materials improves understanding and memory and encourages action. Excel provides many graphical layouts and styles that you can use to effectively communicate your message. SmartArt graphics can be used with other images and decorative text.

→ USE SMARTART GRAPHICS

OPEN *Cruise Dates* from the data files for this lesson.

CD

The *Cruise Dates* workbook is available on the companion CD-ROM.

1. On the Mexico worksheet, select **C24**.
2. On the Insert tab, in the Illustrations group, click **SmartArt**. The Choose a SmartArt Graphic dialog box is displayed as shown in Figure 10-5.

Figure 10-5

Select layout for SmartArt graphic

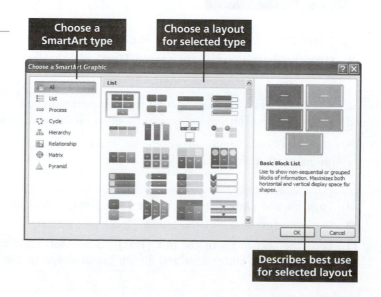

3. On the Choose a SmartArt Graphic dialog box, click **Cycle** in the type pane.

4. Click **Block Cycle** in the layout pane of the dialog box. Click **OK**.

5. The cycle graphic image is inserted and SmartArt Tools are available on the Design and Format tabs. On the Design tab, shown in Figure 10-6, click **Text Pane** in the Create Graphic group if the Text pane is not displayed when the graphic is inserted.

Figure 10-6

Design tab with SmartArt Tools

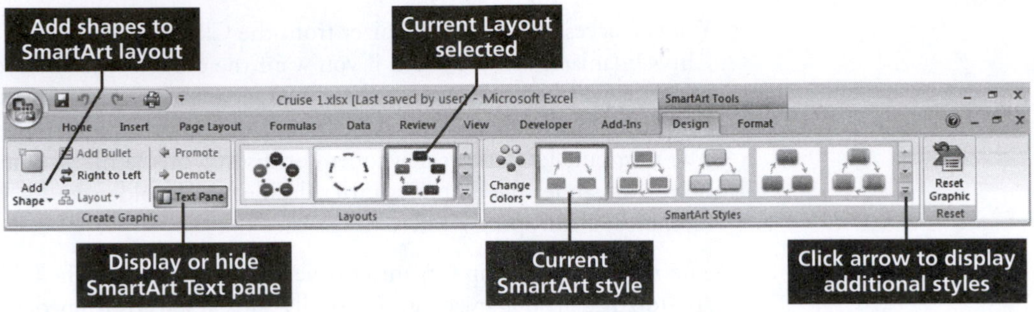

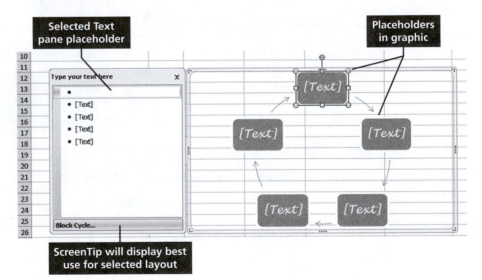

6. Select the first **[Text]** placeholder in the Text pane shown in Figure 10-7. Key **May 20**. As you key text in the Text pane, it is displayed in the first block of the graph.

Figure 10-7

Key or paste text in text boxes

7. Select **E5** in the data range and click **Copy**.

8. Click the graphic, select the second **[Text]** placeholder, and click **Paste**.

TROUBLESHOOTING

If you press Enter when you key or copy text to a text placeholder, a new block is added to the diagram. You can delete an unwanted block by deleting the placeholder.

When you click outside the SmartArt graphic, the Text pane closes. Click the graphic to display the pane to insert or paste additional text.

9. Copy **E6** and paste the date in the third **[Text]** placeholder.

10. Copy the text in **E7** to the fourth **[Text]** placeholder.

11. Copy the text in **E8** to the last **[Text]** placeholder. Press **Enter** to add an additional text placeholder and an additional shape to the design.

12. Copy the text in **E9** to the last block.

13. Click outside the image to view the display.

14. **SAVE** the workbook as *Cruise 1*.

   PAUSE. LEAVE the workbook open to use in the next exercise.

The *Text pane* should appear to the left of a SmartArt graphic. You can use the pane to enter and edit the text that appears in the graphic.

When choosing a layout for a SmartArt graphic, determine what you want to convey and how your information should appear. You can try different layouts until you find the one that best illustrates your message. Your graphic should be clear and easy to follow.

The description of the best use for a selected SmartArt layout that was shown on the right pane of the Choose a SmartArt Graphic dialog box (Figure 10-5) can be seen in a ScreenTip when you point to the layout name that appears at the bottom of the Text pane. Table 10-1 lists the seven types of SmartArt graphics and a short description of the purpose of each type.

Table 10-1

SmartArt graphic types and purposes

Graphic Type	Purpose of Graphic
List	Show non-sequential information
Process	Show steps in a process or timeline
Cycle	Show a continual process
Hierarchy	Show a decision tree
	Create an organization chart
Relationship	Illustrate connections
Matrix	Show how parts relate to a whole
Pyramid	Show proportional relationships with the largest component on the top or bottom

If you cannot find the exact layout that you want, you can add and remove shapes in your SmartArt graphic to adjust the structure of the layout. For example, the Block Cycle layout you inserted had five blocks, and the process you wanted to display needed six blocks. You added another block in the Text pane. When you add or remove shapes and edit the text, the arrangement of the shapes and the amount of text within those shapes is updated automatically. The original design and border of the layout is maintained.

Each bullet in the Text pane represents a shape in the graphic. The Text pane works like an outline or a bulleted list that maps information directly to the graphic. The Text pane and the SmartArt graphic have placeholder text that you can replace with your information. You can edit the text at the top of the Text pane, and you can point to the bottom of the Text pane to view additional information about the SmartArt graphic.

Although you cannot drag text into the Text pane, you can copy and paste to the pane. Also, you can copy from the Text pane to any Microsoft Office program. When you click away from the SmartArt graphic, the Text pane disappears. You can show or hide the Text pane by clicking the control on the left side of the SmartArt graphic or by clicking Text Pane on the Design tab.

In general, SmartArt graphics work best with small amounts of text. Larger amounts of text detract from the visual appeal of the graphic and make it more difficult to convey your message visually. Each SmartArt graphic contains a fixed number of spaces. If you enter too much information, it will not be displayed. Content that is not displayed is identified with a red X in the Text pane. The content is still available if you switch to another SmartArt layout with more space, but if you close the workbook with the same layout, the hidden information is lost.

■ Adding Shapes

↓
THE BOTTOM LINE
You can add a shape to a workbook or combine multiple shapes to create a drawing or a more complex shape. Available shapes include lines, basic geometric shapes, arrows, equation shapes, flow chart shapes, stars, banners, and callouts.

Inserting Basic Shapes

You can use a shape to call attention to an important aspect of worksheet data. Excel provides a variety of basic shapes that you can insert. You can add shapes to a chart or add shapes on top of a SmartArt graphic to customize the chart or SmartArt graphic.

⊕ INSERT BASIC SHAPES

USE the workbook from the previous exercise.

1. On the Alaska worksheet, select **A5**. Click **Shapes** in the Illustrations group on the Insert tab. The Shapes gallery shown in Figure 10-8 opens.

Figure 10-8

Select a shape from the Shapes gallery

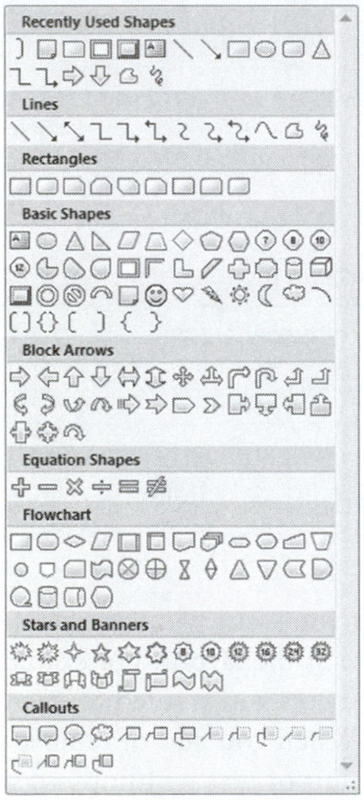

2. Click **Rounded Rectangle** in the Rectangles group in the Shapes gallery and click **A5** to place the rectangle. Use the handles on the rectangle to resize the rectangle to hide the text in row 5 from A5 to the right boundary of F5 of the worksheet.

3. On the Format tab, in the Shape Styles group, click **Colored Outline – Accent 6** (first outline style).

4. Click **Shape Fill** in the Shape Styles group and click **No Fill**. Click an empty cell to deselect the rectangle. The shape calls attention to the Southbound Glacier Discovery cruise that leaves Seattle on June 4.

5. Click **WordArt** in the Text group on the Insert tab. On the WordArt gallery, click **Fill – None, Outline – Accent 6, Glow – Accent 6** (second row, second style). The WordArt sample text is placed on the worksheet.

6. Select **Your Text Here**. On the Home tab, select the number in the Font Size box and key **36**. Press **Enter**.

7. Select the WordArt text. Key **Lowest Price of the Summer** in the WordArt text box.

8. Position the WordArt text box so that it is several rows directly below the last row of data and aligned with the data range.

9. On the Insert tab, click **Shapes** and click **Double Arrow** in the Lines group. Click **C5** to position the arrow from C5 to the WordArt below the data range.

10. Click the **Insert** tab. On the Mexico worksheet, click **Shapes**. In the Rectangles group, click **Snip Same Side Corner Rectangle**. Click in the center of the existing SmartArt to place the new shape.

11. Click **Colored Outline – Accent 6** in the Shape Styles group.

12. Use the shape's handles to resize the rectangle and drag the rectangle to cover the SmartArt graphic. Click **Send to Back** in the Arrange group on the Format tab.

13. **SAVE** your workbook.

   PAUSE. LEAVE the workbook open to use in the next exercise.

CERTIFICATION READY?
How do you add a basic shape to a worksheet?
4.4.3

In this exercise, you placed one shape on top of another to achieve a desired result. When you use more than one shape, it does not matter which shape you insert first. Use the Bring to Front and Send to Back commands to place the shape containing text on top so that the text is visible.

Drawing Lines

You may want to add a line to point to data in a specific location, create a signature line, or separate text. A **connector** is a line that has connection points at the ends of the line and stays connected to the shape to which you have connected it. Straight, elbow, and curved lines are available.

⊙ DRAW LINES

USE the workbook from the previous exercise.

1. On the Advertising worksheet, click **Text Box** in the Text group on the Insert tab.

2. Select **A2** and draw a text box that covers **A2:A4**.

3. Key **Cruise**.

4. Click the **Insert** tab. Click **Text Box** and select **C5**. Draw a text box that covers **C5:C7**.

5. Key **Relax**.

6. Click the **Insert** tab. Click **Text Box** and select **E8**. Draw a text box that covers **E8:E10**.

7. Key **Enjoy**.

8. Click **Shapes** in the Illustrations group. Under Lines, click **Elbow Double-Arrow Connector**. Red circular dots appear on the text boxes as you move your pointer over them.

9. Click the right connection point on the Cruise textbox and drag the connection arrow to the left connection point on the Relax text box.

10. Click **Shapes** and connect the Relax text box to the Enjoy text box. Your worksheet should look like Figure 10-9.

TAKE NOTE*

To create a perfect line, press and hold **Shift** while you drag the shape to the size you want.

Figure 10-9

Use connector lines to connect shapes

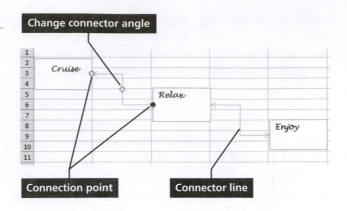

11. Click the border of the Cruise text box to display the move arrow. Drag the box to A8. The connection line remains with text box.

12. Move the text box to A2:A4.

> **TAKE NOTE** *
>
> After you have connected the text boxes, you can move the connection line independently, but not the boxes that the connector links.

CERTIFICATION READY?
How do you draw lines to connect shapes?
4.4.3

13. **SAVE** your workbook.

   PAUSE. LEAVE the workbook open to use in the next exercise.

In this exercise, you inserted connector lines to connect text boxes. After you choose a connector, red circular dots appear on shapes as you move the pointer over them. The dots indicate where you can attach a connector.

When you rearrange shapes that are joined by connectors, the connectors move with the shapes. You can move the end of a connector to detach it from the shape. You can then attach it to another connection site on the same shape, attach it to another shape, or delete the connector. When you select the connector, you can click the diamond shape in the center of the connector and change the angle of the connector line.

If you want to draw a line without connection points, click Freeform in the Shapes gallery. Click one position in the document, move your pointer to a different location, and click again. When you are finished drawing the line, double-click.

If you attach shapes with a line without arrow points, you can add an arrowhead to the line after it has been attached to a shape. Under Drawing Tools on the Format tab, click the arrow next to Shape Outline and point to Arrows. Click the arrow style you want.

Inserting a Block Arrow

> Insert block arrows when you want to show steps in a process or show a timeline. You can insert a block arrow from the Shapes gallery, or you can insert a SmartArt graphic and select the Continuous Arrow Process.

⊙ **INSERT A BLOCK ARROW**

USE the workbook from the previous exercise.

1. On the Hawaii worksheet, click the **Insert** tab if necessary and then click **Shapes**. Under Block Arrows, click **Right Arrow**.

2. Move the insertion crosshairs to **A11** and drag the block so that the arrow point touches the right boundary of column B.

3. Click the block arrow if necessary, and key **Explore the Islands!**

4. On the Insert tab, click **SmartArt**, and click **Process** in the SmartArt type pane.

5. Click **Continuous Arrow Process** and click **OK**.

6. Click the edge of the SmartArt image to display the move pointer and drag the image below the block arrow shape.

7. Click the first placeholder and key **Call Today!**

8. In the second placeholder, key **Sail this Summer!**

9. Select the third **[Text]** placeholder and press Delete. Press Backspace if necessary to delete the third placeholder bullet.

10. **SAVE** and **CLOSE** the workbook.

    PAUSE. LEAVE Excel open to use in the next exercise.

CERTIFICATION READY?
How do you insert a block arrow into a worksheet?
4.4.3

There is little difference between the two block arrows you inserted in this exercise. The SmartArt Continuous Arrow Process arrow is used to show a timeline or sequential steps in a task, process, or workflow. The standard block arrow can serve the same purpose or be used to call attention to data in the worksheet. You can size either arrow to fit your needs. The major difference is that text entered in the SmartArt graphic is entered in a text box so messages can be separated, as illustrated in the exercise.

Creating a Flowchart

A *flowchart* is a schematic representation of a process. It shows what comes first, second, third, etc. It is a basic tool of quality control. Examples include instructions for assembling the components for a new computer, a diagram of a manufacturing plant's work flow, and the process to be completed when a travel agency determines whether to respond to a request for proposal (RFP) for a corporate travel contract. It is a working map of your final product or decision. You can create a flowchart by inserting Flowchart shapes and connectors or use a Process SmartArt graphic.

⊕ CREATE A FLOWCHART

OPEN *Graphics* from the data files for this lesson.

1. On the Flowchart 1 worksheet, click the **Insert** tab, and then click **Shapes**.

2. Under Block Arrows, click **Down Arrow**. Place the arrow at the bottom point of the last diamond shape. Adjust the arrow's size and position to resemble the existing arrows if necessary.

3. Click the **Insert** tab and click **Shapes**. Click the **Flowchart: Process** shape. Insert the image below the arrow. Make the symbol the approximate size of the existing shapes.

4. In the Process shape, key **Prepare worksheet to calculate potential earnings**.

5. Click **Sheet2** and rename it **Flowchart 2**.

6. On the Insert tab, click **SmartArt**.

7. Click **Process** in the Type pane. Click **Vertical Process** in the Layout pane. Click **OK** to place the graphic.

8. On the Design tab, click **Text Pane** in the Create Graphic group if necessary.

9. Click the first **[Text]** placeholder in the Text pane and key **Review RFP**.

10. In the second placeholder, key **Personnel?**

11. In the third placeholder, key **Time?** and press Enter.

12. Key **Prepare worksheet**. The size and shape of the rectangles in the diagram change when you enter a longer text string.

13. **SAVE** the workbook as *Graphics 1*.

    PAUSE. LEAVE the workbook open to use in the next exercise.

The *Graphics* workbook is available on the companion CD-ROM.

CERTIFICATION READY?
How do you use shapes and SmartArt graphics?
4.4.3

Flowchart shapes provide an indication of what happens during the flow of work. In the Flowchart worksheet you used in this exercise, the chart began with a Preparation shape. A diamond shape is used to indicate a decision. Connector arrows point one direction if the decision is no, and point the other direction if the decision is yes.

The SmartArt Vertical Process layout is used to show a progression or sequential steps in a task, process, or workflow from top to bottom. This SmartArt layout works best with Level 1 text without a great deal of detail.

You can add more detail when you create a flowchart by using the flowchart shapes. The SmartArt graphic saves time but provides less detail. The flowchart's intended use and the amount of detail needed determine which style should be used.

Creating an Organization Chart

One of the most common uses for the Hierarchy layout is a company organization chart. An *organization chart* graphically illustrates the management structure of an organization. When you choose this layout, additional functionality, such as the assistant shape and hanging layouts, become available.

⊙ **CREATE AN ORGANIZATION CHART**

USE the workbook you saved in the previous exercise.

1. Click the **Sheet3** tab. On the Home tab, click **Format** and click **Rename Sheet**.
2. Key **Organization Chart** and press Enter.
3. On the Insert tab, click **SmartArt**.
4. Click **Hierarchy** in the Shape Type pane. Click **Organization Chart** in the layout pane and click **OK**.
5. In the Text pane, click the first **[Text]** placeholder if necessary, key **Margie Shoop, CEO**, and press Enter.
6. Click **Demote** in the Create Graphic group on the Design tab to demote the box to Level 2. Key **John Y. Chen** and press Enter.
7. Click **Demote** and key **Jamie Reding**. Press Enter.
8. Key **Stephanie Conway** and press Enter.
9. Click **Promote** and key **Ciam Sawyer**. Press Enter.
10. Click **Demote** and key **Jeffrey Ford**.
11. Click the first bulleted item in the Text pane and click the arrow under **Add Shape** in the Create graphic group on the Design tab.

TAKE NOTE ✱ You can select a diagram shape and click Add Shape. You can then choose the position and shape type that should be added.

12. Click **Add Assistant**. Key **Brenda Diaz, Assistant** in the Text pane.
13. Select any blank placeholders in the Text pane and click Delete.

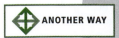 **ANOTHER WAY** When you key text in a Text pane placeholder, you can select the next placeholder rather than pressing Enter. Press **Enter** when you need additional positions in the organization chart.

14. Click outside the graphic. Your organization chart should look like Figure 10-10.

Figure 10-10

Organization chart created with SmartArt tools

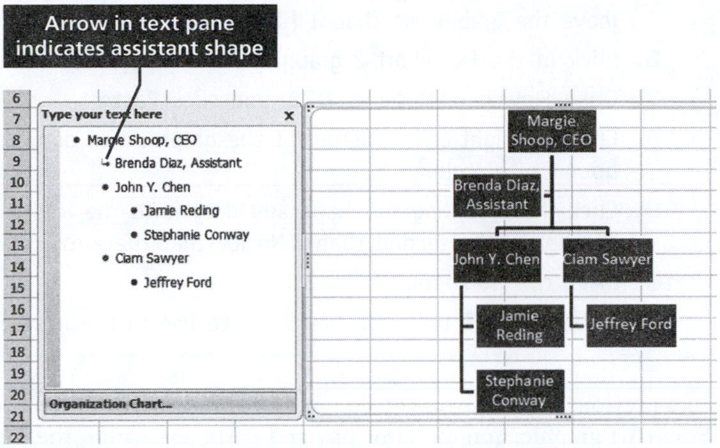

TAKE NOTE

In the Text pane of an organization chart, the Assistant shape is indicated by a bullet with a line attached.

TROUBLESHOOTING If necessary, select the shape and click Promote to move an individual to a higher level. Click Demote to move an individual to a lower level.

CERTIFICATION READY?
How do you use SmartArt?
4.4.2

15. **SAVE** your workbook.

PAUSE. LEAVE the workbook open to use in the next exercise.

In this exercise you created a standard organization chart for Margie's Travel. In a subsequent exercise, you will modify the SmartArt graphic by changing the reporting level of some positions. You can adjust levels in the organizational chart by selecting the shape or the bulleted item in the Text pane and then clicking Promote or Demote.

When two individuals share the top-level responsibilities, their positions should be connected by a broken line. The SmartArt Organization Chart layout does not provide this type of connection. You can insert a broken line and connect the two blocks.

Character formatting such as bold or italic can be applied in the Text pane. This formatting will be displayed in the graphic, but not in the Text pane.

■ Copying or Moving a Graphic

THE BOTTOM LINE Pictures, clip art, shapes, and SmartArt graphics are not always inserted where you want them for an effective presentation. You can move a graphic manually, or specify its exact size by using options in the Size group on the Format tab.

⊙ COPY OR MOVE A GRAPHIC

USE the workbook you saved in the previous exercise.

1. Click the **Close** (**X**) button on the Text pane of the organizational chart.

2. Click in the organization chart to select the SmartArt graphic.

3. Click the border of the SmartArt graphic and drag the graphic to the upper-left corner of the worksheet.

TROUBLESHOOTING If you click the dots on the corners and sides of the border, you will resize the graphic rather than move it.

4. Click the **Flowchart 2** tab to open the worksheet.

5. Click the SmartArt graphic to select it. Press the up, down, left, or right arrows to move the graphic so that it fills F4:H18.

6. Click in the Flowchart 2 graphic. Click **Copy** on the Home tab.

7. Open Flowchart 1, select **D32**, and click **Paste**.

8. Click the right-center border of the graphic and drag the border to the right boundary of column M.

9. Click the first diagram shape and drag it to the left and down so that it is parallel to the second shape. Notice that the arrow now points to the right.

10. **SAVE** the workbook.

PAUSE. LEAVE the workbook open to use in the next exercise.

In a previous exercise, you copied text from worksheet cells and pasted it in a bullet point in a SmartArt graphic. You can also copy and paste text within the Text pane. You can copy a SmartArt graphic, or any other graphical display, and paste it to another location within the worksheet, paste it to another worksheet or workbook, or paste it to another Microsoft Office program.

You can move a shape in a SmartArt graphic, or you can move the whole graphic. This flexibility allows you to customize the design of the graphical display. When you want to move a graphic incrementally, use the arrow keys, which provide precision. Click the graphic border and move the graphic for a significant change in location.

■ Formatting Graphics

THE BOTTOM LINE

The formatting styles such as font, fill color, and effects that are applied when you insert a shape or SmartArt graphic are based on the underlying document theme of the worksheet. You can apply a Quick Style to an entire graphic or apply formatting components to various parts of a graphic.

Applying Styles to Shapes

Quick Styles are combinations of different formatting options. They are displayed in a thumbnail in various Quick Style galleries on the Format tab that is added to the Ribbon when a graphic is inserted in a worksheet. When you place your pointer over a style thumbnail on the Format tab, you can see how applying that style will affect your SmartArt graphic or shape.

➔ APPLY STYLES TO SHAPES

USE the workbook from the previous exercise.

1. On the Flowchart 1 worksheet, select the **Start** shape. Click the **Format** tab and click **More** next to the predefined Shape Styles group.

2. In row 4, click **Subtle Effect – Accent 3**.

3. Select the first diamond shape, press ⌈**Shift**⌋, and select the second diamond.

4. Click **Shape Fill** and click **Red**.

5. With the shapes still selected, click **Shape Outline**.

6. Click **Dashes** and click **Round Dot**.

7. Click **Shape Effects**, point to **Glow**, and click the first option under Glow.

8. Click **Text Fill** in the WordArt Styles group and click **Dark Blue**.

PAUSE. LEAVE the workbook open to use in the next exercise.

CERTIFICATION READY?
How do you apply a style to SmartArt?
4.4.2

A word of caution is in order: To prevent the formatting of a graphic from overpowering the message, apply formatting sparingly. In this exercise, you changed the appearance of the graphic by applying formatting to flowchart components to preview various formatting styles. After trying several effects, you would select a basic style to use throughout the flowchart rather than have such varying styles in one graphic.

When a graphic is composed of individual shapes, you must select the shapes to which you want to apply formatting. As you will see in the next exercise, you can apply a predefined style to shapes or apply a style to the entire SmartArt graphic.

Applying Quick Styles to Graphics

SmartArt styles reflect the document theme that was chosen when the worksheet was created. You can apply a different style from those displayed on the Design tab, or you can modify elements within the graphic by changing the shape fill, outline, or effects.

⊙ APPLY QUICK STYLES TO GRAPHICS

USE the workbook from the previous exercise.

1. On the Flowchart 2 worksheet, select the SmartArt graphic. Click the **Design** tab. In the SmartArt Styles group, the style that is currently applied to the graphic is selected.

2. Point to each style that is displayed to see the changes that applying the style would have on the SmartArt graphic. Click **White Outline**.

3. Click **More** and point to various styles in the Best Match for Document list to observe changes to the graphic.

4. Preview the styles in the 3-D group and click **Metallic Scene**.

5. Click **Change Colors** and click **Colorful – Accent Colors**. Notice that choices in the SmartArt Styles group have changed based on changing the graphics colors.

6. On the Organization Chart worksheet, click the SmartArt graphic. Click Subtle Effect in the SmartArt Styles group.

7. **SAVE** the workbook as *Graphics 2*.

   PAUSE. LEAVE the workbook open to use in the next exercise.

CERTIFICATION READY?
How do you modify the style applied to a SmartArt graphic?
4.4.2

The ability to point to a style and see how that style will look in your display is an Excel 2007 new feature. Rather than try a style, click Undo, try another style, etc., you can see the effect without changing anything on your worksheet.

The default SmartArt style that was applied to the graphic when it was created was based on the Office theme. The style choices that are available in the SmartArt Styles group on the Design tab are based on the colors, fonts, and effects that comprise the Office theme. If you change the worksheet's theme, the options in the styles gallery change to reflect the new theme that you applied to the worksheet.

When you insert a SmartArt graphic, a color diagram of the style you select is displayed on the Choose a SmartArt Graphic dialog box. The color combination displayed in that sample was applied to your graphic when you clicked Change Colors.

Resizing a Graphic

You can resize one or more shapes within a graphic or resize the complete SmartArt graphic. You can use the sizing handles on the side or corner of a graphic to increase or decrease its size, or you can specify a specific size for the height and width of a graphic or shape within the graphic.

TAKE NOTE*

You can change the Zoom to see the entire graphic without changing the size.

CERTIFICATION READY?
How do you resize a SmartArt graphic?
4.4.2

RESIZE A GRAPHIC

USE the workbook from the previous exercise.

1. On the Organization Chart worksheet, click in the SmartArt graphic to select it.
2. Click the left-center sizing handle and drag it to the column G right boundary.
3. On the Format tab, click **Size**. In the Height box, key **5.5**. In the Width box, key **6**.
4. Click the shape at the top of the diagram (Margie Shoop, CEO). Click the right sizing handle and drag to the right until the shape extends over the diagram.
5. **SAVE** and **CLOSE** the workbook.

   PAUSE. LEAVE Excel open to use in the next exercise.

Rotating a Graphic

You can change a shape's position by rotating or reversing it. Reversing a shape is also referred to as creating a mirror image or flipping. When you rotate multiple shapes, they are not rotated as a group, but each shape is rotated around its own center.

ROTATE A GRAPHIC

The *Take a Summer Cruise* workbook is available on the companion CD-ROM.

OPEN *Take a Summer Cruise* from the data files for this lesson.

1. On the Hawaii worksheet, select the text in the standard block arrow. Key **Pick a Cruise!**
2. Select the graphic and click the **Format** tab. In the Arrange group, click **Rotate** and click **Flip Horizontal**. The arrow and the text are reversed.
3. Click **Rotate** and click **Rotate Right 90°**.
4. Click the graphic, display the move pointer, and move it so that the arrow tip is centered in the white space in A6.
5. Click the SmartArt graphic. On the Design tab, click **Right to Left** in the Create Graphics group. The graphic is reversed horizontally.
6. On the Format tab, click **Arrange**, and then click **Selection Pane**. On the Selection and Visibility pane, click **Right Arrow 10**.
7. Click **Rotate** and then click **More Rotation Options**. The Size and Properties dialog box is displayed.
8. On the Size and Properties dialog box, click the down arrow in the **Rotation** field until the graphic rotation is **70°**. Click **Close**.
9. If necessary, move the graphic so that all text is visible and the point is centered in the white space in A6.
10. Close the Selection and Visibility pane. Also, hide the cell gridlines.
11. **SAVE** the workbook as *Cruise 2*.

    PAUSE. LEAVE the workbook open to use in the next exercise.

CERTIFICATION READY?
How do you modify SmartArt and shapes?
4.4.2, 4.4.3

The predefined rotation options limit you to flipping the graphic. When you open the Size and Properties dialog box, you can rotate a graphic one degree at a time, which gives you a great deal of flexibility in placing the graphic at exactly the angle that calls attention to the most significant data in a worksheet.

If you have more than one graphic in a worksheet, display the Selection and Visibility pane so that you can easily select the graphic that you want to modify or format. Options on the Selection and Visibility pane allow you to hide graphics temporarily and to reorder the shapes on a worksheet. This feature is useful when you want to print a draft, but you do not need the graphics to display until you are ready to print the final document.

Resetting a Picture to Its Original State

Sometimes you make formatting changes and then want to restore a picture or graphic to its original formatting. The Reset Picture command on the Picture Tools Format tab will reset picture formatting to the formatting present when the file was last saved.

➔ RESET A PICTURE TO ITS ORIGINAL STATE

USE the workbook from the previous exercise.

1. On the Mexico worksheet, select the picture and click the **Format** tab.
2. Click **Picture Shape**. On the dropdown list, click **Snip Same Side Corner Rectangle**.
3. In the Picture Styles group, click **Metal Frame**.
4. Click **Brightness** in the Adjust group and click **+20%**.
5. Click **Contrast** and click **−40%**.
6. Click **Recolor**. Click **Text color 2 Dark**.
7. Click **Reset Picture** in the Adjust group.
8. **SAVE** the workbook with the same name. **CLOSE** the workbook.

   CLOSE Excel.

CERTIFICATION READY?
How do you reset a picture to its original state?
4.4.1

In the previous exercise, you made multiple formatting changes to the picture and then restored the picture to its original formatting. The same option is available when you work with SmartArt graphics so that when you are not pleased with formatting changes, you have not lost the original.

SUMMARY SKILL MATRIX

IN THIS LESSON YOU LEARNED	MATRIX SKILL	SKILL NUMBER
To insert pictures from files on your computer and from online resources		
To insert digital photographs from a file	Insert and modify pictures from files	4.4.1
To insert SmartArt graphics into a worksheet	Insert and modify SmartArt graphics	4.4.2
To add predefined shapes to a worksheet	Insert and modify shapes	4.4.3
To copy and move graphics within a worksheet		
To apply formatting options to graphics		
To apply predefined styles to shapes	Insert and modify shapes	4.4.3
To apply Quick Styles to graphics	Insert and modify SmartArt graphics	4.4.2
To resize graphics to desired dimensions	Insert and modify SmartArt graphics	4.4.2
To rotate a graphic image to a desired angle	Insert and modify shapes	4.4.3
To restore a picture to its original formatting without reverting to a saved file	Insert and modify pictures from files	4.4.1

■ Knowledge Assessment

Matching

a. clip
b. clip art
c. Clip Organizer
d. connector
e. Drawing Tools

f. flowchart
g. Quick Styles
h. SmartArt Graphic
i. SmartArt Tools
j. Text pane

_____ **1.** Commands added to Excel's Ribbon when you insert a SmartArt graphic.

_____ **2.** A listing of clips that is easily accessible so that you can locate and insert them into documents.

_____ **3.** A visual representation of information and ideas.

_____ **4.** The pane that appears to the left of a SmartArt graphic that you use to enter and edit text that appears in the graphic.

_____ **5.** Commands added to Excel's Ribbon when you insert a shape.

_____ **6.** A schematic representation of a process.

_____ **7.** A line that has connection points at the end of the line and stays connected to the shapes to which you add it.

_____ **8.** A single piece of ready-made art, often appearing as a bitmap or combination of drawn shapes.

_____ **9.** A single media file including art, sound, animation, or movies.

_____ **10.** Collections of formatting options that make formatting documents and objects easier.

True / False

Circle T if the statement is true or F if the statement is false.

T F **1.** When you insert a SmartArt graphic, the formatting is preset and cannot be changed.

T F **2.** You can insert multiple images into one worksheet.

T F **3.** The colors, fonts, and effects in a SmartArt graphic are based on the document theme that was applied to the worksheet.

T F **4.** When you move a shape that has a connector line attached, you must select the connector to move it as well.

T F **5.** You can hide a graphic on a worksheet without deleting it.

T F **6.** You can rotate a SmartArt graphic, but you cannot rotate the individual parts of the graphic.

T F **7.** When you create an organization chart, an assistant position is at the same level as the individual who is being assisted.

T F **8.** You can rotate a graphic to any desired angle.

T F **9.** You can restore a picture to its original formatting without reverting to a saved file.

T F **10.** You can change a graphic without deleting the original.

■ Competency Assessment

Project 10-1: Insert Pictures and Clip Art

An employee at Blue Yonder Airlines wants to add graphics to a worksheet that summarizes annual sales.

GET READY. Launch Excel.

CD

The *Annual Sales* workbook is available on the companion CD-ROM.

1. **OPEN** *Annual Sales* from the data files for this lesson.
2. On the Insert tab, click **Clip Art**. The Clip Art task pane opens.
3. In the *Results should be* field, select **Photographs**. All other media types should be deselected.
4. Key **Airplane** in the *Search for* field and click **Go**.
5. Scroll through the search results and select an image of an airplane in an open sky.
6. Click the picture and display the Format tab. Click the text in **Shape Height**, key **1**, and press Enter.
7. Click the picture and move it to the blank space on the right side of **A1**.
8. Use the sizing handles to shrink the picture so that it fits into the blank space to the right of the title.
9. With the picture selected, use the arrow keys to align the picture against the right boundary of column B.
10. In the Picture Styles group, click **Soft Edge Rectangle**.
11. **SAVE** the workbook as *Annual Sales 10-1*. **CLOSE** the workbook and the Clip Art task pane.

    LEAVE Excel open to use in the next project.

Project 10-2: Format and Resize a SmartArt Graphic

The School of Fine Art has created a SmartArt graphic to represent the steps a department must complete in order to add a new course to the department course offerings.

CD

The *Curriculum* workbook is available on the companion CD-ROM.

1. **OPEN** *Curriculum* from the data files for this lesson.
2. Select the **WordArt** box at the top of the worksheet.
3. On the Format tab, click **More** in the WordArt Styles group.
4. On the WordArt gallery, click **Fill – Accent2, Matte Bevel** (last row).
5. Click in the SmartArt graphic. Close the Text pane if necessary.
6. On the Design tab, click **Change Colors** and click the first choice under Accent 2.
7. Use the right-center sizing handle to decrease the graphic's width and align the graphic pane with the title.
8. Click **Text Box** on the Insert tab. Draw the text box in the center of the graphic.
9. Key **New Course Cycle** in the box.
10. Select the text box and click **Shape Fill** on the Format tab. Click **Dark Red**.
11. Click **Shape Height** and key **0.3**. Press Enter.
12. Use the arrow keys to center the text box within the graphic.
13. **SAVE** the workbook as *Curriculum 10-2* and then **CLOSE** the file.

    LEAVE Excel open for the next project.

■ Proficiency Assessment

Project 10-3: Insert Pictures and Shapes into SmartArt

1. **OPEN** *Curriculum* from the data files for this lesson.
2. On the Insert tab, click **Picture**.
3. Select **Book** and click **Insert**.
4. Resize the picture so it is the same size as the graphic. Move the picture so that the graphic is hidden.
5. On the Format tab, click **Contrast** and click **−40%**.
6. Click **Brightness** and click **+40%**.
7. Click **Send to Back**.
8. Click in the graphic and press Ctrl + A to select the shapes in the graphic.
9. In the Shape Styles group on the Format tab, click **Colored Outline – Accent 2**.
10. **SAVE** the workbook as *Curriculum 10-3* and **CLOSE** the file.

   LEAVE Excel open for the next project.

Project 10-4: Format and Reset a Picture to Its Original State

1. **OPEN** *Pictures* from the data files for this lesson.
2. Click a picture. On the Format tab, click **Selection Pane**.
3. In the Selection and Visibility pane, click **Picture 1**.
4. In the Picture Styles group, click **Reflected Rounded Rectangle**.
5. Click **Recolor** and click **Sepia**.
6. Click **Picture 2** in the task pane. Click **Picture Effects**.
7. Point to **Glow** and click **Accent Color 2, 5 pt glow**.
8. Select **Picture 3** in the task pane and click **Crop**. Place the crop tool at the lower-right corner and drag up to the desktop in the picture. Click **Crop** to complete the crop.
9. Select **Picture 4** in the task pane. Click **Change Picture** and select **Book**. Click **Insert**.
10. Click **Picture 2** and click **Reset Picture**.
11. **SAVE** the workbook as *Pictures 10-4*. **CLOSE** the workbook.

   LEAVE Excel open for the next project.

■ Mastery Assessment

Project 10-5: Create an Organization Chart

Blue Yonder Airlines wants to create an organization chart. Use SmartArt graphics to create and format an organization chart.

1. **OPEN** a new blank workbook.
2. On the Insert tab, click **SmartArt**.
3. Click **Hierarchy** and click **Organization Chart**.

4. Enter the following information in the Text pane. When you have entered the names, the assistant shape should be connected to the line between the CEO and the two managers. Click **Promote** to move a shape to a higher level and click **Demote** to move a shape to a lower level as needed.

Name	Position	Reports to
Kim Ralls	CEO	
Mikael Sandberg	Corporate Sales and Charter Flights	CEO
John Evans	Flight School and Sky Diving	CEO
Frank Pellow	Sales Representative	Mikael Sandberg
Linda Randall	Sales Representative	Mikael Sandberg
Scott Seely	Sales Representative	John Evans
Tracy Tallman	Flight Instructor	John Evans
Katie Jordan	Sky Diving Instructor	John Evans
Elsa Leavitt	Assistant	

5. Move the SmartArt graphic to the upper-left edge of the worksheet.
6. Use a corner sizing handle to expand the graphic so that it fits in A1:I20.
7. On the Design tab, click **Subtle Effect**.
8. **SAVE** the workbook as *Blue Yonder 10-5*. **CLOSE** the file.

    LEAVE Excel open for the next project.

Project 10-6: Format Shapes

CD

The *Advertising* workbook and the *Ship* image file are available on the companion CD-ROM.

1. **OPEN** *Advertising* from the data files for this lesson.
2. Press Shift to select the shapes and change the height of the shape to **1 inch** high by **1.35 inches** wide.
3. Apply **Colored Outline – Accent 5** style to the shapes.
4. Rotate the shapes **20°**.
5. Select the connectors and change the shape outline weight to **1½ pt** and the shape outline to **dark red**.
6. Insert the *Ship* picture from the data files for this lesson.
7. Set shape height at **4.5 inches** and accept the default width.
8. Change the picture brightness to **+40%**.
9. Send the picture behind the connected shapes.
10. **SAVE** the workbook as *Advertising 10-6*. **CLOSE** the workbook.

    LEAVE Excel open for the next project.

INTERNET READY

Use Web search tools to find a travel agency that you could use to plan your next vacation. View the pictures and vacation descriptions on the Web page that represents the type of vacation you would like to take (i.e., the beach, the mountains, cruise, etc.).

Open a new Excel workbook. Open the Clip Art task pane and click Clip Art on Office Online. Locate at least two pictures that represent your vacation. Download the selected images to your Clip Organizer in a Vacation Folder.

Insert the pictures into the open worksheet. Title the worksheet Vacation Plan. **SAVE** the workbook as *Vacation Plan*. **CLOSE** Excel.

11 Securing and Sharing Documents

Contoso, Ltd. is concerned with information security on three levels:

- Protecting employees' Social Security numbers and other personal information.
- Protecting employees' performance evaluations.
- Protecting patients' personal and medical information.

Jim Giest, the office manager, is in the process of establishing policies to protect private and confidential information. Although Social Security numbers must be used when payroll tax

KEY TERMS
authenticate
certificate authority (CA)
change history
change tracking
digital certificate
digital signature
password
shared workbook
strong password

information is transmitted to governmental agencies, the office manager assigns employee ID numbers that will be used on all other documents such as employee checks and electronic and printed materials.

Workbooks that contain employee or patient information will be password protected to limit access to information. Only those who have a legitimate need for information will be able to view any employee information. Only Dr. Bourne, the owner, and the office manager will be able to modify information related to payroll.

■ SOFTWARE ORIENTATION

The Review Tab

Microsoft Excel provides several layers of security and protection that allow you to control who can access and change your Excel data. You can protect an entire workbook file so that only authorized users can view or modify your data. This provides the highest level of protection. You can also protect certain worksheet or workbook elements to prevent users from accidentally or deliberately changing, moving, or deleting important data. Data protection is especially important when files are shared and edited by multiple users.

Figure 11-1

Review tab

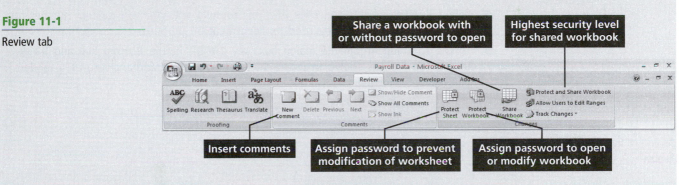

Use this illustration as a reference throughout this lesson as you learn to share and edit files using Excel's security and protection options.

■ Securing Your Work Before Sharing It with Others

↓
THE BOTTOM LINE

A *password* is text that must be keyed before a user can access a workbook, worksheet, or worksheet elements. You can secure an entire workbook by restricting who can open and/or use the workbook data and by requiring a password to view or to save changes to the workbook. You can provide additional protection for certain worksheets or workbook elements with or without a password.

Protecting a Worksheet

In a work environment, workbooks are frequently used by more than one employee. When you create a worksheet that will be accessed by multiple users, you often need to protect it so that a user does not accidentally or intentionally change, move, or delete important data.

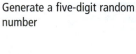

CD

The *Employee Data* workbook is available on the companion CD-ROM.

→ PROTECT A WORKSHEET

GET READY. Before you begin these steps, launch Microsoft Excel.

1. **OPEN** *Employee Data* from the data files for this lesson.

2. Select **G4** on the SSN worksheet. On the Formulas tab, click **Insert Function**. The Insert Function dialog box is displayed.

3. Key **Rand** in the *Search for a function* box and click **Go**. As shown in Figure 11-2, two random number functions are displayed in the *Select a function* box.

Figure 11-2

Functions to generate random numbers

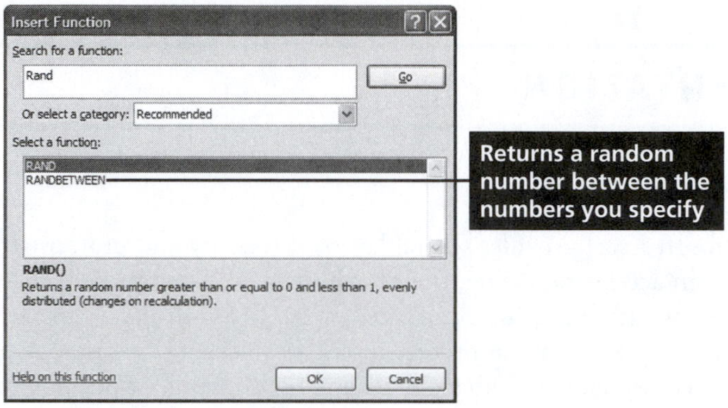

Insert Function

Search for a function:

Rand   [Go]

Or select a category: Recommended

Select a function:

RAND
RANDBETWEEN ────── **Returns a random number between the numbers you specify**

RAND()
Returns a random number greater than or equal to 0 and less than 1, evenly distributed (changes on recalculation).

Help on this function   [OK]   [Cancel]

4. Select **RANDBETWEEN** and click **OK**. This formula will create a random number for each employee that can be used for identification purposes.

5. In the Function Arguments dialog box, key **10000** in the Bottom box and **99999** in the Top box, as shown in Figure 11-3. Click **OK**. The formula returns a random number between the two values.

Figure 11-3

Generate a five-digit random number

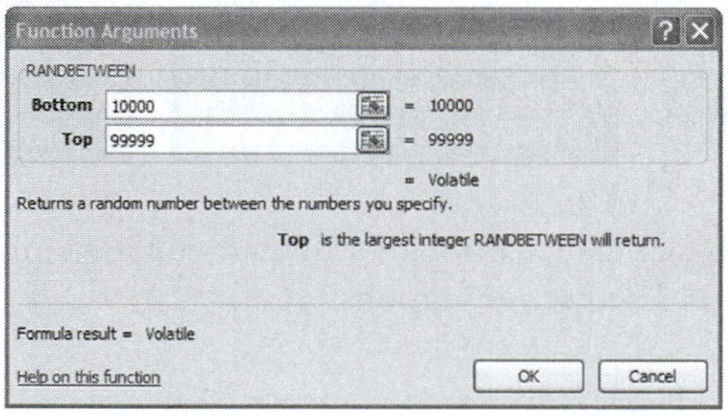

Function Arguments

RANDBETWEEN

Bottom 10000   = 10000
Top   99999   = 99999

= Volatile
Returns a random number between the numbers you specify.

Top is the largest integer RANDBETWEEN will return.

Formula result = Volatile
Help on this function   [OK]   [Cancel]

6. Copy the formula in G4 to **G5:G33**. Each employee is assigned a random five-digit ID number.

7. Select **G4:G33**. On the Home tab, click **Copy**. Click the **Paste** arrow, and click **Paste Values**.

TROUBLESHOOTING

The RANDBETWEEN formula generates a new random number each time a workbook is opened. To retain the Employee ID numbers created by the formula, you must replace the formula with the values.

8. With G4:G33 selected, click **Format** and click **Format Cells**.

9. On the Protection tab of the dialog box, select **Locked** and click **OK**. This prevents employee ID numbers from being changed when the worksheet has been protected.

10. On the Review tab, in the Changes group, click **Protect Sheet**.

11. Key **L11!e01** in the *Password to unprotect sheet* box. The password is not displayed on the screen. Click **OK**.

12. You are asked to confirm the password. Key **L11!e01** and click **OK**. The worksheet is locked. You cannot edit any cell.

13. **SAVE** the workbook as *Payroll Data*. **CLOSE** the workbook.

    PAUSE. LEAVE Excel open to use in the next exercise.

As a first step in information security, you are assigned an Employee ID number that can replace Social Security numbers on all documents. Excel has two random number functions: RAND and RANDBETWEEN. RAND does not require function arguments so you cannot specify the number of digits you want in the number returned by a RAND formula. RANDBETWEEN allows you to determine the beginning and ending numbers. Your formulas returned a five-digit number for each employee.

The Payroll Data workbook you saved in this exercise can be viewed by anyone who has access to the computer system. You restricted the modification of the file, but did not restrict access to the data. In the next exercise, you will limit access to the workbook by requiring a password to open the document.

Excel passwords can be up to 255 letters, numbers, spaces, and symbols. Passwords are case sensitive, so you must type uppercase and lowercase letters correctly. If possible, select a strong password that you can remember so that you do not have to write it down. A ***strong password*** is one that that combines uppercase and lowercase letters, numbers, and symbols such as L11!e01 that you used in this exercise. A password that uses 14 or more characters, however, is considered to be more secure. Passwords that use birthdates, house numbers, pet names, etc., provide little protection.

 It is vitally important that you remember passwords assigned to workbooks or worksheets. If you forget your password, Microsoft cannot retrieve it. If necessary, write down passwords and store them in a secure place away from the information that you want to protect.

When you protect a worksheet, you can hide any formulas that you do not want to be visible. Select the cells that contain the formulas that you want to hide. On the Protection tab of the Format Cells dialog box, select the Hidden checkbox.

 Workbook and worksheet element protection should not be confused with workbook-level password security. Element protection cannot protect a workbook from users who have malicious intent.

Protecting a Workbook

Assigning a password is an effective way to prevent any user who does not know the password from opening the workbook. To protect the entire workbook, you can require a password to open and view the workbook. You can also require one password to open and view the workbook and a second password to modify workbook data. Passwords that apply to the entire workbook provide optimal security for your data.

 PROTECT A WORKBOOK

1. **OPEN** *Payroll Data* that you saved and closed in the previous exercise.

2. Click **D11** and try to key a new value in the cell. You are unable to modify the cell because the worksheet is protected.

3. Click the **Performance** worksheet tab and select **D6**.

4. On the Home tab, click the **Delete** arrow, and click **Delete Sheet Rows**. Dr. Bourne's data is removed from the worksheet.

5. Click the **SSN** worksheet tab. Click **Unprotect Sheet** in the Changes group on the Review tab.

6. Key **L11!e01** (the password you created in the previous exercise) and click **OK**.

7. Select **D11**, key **25**, press Tab, and key **17000**. Press Tab.

8. On the Review tab, in the Changes group, click **Protect Workbook**. Click **Protect Structure and Windows**. The Protect Structure and Windows dialog box shown in Figure 11-4 opens.

Figure 11-4

Protect the structure of a protected workbook

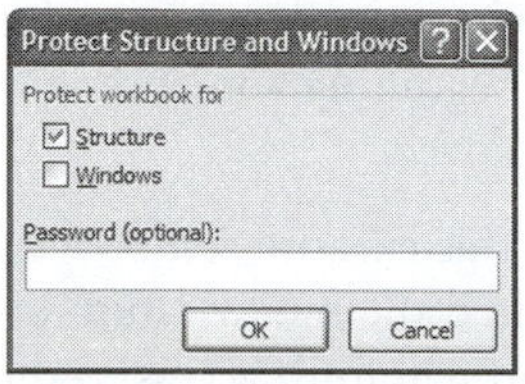

9. Key **L11&E02** in the password box and click **OK**. Confirm the password as shown in Figure 11-5 and click **OK**.

Figure 11-5

Confirm password to open workbook

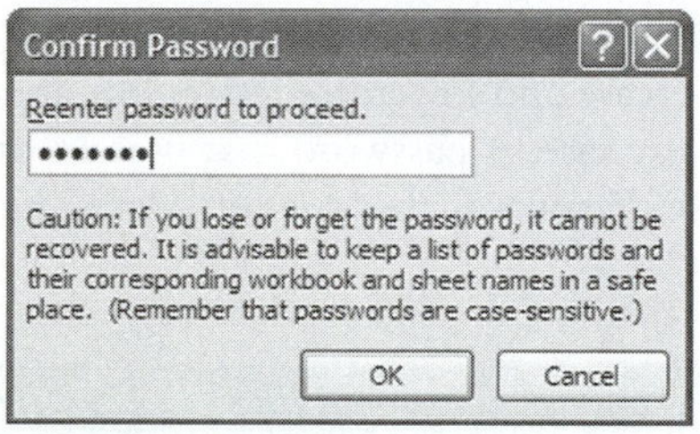

TAKE NOTE
The workbook password is optional, but if you do not supply a password, any user can unprotect the workbook and change the protected elements.

10. Click the **Microsoft Office Button** and click **Save As**.

11. On the Save As dialog box, click **Tools** and click **General Options** as shown in Figure 11-6.

Figure 11-6

Use Tools options to restrict access to workbook

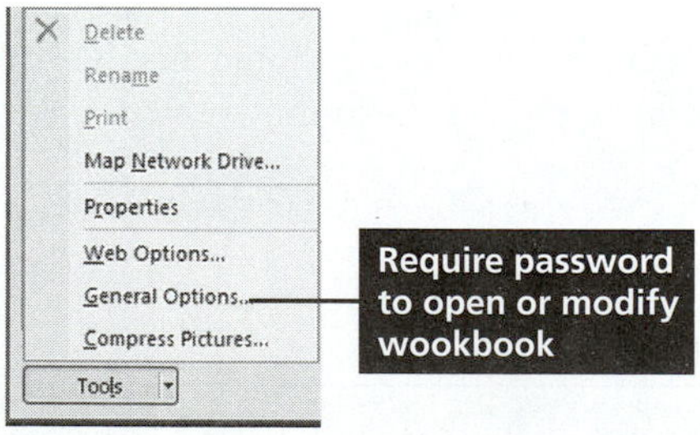

12. On the General Options dialog box shown in Figure 11-7, in the *Password to open* box, key **L11&E02** and click **OK**.

Figure 11-7

Create a strong password to restrict access to workbook

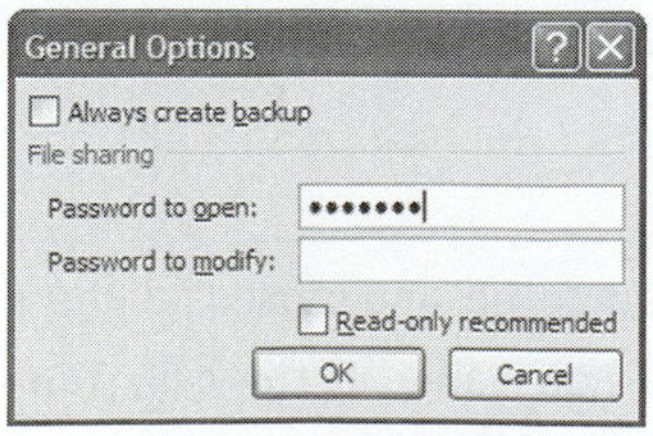

13. Reenter the password on the Confirm Password dialog box and click **OK**. The passwords must match exactly.

14. Click **Save**. Select **Yes** to replace the existing file.

When you confirm the password to prevent unauthorized viewing of a document, you are reminded that passwords are case-sensitive. If the password you enter on the Confirm Password dialog box is not identical to the one entered on the previous dialog box, you will receive an error message. Click OK to close the error message and reenter the password on the Confirm Password dialog box.

CERTIFICATION READY?
How do you prevent a workbook from being viewed or modified?
5.2.1

PAUSE. LEAVE the workbook open to use in the next exercise.

When you saved the *Payroll Data* workbook in the first exercise, it could be viewed by anyone with access to your computer system or network. As you saw when you opened the file in this exercise, the workbook could be viewed, but the SSN worksheet could not be modified. If you saved the file with a different name, that file also would be protected, and you could not alter the data without the password that protects that worksheet.

In this exercise, you established a password to open the document. As the document is now saved, anyone who has the password can open the workbook and modify data contained in the Performance worksheet, because that worksheet is not protected. To modify the SSN worksheet, the user must also know the password you used to protect that worksheet in the first exercise.

Protecting the structure of a workbook prevents users from viewing worksheets that you have hidden; inserting new worksheets; or moving, deleting, hiding, or changing the names of worksheets. Selecting the Windows box on the Protect Structure and Windows dialog box (Figure 11-4) prevents the user from changing the size and position of the windows when the workbook is opened.

Setting Access Permissions to a Workbook

Information Rights Management (IRM) allows individuals and administrators to specify access permissions to workbooks. After permission for a file has been restricted using IRM, access to and use of the information is enforced, regardless of the location of the information, because the permission to a file is stored in the document itself. This helps prevent confidential or sensitive information from being printed, copied, or sent to unauthorized people. Authors can restrict permission for workbooks on a per-user or per-document basis.

⊙ SET ACCESS PERMISSIONS TO A WORKBOOK

USE the workbook you saved in the previous exercise. Your computer must be configured to use IRM to complete this exercise.

1. Click the **Microsoft Office Button**, point to **Prepare**, and click **Restrict Permission**. As shown in Figure 11-8, there is currently unrestricted access to the workbook.

If you are not using Microsoft office 2007 Professional Plus, Enterprise, or Ultimate, with IRM installed, you will not see the Restrict Permission option on the Prepare menu.

Figure 11-8

Restrict access to workbook

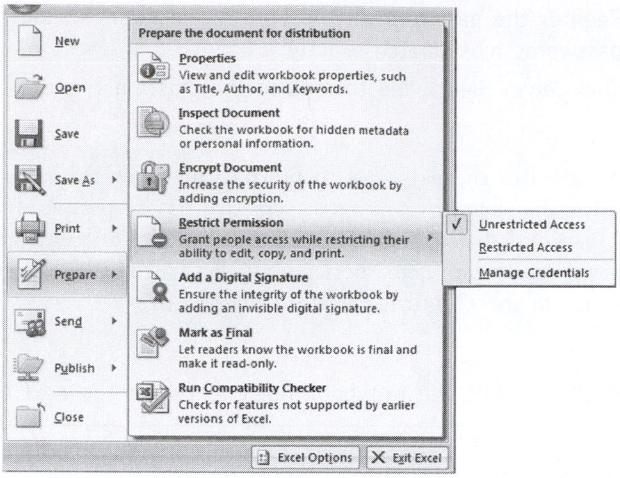

Prepare the document for distribution

New

Open

Save

Properties
View and edit workbook properties, such as Title, Author, and Keywords.

Inspect Document
Check the workbook for hidden metadata or personal information.

Encrypt Document
Increase the security of the workbook by adding encryption.

Save As

Print

Prepare

Restrict Permission
Grant people access while restricting their ability to edit, copy, and print.

✓ Unrestricted Access

Restricted Access

Manage Credentials

Add a Digital Signature
Ensure the integrity of the workbook by adding an invisible digital signature.

Send

Mark as Final
Let readers know the workbook is final and make it read-only.

Publish

Close

Run Compatibility Checker
Check for features not supported by earlier versions of Excel.

Excel Options   ✕ Exit Excel

TROUBLESHOOTING

If your computer has not been configured for IRM, the first time you attempt to restrict access, you will receive a message that says to use IRM, you need to install the Windows Rights Management client. You can use the installation wizard to install the add-in if you have permission to do so.

2. Click **Restricted Access** to open the Permission dialog box. If IRM is not installed, you cannot proceed with this exercise unless you install the add-in.

3. Select the **Restrict permission to this workbook** checkbox to enable the Read and Change boxes. In the Read box, key **jgiest@contoso.com; sbourne@contoso.com**. In the Change box, key **jgiest@contoso.com; sbourne@contoso.com** as shown in Figure 11-9. Click **OK**.

Figure 11-9

Grant permission to read and/or change a workbook

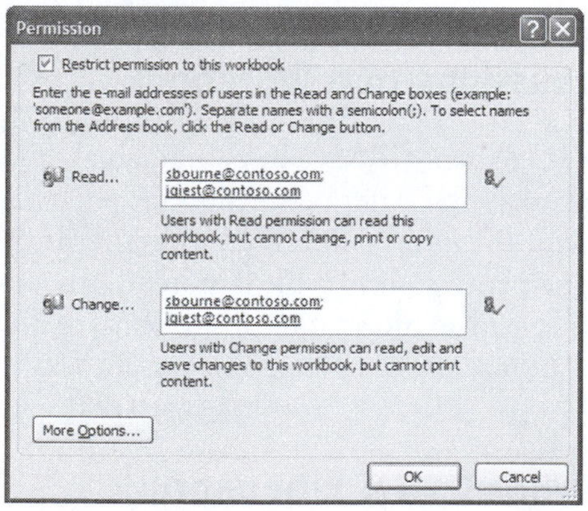

Permission

☑ Restrict permission to this workbook

Enter the e-mail addresses of users in the Read and Change boxes (example: 'someone@example.com'). Separate names with a semicolon(;). To select names from the Address book, click the Read or Change button.

Read...   sbourne@contoso.com; jgiest@contoso.com

Users with Read permission can read this workbook, but cannot change, print or copy content.

Change...   sbourne@contoso.com; jgiest@contoso.com

Users with Change permission can read, edit and save changes to this workbook, but cannot print content.

More Options...

OK   Cancel

4. **SAVE** the workbook as *Payroll Data Restricted*.

5. **CLOSE** the workbook.

6. Click the **Microsoft Office Button** and click *Payroll Data Restricted* in the Recent Documents list. The Password window is displayed.

7. Key **L11&E02** in the Password field and click **OK**. The workbook opens with the Restricted Access notation shown between the Ribbon and the formula bar.

TROUBLESHOOTING

Although you granted permission to read or change the file to only two individuals, you are able to change data in the Payroll Data workbook. Because you created the permissions, you are automatically given full control of the workbook. You cannot change your access level.

8. **CLOSE** the workbook.

   PAUSE. LEAVE Excel open to use in the next exercise.

IRM helps individuals enforce their personal preferences about sharing personal or private information. It also helps organizations enforce corporate policy related to the control and dissemination of confidential or proprietary information.

To use IRM in Excel 2007, the minimum requirement is Windows Rights Management, which can be downloaded the first time you attempt to restrict permission to a workbook.

The individual who grants access rights is automatically given full control of the document. Click More Options at the bottom of the Permission dialog box (Figure 11-9) to change permission after it has been granted, to set an expiration date for the permission, or to change the access level.

Allowing Multiple Users to Edit a Workbook Simultaneously

Creating and updating workbooks is frequently a collaborative process. A worksheet or workbook is often routed to other employees so that they can verify data or make changes. If you want to allow more than one other person to add or modify data simultaneously in your workbook, you can set up and save the workbook as shared. The Protect and Share Workbook command prevents a user from disabling the change tracking option.

⊙ ALLOW MULTIPLE USERS TO EDIT A WORKBOOK SIMULTANEOUSLY

1. **OPEN** a new blank workbook.
2. Select **A1:D1** and click **Merge and Center** in the Alignment group on the Home tab.
3. Key **Sample Drugs Dispensed** and press Enter.
4. Select **A1**, click **Cell Styles**, and then click **Heading 1**.
5. Beginning in A3, enter the following data.

Medical Assistant	Drug	Patient	Date
Delamore, Luca	Cipro	Chor, Anthony	(current date)
Hamilton, David	Ketek	Brundage, Michael	(current date)
Hoeing, Helge	Lipitor	Charles, Matthew	(current date)
Hamilton, David	Altace	Bishop, Scott	(current date)
Esteves, Janeth	Zetia	Anderson, Nancy	(current date)
Esteves, Janeth	Cipro	Coleman, Pat	(current date)
Hagens, Erin	Avelox	Nayberg, Alex	(current date)
Hagens, Erin	Norvasc	Kleinerman, Christian	(current date)

6. Select **A3:D3** and apply the **Heading 3** style.
7. **SAVE** the workbook as *Sample Medications*.
8. On the Review tab, click **Share Workbook** in the Changes group.
9. On the Share Workbook dialog box, click **Allow changes by more than one user at the same time. This also allows workbook merging.** Your identification will appear in the *Who has this workbook open now* box as shown in Figure 11-10. Click **OK**.

Figure 11-10

Share a workbook

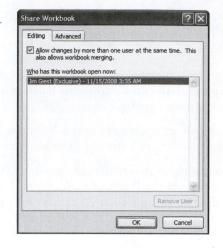

10. Click **OK** when the dialog box shown in Figure 11-11 opens.

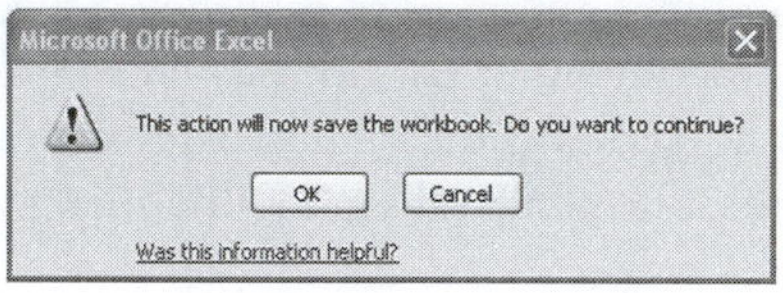

Figure 11-11

Save and close a shared workbook.

CERTIFICATION READY?
How do you enable a workbook to be modified by multiple users?
5.2.2

11. Click **Protect Shared Workbook** in the Changes group. Select the **Sharing with track changes** checkbox on the Protect Shared Workbook dialog box. Click **OK**.

12. Notice that (Shared) appears in the title bar. Save and close the workbook.
PAUSE. LEAVE Excel open to use in the next exercise.

Creating and updating workbooks is frequently a collaborative process. A worksheet or workbook is often routed to other employees so that they can verify data or make changes. You can create a ***shared workbook***, one that is set up to allow multiple users on a network to view and make changes at the same time. When a user opens a shared workbook, he or she can see the changes made and saved by other users.

In a shared workbook, information is maintained about changes made in past editing sessions. The ***change history*** includes the name of the person who made each change, when the change was made, and what data was changed.

The workbook you created in this exercise will be used by the medical assistants, who will record all sample medications the physicians prescribe for patients. Sharing the workbook means that more than one medical assistant can access the workbook and enter data at the same time.

A shared workbook does not support all Excel features. For example, you can include merged cells, conditional formats, data validation, charts, etc., before a workbook is shared, but these features cannot be added by those who edit a shared workbook.

When you protected your shared workbook, you prevented those who use the workbook from removing the change history. By default, changes made in the workbook will be retained for 30 days. You can increase that time frame on the Advanced tab of the Share Workbook dialog box (Figure 11-10).

If you want to assign a password to a shared workbook, you must assign it before the workbook is shared. You can unshare the workbook and add the password. However, when you unshare a shared workbook, the change history is lost.

Change history will be
discussed in detail later
in this lesson.

Using the Document Inspector

Before you share an important document with colleagues or individuals outside your
organization, you should always spell check, proofread, and review the contents to ensure
that everything is correct and the document does not contain anything you do not want
to share with others. You should also review the document for hidden data or personal
information that might be stored in the workbook or in the document properties.

➔ USE THE DOCUMENT INSPECTOR

OPEN *Employee ID* from the data files for this lesson.

1. Click the **Microsoft Office Button**; click **Save As**, and key *Employee ID Copy* in
   the *File name* box to save a copy of the workbook. Click the **Save** button.

TROUBLESHOOTING

It is a good idea to perform the inspection on a copy of the worksheet because you
might not be able to restore hidden content that you remove in the inspection process.
If you attempt to inspect a document that has unsaved changes, you will be prompted
to save the document before completing the inspection.

2. In the copy of your original workbook, click the **Microsoft Office Button**, point to
   Prepare, and click **Inspect Document**. The Document Inspector dialog box opens.
3. Click **Inspect**. The Document Inspector results shown in Figure 11-12 are returned.

Figure 11-12

Document inspection results

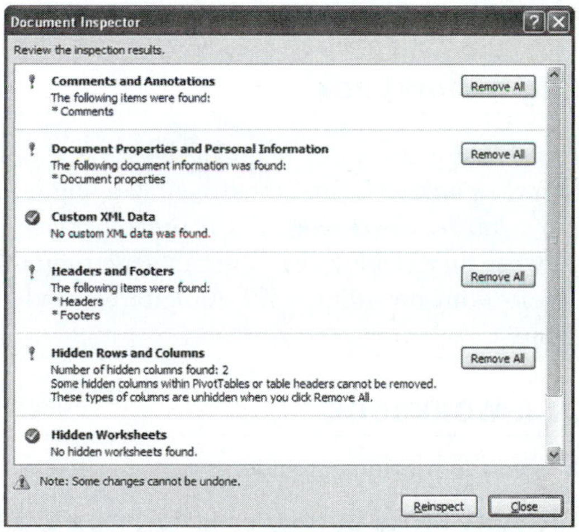

Document Inspector

Review the inspection results.

⚠ **Comments and Annotations**   [Remove All]
   The following items were found:
   * Comments

⚠ **Document Properties and Personal Information**   [Remove All]
   The following document information was found:
   * Document properties

✓ **Custom XML Data**
   No custom XML data was found.

⚠ **Headers and Footers**   [Remove All]
   The following items were found:
   * Headers
   * Footers

⚠ **Hidden Rows and Columns**   [Remove All]
   Number of hidden columns found: 2
   Some hidden columns within PivotTables or table headers cannot be removed.
   These types of columns are unhidden when you click Remove All.

✓ **Hidden Worksheets**
   No hidden worksheets found.

⚠ Note: Some changes cannot be undone.

[Reinspect] [Close]

4. Click **Remove All** for Comments and Annotations.

TAKE NOTE*

You must remove each type of hidden data individually. You can re-inspect the
document after you remove items.

CERTIFICATION READY?
How do you remove private
and other inappropriate data
from workbooks?
5.3.1

5. Click **Remove All** for Document Properties and Personal Information.
6. Click **Remove All** for Hidden Rows and Columns. Headers and Footers should be the
   only hidden item remaining. Click the **Close** button.
7. **SAVE** the workbook.

   PAUSE. LEAVE the workbook open to use in the next exercise.

It is a good idea to use the Document Inspector to find and remove hidden data and personal information before you share an electronic copy of a workbook. When you opened the data file, it contained hidden columns as well as other information that you did not want to share with others. You should use the Document Inspector on a copy of your original worksheet because it is not always possible to restore data that the Document Inspector removes. For that reason, you removed sensitive information from the copy; the complete data is retained in the original workbook.

Several types of hidden data and personal information can be saved in an Excel workbook. This information might not be immediately visible when you view the document, but it might be possible for others to view or retrieve the information. In this exercise, the document inspection revealed the following hidden content.

- Comments and annotations. This information would enable other people to see the names of people who worked on your workbook, their comments, and changes that were made to the workbook.

- Document properties and personal information. Document properties include the author, subject, and title, but also include the name of the person who most recently saved the workbook and the date the workbook was created.

- Headers and footers. Headers and footers may include author, date the file was created, etc.

- Hidden rows, columns, and worksheets. Columns D and E were hidden in the SSN worksheet to protect salary data. Before removing hidden rows or columns, be sure that their removal will not change calculations in your worksheet.

Document inspection will also locate custom XML data, hidden worksheets, and invisible content.

If the original workbook was protected, the copy will also be protected. Read-Only would display in the title bar.

Digitally Signing a Workbook

You can digitally sign a document for many of the same reasons you would sign a paper document. A *digital signature* is used to authenticate digital information using computer cryptography. *Authenticate* refers to the process of verifying that people and products are who and what they claim to be. You can get a digital ID from a Microsoft partner, or you can create your own digital ID. A digital signature is not visible within the document's contents.

⊙ DIGITALLY SIGN A WORKBOOK

USE the workbook from the previous exercise.

1. Click the **Microsoft Office Button**, point to **Prepare**, and click **Add a Digital Signature**. A dialog box opens that explains digital signatures. Read the message and click **OK**. If you or your organization does not have a valid digital certificate, the Get a Digital ID dialog box shown in Figure 11-13 opens.

Figure 11-13

Get a digital ID

The Get a Digital ID dialog box opens only if you select Add a Digital Signature and you do not have a digital certificate. If the document contains unsaved changes, the file is automatically saved when you click Add a Digital Signature.

If one or more digital certificates are available on your computer or network, a Sign dialog box opens so that you can sign the document.

2. Click **OK**. On the Get a Digital ID dialog box, click **Create your own Digital ID** and click **OK**.

3. Enter the information shown in Figure 11-14 and click **Create**.

Figure 11-14

Create your own digital ID

Create a Digital ID	? ✕
Enter the information to be included in your digital ID.	
Name:	Jim Giest
E-mail address:	jgiest@contoso.com
Organization:	Contoso, Ltd.
Location:	Office
	Create Cancel

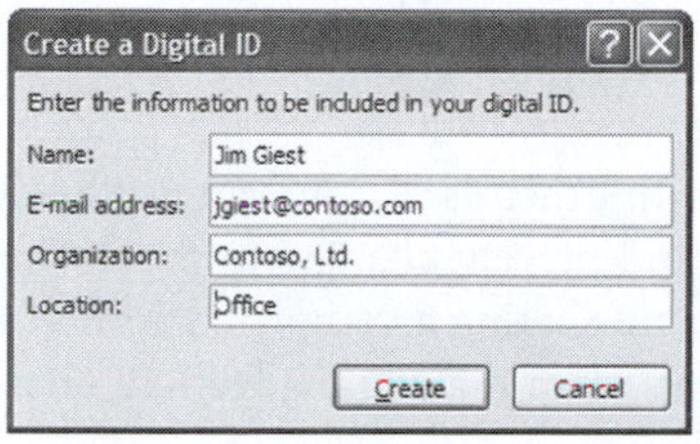

4. In the *Purpose for signing this document* box, key **Transmission to CPA for tax purposes**. Click **Sign**. A message is displayed indicating that your signature has been successfully saved with the document. If the document is changed, the signature will become invalid. Click **OK**. The Signatures pane is displayed.

5. On the Status bar at the bottom of the Excel window, point to the **Signature** icon. A ScreenTip stating *This document contains signatures* is displayed.

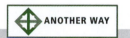
ANOTHER WAY

You can click the Signatures icon on the Status bar to display the Signatures task pane.

6. If the Signatures task pane is not displayed, click the **Microsoft Office Button**. Point to **Prepare** and click **View Signatures**. The signature and the date are displayed in the Signatures pane.

7. In the Signatures task pane, select the signature and click the arrow to display the dropdown menu.

8. Click **Signature Details**. The Signature Details dialog box indicates that the signature and the signed content have not been modified since the signature was applied. The worksheet is now protected so that the signature can be authenticated. Click the **Close** button to close the dialog box.

9. **CLOSE** the workbook.

TAKE NOTE *

The workbook was saved when you created the signature. There is no need to save again. If you use the Save As command after a signature has been added to a document, the signature will become invalid.

CERTIFICATION READY?
How do you add a digital signature to a workbook?
5.3.4

PAUSE. LEAVE Excel open to use in the next exercise.

To digitally sign a workbook, you must have a current digital certificate. A ***digital certificate*** is a means of proving identity and authenticity. Digital certificates make it possible for digital signatures to be used as a way to authenticate digital information. If you plan to exchange digitally signed documents, you should obtain a digital certificate from a reputable certificate authority. A ***certificate authority (CA)*** is a third-party entity that issues digital certificates to be used by others, keeps track of who is assigned to a certificate, signs certificates to verify their validity, and tracks which certificates are revoked or expired. Many organizations issue their own certificates, as you did in the exercise on behalf of Contoso, Ltd.

If you select the Get a digital ID from a Microsoft Partner option when you want to add a digital signature, you will be redirected to the Microsoft Office Marketplace where you can purchase a certificate.

If you do not want to purchase a digital certificate from a CA, you can create your own digital certificate as you did in this exercise. However, other people cannot verify the authenticity of your digital signature. It can be authenticated only on the computer on which you created the certificate.

When you review a signed document, you should look at the signature details and the certificate used to create that signature to find out if there are potential problems. If a workbook contains a signature, a Signature icon displays in the Status bar, as shown in Figure 11-15.

Figure 11-15

Signature icon on Status bar

Marking a Document as Final

Before you share a workbook with other users, you can use the Mark as Final command to make the document read-only and prevent changes to the document. Marking a document as final communicates that you are sharing a completed version of the document, and it helps prevent reviewers or readers from making inadvertent changes to the document.

➡ MARK A DOCUMENT AS FINAL

OPEN *Employee ID* from the data files for this lesson.

The *Employee ID* workbook is available on the companion CD-ROM.

1. **SAVE** the workbook as *Employee ID Final*.
2. Click the **Microsoft Office Button**, point to **Prepare**, and click **Mark as Final**.
3. The Excel message dialog box shown in Figure 11-16 opens indicating that the workbook will be marked as final and saved. Click **OK**.

Figure 11-16

Mark a workbook as final

> Microsoft Office Excel
>
> ⚠ This workbook will be marked as final and then saved.
>
> [OK] [Cancel]

4. An Excel message explains that the document has been marked as final. Click **OK**. If another dialog box is displayed indicating that this is the final version of the document, click **OK**. As shown in Figure 11-17, a Marked as Final icon appears in the Status bar.

Figure 11-17

Marked as Final icon on Status bar

> Ready

Marked as Final icon

CERTIFICATION READY?
How do you mark a workbook as final?
5.3.5

PAUSE. LEAVE the workbook open to use in the next exercise.

Marking a workbook as final indicates that editing is complete. Editing is turned off and the workbook is saved as a read-only document.

The Mark as Final command is not a security feature. Anyone who opens a workbook that has been marked as final can edit the document by removing the Mark as Final status from the document. Documents marked as final in an Excel 2007 workbook will not be read-only if they are opened in an earlier Excel release because Mark as Final was not an option in previous Excel versions.

To enable editing for a document that is marked as final, click the Microsoft Office Button, point to Prepare, and click Mark as Final. The Read-Only designation is removed from the workbook.

■ Distributing a Workbook by Email

One of the most common ways to share Excel data is by sending workbooks via email. You can send a workbook as an attachment from Excel or from your email program. You can also send a worksheet as an email message rather than as an attachment.

➔ DISTRIBUTE A WORKBOOK BY EMAIL

USE the workbook you saved in the previous exercise. You must have an email program to complete the following exercise.

To send a workbook from Excel:

1. Click the **Microsoft Office Button** and point to **Send**. Click **E-mail**. The default email program will open.
2. Key your instructor's email address in the To field.
3. Key a subject line if necessary.
4. Key **The Employee ID Final workbook is attached**. as the email message body.
5. Click **Send**.
6. **CLOSE** the workbook.

To send a worksheet as an email message:

If the Send to Mail Recipient command appears on your Quick Access Toolbar, skip Steps 1–3.

1. **OPEN** *Employee ID Final* if necessary. Click the Microsoft Office Button, Point to Prepare, and click Mark as Final
2. Click the **Microsoft Office Button** and click **Excel Options**.
3. Click **Customize**. In the *Choose commands from field*, click **All Commands**.
4. Click **Send to Mail Recipient** on the list of commands and click **Add**. Click **OK**.
5. Click **Send to Mail Recipient** on the Quick Access Toolbar. The E-mail dialog box opens.
6. Click **Send the current sheet as the message body** and click **OK**.
7. Key your instructor's email address in the To field.
8. Key a subject line if necessary.
9. Click **Send this Sheet** in the toolbar above the email information. Click OK when you are warned about hidden rows or columns.

To send a workbook from your email program:

1. Launch your email program. Create a new message.
2. Key your instructor's email address in the To field.
3. Key a subject line.
4. Click **Attach File**.
5. Navigate to the location where you saved *Employee ID Copy*. Click the filename and click **Open**.
6. Key **The Employee ID Copy workbook is attached**. in the email message.
7. Send the message.
8. **CLOSE** the workbook.

Some email programs will not send attachments if the document is open. If you receive such a message, close the Excel workbook and click Send again.

PAUSE. LEAVE Excel open to use in the next exercise.

The most common ways to share Excel data are by sending workbooks through email, by faxing workbooks, and by printing and distributing hard copies. Email allows you to share a workbook by routing it to one user who makes changes or comments and routes it to the next user. Changes can then be incorporated into a final document.

The option to send a worksheet as an email message is available only from the Send to Mail Recipient on the Quick Access Toolbar. When you add this command to the toolbar, you can use this option as a shortcut to send a workbook as an attachment.

 Tracking Changes to a Workbook

↓ THE BOTTOM LINE

Change tracking is the ability to mark and keep track of changes that have been made to a workbook, especially for a workbook that is shared and modified by multiple users. When you turn on change tracking, the workbook automatically becomes a shared workbook.

Turning Change Tracking On and Off

You can turn on change tracking using the Track Changes command, the Share Workbook command, or the Protect and Share Workbook command. The Protect and Share Workbook command provides the highest level of security.

When workbooks are shared, it is often important to know what changes were made by each user. The owner (creator) of the workbook can use change-tracking functions to manage the data in a shared workbook. The owner can use the change history record to manage the shared workbook by adding or removing users and resolving conflicting changes.

⊕ TURN CHANGE TRACKING ON AND OFF

1. **OPEN** *Sample Medications* from the data files for this lesson.
2. **SAVE** the workbook as *Samples*.
3. On the Review tab, in the Changes group, click **Protect and Share Workbook**.
4. Click **Sharing with track changes**.
5. Click **OK** when asked if you want to continue.

PAUSE. LEAVE the workbook open to use in the next exercise.

◎ CD

The *Sample Medications* workbook is available on the companion CD-ROM.

CERTIFICATION READY
How do you insert, display, modify, and resolve tracked changes?
5.1.1

You can turn change tracking on and off in several ways. Using the Protect and Share Workbook command provides the highest level of security. Before the workbook is shared, the creator can enter a password that must be used to turn off change tracking. This protects the change history.

When you click the Share Workbook command, change tracking is automatically turned on. To prevent users from turning off change tracking, use the Protect Shared Workbook command. This shares the workbook and prevents change tracking from being removed.

X REF

The Track Changes command allows you to determine how changes are displayed on the screen. You will use this option in a subsequent exercise.

TAKE NOTE Turning off change tracking removes the change history and removes the shared status of the workbook.

Setting Track Change Options

The Advanced tab on the Share Workbook dialog box allows you to customize the shared use of the workbook. These options are normally set by the workbook author before the workbook is shared.

→ SET TRACK CHANGE OPTIONS

USE the workbook from the previous exercise.

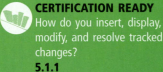
CERTIFICATION READY
How do you insert, display, modify, and resolve tracked changes?
5.1.1

1. On the Review tab, in the Changes group, click **Share Workbook**.
2. Click the **Advanced** tab.
3. In the *Keep change history for* box, click the up arrow until it displays **35**.
4. Click **OK** to accept the default settings in the remainder of the options.

    PAUSE. LEAVE the workbook open to use in the next exercise.

The Advanced tab contains four options. *Track changes* determines whether a change history is kept and the length of time it is kept. In a shared workbook, the change history documents changes made in past editing sessions. The information includes the name of the person who made each change, when the changes were made, and what data was changed. The default setting is 30 days. Contoso maintains a monthly record of the distribution of samples. Setting the change history to 35 days ensures that the office manger has sufficient time to review the workbook and resolve any conflicting changes before the change history is deleted.

Update changes controls when changes made to the shared workbook are incorporated into the workbook. *Conflicting changes between users* determines whose edits become part of the file if two or more people are attempting to edit at the same time. The workbook owner's changes usually take precedence. *Include in personal view* enables each user who edits the workbook to see a personal view of the workbook.

Inserting Tracked Changes

When you open a shared workbook, change tracking is automatically turned on. In most cases, the workbook owner would have entered a password to prevent a user from turning off change tracking. Any text you key in the workbook will be tracked.

→ INSERT TRACKED CHANGES

USE the workbook from the previous exercise.

1. On the Review tab, in the Changes group, click **Track Changes**.
2. Click **Highlight Changes**. The *Track changes while editing* box is inactive because change tracking was activated when you shared the workbook. As shown in Figure 11-18, select **When** and select **All**. Select **Who** and select **Everyone**. If necessary, select **Highlight changes on screen**. Click **OK**.

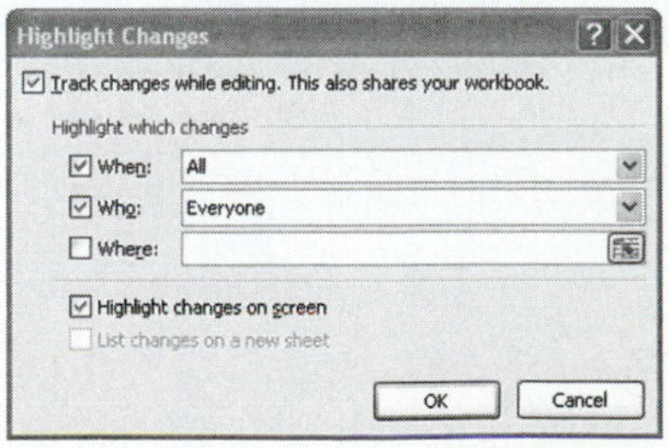

Figure 11-18

Change tracking options.

3. Click the **Microsoft Office Button** and click **Excel Options**.

4. In the Popular category, under *Personalize your copy of Microsoft Office*, in the User name box, key **Luca Delamore**. Click **OK**.

5. Select **A12** and enter the following information.

Delamore, Luca	Avelox	LaMee, Brian	14-Nov
Delamore, Luca	Ketek	Miller, Ben	14-Nov
Delamore, Luca	Cipro	Kearney, Bonnie	14-Nov

6. Save the changes made by Luca Delamore.

7. Click the **Microsoft Office Button** and click **Excel Options**.

8. In the User name box, key **Billie Jo Murray**. Click **OK**.

9. Select **A15** and key the following data.

Murray, Billie Jo	Zetia	Peters, James	15-Nov
Murray, Billie Jo	Cipro	Smith, Samantha	15-Nov
Murray, Billie Jo	Ketek	Ruth, Andy	15-Nov

10. Point to the colored triangle in the upper-left corner of one of the cells in which you entered data. A box opens with information about the change made to that cell.

11. **SAVE** the changes made by Billie Jo Murray.

   PAUSE. LEAVE the workbook open to use in the next exercise.

On a network, you do not see changes made by other users until they and you save your changes. To save your changes to a shared workbook and to see the changes that other users have saved since your last save, click Save on the Quick Access Toolbar. When you are working in a network environment, you can click Share Workbook in the Changes group and see a list of other users who have the workbook open.

Sometimes conflicts occur when two users are editing a shared workbook and try to save changes that affect the same cell. When the second user tries to save the workbook, Excel displays the Resolve Conflicts dialog box. Depending upon the options established when the workbook was created and shared, you can keep your change or accept the change made by the other user.

You can display a list that shows how past conflicts have been resolved. These can be displayed on a separate worksheet that displays the name of the person who made the change, when and where it was made, what data was deleted or replaced, and how conflicts were resolved.

Deleting Your Changes

As noted previously, changes you make in a shared workbook are not visible to other users until you save your work. Changes become a part of the change history when you save. If you change your mind before saving, you can edit or delete any change. When you have saved your workbook and you want to delete the change, you can enter new data or reject the change you made before saving.

→ **DELETE YOUR CHANGES**

USE the workbook from the previous exercise.

1. Click the **Microsoft Office Button** and click **Excel Options**.
2. In the Popular category, under *Personalize your copy of Microsoft Office*, in the User name box, key **Erin Hagens**. Click **OK**.
3. Select **A17** and enter the following data. You will replace data in row 17.

Hagens, Erin	Cipro	Berry, Jo	15-Nov
Hagens, Erin	Norvasc	Corets, Eva	15-Nov
Hagens, Erin	Altace	Beebe, Ann	15-Nov

TAKE NOTE * Undo is inactive in a shared workbook. If you accidentally replace your data or another user's, you will need to reject the change to restore the data you replaced.

4. Click **Track Changes** and click **Accept/Reject Changes**. The Excel message shown in Figure 11-19 is displayed.

Figure 11-19

Workbook must be saved

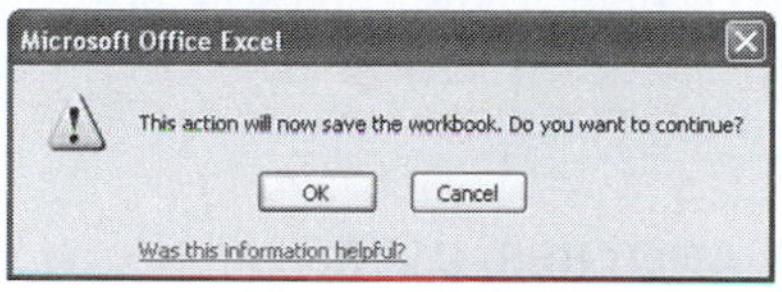

Microsoft Office Excel dialog box: "This action will now save the workbook. Do you want to continue?" with OK and Cancel buttons. "Was this information helpful?"

5. Click **OK**. On the Select Changes to Accept or Reject dialog box, click the arrow in the Who box and select **Erin Hagens** and click **OK**.
6. A17 is selected on the worksheet and the change you made to A17 is displayed. Click **Reject**. A17 displays the text you replaced and the cell selector moves to B17.
7. Reject the changes to **B17**, **C17**, and **D17**. Click **Close**.
8. Key the following information, beginning in A20.

| Hagens, Erin | Cipro | Berry, Jo | 15-Nov |

9. **SAVE** the workbook.

PAUSE. LEAVE the workbook open to use in the next exercise.

CERTIFICATION READY
How do you insert, display, modify, and resolve tracked changes?
5.1.1

Changes must be saved before you can accept or reject them. If you do not save, Excel displays a message that the workbook must be saved before you can accept or reject changes.

If you replace another user's data and you want to restore the original data, you should reject your change. If you delete text you entered as a replacement for other text, you will leave the cell or range blank. Rejecting your change restores the entry that you replaced.

Accepting Changes from Another User

After a shared workbook has been edited, you can easily identify which cells have been changed and determine whether you want to keep or reject the changes. You can choose to accept or reject all changes at one time without reviewing each change or you can accept or reject them individually.

⊕ ACCEPT CHANGES FROM ANOTHER USER

1. Click the **Microsoft Office Button** and click **Excel Options**.

2. In the Popular category, under *Personalize your copy of Microsoft Office*, in the User name box, key **Jim Giest**. Click **OK**.

3. Click **Track Changes** and click **Accept/Reject Changes**.

4. If necessary, select **Not yet reviewed** in the When box and **Luca Delamore** in the Who box. Click **OK**. The Accept or Reject Changes dialog box is displayed.

5. Click **Accept** as each change is displayed. The Accept or Reject Changes dialog box closes when you have accepted all changes made by Luca Delamore.

   PAUSE. LEAVE Excel open to use in the next exercise.

> **CERTIFICATION READY?**
> How do you insert, display, modify, and resolve tracked changes?
> **5.1.1**

You can click the Collapse Dialog button in the Where box on the Select Changes to Accept or Reject dialog box and select the cells that contain changes. You can then accept or reject the changes in their entirety. In this exercise, some changes were highlighted by cell and others were highlighted by row and you could accept or reject changes to the selected cell or range.

Rejecting Changes from Another User

As the owner of the Samples workbook, the office manager has the authority to accept or reject changes by all users. Rejecting changes, however, does not prohibit a user from changing the data again. When all users have made necessary changes, the owner can remove users and unshare the workbook.

⊕ REJECT CHANGES FROM ANOTHER USER

1. Click **Track Changes** and click **Accept/Reject Changes**.

2. Click the **Collapse Dialog** button on the right side of the Where box.

3. Select the data in row 16 and click the **Expand Dialog** button. Click **OK** to close the Select Changes to Accept or Reject dialog box. The Accept or Reject Changes dialog box is displayed.

4. Click **Reject** for each cell containing data in the row. The data is removed and row 16 is blank. Click **Close**.

5. **SAVE** the workbook as *Samples Edited*.

   PAUSE. LEAVE the workbook open to use in the next exercise.

> **CERTIFICATION READY?**
> How do you insert, display, modify, and resolve tracked changes?
> **5.1.1**

When you have the opportunity to work with a shared workbook that is saved on a network, you will likely encounter conflicts when you attempt to save a change that affects the same cell as another user. In the Resolve Conflicts dialog box, you should read the information about each change and the conflicting changes made by another user. The options set on the Advanced tab of the Share Workbook dialog box determine how conflicts are resolved.

Removing Shared Status from a Workbook

Before you stop sharing a workbook, make sure that all other users have completed their work and that you have accepted or rejected all changes. Any unsaved changes will be lost when you stop sharing and the history worksheet will be deleted. Before you remove the shared status from a workbook, you should print the history worksheet and/or copy it to another workbook.

⊕ **REMOVE SHARED STATUS FROM A WORKBOOK.**

USE the workbook from the previous exercise.

1. On the Review tab, in the Changes group, click **Track Changes**, and then click **Highlight Changes**.

2. In the When box, select **All**.

3. Clear the **Who** and **Where** checkboxes.

4. Click the **List changes on a new sheet** checkbox. Click **OK**. A History sheet is added to the workbook.

5. On the History worksheet, click the **Select All** button. Click **Copy** on the Home tab.

6. Press ⎡Ctrl⎤+⎡N⎤ to open a new workbook.

7. Select **A1** in the new workbook and click **Paste**.

8. **SAVE** the new workbook as *Medications History*. Close the workbook.

> **TAKE NOTE** ✱ It is a good idea to print the current version of the shared workbook as well as the change history because cell locations in the copied history may no longer be valid if additional changes are made.

9. In the shared workbook, on the Review tab, click **Unprotect Shared Workbook**.

10. Click **Share Workbook**. The Share Workbook dialog box is displayed. On the Editing tab, make sure that you (Jim Giest) are the only user listed in the *Who has this workbook open now* list.

11. Clear the **Allow changes by more than one user at the same time. This also allows workbook merging** checkbox. Click **OK** to close the dialog box.

12. A dialog box opens to prompt you about removing the workbook from shared use. Click **Yes**. *Shared* is removed from the title bar.

13. **SAVE** and close the workbook.

PAUSE. LEAVE Excel open to use in the next exercise.

When shared status has been removed from a workbook, changes can be made like they are made in any workbook. You can, of course, turn on change tracking again, which will automatically share the workbook.

■ Adding Comments to a Workbook

↓ **THE BOTTOM LINE**   In Excel, you can add a note to a cell by inserting a comment. You can edit the text in comments and delete comments that you no longer need. Comments are marked by a red triangle in the upper-right corner of the cell. When you point to the triangle, the comment appears in a box next to the cell with the name of the user logged on to the computer at the time the comment was created.

Inserting a Comment

Comments are a useful technique for calling attention to important or significant data and providing insights from the user that explains more about the data. Contoso's employees are evaluated on three performance measures. The manager uses comments to note incidents related to the measures.

CERTIFICATION READY?
How do you insert comments?
5.1.2

→ **INSERT A COMMENT**

1. OPEN *Personnel Evaluations* from the data files for this lesson.
2. Select **F11**. On the Review tab, in the Comments group, click **New Comment**.
3. Key **Frequently late to work**. Click outside the comment box.
4. Select **E8**. Click **New Comment** and key **Currently completing Masters degree program for additional certification**. Click outside the comment box.
5. Select **F20**. Click **New Comment** and key **Adjusted hours for family emergency**. Click outside the comment box.
6. Select **G4**. Click **New Comment** and key **Consider salary increase**. Click outside the comment box.
7. SAVE the workbook as *Performance Evaluation*.

   PAUSE. LEAVE the workbook open to use in the next exercise.

Contoso, Ltd. conducts an annual employee performance review. The manager uses comments to note events or actions that he wants to recall when he conducts the annual performance review. Excel automatically displays the name that appears in the Name box under Global Office Settings on the Excel Options dialog box. If you don't want to use a name, you can select it in the comment and press Delete.

Viewing Comments

When you rest the pointer over the red triangle that indicates that a cell has a comment attached to it, the comment is displayed. You can keep selected comments visible as you work, or you can display all comments using commands in the Comments group on the Review tab.

→ **VIEW COMMENTS**

USE the workbook you saved in the previous exercise.

1. Select **E8** and click **Show/Hide Comment** in the Comments group on the Review tab. The comment remains visible when you click outside the cell.
2. Select **G4** and click **Show/Hide Comment**.
3. Select **E8** and click **Show/Hide Comment**. The comment is hidden.
4. In the Comments group, click **Next** twice. The comment in **F11** is displayed.
5. Click **Show All Comments**. Your comments and those entered by others are displayed.
6. Click **Show All Comments**. All comments are hidden.

   PAUSE. LEAVE the workbook open to use in the next exercise.

 **ANOTHER WAY**

You can right-click a cell that contains a comment and click Show/Hide Comments.

CERTIFICATION READY?
How do you display comments?
5.1.2

The Show/Hide Comment and Show All Comments commands allow you to display or hide comments as needed. The Previous and Next commands allow you to move from one comment to another without selecting the cells.

Editing a Comment

Comments can be edited and formatted as needed. To edit a comment, select the cell containing the comment and click Edit Comment. The comment opens in edit mode.

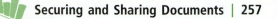

→ EDIT A COMMENT

USE the workbook from the previous exercise.

1. Select **F11** and click **Edit Comment** on the Review tab.
2. Following the existing text, key **Placed on probation**. Click any cell between F11 and E8.
3. Click **Previous**. The comment in E8 is displayed.
4. Select the existing text and key **MA completed; can now prescribe medications**.
5. Select **G4** and click **Edit Comment**.
6. Select the text. On the Home tab, click **Bold**.
7. Select **F14** and click **Edit Comment**.
8. Select the name and the comment text. Right-click and click **Format Comment**.
9. On the Format Comment dialog box, click the arrow in the Color box and click **Red**. Click **OK** to apply the format and close the dialog box.
10. **SAVE** the workbook.

    PAUSE. LEAVE the workbook open to use in the next exercise.

CERTIFICATION READY?
How do you modify comments?
5.1.2

You can format a comment using most of the formatting options on the Home tab in the Font group. However, the Fill Color and Font Color options are not available for comment text.

Deleting a Comment

You can delete comments when they are no longer needed. Unless the workbook is protected, any user can delete comments. Consider protecting a workbook that contains sensitive or confidential information.

→ DELETE A COMMENT

USE the workbook from the previous exercise.

1. Select **F20**. The comment is displayed.
2. On the Review tab, click **Delete**.

◆ ANOTHER WAY

To delete a comment, you can click Show/Hide on the Review tab to display the comment and then double-click the comment text box and press **Delete**.

---

3. **SAVE** the workbook with the same name.

   PAUSE. LEAVE the workbook open to use in the next exercise.

CERTIFICATION READY?
How do you delete comments?
5.1.2

TAKE NOTE ✱

You can edit comments others have entered as well as comments you entered.

▪ Printing Comments

↓ THE BOTTOM LINE

Anyone with access to a workbook can view the comments made by all users. As you learned in a previous exercise, comments can be removed from a workbook before the workbook is shared or copies are distributed. Comments can be printed as they appear in the worksheet or on a separate page following the workbook.

➔ PRINT COMMENTS

USE the workbook from the previous exercise.

1. On the Review tab, click **Show All Comments**. The comment in E8 slightly overlaps the comment in F11, and the comment in F11 slightly overlaps the comment in F14.

2. Click the border of the comment box in E8. Select the center sizing handle at the bottom of the box and drag upward until the comment in F11 is completely visible. Repeat this process with the F11 comment.

3. On the Page Layout tab, in the Page Setup group, click **Orientation**. Click **Landscape**.

4. In the Page Setup group, click the **Page Setup** Dialog Box Launcher.

5. On the Sheet tab, in the Comments box, select **As displayed on sheet** and click **Print Preview**. Page 2 contains one line.

6. Click **Page Setup** on the Print Preview tab. Click **Fit to 1 page wide**.

7. Click **Print**.

8. **SAVE** and **CLOSE** the workbook.

   CLOSE Excel.

When you print comments as they appear on the worksheet, the data in some cells may be covered. To print comments on a separate page, select *At end of sheets* in the Comments box on the Sheet tab of the Page Setup dialog box.

SUMMARY SKILL MATRIX

In This Lesson You Learned	Matrix Skill	Skill Number
To secure your work before sharing it with others		
To protect a worksheet to prevent unauthorized changes	Protect workbooks and worksheets	5.2.1
To protect a workbook to prevent unauthorized changes	Protect workbooks and worksheets	5.2.1
To protect a workbook from unauthorized access	Restrict permissions to a workbook	5.3.2
To share a workbook so that multiple users can edit it simultaneously	Enable workbooks to be changed by multiple users	5.2.2
To use the Document Inspector to remove private or sensitive data from a workbook.	Remove private and other inappropriate data from workbooks	5.3.1
To create and add a digital signature to a workbook	Add digital signatures	5.3.4
To mark a document as final	Mark workbooks as final	5.3.5
To distribute a workbook by email		
To insert, accept, and resolve changes to a workbook	Insert, display, modify, and resolve tracked changes	5.1.1
To add, modify, and delete comments in a workbook	Insert, display, modify, and delete comments	5.1.2
To print comments as they are displayed in the worksheet or print them on a separate page		

Knowledge Assessment

Fill in the Blank

1. A workbook set up to allow multiple users on a network to view and make changes at the same time is called a(n) _____.

2. Assigning a(n) _____ is one way to restrict access to a workbook, worksheet, or part of a worksheet.

3. The process of verifying that people and products are who and what they claim to be is called _____.

4. A(n) _____ is an electronic notation encrypted into a document to authenticate the content of a workbook.

5. _____ allows you to mark and keep track of changes that have been made in a workbook that is shared and modified by multiple users.

6. A trusted third-party entity, known as a(n) _____, issues digital certificates for use by other parties.

7. For a shared workbook, a(n) _____ is a log of changes made in past editing sessions.

8. A(n) _____ is a means of proving identity and authenticity.

9. When you stop sharing a workbook and create a record of changes, a(n) _____ is added to the workbook.

10. Jgiest223$! would be considered a(n) _____ password.

Multiple Choice

Circle the choice that best completes the following statements.

1. Which of the following ways to share a workbook provides the highest level of workbook protection?
   a. Share Workbook
   b. Protect and Share Workbook
   c. Track Changes
   d. Assign Password

2. Which of the following scenarios allows a workbook to be viewed but not modified?
   a. The user knows the password and opens a password-protected workbook.
   b. The user has access to a shared workbook.
   c. The user opens a workbook; the worksheet has been protected with a password.
   d. The user opens a workbook that does not require a password.

3. Which of the following prevents a workbook user from viewing worksheets that are hidden or inserting new worksheets?
   a. The workbook requires a password to open.
   b. The workbook structure has been protected.
   c. The workbook is shared.
   d. The workbook was opened using Information Rights Management.

4. Which of the following describes a digital signature?

    a. The workbook author's name appears on the worksheet.

    b. The digital signature appears in a new workbook.

    c. The signature is encrypted. You can view details from the Signatures task pane.

    d. The digital signature appears on a new worksheet.

5. When multiple users are permitted to edit a workbook simultaneously,

    a. the user whose changes are saved last overrides those previously saved.

    b. a second user cannot save changes to the same cell that another user has already changed.

    c. both changes are saved and the workbook owner must resolve the conflict.

    d. options set before the workbook was shared determine which change is saved.

6. Marking a document as final means that

    a. all changes have been made. The Final notation can be removed.

    b. all changes have been made. The Final notation cannot be changed.

    c. changes are being made to the document.

    d. no further changes can be made to the document.

7. Which of the following will **not** be found by the Document Inspector?

    a. hidden rows or columns

    b. comments

    c. visible objects

    d. headers and footers

8. From the following statements, select the one that is **false**.

    a. You can make a comment without displaying your name in the comment box.

    b. You can change the size of the comment box.

    c. You can change the font color of a comment.

    d. Comments will not appear on a printed worksheet.

9. Changes made in a shared workbook

    a. expire after a specified period of time.

    b. are permanently retained when the workbook is saved.

    c. can be accepted or rejected only by the workbook owner.

    d. cannot be changed a second time.

10. Which of the following formulas allows you to specify the number of digits in a random number?

    a. RAND

    b. RANDNUMBER

    c. RANDBETWEEN

    d. RANDOM

■ Competency Assessment

Project 11-1: Protect a Workbook

The manager at Litware, Inc. needs to password protect a workbook that will be used to determine the semiannual bonus paid to its sales representatives. You will create a password to open the workbook and a different password to modify the workbook.

GET READY. Launch Excel.

1. **OPEN** *Litware Sales* from the data files for this lesson.
2. Click the **Microsoft Office Button** and click **Save As**.
3. On the Save As dialog box, click **Tools** and click **General Options**.
4. On the General Options dialog box, in the *Password to open* box, key **Sales$LitW**.
5. In the *Password to modify* box, key **LitW$Sales** and click **OK**.
6. On the Confirm Password dialog box, reenter the password to open the workbook and click **OK**.
7. Reenter the password to modify the file and click **OK**.
8. In the *File name* box, key *Litware Sales 11-1* and click **Save**.
9. **CLOSE** the workbook.

   LEAVE Excel open to use in the next project.

Project 11-2: Add Comments to a Workbook

Jim Giest, office manager for Contoso, Ltd., has prepared a draft of the budget for the medical practice for the coming year. He plans to meet with the physicians and office staff to discuss the budget. He will insert comments for budget items that may need revision.

1. **OPEN** *Budget Draft* from the data files for this lesson.
2. Click the **Review** tab if it is not active. Select **B4** and click **New Comment**.
3. Key **Dr. Bourne expects an increase in liability premiums. Check with insurance agent.**
4. Select **B7** and click **New Comment**. Key **Investigate changing cell phone service for physicians.**
5. Insert a comment in **B12**. Key **Retainer for attorney expected to increase.**
6. In **B15**, key the comment **PA has completed his advanced training. Reduce this amount.**
7. Click **Show All Comments**. If any comments overlap, adjust the size of the comment box so that all comments are visible.
8. On the Page Layout tab, click the **Page Setup** Dialog Box Launcher.
9. On the Sheet tab, in the Comments box, select **As displayed on sheet**.
10. Click **Print**.
11. **SAVE** the workbook as *Budget Draft 11-2*. **CLOSE** the workbook.

    LEAVE Excel open for the next project.

■ Proficiency Assessment

Project 11-3: Digitally Sign a Workbook

Contoso's budget has been finalized. The manager will attach a digital signature to the workbook before he transmits it to Contoso's accountant.

1. **OPEN** *Budget* from the data files for this lesson.
2. **SAVE** the workbook as *Budget 11-3*.
3. Click the **Microsoft Office Button** and point to **Prepare**.
4. Click **Add a Digital Signature**.
5. Click **OK** on the dialog box that explains digital signatures.

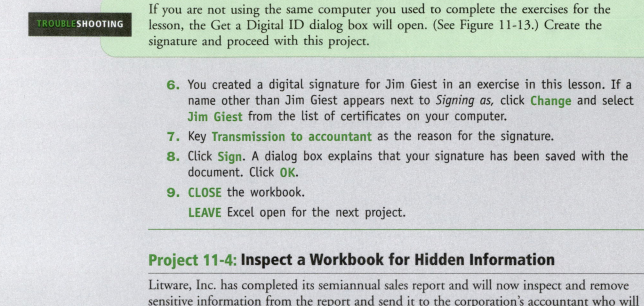

TROUBLESHOOTING If you are not using the same computer you used to complete the exercises for the lesson, the Get a Digital ID dialog box will open. (See Figure 11-13.) Create the signature and proceed with this project.

6. You created a digital signature for Jim Giest in an exercise in this lesson. If a name other than Jim Giest appears next to *Signing as*, click **Change** and select **Jim Giest** from the list of certificates on your computer.

7. Key **Transmission to accountant** as the reason for the signature.

8. Click **Sign**. A dialog box explains that your signature has been saved with the document. Click **OK**.

9. **CLOSE** the workbook.

   LEAVE Excel open for the next project.

Project 11-4: Inspect a Workbook for Hidden Information

Litware, Inc. has completed its semiannual sales report and will now inspect and remove sensitive information from the report and send it to the corporation's accountant who will issue a bonus check.

The *Litware Sales* workbook is available on the companion CD-ROM.

1. **OPEN** *Litware Sales* from the data files for this lesson.

2. Save the workbook as **Copy of Litware Sales**.

3. Click the **Microsoft Office Button**.

4. Point to **Prepare** and click **Inspect Document**.

5. On the Document Inspector dialog box, click **Inspect**.

6. For Comments and Annotations, click **Remove All**.

7. For Document Properties and Personal Information, click **Remove All**.

8. For Headers and Footers, click **Remove All**.

9. Click **Close**.

10. **SAVE** the file as *Litware Sales 11-4* and **CLOSE** the workbook.

    LEAVE Excel open for the next project.

■ Mastery Assessment

Project 11-5: Track Changes in a Shared Workbook

The sales manager at Litware has established a sales quota for each sales representative for the coming year. Some representatives have made changes and inserted comments related to their changes. The sales manager will accept or reject the changes to arrive at the final quotas.

The *Sales Quotas* workbook is available on the companion CD-ROM.

1. **OPEN** *Sales Quotas* from the data files for this lesson.

2. **SAVE** the workbook as *Sales Quotas 11-5*.

3. Display all comments and print the worksheet with the comments displayed on the sheet.

4. Click **Track Changes**, click **Highlight Changes**, and clear the When checkbox. List the changes on a new worksheet.

5. Print the History worksheet.

6. Click **Track Changes** and click **Accept/Reject Changes**.

7. Accept all changes.

8. Delete all comments.

9. Turn off change tracking and click **Yes** to remove the workbook from shared use.

10. **SAVE** and close the workbook.

   LEAVE Excel open for the next project.

Project 11-6: Mark a Document as Final

Contoso's budget amounts are final. The office manager will protect the worksheet and mark the workbook as final. Employees will be able to view the budget but will not be able to modify it.

The **Budget** workbook is available on the companion CD-ROM.

1. **OPEN** *Budget* from the data files for this lesson.

2. **SAVE** the workbook as *Budget 11-6*.

3. Click **Protect Sheet**. Key **Bud*JG** as the password to unprotect the sheet.

4. Mark the workbook as final. The workbook will be automatically saved.

5. **CLOSE** the workbook.

TROUBLESHOOTING

Before you exit Excel, restore the default setting to the user name for the computer you used for this lesson. Click the Microsoft Office Button and click Excel Options. Select the Popular category. In the User name box, key the default name that you removed in an exercise for this lesson.

   CLOSE Excel.

INTERNET READY

As you learned in this lesson, assigning a strong password is an important security precaution. Visit http://www.microsoft.com/athome/security/privacy/password.mspx to learn more about creating a strong password.

Based on your review of the suggestions for creating strong passwords, create a list of passwords that you need to change to secure your personal information and protect the integrity of data you create. Do not list the actual password; identify the password usage. For example, change the password that you use to access your college email account or your personal email account. Determine a safe storage vehicle for passwords you create (in case you forget the new password).

✳ Workplace Ready

Working Collaboratively in a Global Business Arena

In the past, work was structured around independent functions, which were usually coordinated by management. Today, whether you work for a small business enterprise or a major international corporation, collaboration and teamwork are the norm. An increasing number of businesses work across geographic and organizational boundaries. In such an always-on, always-connected business environment, team members must have access to current, accurate information.

There are many ways to share, analyze, and communicate business information and data in Excel 2007. The way you choose to share data depends on many factors, including how you want others to view or work with the data. For example, do you want to limit access to sensitive information? Do you want to prevent important information from being modified, or do you want to allow users to change and edit the data? Perhaps you need to share data with users who do not have Microsoft Office Excel or have different versions of Excel.

In Lesson 11, you explored techniques to protect confidentiality and maintain data integrity while sharing access with specific users. Those techniques are sufficient when team members are centrally located and have access to the server where the Excel files are stored.

The travel consultants at Margie's Travel work with clients from around the world. The consultants often work from home or while traveling. Because they depend on up-to-the-minute information about availability and costs, Margie's Travel chose to use Excel Services, a part of Microsoft Office SharePoint Server 2007. Using this service allows an office associate or consultant to save a workbook to the SharePoint server so that other users can access all or parts of it in a browser.

After workbooks have been saved to the server, consultants can view and interact with the worksheet data in a browser environment. They are not required to have Microsoft Office Excel 2007 installed on local computers. Thus, consultants have access from any Internet-connected computer.

Excel Services enables Margie's Travel to maintain a single copy of a workbook in a central, secure location. From that location, users can perform calculations, analyze, chart, and interact with data by using a browser.

When you save a workbook to Excel Services, the entire workbook is placed on the server, but you can specify the parts of the workbook (such as individual worksheets, named ranges, or charts) that you want to display in the browser. You can also specify cells that can be edited on the worksheet

You can grant users view-only permissions so that users can view the worksheet in the browser. You also can control the parts of the worksheet that users are allowed to view in the browser. View-only users cannot access the worksheet directly by using Excel or any other program.

⟳ Circling Back

Cross-Cultural Solutions (CCS) is a nonprofit organization and a registered charity, which means that contributions made by companies and individuals are tax deductible. The organization is preparing for one of its annual fundraising events—a formal dinner and charity auction.

As a CCS employee, you have created a workbook to track corporate and individual contributions. The director has asked you to create charts to illustrate his presentation to potential contributors who will attend the fundraising event.

➔ Project 1: Create a Summary Worksheet and Pie Chart

Subtotal contributions by the budget category to which the contributions are to be applied and create formulas in a summary worksheet that references the subtotals. Use the summary worksheet to create a pie chart that illustrates the distribution of contributions among the organization's budget categories.

GET READY. Launch Excel if it is not already running.

The *Contributions 1* workbook is available on the companion CD-ROM.

1. **OPEN** *Contributions 1* from the data files.
2. Click the **Data** tab. Select any cell in the data. Click **Sort** in the Sort & Filter group.
3. The Sort dialog box opens. In the *Sort by* field, select **Fund**. Click **OK**.
4. **SAVE** the document as *Contributions Project 1*.
5. Click **Subtotal** on the Outline group. In the *At each change in* field, select **Fund**. Click **OK**.
6. Click the **Summary** tab and click **B5**. Key **=** and click the **Year-to-Date Contributions** tab. Click **C12** and press ⎣Enter⎦.
7. Select **B6** and enter a formula that references the subtotal for general operating fund contributions.
8. Enter formulas in **B7** and **B8** that reference the appropriate subtotals.
9. Select **B9** and click **AutoSum** on the Formulas tab to total the contributions.
10. Select **B5:B8** and click **Copy** on the Home tab.
11. Click the arrow under **Paste** and click **Paste Values**.
12. Click the **Insert** tab. Select **A4:B8** and click **Pie** in the Chart group. Click **Pie** in the 2-D Pie category.
13. Click the **Design** tab and click **Layout 1** in the Chart Layouts group.
14. Click the **Layout** tab and select **Chart Title** in the Current Selection group.
15. Key **Year-to-Date Contributions**. Press ⎣Enter⎦.
16. Select the **chart title** and click the **Format** tab.
17. Click **Shape Fill** and click **Orange** under Standard Colors.
18. Click the **Design** tab and click **Move Chart**. Click **New sheet** and click **OK**.
19. **SAVE** and **CLOSE** the workbook.

    LEAVE Excel open for the next project.

Project 2: Create a Column Chart

The *Contributions 2* workbook is available on the companion CD-ROM.

Create a chart that compares budgeted amounts with contributions received to date. This comparison will be used to establish the fundraising goal.

1. **OPEN** *Contributions 2* from the data files.
2. Click the **Insert** tab. On the Budget worksheet, select **A4:C8** and click **Column**.

3. Click **3-D Clustered Column**.

4. **SAVE** the document as *Contributions Project 2*.

5. Select **Layout 2.**

6. Select **Chart Title** in the Current Selection group on the Layout tab and key **Budgeted vs. Received**. Press Enter.

7. Delete the legend.

8. Select **Budgeted** in the chart title, click **Text Fill** on the Format tab, and click **Pink, Accent 1** under Theme Colors.

9. Select **Received** in the chart title, click **Text Fill**, and click **Purple**.

10. Select **Series "Budgeted Amount" Data Labels** in the Current Selection group on the Layout tab and apply **Pink, Accent 1** text fill.

11. Select **Series "Received to Date" Data Labels** and apply **Purple** text fill.

12. Move the chart to a new sheet.

13. Name the chart sheet **Budgeted vs. Received**.

14. Select the **Horizontal (Category) Axis** and select **Text Fill**. Click **Purple.**

15. If necessary, select and move the series amounts so that they are completely visible.

16. **SAVE** and **CLOSE** the workbook.

   LEAVE Excel open for the next project.

⊙ Project 3: Add Pictures to a Worksheet

Enhance a worksheet's appearance by adding pictures and a background.

OPEN *CCS Locations* from the data files.

1. Click the **Locations** worksheet tab if necessary. Click the **Insert** tab and click **Picture**.

2. Select *Africa* from the data files for this lesson. Click **Insert**.

3. Select the picture and move it to cell A5. Use the sizing handles to shrink the picture so that it fits within A5 without covering the text.

4. Click the **Insert** tab and click **Picture**.

5. Select *Asia* from the data files for this lesson. Click **Insert**

6. Click the **Format** tab. In the size group, click **Shape Height** and key **1**. The width of the picture should size proportionately.

7. Align the picture with the right boundary of A8.

8. Insert *Latin America* into cell A13. Size the picture so that it is centered below the text in the cell.

9. Insert *Europe* from the data files. Set shape width to **1.2**. The height of the picture should size proportionately. Align the picture with the top and right boundaries of cell A19.

10. Select the picture in **A19** and click **Picture Effects**. Select **Accent color 2, 5pt glow**.

11. Click the **Welcome** worksheet tab and select **A1:O32**. In the Alignment group on the Home tab, click **Merge & Center**.

12. Click **Middle Align** and click **Center Text**. Key **Welcome to Cross-Cultural Solutions' Annual Charity Auction**.

13. Select the text and change the font to **Lucida Calligraphy** and the font size to **36**. Click **Wrap Text**.

14. Click the **Page Layout** tab and click **Background**. Click **Sunset** from the data files and click **Insert**.

15. Remove gridlines and headings from the view. Double-click a Ribbon tab to minimize the Ribbon. Increase or decrease the zoom so that the message background fills the screen.

16. **SAVE** the workbook as *CSS Locations Project 3* and **CLOSE** the file.

    LEAVE Excel open for the next project.

Project 4: Track Changes in a Shared Workbook

As a result of the fundraising event, several organizations and individuals have increased their contributions. Use change-tracking to record the increases and to add comments related to the changes.

OPEN *Contributions 1* from the data files.

The *Contributions 1* workbook is available on the companion CD-ROM.

1. Click the **Microsoft Office Button** and click **Save As**.
2. Click **Tools** and click **General Options**.
3. Key **Cont4!** in the *Password to modify* box and click **OK**.
4. Reenter the password.
5. **SAVE** the workbook as *Contributions Project 4*.
6. Click the **Review** tab. Click **Track Changes** and click **Highlight Changes**.
7. Click **Track changes while editing. This also shares your workbook.** Click **Who** and click **OK**.
8. Click **OK** to save the workbook.
9. Click **C7** and key **1500**. Press Enter. In C7, click **New Comment** and key **Increased by Jim Hance**.
10. Select **A15** and click **New Comment**. Key **Call Maria Hammond next week**.
11. Select **B27** and key **Scholarship**. Press Enter. In B27, insert a comment that reads **Mark Hassal, General Manager, changed fund allocation**.
12. **SAVE** and **CLOSE** the file.

    CLOSE Excel.

Appendix A
Microsoft Certified Application Specialist (MCAS) Skills

Matrix Skill	Skill Number	Lesson Number
Fill a series	1.1.1	2
Copy a series	1.1.2	2
Restrict data using data validation	1.2.1	6
Remove duplicate rows from spreadsheets	1.2.2	6
Cut, copy, and paste data and cell contents	1.3.1	2
Change views within a single window	1.4.1	1
Split windows	1.4.2	1
Open and arrange new windows	1.4.3	1
Copy worksheets	1.5.1	5
Reposition worksheets within workbooks	1.5.2	5
Rename worksheets	1.5.3	5
Hide and unhide worksheets	1.5.4	5
Insert and delete worksheets	1.5.5	5
Use themes to format worksheets	2.1.1	4
Show and hide gridlines and headers	2.1.2	4
Add color to worksheet tabs	2.1.3	4
Format worksheet backgrounds	2.1.4	4
Insert and delete cells, rows, and columns	2.2.1	3, 4
Format rows and columns	2.2.2	4
Hide and unhide rows and columns	2.2.3	4
Modify row height and column width	2.2.4	4
Apply number formats	2.3.1	3
Create custom cell formats	2.3.2	3
Apply and modify cell styles	2.3.3	3
Format text in cells	2.3.4	3
Convert text to columns	2.3.5	8
Merge and split cells	2.3.6	3
Add and remove cell borders	2.3.7	3
Insert, modify, and remove hyperlinks	2.3.8	3
Apply Quick Styles to tables	2.4.1	6
Add rows to tables	2.4.2	6
Insert and delete rows and columns in tables	2.4.3	6
Create formulas that use absolute and relative cell references	3.1.1	7
Create formulas that reference data from other worksheets or workbooks	3.1.2	7
Manage named ranges	3.1.3	7
Use named ranges in formulas	3.1.4	7
Use SUM, COUNT, COUNTA, AVERAGE, MIN, and MAX	3.2.1	7

continued

MATRIX SKILL	SKILL NUMBER	LESSON NUMBER
Create and modify list ranges	3.3.1	7
Use SUMIF, SUMIFS, COUNTIF, COUNTIFS, AVERAGEIF, and AVERAGEIFS	3.4.1	8
Use VLOOKUP and HLOOKUP	3.5.1	8
Use IF, AND, OR, NOT, IFERROR	3.6.1	8
Use PROPER, UPPER, LOWER, SUBSTITUTE	3.7.1	8
Convert text to columns	3.7.2	8
Display and print formulas	3.8	7
Select appropriate data sources for charts	4.1.1	9
Select appropriate chart types to represent data sources	4.1.2	9
Format charts using Quick Styles	4.1.3	9
Add and remove chart elements	4.2.1	9
Move and size charts	4.2.2	9
Change chart types	4.2.3	9
Manage conditional formats using the rule manager	4.3.1	3
Allow more than one rule to be true	4.3.2	3
Apply conditional formats	4.3.3	3
Insert and modify pictures from files	4.4.1	10
Insert and modify SmartArt graphics	4.4.2	10
Insert and modify shapes	4.4.3	10
Group and ungroup data	4.5.1	6
Subtotal data	4.5.2	6
Sort data using single or multiple criteria	4.6.1	6
Filter data using AutoFilter	4.6.2	6
Filter and sort data using conditional formatting	4.6.3	6
Filter and sort data using cell attributes	4.6.4	6
Insert, display, modify, and resolve tracked changes	5.1.1	11
Insert, display, modify, and delete comments	5.1.2	11
Protect workbooks and worksheets	5.2.1	11
Enable workbooks to be changed by multiple users	5.2.2	11
Remove private and other inappropriate data from workbooks	5.3.1	11
Restrict permissions to a workbook	5.3.2	11
Add key words and other information to workbook properties	5.3.3	2
Add digital signatures	5.3.4	11
Mark workbooks as final	5.3.5	11
Save workbooks for use in a previous version of Excel	5.4.1	2
Using the correct format, save a workbook as a template, a Web page, a macro-enabled document, or another appropriate format	5.4.2	2
Define the area of a worksheet to be printed	5.5.1	2
Insert and move a page break	5.5.2	4
Set margins	5.5.3	4
Add and modify headers and footers	5.5.4	4
Change the orientation of a worksheet	5.5.5	4
Scale worksheet content to fit a printed page	5.5.6	4

TO USE MICROSOFT OFFICE PROFESSIONAL 2007, YOU WILL NEED:

COMPONENT	REQUIREMENT
Computer and processor	500 megahertz (MHz) processor or higher[1]
Memory	256 megabyte (MB) RAM or higher[1, 2]
Hard disk	2 gigabyte (GB); a portion of this disk space will be freed after installation if the original download package is removed from the hard drive.
Drive	CD-ROM or DVD drive
Display	1024x768 or higher resolution monitor
Operating system	Microsoft Windows XP with Service Pack (SP) 2, Windows Server 2003 with SP1, or later operating system[3]
Other	Certain inking features require running Microsoft Windows XP Tablet PC Edition or later. Speech recognition functionality requires a close-talk microphone and audio output device. Information Rights Management features require access to a Windows 2003 Server with SP1 or later running Windows Rights Management Services.
	Connectivity to Microsoft Exchange Server 2000 or later is required for certain advanced functionality in Outlook 2007. Instant Search requires Microsoft Windows Desktop Search 3.0. Dynamic Calendars require server connectivity.
	Connectivity to Microsoft Windows Server 2003 with SP1 or later running Microsoft Windows SharePoint Services is required for certain advanced collaboration functionality. Microsoft Office SharePoint Server 2007 is required for certain advanced functionality. PowerPoint Slide Library requires Office SharePoint Server 2007. To share data among multiple computers, the host computer must be running Windows Server 2003 with SP1, Windows XP Professional with SP2, or later.
	Internet Explorer 6.0 or later, 32 bit browser only. Internet functionality requires Internet access (fees may apply).
Additional	Actual requirements and product functionality may vary based on your system configuration and operating system.

[1] 1 gigahertz (GHz) processor or higher and 512 MB RAM or higher recommended for **Business Contact Manager**. Business Contact Manager not available in all languages.
[2] 512 MB RAM or higher recommended for **Outlook Instant Search**. Grammar and contextual spelling in **Word** is not turned on unless the machine has 1 GB memory.
[3] Office Clean-up wizard not available on 64 bit OS.

Glossary

A

absolute cell reference In a formula, a reference to a specific cell. Absolute references point to the same cell even when the formula that contains the reference is copied or moved to a different cell.

active cell The cell in which you can enter data. A thick black border surrounds the active cell.

add-in A supplemental program that can be installed to extend the capabilities of Excel by adding custom commands and specialized features.

arguments The values that a function uses to perform operations or calculations.

array Used to build single formulas that produce multiple results or operate on a group of arguments that are arranged in rows and columns. An array range shares a common formula.

ascending order Sort order in which alphabetic data appears A to Z, numeric data appears from lowest to highest or smallest to largest, and dates appear from oldest to most recent.

attribute A formatting characteristic of text or a cell.

authenticate The process of verifying that people and products are who and what they claim to be.

auto fill An Excel feature that automatically fills cells with data from another cell or range of cells or completes a data series.

AutoComplete A feature in Microsoft Office Excel that completes text entries that you start to key in a column of data if the first few letters that you key match an existing entry in that column.

AutoFilter A built-in set of filtering capabilities that you can apply to worksheet data.

axis A line bordering the chart plot area used as a frame of reference for measurement.

B

boundary The line that divides columns or rows on an Excel worksheet.

C

cell The intersection of a column and a row in a worksheet.

certificate authority (CA) A trusted third-party entity that issues digital certificates for use by other parties.

change history In a shared workbook, information that is maintained about changes made in past editing sessions. The information includes the name of the person who made each change, when the change was made, and what data was changed.

change tracking The ability to mark and keep track of changes that have been made to a workbook, especially for a workbook that is shared and modified by multiple users.

character A letter, number, punctuation, mark, or symbol.

chart A graphical representation of numeric data in a worksheet.

chart area The entire chart and all its elements.

chart sheet A sheet in a workbook that contains only a chart.

clip A single media file including art, sound, animation, or movies.

clip art A single piece of ready-made art that can be inserted into a document. Clip art often appears as a bitmap or a combination of drawn shapes.

Clip Organizer A listing of clips that is easily accessible so that you can locate and insert them into documents.

column A vertical line of cells. Columns are identified by a letter or letters.

column heading The letter that appears at the top of the columns on a worksheet.

column width The number of characters that will fit in a column. Default column width is 8.43 characters.

command groups Organization of subtasks on Excel's Ribbon.

command tab Tab that contains commands, buttons, and galleries. Command tabs appear on the Ribbon.

comparison operator A sign used in comparison criteria to compare two values.

conditional formatting Formatting that is applied based on established criteria.

conditional formula A formula in which the result is determined by the state of a particular condition.

connector A line that has connection points at the ends of the line and stays connected to the shapes to which you attach it.

constant Numbers text value entered directly into a formula. Constant values are not calculated.

copy Place a duplicate of a selection on the Office Clipboard.

copy pointer A + (plus) symbol that allows you to use the mouse to copy data from a selected range to a new location.

criteria Conditions you specify to limit which records are included in the result of a sort, query, or filter.

cut Remove a selection from a worksheet and place it on the Office Clipboard.

D

data Information keyed into an Excel workbook cell.

data labels Text that provides additional information about a data marker, which represents a single data point or value that originates from a worksheet cell.

data marker A bar, area, dot, slice, or other symbol in a chart that represents a single data point or value that originates from a worksheet cell. Related data markers in a chart constitute a data series.

data series Related data points that are plotted in a chart.

default A predefined setting. You can accept Excel's default option settings or you can change them.

descending order Sort order in which alphabetic data appears Z to A, numeric data appears from highest to lowest or largest to smallest, and dates appear from most recent to oldest.

dialog box A box that displays options or information you can specify to execute a command.

Dialog Box Launcher An arrow located in the lower-right corner of a command group that opens a dialog box or a task pane.

digital certificate A means of proving identity and authenticity which verifies that the signer of a document is the person he or she claims to be and the content has not been changed since it was signed.

digital signature An electronic notation encrypted into a document to authenticate the content of a workbook.

document properties Details about a file that describe or identify it and include information such as title, author, name, subject, and key words that identify the topic or contents.

document theme A set of predefined formatting options that include sets of theme colors, fonts, and effects.

duplicate value Values in the row are an exact match of all the values in another row.

E

embedded chart A chart that is placed on a worksheet rather than on a separate chart sheet.

external reference A reference to a cell or range on a worksheet in another Excel workbook, or a reference to a defined name in another workbook. External references are sometimes called links.

F

fill handle A small black square in the lower-right corner of selected cells. You can click the handle to drag the contents of one cell to adjacent cells or to create a series such as a series of dates.

filter A rule that Excel uses to determine which worksheet rows to display.

flowchart A schematic representation of a process.

font A set of text characters designed to appear a certain way. Calibri is the default font for Excel 2007.

footer A line of text that appears at the bottom of each page of a printed worksheet.

Format Painter An Excel feature that allows you to copy formatting from a cell or range of cells to another cell or range of cells.

formula An equation that performs calculations on values in a worksheet.

formula bar A bar at the top of the Excel window where you can enter or edit cell entries or formulas.

freeze Make certain rows or columns visible on your screen even when you scroll your worksheet.

function A predefined formula that performs a calculation.

G

gridlines The lines that display around the worksheet cells.

group Organization within the Ribbon tabs that breaks a task into subtasks.

group worksheets Selecting multiple worksheets to enter and edit data on them or format them at the same time.

grouping Organizing data so that it can be viewed as a collapsible and expandable outline.

H

header A line of text that appears at the top of each page of a printed worksheet.

hide To make a row, column, worksheet, or workbook invisible.

hyperlink A shortcut or jump that opens a document stored on a network server, an intranet, or the Internet.

L

label Entries that identify the numeric data in a worksheet.

landscape orientation Page setup in which a page is wider than it is tall.

legend A box that identifies the patterns or colors that are assigned to a data series or categories in a chart.

legend keys Color-coded icons that appear to the left of legend entries that identify the data series in a chart.

lookup functions Functions used to look up information stored in a table in an Excel worksheet. You can look up information by rows (HLOOKUP) or by column (VLOOKUP).

M

mathematical operator The formula component that specifies what calculations are to be performed. The most common operators are = (equal), + (addition), − (subtraction), * (multiplication), and / (division).

merged cell A single cell that is created by combining two or more selected cells.

Microsoft Office Button Displays a menu of basic commands for opening, saving, and printing files as well as more advanced options.

Mini toolbar A miniature formatting toolbar that displays above the right-click shortcut menu.

mixed reference In formulas, a cell reference in which the column is absolute and the row is relative or vice versa.

move pointer A four-point symbol that allows you to use the mouse to move data from one worksheet location to another.

N

name A meaningful shorthand that makes it easier to understand the purpose of a cell reference, constant, formula, or table.

O

Office Clipboard An area in memory for storing up to 24 copied or cut items so they can be selectively pasted in other locations.

operand The components of a formula that identify the values to be used in the calculation. These can be a constant value, a cell reference, a range of cells, or another formula.

organization chart Graphically illustrates the management structure of an organization.

orientation A setting that specifies the direction a worksheet appears on a printed page, either vertically (portrait orientation) or horizontally (landscape orientation).

outline symbols Symbols that you use to change the view of an outlined worksheet. You can show or hide detailed data by pressing the plus sign, minus sign, and the numbers 1, 2, 3 indicating the outline level.

P

page break Divider that breaks a worksheet into separate pages for printing.

Page Break Preview: A view that allows you to see the dividers that break a worksheet into separate pages for printing.

password Text that must be keyed before a user can access a workbook, worksheet, or worksheet elements.

paste A command used to insert a cut or copied selection stored on the Office Clipboard to a cell or range in a worksheet.

plot area The area bounded by the axes.

point A measurement of the height of characters in a cell or the height of a row. One point is equal to 1/72 inch.

Print Preview The Excel window that allows you to view a full-page preview of what your worksheet will look like when it is printed.

Q

Quick Access Toolbar A customizable toolbar containing the most-frequently used commands. The Quick Access Toolbar is displayed regardless of the tab that is currently displayed on the Ribbon.

Quick Styles Collections of formatting options that make formatting documents and objects easier.

R

range A group of adjacent cells that you select to perform operations on all of the selected cells.

reference Identifies a cell or a range of cells on a worksheet and tells Excel where to look for the values you want to use in a formula.

relative cell reference In formulas, a cell reference that changes "relative" to the location to which they are copied or moved.

Ribbon A band that runs across the top of the Excel window. The Ribbon is organized into task-oriented command tabs that replace the menus and toolbars in earlier versions of Excel.

row A horizontal line of cells.

row heading The row number that appears to the left of a worksheet.

row height The top-to-bottom height of a row, given in points or in pixels. You can change row height by using the Format command in the Home tab Editing group or by dragging the bottom boundary of the row.

S

scaling Expanding or shrinking how a worksheet appears on a printed page.

scope Location within which a defined name is recognized without qualification.

ScreenTip A small window that displays descriptive text when you rest the pointer on a command or control.

Select Identify the cell or range of cells in which you want to enter data or apply formatting.

shared workbook A workbook set up to allow multiple users on a network to view and make changes at the same time. Each user who saves the workbook sees the changes made by other users.

SmartArt graphic A visual representation of information and ideas with built-in layouts and formats.

string Any sequence of letters or numbers that you key.

strong password A password that combines uppercase and lowercase letters, numbers, and symbols, and uses 14 or more characters.

style A set of formatting attributes you can apply as a group to a cell or range of cells.

T

table In an Excel worksheet, a range of cells that can be used by a lookup function.

template Worksheets that are already set up to track certain kinds of data, such as sales reports, invoices, and purchase orders.

Text pane The pane that appears to the left of a SmartArt graphic that you can use to enter and edit the text that appears in the graphic.

title Descriptive text that is automatically aligned to an axis or centered at the top of a chart.

U

unhide To make a hidden workbook, worksheet, row, or column visible.

W

workbook An Excel file that can contain multiple worksheets.

worksheet An individual sheet within an Excel workbook.

Z

zoom Make a worksheet appear bigger (zoom in) or smaller (zoom out) on your screen.